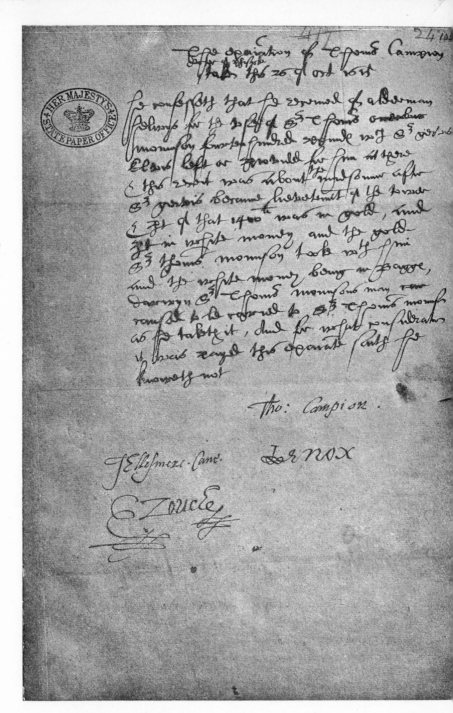

Minutes of the examination of Thomas Campion on the 26th Oct. 1615,
prior to the arrest of Sir Thomas Monson for complicity in
the Overbury murder. [S. P. Dom. James I. lxxxii.]

See p. xliv. The signatures of the poet and his examiners are in autograph.

CAMPION'S WORKS

EDITED BY

PERCIVAL VIVIAN

OXFORD
AT THE CLARENDON PRESS

Oxford University Press, Ely House, London W. 1

GLASGOW NEW YORK TORONTO MELBOURNE WELLINGTON
CAPE TOWN SALISBURY IBADAN NAIROBI LUSAKA ADDIS ABABA
BOMBAY CALCUTTA MADRAS KARACHI LAHORE DACCA
KUALA LUMPUR HONG KONG

FIRST PUBLISHED 1909

REPRINTED LITHOGRAPHICALLY IN GREAT BRITAIN
AT THE UNIVERSITY PRESS, OXFORD
BY VIVIAN RIDLER
PRINTER TO THE UNIVERSITY
1966, 1967

PREFACE

Some time ago, when working upon a small edition of Campion's English poems for Messrs. Routledge's 'Muses' Library', I had the good fortune to come across certain information concerning the poet's descent and early circumstances which had not, so far as I am aware, been previously noticed. The original clues, when fully pursued, provided a mass of material too great for inclusion in that volume, and I was obliged to content myself with a promise of dealing with the subject more completely in a subsequent work. The present edition was undertaken by way of redemption of that promise, partly with the object of placing the facts on record, and partly to provide for general access a complete collection of Campion's works, the fullest edition hitherto produced (Mr. Bullen's 1889 volume) having been privately printed and limited by subscription.

The text has everywhere been given in the old spelling (reduced to consistency in the Latin works); and I have striven to reproduce the character of the originals in typography, indentation, and punctuation, though discretion has been used in the last-named. MS. records have been quoted in their native garb of spelling and abbreviation; and here let me anticipate a criticism which I have heard in respect of other books by stating that I am fully aware that the current MS. abbreviation for 'th' is not 'y', though I have employed that letter as nearest to the character in question. Except in a very few passages I have adhered to and occasionally restored the reading of the original texts.

I think I ought at this point to explain the course of reasoning which led me to my conclusions as to Thomas Campion's identity, so as to lay my grounds open to examination. Egerton MS. 2599 was first pointed out to me by Mr. Flower of the British Museum, but, beyond the fact that it referred to a Thomas Campion at Cambridge, I could at first find no sure footing for identification. Finally, however, a laborious search through accounts and title-deeds, Latin and English, disclosed the allusion to 'Thomas Campion de Grayes ynne'. This was the keystone to the whole structure of material. It had been shown by Mr. Bullen that the poet was a member of Gray's Inn, and the records of the Inn make it clear that it only boasted one Campion at this date. This proved, the MS. afforded clues which ramified in every direction, frequently providing corroborative evidence of the truth of my original identification.

My obligations are almost too numerous to be acknowledged in detail, though shift must be made to mention the greater. To Professor Raleigh, and that veteran of literature, Dr. Furnivall, I am indebted for encouragement and advice; and I have to thank Mr. Bullen, the pioneer of the study to which I am a mere apprentice, for his assistance, and for kind permission to quote several notes from his own editions. I owe much to Dr. Walker, Librarian of Peterhouse, who at my instance and armed with clues of my providing, made successful research among the College records for proof of Campion's membership; and who has shown untiring courtesy in affording me subsequent assistance.

Among other literary creditors mention must be made of my friend Robin Flower of the British Museum, who, as already explained, was in a sense the only begetter of the present work; of Dr. Thomas Lea Southgate, with whose authoritative voice I speak on technical questions of music; of my friend Adrian Collins, for the recollection of many fruitful discussions upon music and prosody; of the Rev. F. R. Williams, Rector of Anstey, for the courtesy of access to the registers of his parish; of Messrs. Routledge and Son, for their kind permission to quote notes from my small edition in their 'Muses' Library'; of Mr. Madan of the Bodleian, and the Librarian of the Cambridge University Library, for assistance which has saved me time and labour; and, finally, of the officials of the Clarendon Press, for considerate help and useful suggestions, and for a liberality in the matter of reproductions and illustrations which will have contributed no little to any success with which this book may meet.

P. V.

CONTENTS

PEDIGREE OF THOMAS CAMPION.

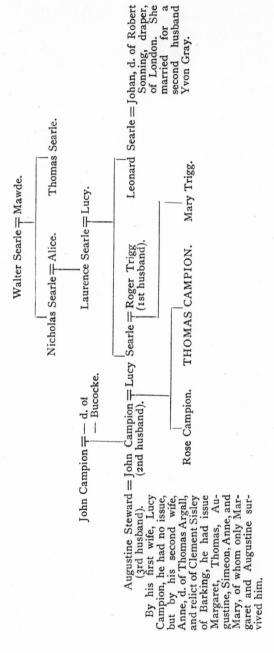

Walter Searle = Mawde.

Nicholas Searle = Alice. Thomas Searle. Laurence Searle = Lucy.

Leonard Searle = Johan, d. of Robert Sonning, draper, of London. She married for a second husband Yvon Gray.

John Campion = — d. of — Bucocke.

Augustine Steward = John Campion = Lucy Searle = Roger Trigg
(3rd husband).   (2nd husband).   (1st husband).

Rose Campion. THOMAS CAMPION. Mary Trigg.

Augustine Steward = Lucy (3rd husband). By his first wife, Lucy Campion, he had no issue, but by his second wife, Anne, d. of Thomas Argall, and relict of Clement Sisley of Barking, he had issue Margaret, Thomas, Augustine, Simeon, Anne, and Mary, of whom only Margaret and Augustine survived him.

INTRODUCTION

CHAPTER I. BIOGRAPHICAL.

FOR some generations prior to his date, it is probable that the forefathers of Thomas Campion were settled in that district of Hertfordshire which abuts upon the extreme north-eastern border of the county; and, to limit their locality still further, in a group of scattered villages in this neighbourhood,* mention of which will occur hereafter. The facts upon which this inference is based cannot now be stated without undue anticipation, but they will be sufficiently apparent.

There was, of course, an armigerous family of the name whose pedigree is recorded in the heraldic visitations of the period. These people appear to have been resident chiefly in London and Essex; but some of them undoubtedly had landed interests in the neighbouring county of Herts.[1] From such indications it seems likely that the poet's ancestors had an origin in common with the Essex Campions; but while the latter had become prosperous merchants, the former had not flourished to the same extent.

The earliest of the poet's ancestors in the male line of whom we have any trace is John Campion, his grandfather, described in 1565 as 'John Campion, late of Dublin, Ireland, deceased'.[2] I can find, however, no certain trace of him in Ireland; and I believe that he was not a native of that country, but had either visited it on some venture, commercial or otherwise, or held a petty office there; for he seems to have originally sprung from Anstey,* one of the small villages above mentioned. From the Subsidy Rolls for Herts., we find that at Anstey, 'John

---

[1] In illustration of the connexion between the Essex and Herts. Campions see Feet of Fines, Herts. (1601) Abraham Campion: Robert Curtis and Isabel his wife. Land in Chesthunt. (1598) Thos. Hitchin: Thomas Campion and Anastasia his wife. Messuage and land in Stevenage. (1591) Edm. Nodes senior gent. and Edw. Norwood, gent.: William Campion and Susan his wife. Land in Stevenage and Graveley. The Campions mentioned in these documents belonged to the Essex family. The fact is also suggestive that Margaret, daughter of Thomas Campion of Essex, married Henry Brograve at Buntingford in 1574, and on his death married Edward Gyll of Anstey, where she was buried in 1605. A child of the first marriage was Sir John Brograve, who married Margaret, daughter of Simeon Steward of Ely, and sister of Augustine Steward, of whom see p. xix.   [2] v. infra, p. xiii.

* See map. The Subsidy Rolls and Feet of Fines are transcribed in the *Herts. Genealogist and Antiquary.*

Campion, g.' paid iij*s*. iiij*d*., and the registers[1] of the parish
disclose the existence of a large family of Campions resident
there. The Christian name of John is very frequent among
these people, and it is accordingly harder to identify the
poet's grandfather. But, as will be seen hereafter,[2] he seems
to have married into a family equally prevailing in the neigh-
bourhood,[3] which bore a name rendered indifferently as Bawcock,
Beaucock, or Bucock ; the middle form, I take it, being that
which reconciles the dissimilarity of the others. The fruit of this
union was John Campion, the younger.

So far, with the exception of one piece of documentary
evidence, we have been mainly on the ground of inference, but
with this next generation we gain more certain footing.

Of John Campion, the poet's father, we learn nothing until
1564, when he espoused a widow who was a small heiress in her
own right and comfortably off besides. From Chester's *London
Marriage Licences* we gather that ' John Campion, of St. Clement
Danes, gent. and Lucy Trigg, widow, of St. Andrew's, Holborn ',
obtained a licence on June 21, 1564, for marriage at St. Andrew's,
Holborn. The marriage was accordingly solemnized at St.
Andrew's, in the registers of which parish stands the entry
' William Campion, gent. and Lucy Trigg maried the 26 June'
(1564), a curious instance of an undeniable error in what is
usually such a reliable class of records.

It will now be not amiss to give some account of the origin of
Lucy Campion, the poet's mother, whose maiden name was
Searle. Walter Searle, Mawde his wife, and Thomas Searle

---

[1] The registers show 24 baptisms between 1545 and 1594; 6 marriages between
1541 and 1564 ; and 13 burials between 1541 and 1592,—of persons bearing this
name.   [2] *v. infra*, p. xxii.

[3] There were also Campions at Brent Pelham in the same neighbourhood.
In a bill dated 17 April, 12 Elizabeth (1570), Thomas Campion sued John
Rowley in the Court of Requests (XXXVII, 71) for the recovery of certain
copyhold property in Brent Pelham, formerly the possession of Raafe Campion,
from whom it devolved upon his brother John Campion, the complainant's
father. It is clear from the date, however, that this Thomas Campion was not
the poet, but they must have been of the same family.

Rauf or Ralph Campion was vicar of Brent Pelham shortly before this time ;
his will was proved in the P.C.C. in 1552 (16 Powell). On the dissolution
of the Abbey of St. Albans in 1539 he was granted by Henry VIII an annuity
of £6 13*s*. 4*d*., by a charter dated December 14, 1539, making compensation to
the dispossessed monks. He is also mentioned in the Composition Papers
(P.R.O.) for Herts. as ' Radulphus Campyon, Pelham Arsa, 4 Nov., 33
Henry VIII '.

Introduction.

their son, who were living in 22 Edward IV (1483), are the earliest of her ancestors whom we can trace; and Nicholas Searle,[1] described as a 'monyer', i. e. a money-changer, or banker, son and heir of the bodies of Walter and Mawde, was a brother of Thomas, and became the grandfather of Lucy Searle. By his will made on January 6, 1535, he devised some property in Hoxton and Hornsey, of which that in the former neighbourhood afterwards devolved upon Lucy, and became the subject of considerable litigation. He died on February 2, 27 Henry VIII (153$\frac{5}{6}$), and his wife Alice, surviving him by a few years, died in or about 31 Henry VIII (1540).

His son Laurence was a member of a body of officers of whose functions at this time little seems to be known, the Serjeants-at-Arms in attendance upon the sovereign. As originally created the office stood limited to persons of knightly rank: whether this was so or not in the sixteenth century, the posts were reserved for gentlemen of good standing, and the appointment was presumably deemed an honour. Besides attendance on the sovereign as a kind of guard of honour, their duties comprised the arrest and possibly custody of noble offenders and those charged with breaches of parliamentary privilege; which province of their function survives to the present day, the Serjeants-at-Arms at the Houses of Parliament being in theory deputed by the sovereign to attend the Lord Chancellor and Speaker respectively, to guard the observance of due privilege, and to execute the warrants and orders of each House during Session.

Laurence Searle and his wife Lucy had two children, a son, Leonard, and a daughter, Lucy, afterwards the poet's mother. Leonard, who had married Johan, daughter of Robert Sonning, draper, of London, predeceased his father, dying about July 17, 1568; and letters of administration of his estate issued to his relict out of the Commissary Court of London, on July 27, 1568. Laurence Searle himself died on January 26, 156$\frac{8}{9}$, and administration of his estate issued out of the same Court—his wife, who

---

[1] As to Nicholas Searle and his descendants, see Feet of Fines, Middlesex, 24 Henry VIII, Mich.:—Nich. Serle, Thos. Armerer, Laur. Serle, and Thomas Austen: John Williams and Elizabeth his wife. Land in Hoxton and Fynnesbury. 2 and 3 Ed. VI. Hil.:—Sir Clement Smythe, Kt., and Thomas Curtis: Henry Searle and Alice his wife. The manor of Wyke and premises in Wyke, Hackeney, Stebenheth, Hoxton, Islington, and Shordych, &c., Co. Middlesex, and premises in Counties Cambs. and Essex. 10 Eliz. Trin.:—Thomas Estfielde and John Kaye, gen.: Leonard Searle and Joan his wife. Premises in Hoxton and Hornsey. (Hardy & Page.)

died about October 29, 1553, having predeceased him—to his daughter Lucy, then the wife of John Campion, on August 27, 1569. Several years before this, Lucy had married Roger Trigg, an attorney of the Common Pleas, by whom she had one child, a daughter named Mary. But he had died, presumably in 1563, for letters of administration of his estate were granted on November 11, 1563, to Lucy Trigg, out of the Prerogative Court of Canterbury.

An investigation into the probable means by which the persons concerned in this history came together is instructive as illustrating our previous assumption as to the local origin of the Campion family. The Searles were apparently settled in Hackney, while their landed interests were in Hoxton, Hornsey, and Shoreditch. At the same time Laurence Searle is referred to as 'ar(miger)',[1] and there was an armigerous family resident at Epping, North Weald, and Bobbingworth in Essex, to which he may have belonged. The Triggs were Hertfordshire people, and from the same neighbourhood as the Campions. There were Triggs at Barkway,* Furneaux Pelham,* and Wyddial,* all villages within a few miles of each other and Anstey ; while Roger Trigg himself was concerned,[2] either professionally or in his own interests, with property in Brent Pelham* and Stocking Pelham,* as we learn from the Feet of Fines. But he was also similarly concerned with London property ; and, of course, as an attorney he must have spent much time in London, where he probably met and married Lucy Searle. Roger Trigg was probably, therefore, the means by which his wife became acquainted with the Campions ; and to their proximity as neighbours we may assign another intimacy, that of Augustine Steward (of whom more hereafter) with this little circle. Steward, Campion, and Trigg were either originally neighbours in Hertfordshire or sprang from families who had become acquainted in this way.

In 1564, then, John Campion married the widow of Roger

---

[1] Eg. MS. 2599, f. 1.

[2] See Feet of Fines, Herts., 2 & 3 Phil. and Mary, Trin. :—Roger Trigg, gent. & Robert Aprice : William Walgrave, gent. & Katherine, his wife. Manor of Brent Pelham alias Grays & Chamberlens, & messuages & lands in Brent Pelham & Stokkyng Pelham. 2 & 3 Eliz. Mich. :—Tho. Brand : Roger Tryg, gent. & Robert Aprice. Lands in Brent Pelham.

Feet of Fines, London, 1 & 2 Phil. & Mary, Mich. :—Roger Trygge, gen.: Thos. Devyne als. Deane, & Elizabeth, his wife, late the wife of Giles Harryson deceased. A messuage & brewhouse called le Reed Lyon & 2 gardens in the parish of St. Botolph in Est Smythfelde.

* See map.

Trigg. They had two children, the elder a girl, Rose, who was christened at St. Andrew's on June 21, 1565, and a son, Thomas Campion, the poet, ' borne upon Ash Weddensday being the twelft day of February, An. Rg. Eliz. nono,[1] and cristened at St. Andrewes Church, in Houlborne,' as the registers of that church inform us, on the day following his birth.

Whether John Campion was possessed of any considerable means prior to his marriage, or whether, as appears rather likely, he was indebted to a prudent marriage for a start in life, all the facts at present extant concerning his career date subsequently to that event. In 1565 he was admitted to the Middle Temple. The Minutes of a Parliament held at that Inn on July 26, 1565, record the admission of ' John Campion, son and heir of John Campion of Dublin, Ireland, deceased'; while the Latin entry runs, 'Johẽs Campion fĩs & heres Johñis Campion nup. de Dublina in Hibñia defunct. admissus est in societatẽ medij Templi spec(ialiter)[2] xxvi^{to} die Julij A^o Eliz. reginae Septimo p. (per) mr̃um (magistrum) Bell Lectorẽ'. He does not appear to have been ever called to the Bar, but possibly this was not his object; for in or after 1566 we find him in enjoyment of the post and privileges of a Cursitor[3] of the Chancery Court, for which it was, no doubt, necessary to qualify by a course of legal study. These Cursitors, Clerks of Course (*clerici de cursu*, to follow the traditional derivation) were a body of 24 or (according to one account) 19 officers, who drew up the writs of the Court *de cursu*, i. e. according to routine. These posts, though not so valuable as those of the Six Clerks, were yet worth having, for according to the MS. below cited,[4] the remuneration of the whole 19 was 'not so little as 2000^{li} per ann.', and, originally in the gift of the Lord Chancellor, the posts ' are ordinarily conferred to others at the Rates of a thousand pounds a thousand markes, vc^{li}, and viijc^{li}'; from which we may infer that some of them were of more value than others as involving larger salaries. Doubtless, therefore, some ready money was required to secure the appointment, and possibly it was furnished by Lucy Campion.

The knowledge of his occupation may help us to make at least a plausible guess as to the exact locality of John Campion's

---

[1] Eg. MS. 2599, f. 30 : that is, Feb. 12, 1567.

[2] 'Special' admission was, as a matter of fact, the rule, and implied admission to the whole Inn with all its privileges. 'General' admission was exceptional, and implied partial admission only, as, e. g. to chambers.

[3] *v. infra*, p. xvi.   [4] MS. Titus Bv., f. 302.

residence. It appears that there was a Cursitors' Office or Inn in Chancery Lane for the reception of these officers, in fact, an official residence for them. Stow says (p. 163): 'In this street (Chancery Lane) the first fair building to be noted on the east side is called the Cursitors' Office, built with divers fair lodgings for gentlemen, all of brick and timber, by Sir Nicholas Bacon, late Lord Keeper of the Great Seal.' Stow is apparently working from the north, but if we assume this Inn to have been somewhere at the present junction of Cursitor Street and Chancery Lane, it fulfils the necessary conditions of John Campion's residence, which must have been both in the parish of St. Andrew's, and within the city boundaries.[1] These ran, and still run, from the spot where a stone now stands by Staple Inn down to Temple Bar, cutting through Chancery Lane obliquely, and including its south-eastern portion together with Cursitor Street. In this 'fair building', therefore, we may, with some show of likelihood, conjecture the poet's early days to have been spent.

In his wife's right John Campion was involved in considerable litigation. In 1567 he was sued in the Court of Requests by Henry Lord Morley for the restitution of the title-deeds and court-rolls of the manors of ' Brent Pelham, Greyes, and Chamberlyns', which had come into his hands in a somewhat curious fashion. Roger Trigg had in some way gained possession of these title-deeds, but in what capacity is not clear. From the Feet of Fines already quoted (footnote to p. xii), it is clear that he was concerned with these manors; and upon his death the title-deeds and court-rolls passed to his relict, in whose right John Campion stood possessed of them. Lord Morley, by reciting the legal devolution of the property, proves that the deeds should be in the possession of one William Walgrave (who was, as a matter of fact, merely trustee for himself[2]). John Campion acknowledges the manner in which the deeds came into his hands, but declines to give them up without an order from the Court, inasmuch as there were rival claimants to them, viz. William Walgrave and one Thomas Brand.[3] Finally, however, he offered to lodge them with

---

[1] *v. infra*, p. xvii.

[2] See Sir H. Chauncey's *Herts.* 'Henry Lord Morley convey'd the Mannor (Brent Pelham) to — Walgrave, Esq., who held Courts here in his own Name, but it seems it was only in Trust, for this Henry and Elizabeth his wife, daughter of Edward Earl of Derby, by whom he had issue Edward. . . . Edward by deed of the 14 of June, 27 Eliz., convey'd this Mannor . . . to John Lord Sturton' (p. 141).

[3] See Feet of Fines, Herts., in footnote to p. xii.

the Court, to be awarded at its decision. It was alleged by Morley that Trigg was enfeoffed of the property merely to the uses of William Walgrave's father. This seems on the whole likely, and Campion, while acting judiciously in refusing to part with the documents while there was a disputed title to them, made no effort to retain them for himself.

In 1569, however, he was involved in a far more tedious course of litigation, pursued through both the Chancery Court and the Star Chamber, though with, ultimately, greater profit. On the death of Laurence Searle in 1569, certain property at Hoxton [1] should have devolved upon Lucy, but her husband had to resort to law to establish her rights. Briefly, without entering into the numerous side issues of the case, the facts were these. By the will of Nicholas Searle the property was entailed ; and on the death of Laurence Searle—his only son, Leonard, having predeceased him and died without issue—it descended to Lucy. Leonard Searle's relict, Johan, had, however, married one Yvon Gray, who, claiming in her right, alleged the feoffment of certain persons in the property by Laurence and Leonard Searle, as trustees for the latter and Johan Sonning on the occasion of their marriage, equivalent, in fact, to the barring of the entail and resettlement of the property in their favour. That the feoffment was contemplated and partly carried out, was not denied, but the litigation turned mainly upon the question as to whether the memorandum of livery of seisin endorsed on the deed of feoffment was authentic, and whether, in fact, possession was ever formally surrendered to the feoffees.

The first suit was commenced in the Court of Chancery,[2] when John and Lucy Campion filed a bill dated April 27, 1569, against Yvon Gray and Joan his wife, apparently for restitution of the title-deeds. The facts as already stated were recited at great length, but from the state of the papers it is not possible to arrive at the upshot of the case, except that (as we learn from the subsequent proceedings) by an Order of the Court of April 29, 1569, it was decreed that Gray should bring an action of eviction against Campion in the Common Pleas, and that, instead of doing

---

[1] By the aid of a quaint map in Eg. MS. 2599 it is possible to identify the position of this property, a house and about three acres of land. It formed a strip running east and west ; abutting eastwards on the ' via regia ', or king's high road, to Ware, now the Kingsland Road, and westwards on the Hoxton High Street. It occupied roughly the site of the present Drysdale Road, though, of course several times wider.

[2] Chancery Proceedings, Eliz. xliv. 36.

this, he granted a lease of the property to certain persons, who themselves brought actions for eviction against Campion's tenants.

The proceedings were followed by two suits in the Star Chamber. In the first[1] of these, Campion and his wife sued John Turner, in a bill dated November 24, 1572, for forgery in the matter of the feoffment above referred to, and perjury in the subsequent proceedings; it being alleged that the defendant, as the attorney who acted in the matter of the feoffment, forged the name of Thomas Dunkyn, tenant of the property, as witness to its livery of seisin, and committed perjury in giving evidence at the previous trial. The second suit,[2] begun in the following year by John and Lucy Campion, pressed the same charges against Turner, with the additional allegation that, whereas the deed of feoffment was never properly executed by reason of the absence of the chief parties on the occasion of livery of seisin, Turner, when confronted with this fact at the first trial, declared that he was empowered to act for the parties by Letters of Attorney, and when pressed for the production of these Letters of Attorney, first temporized and finally produced a document which, as the condition of the writing and seals proclaimed, was obviously ' faked '.

As these latter papers merely consist of lists of interrogatories to be administered and the replies thereto, it is not possible to ascertain the result of the action, but in the end John and Lucy Campion were successful and gained possession of the property.[3]

But the interests to which John Campion became entitled in right of his wife were not always beneficial. He was sued in the Chancery Court[4] by one John Box, in respect of a debt of £6 11s. 7d. due to the complainant from Thomas Trigg, Roger Trigg's brother, for £4 of which the latter had become surety. His liability had devolved upon John and Lucy Campion through the latter's grant of representation to her first husband. The papers are badly damaged, and it is accordingly difficult to glean a coherent story from them; but we learn that Box had already got a judgement in some other court against Campion, who denied its jurisdiction, pleading the privilege to which, as a Cursitor, he was entitled, of being sued in the Chancery Court alone. The upshot of the matter is entirely obscure.

It is clear that the poet's father during these years must have occupied a position of comfort, if not affluence, for in 1569[5] he

---

[1] Star Chamber Proceedings, xxx. 35. [2] Ibid., xxxix. 40.
[3] See Eg. MS. 2599 *passim*. [4] Chancery Proceedings, Eliz. xxxvi. 46.
The papers bear no date, but the litigation must have been later than 8 Eliz., by which time Trigg's estate had been administered. [5] Eg. MS. 2599, f. 65.

purchased the leasehold property, Aveley or Alveleigh Parsonage (near Purfleet,[1] in Essex), from Henry Northey, of Lambeth ; while he occupied property in Brokenborough [2] (near Malmesbury, in Wiltshire), and rented other farms, possibly in the same neighbour-hood. He was also a pillar of the Church, having been elected one of the Assistants or Vestrymen of St. Andrew's. Stowe MS. 795 (f. 152) contains a document which is almost an exact copy of an original memorandum in the registers of that parish, relating to a 'Confirmation of Assistants'. It runs :—'Where (as) Hugh Wadylow one of the assistants hath misbehaved himself We the parson and assistants now being have in his place chosen John Campion, Gen. 3 Nov. A.D. 1573.' The original document in the registers adds the information that he was chosen assistant 'within the barres', i. e. for that part of the parish which fell within the city boundaries ; and, as we have already seen, the residence which we have assigned him on presumption fulfilled this condition.

John Campion is always described as 'gentleman', or 'gen-(erosus)', but it is possible that he may have aspired in his prosperity to the more honourable title of 'armiger'. Harl. MS. 1072, which contains collections of coats-of-arms borne by different families of the same name, includes such a collection of those borne by persons of the name of Campion, hastily tricked in pen and ink (f. 4). Among these is the following coat stated to belong to ' John Campyon '.

Now, I have not come across one other John Campion of any

---

[1] There were Campions in the neighbourhood of Purfleet, of what family is not clear. The will of John Weme or Wembe, alias Campion, proved in the P.C.C. in 1568 (21 Babington) refers to a limekiln in Purfleet ; and on the same matter of a limekiln in Purfleet John Campion sued Henry Griffin in Chancery (Chancery Proceedings, Series II, xxxi. 57).

[2] *v. infra*, pp. xxii, xxiii.

standing besides the object of the present narrative. Further, I take the central object, which is very rudely sketched in the MS., to be a campion flower, and such 'canting' arms would be precisely the kind that a man of the name would devise for himself, having none by right of inheritance. This charge of a campion flower is met with in none of the other bearings, and the only point of similarity between this coat and any of the others is the bordure engrailed, which is found upon the shield of Sir Richard Campion, one time Lord Mayor of London, of whom I can learn nothing. But these arms were never granted by the Heralds' College, and if they had any connexion with John Campion, he must either have worn them without licence, or, which is equally likely, devised them with a view to securing a grant, which, however, was forestalled by his death.

For he died in October, 1576, at an age which, without having certain knowledge as to the date of his birth, we can only conjecture by reference to his contemporaries to have been extremely early. He was buried at St. Andrew's on October 8, when the large sum of £50 [1] was expended on his funeral. If there was a monument, as appears likely from the amount of the expenditure, it has disappeared. On October 10, letters of administration of his estate issued to Lucy Campion, relict, out of the Prerogative Court of Canterbury, and soon afterwards the parish church records his vacation of the post of Assistant in the same way as it announced his appointment: 'Whereas John Campion, Gent. one of the Assistants is Deceased. We the Parson and Assistants now being have in his place chosen John Cowper Gent. 6 Dec. A. D. 1576.'

After her bereavement, Lucy Campion shook the dust of London from her shoes and departed to her late husband's property at Brokenborough, where she resided, presumably with her children, for the better part of a year. But she was not destined to mourn alone. Before the expiration of a year she was negotiating with a view to a third venture into matrimony, this time with Augustine Steward, whose name has already been mentioned in these pages.

Augustine Steward was the sixth son of Symeon Steward of Lakenheath, Suffolk, and grandson of Nicholas Steward, of a family spread over the north-easterly home counties which was of considerable standing and importance, and from which Oliver

---

[1] *v. infra*, p. xxii.

Cromwell,[1] the Protector, was descended through his mother, Elizabeth Steward. The generation to which Augustine belonged included several brothers who appear to have won a reputation as examples of brotherly love and amicable concord.[2] Augustine Steward himself was born in 1542 ; he was, in 1573 at any rate, one of the Queen's Serjeants-at-Arms, and he appears to have been a friend of the Campion family, for he gave evidence in that year in the Star Chamber suit against John Turner, and in 1574 John Campion apparently witnessed a deed [3] of his. Steward had considerable landed interests in Hertfordshire and the neighbouring counties, while a branch of the family, that of his brother John, had actually settled in Braughing,[4] within a few miles of the

[1] The Protector's mother, Elizabeth Steward, was grand-daughter of Nicholas Steward, Augustine's grandfather.

[2] MS. Rawl. C. 929, f. 65b.

[3] Eg. MS. 2599, f. 17.

[4] Augustine's brothers, John Steward and Nicholas Steward, D.C.L., purchased the manor of Braughing from Thomas, Lord Howard. Nicholas first held a court there on 24 Oct. 4 Eliz. Eg. MS. 2599 is Steward's book of accounts, containing also copies of the title-deeds of his properties. These included estates in Wisbech, Guilden Morden, Bassingbourn, Ely, Hoxton, London (Glastonbury Place, in Smithfield), Stradsett, Outwell, Aveley, Barking, Canewdon Rectory, and Hadham. There is also the title-page of a volume which belonged to him in the Bodleian (MS. Rawl. D. 1387, fo. 205) containing his signature, and coat-of-arms. He is also mentioned in the following records :—

Feet of Fines, Herts., 37 Eliz. Hil. : Augustine Steward : Simeon Brograve and Dorothy his wife. Manors of Alburye, Braughin, and Pelham. (See map.) Close Rolls, 26 Eliz. Pt. 10 ; 27 Eliz. 4 ; 28 Eliz. 1, 18, 24, 27 ; 29 Eliz. 23 ; 30 Eliz. 14, 16. Court of Requests, cxxxiii. 39 : Sir Henry North against Thomas, Augustine, and Nicholas Styward, concerning the purchase and removal of firewood. (Suffolk) xxxvi. 22 : Rowland Argall and Dorothy his wife against Augustine Steward and others, concerning a sum of money required to procure the office of the Clerk to the Council of Connaught. xxx. 104 : Nicholas Walterton against Augustine Steward and others, concerning a tenement in Fleet Lane, London.

' Augustine Steward, Lakenheath, Suffolk,' was admitted to the Inner Temple in April, 1564. By his second wife, Anne, he had issue : Margaret, Thomas, Augustine, Simeon, Anne, and Mary. Of these children only one of each sex survived him—a daughter, Margaret, and a son, Austen, who succeeded to his estates, and, described as of ' Hogsden, Middlesex ', was admitted to Gray's Inn on January 29, 1622. Augustine Steward, the elder, died in 1597, and his will was proved in the P.C.C. in that year (45 Cobham). Thomas Campion is not mentioned therein. He was buried at Braughing, in Herts., in which church a mural monument was erected to him. This monument, which is in the chapel north of the aisle, consists of a half-length portrait figure in armour and a ruff, with his arms above : or, a fess checky arg. and az. surmounted by an inescutcheon of the second charged with a lion rampant of

other Hertfordshire villages mentioned. It was not strange, therefore, that the families should have been acquainted.

In 1575 he apparently held the Patent of Keeper of the Park at Downham, in Cambridgeshire, not far from his parents' home in Lakenheath, and in connexion with this and other matters he fell exceedingly foul of the Bishop of Ely, Dr. Cox. Strype (*Ann.* II, App. i. 51) quotes some interesting papers recording the matter :—

A large book of sundry articles of Complaints against the Bishop of Ely with his answers to each.

XI. Austen Styward having the keeping of the Park at *Downham* demanding his Fee of the Bishop, it was withholden and denyed chalenging the forfeiture of his Office, for that the Chapel within the House of *Downham* was made a Milk-house. The said *Styward* and a minister with him were both indicted for breaking of the Milkpans. The Minister having a living of 16 l. pension in *Ely* he was forthwith suspended from his Living, and ministring within the Dioces of Ely. No Copies can be had of the Indictments : and the said Styward must yield Fine at the Bishop's plesure, or else ly in Prison.

Answer. I never denyed him his Fee, albeit he never did me Service but this : In mine Absence he entered into mine House, and brake up my Chapel Doors. And whereas in the Heat of Summer, for two or three Days in the Time of Thunder my woman had set her Milk pans in a cold place of the Chapel, he spurned them down with his foot. And Dr. *Turner* misliking of his Doings the said *Styward* with lavishing words termed him Dr. Pispot. I suppose this is not the office of an House-Keeper. Notwithstanding I meant not to take any forfeiture of his Patent. For since that time he hath received his Fee. But for his leud Dealing and abusing my House, and breaking up my Doors, he and his chaplain *Peter Tye*[1] was discharged of his service by my Chancellor justly. For divers of *Ely* have been most offended with him for his Negligence in Teaching and Catechizing the Children. And also for that he is a common Dicer, a common Bowler, and a common Hunter and is indicted for killing of Deer. And I ought not to suffer him to be Parish Priest and a Minister in the Cathedral Church also and to keep his Residence in *Ely* having a benefice in *Northfolk*. And yet notwithstanding I cannot drive him from Ely to his Benefice. And no mervail ; for an evil Beginning

the third debruised by a bendlet raguly of the first. This is the coat contained in the book above mentioned. Below the figure is the inscription :—'Augustino filio Symeonis Stewardi de Lakengheath, Suffo' Armigeri, moestissima sua conjux Anna, filia Thomae Argall, armigeri, posuit, per quem habuit filium et filiam, tantummodo virentem tempore mortis suae, anno Domini 1597.'

[1] 'Peter Tye, clarke,' witnessed an indenture and a recognisance for Steward in 1576. See Eg. MS. 2599, f. 51.

seldome hath a good Ending.   His Father Dr. *Ty* hath told me
and others not without grief that he wrote a letter counterfeiting his
Father's hand and carried it to my Lord of *Canterbury*, and by that
means was made Minister.

The Dr. Tye referred to was, be it noted, the famous Dr.
Christopher Tye, composer, and Master of the Choristers at Ely
Cathedral.

Some ten months, then, after the death of John Campion,
Augustine Steward paid his addresses to the former's widow and was
favourably received.   Matters were in the first place put upon a
sound business footing with reference to her property.   By a deed
dated August 19, 1577, she assigned the whole of her possessions
to Steward in consideration of marriage and of certain provisions
for her children which Steward bound himself to make.   These
are set forth in the title-deeds[1] of the Aveley property, which recite
the circumstances and the deed of gift as follows :—

Wd that Lucy Campion administrator of the goods and chattels
of John Campion hir husband decesed by Lr̃es of administraciõn
to hir graunted out of the pr̃ogative Court dated the tenth of
October Anº Dom 1576 did among other things and for and in
consideracion of a mariage wᵗin two dayes followinge between hir
& Austin Steward to be solemnized wᶜʰ accordingly in the Churche
of St. Dunstans in the est was done, & for & in consideracon of
dyvers bonnds wᶜʰ the said Austin entred endorced wᵗʰ condicion
to paye Mary Trigge fifty pounds Rose Campion ijᶜ li. at her
mariage and Thoms̃ Campiõ xl pounds by yere during his lyffe or
xiii score pounds in money being all the children of the said Luce,
she the said Luce by hir dead of gift among other hir chattels did
convaye the said p̃sonage of Alveleighe as followeth

To all to whom this p̃sent writing shall come be it knowen that
I Lucye Campion of houlborne in the suburbes of the Citye of
London wydowe do by theis p̃sents gyve graunt & confirme unto
Augustin Steward gent. his executors administrators and assignes
to the only use and behofe of the said Augustin his executors
administrators and assigns all & all mañ my goods chattels depts
lesses implem̃ts houshold stoffe & things what so ever as well quicke
as dead moveable & unmoveable of what so ever kind qualite or
condicion the same be or in whose so ever hands or possession
the same remayne & be To have hould & enioye to the said
Aug. his executors administrators and assigns as his and thir
owne p̃p̃ goods for ever   In witnesse whereoff to theis p̃sents I the
said Lucye have put my seale.   yeven the xix day of August in
the xix yere of the Raigne of õ Soveraigne Lady Elizabeth by

[1] Eg. MS. 2599, f. 69.

the grace of god quene of Yngland france & Yrland defender
of the faithe etc etc

1577

Lucy Campion

Sealed & delivered in the p̄sence of John Cowp. & John Walker
the writer hereof.

As the recital states, the marriage duly took place at St.
Dunstan's in the East, in Idol Lane, within two days of the
execution of the deed, viz. on the 21st August,[1] and Steward
obtained possession of all the property which had devolved upon
Lucy as Administratrix of Roger Trigg and John Campion. From
his detailed account of the whole transaction given below, it does
not appear that he was much the gainer. [Eg. MS. 2599, f. 62.]

A breif accompt of the goods of Mr. Campion which came to
my handes made 20 novembr. 1577.

First the inventorie of all his goods at London & Brokenborough
exhibited & del. unto the prerogative officer xxiii novembr. Anno
1577 amontinge (to) in both places in all to   1035 12 9

whereof deducted

	for funerall expenses	50li ⎫
Besides ye rents of his farmes, servants wages 55li	for detts mentioned in the inventory	304li ⎪
	To be paid to Mary Trig in consideration y^t divers goods remayning in the hands of mistris Campion were Mr. Trigs and so not administered	50li ⎬ 864li
	To Rose Campion for her porcion	200li ⎪
Paid to him 260li	To Thom̄s Campion an añuite after 40li by ye yere duringe his liffe	260li ⎭

unde remanet   ⎫

de Sm̄a   1035. 12. 9 ⎰ 171li   12   9

nòte that xiiili vis viiid due to the testator mentioned in the
inventory was nevr yet paid as by the bill obligatorye of
Bucocke[2] appēth quia admodum paup. est et Avunculus intestōris.
Of which 171li 12ˢ 9d Mrs. Campion before my mariage had lent
to Mr. Barnard Brocas upon his bill oblig. 76li whch could not
be had nor recovered from him in vii yeres after and until more
was spent in p̄curing him to be arrested then the det amonted

---

[1] The entry under that date is: ' Augusthyne Steward & Lucy Campion.'
[2] *v. supra*, p. x.

vnto and among oth͠r charges expended Wait had xx^li to get him staid in his house. also to Mr. Harecourts men x^li to get him staid in his Mrs Lodginge and last iiij^li to two Sergeants watching in fletstreet ij or three nights for him.

Item ther was sould to him Brocas of the goods mencioned in thinventorye as much as by a bill of the p̃ticulars amonted to 10^li 9^s 10^d which could never be recovered

Item left him to kepe other p̃ticulars wh^h remayned in the house at brokingboroughes till it was sould valued at iiij never yet had againe

Note that margret Jarvis aucthorised by mistres campion to sell her things at Brokingb. sould the hay and other implem̃ts there for lesse then they were prised by   31^li

And divers to whom she sould divers p̃cels being pore folke never were able to pay for them. and so the det still remayneth and mergret Jarvis upõ her accompt was found in arrerage above x^li wh^h she never paid leving w^t me at hir going away a bill of hir hand for it. note also that gomershall upõ the sale of Brokkingb. beside such implem̃ts as he bought ther were left divers p̃ticulars as a stacke of bavine ¹ and a gret deale of tall wood & sundry other things wh^ch after his graunt made could never be had from him

                                        19^li 9^s 6^d

Item I had bought of hir before mariage all hir horses to the value of   xxxv^li 6^s 8^d

Item Mrs. Campion maintayned hir selfe & hir familie one whole yere off the stocke before she was married   cc^li

Item I paid unto Bartholomew fild ² kinsman to Mr Campiõ as det to him due by Mr Campion as by a letter and a bill of filds hand appereth   iiij^li ij^s

Item I paid to one Wm̃ East for a legacy unto him bequethed by alice Bendbrig whose executore Mrs Campion was, as by his acquitance apperith   xl^s

Note Mrs. Campion gave awaye to divers hir husbands pore kinsfolke sundry of his goods and all his apparel

note also all her widdowhood being almost one yere she lyved of the stocke

---

¹ Bundles of brushwood or light underwood, differing from fagots in being bound with one withy instead of two.

² Bartholomew Field. His will was proved in the Commissary Court of London, November 16, 1608. As this will (in which he is described as a citizen and ironmonger of London) was witnessed by one George Searle, it is probable that Field was related to Campion through the latter's wife's family. He was executor of the will of Robert Parminter, proved in the P.C.C. in 1581 (11 Tirwhite) and was sued in the Court of Requests (cxxii. 10) in connexion with his administration by Thomas Hall. He was also sued in Chancery (Eliz. F. vi. 7) by Nicholas Woofe concerning money matters. There was an old and distinguished family of this name in and about Standon, Herts.

further the greter p̃t of the napery and divers other implements valued in the inventory were the very goods of Rogr̃ Trig whose administrator Mrs Campion was and never administered. wherefore they should not have come into the inventory of Mr Campion's goods.

So deductis deducend. & allocat. allocand. there came to my hands the remaynd. of the 171^{li} 12^s 9^d with the charge thereupon depending.

I had also by mrs. Campion as much copi hould land as I sould for 100 marks & the house & land at Hoxton demised w^{t}out fine to Jo. Curwin for x^{li} by the yere wch since I offering to sell because it is liable to a recog. knowledged by Mrs. Campiõ upõ the sale of Brokingb. I could not get for it above 160^{li}.

Au stewarde

I do accompt the expenses of Mrs Campion that yere she was wedow at 200^{li} : detts not paid w^t charge & expenses in the Law about obteyninge them 100^{li} : goods gyven away ; losse on the sale of other goods deteyned by gõmshale lxx^{li}
So in substance hir land excepted she was worse than enything by 200^{li}

Au Stewarde.

The will of Alice Bendbrig is interesting, for Lucy Campion's children were legatees thereunder to a considerable extent. By this will, made June 18, 1574, and proved in the Bishop of London's Court on July 7, 1575 (215 Bullocke), the testatrix, therein referred to as Alice Benbricke, made Lucy Campion her executrix, and bequeathed to Thomas Campion 'a bason, an ewer, a quart wine pott, and a damask napkin'; to Mary Trigg 'a diaper table cloth with open-work, two dishes, and two platters'; and to Rose Campion 'a diaper towell, a wine pottle pott, two dishes, and two platters'. The payment of 40s. to William East referred to appears to have been in satisfaction of a legacy of 'a hart of silver-gilt and a ring gilt' in favour of the testatrix's 'cousin Isabell's boy'. The residue of the estate was given to her three sisters'[1] daughters, and, in default of them, in equal shares among Thomas Campion, Mary Trigg, and Rose Campion.

Lucy had no children by Steward, and did not long survive the marriage. She died in March, 15$\frac{79}{80}$, and was buried in St. Andrew's, the entry running : 'Luce Steward ge^{t}w. (gentlewoman) buried the xvij m^{ch}.' Letters of Administration of her estate, in which she is described as 'Lucy Campion, otherwise Steward' of the parish of St. Andrew's, Holborn, issued some

---

[1] One of these, Alice Bageley, was one of Steward's tenants. (Eg. MS. 2599, f. 231.)

years later, on May 7, 1584, out of the Prerogative Court of Canterbury to Augustine Steward.

Steward, thus saddled with his orphan stepchildren, did not long remain a widower. On the 26th January following his first wife's demise (January 26, 158$\frac{9}{1}$), he married at Great St. Bartholomew's, Anne,[1] daughter of Thomas Argall and relict of Clement Sisley, of Barking, who brought him yet another stepson, Thomas Sisley, a lad of about the same age as Thomas Campion.

There is no evidence of the latter having attended any of the great schools of the time, though we should remember that there was an excellent grammar school in connexion with St. Andrew's, and, close at hand also, the old foundation of St. Thomas Acon.[2] But doubtless it was now high time that his education should be commenced in earnest, and, possibly, Anne Steward may have adopted the attitude usually associated with the title of stepmother. However this may be, the two boys were packed off a few months after the marriage to Peterhouse, Cambridge, where they were entered as gentlemen pensioners. Of Mary Trigg we hear no more ; Rose Campion continued to live unmarried with the Stewards until 1592, after which date we lose sight of her also.

Having regard to the local interests of the Campions and Stewards it was natural that Cambridge should be the University selected. Further, the famous Dr. Perne, who was at this time the Master of Peterhouse, was also Dean of Ely, and it is possible that Steward, who certainly had business dealings with him in his latter capacity soon after,[3] may have been acquainted with him already. But the choice of Peterhouse at this time requires no explanation, for it was passing through one of the most flourishing stages of its whole career.

The two lads did not matriculate, and no admission registers were kept by the College at this period. But the Buttery Books give the surnames of members, and in the entries under the date of May 13, 1581, the name ' Campyon ' first appears, followed by that of ' Sizley ' in the October term next after. The two names gradually approximate by removals until they stand together at the very head of the undergraduate list, their last appearance before finally vanishing being under the date of April 26, 1584.

Steward, who appears to have been a methodical person in all business matters, kept careful accounts of his stepsons' expenditure

---

[1] Eg. MS. 2599, f. 1.   [2] Now the Mercers' School, Holborn.
[3] *v. inira*, p. xxvii.

at Cambridge from Christmas, 1582, which, if not unique, are sufficiently interesting to be given in full. We may note that they occupied a study apiece, but a bedchamber in common, and that the living expenses were calculated upon a basis of fifty-two weeks in the year, from which it may be gathered that they did not return home during the vacations. [MS. Eg. 2599, f. 233.]

Allowance for Thoм̃s Sisley and Thoм̃s Campion at Cambridge beg̃ning at cristmas 1582.

First, eche of them for thir diete weakely ijs. vjd. : in the whole yere it amounteth to	xiij.li.
Item, thir tuition yerely xlv.s. for eche	iiij.li.
Item, rent for thir chamber and studies	xx.s.
Item, ether of them the first day of eche other monethe a payer of shoes at xvj. d. the payre, the whole xij payre of shoes	xvj.s.
Item, ech of them qūterly a quire of paper at iiij.d. the quire	ij.s. viij.d.
Item, a pound of candell betwen them every fortnight from mich^s untill ō Lady daye, in all xij. li. at iij.d. the li.	iij.s. vj.d.
Item, thir washing yerely	x.s.
Item, for mending thir clothes and shoes yerely	vij.s. x.d.
Sм̃	xx.li

Wh^ch I will qūterly deliver to thir tutor aforesaid.

These things they shal have qūterly sent them

At Cristmas, a cap, a band, a shirt, a doblet, a payer of hose, a gowne, a payer of netherstockes.

At ō Lady Day a new payer of netherstockes, and a hatt.

At midsuм̃r a shirt, a band, a doblet, a payre of hose, a payre of netherstockes.

At mich̃s a payre of netherstockes, a band.

And all such bookes as they shall rede from tyme to tyme.

So eche of thir whole yerely allowance is :—

A gowne, a cap, a hat, ij dubletes, ij payres of hose, iiij payres of netherstockes, vj payre of shoes, ij shirts, and two bandes.

The popularity of Peterhouse at this date was doubtless due to the prestige of Dr. Andrew Perne himself, a conspicuous figure in University affairs, and a broad-minded Churchman who has been much maligned. His changes of attitude during the reigns of Mary and Elizabeth, 'lackeying the varying tide' of the alternately predominating creeds, earned him the doubtful honour of having given rise to a new verb in current slang, *pernare*, to be a turncoat [1];

---

[1] Certain letters upon the college weather-vane were interpreted according as the wind blew as ' Andrew Perne, Papist ', or ' Andrew Perne, Protestant '.

but in reality he was a man who realized that by such conformity he could best protect and benefit the establishment under his charge, and do real service to the cause of religion. Where a more stiff-necked single-mindedness might have wrecked the college, it prospered under Perne to an unprecedented extent, while he was enabled to prove the protector of Whitgift through the Marian persecutions, and the patron of Peter Baro. And in some way, either direct or otherwise, the condition of Peterhouse itself reflected the attitude of its great Master. It contained at this time examples of almost every shade of religious creed, from the determined Roman Catholicism of such men as Henry Walpole the Jesuit (afterwards hanged) and the Yelvertons, to the opposite Puritan pole of John Penry, 'Elder Brewster' of the *Mayflower*, Dudley Fenner and Charke, all of whom were contemporary with Campion. The combination was one calculated to rub off the salient angles of creed, and this effect it probably had upon the poet, who, though many of his friends adhered to the older faith, was certainly not imbued with Roman Catholicism.[1] If he had any decided religious views, they were probably those of a moderate Anglicanism, but it is more likely that he was not deeply interested in matters of creed. His hostility to Puritanism cannot be construed as ranking him among the partisans of Church authority ; it was nothing more than the distaste of a scholarly and fastidious nature for the fanatical extravagances which masked the real importance of the movement. Campion probably looked no further.

Of Campion's career at Cambridge we know nothing except that he seems to have imbibed a considerable and varied knowledge of classical literature, together with much reverence for it. Very few of his friendships made at Peterhouse can be traced in his after life. There were two Percys at the college in Campion's time, either of whom may have been William Percy[2] the author of *Cælia*, and the subject of Campion's lines.[3] In the wider field of the University he probably made the acquaintance at this time of Thomas Nashe,[4] with whom from a very early date he was on terms of intimacy.

From the silence of the University records it is clear that the

---

[1] No sincere Catholic, however loyal, could have alluded to Elizabeth as ' Faith's pure shield ' (p. 50). See also *Poemata*, p. 330, *Ad Thamesin* ll. 11–14.

[2] This William Percy is known to have been at Gloucester Hall, Oxford, but he might have migrated thither from Peterhouse ; or, more possibly, these Percys were other members of the family, and the means of Campion's introduction to William Percy. [3] p. 277.

[4] Nashe matriculated as a sizar at St. John's in October, 1582, and remained at Cambridge ' for seven yere together, lacking a quarter '.

poet did not proceed to a degree before his departure in April, 1584. His movements, moreover, for the two years following are un-known to us, except that we occasionally sight him in Steward's account-book. In 1585, for example, he witnessed a bond[1] dated December 10, 1585, entered into by Steward to observe the condi-tions of a lease of a farm and lands in West Fen, Ely, granted to the latter by Dr. Perne, as Dean of Ely, on behalf of the Chapter. He also witnessed the signature to a recognisance[2] of February 10, 158⅚ given by Thomas Grymesdiche to Steward, with the endorsement ' I Thoms Campion, do know the recognitor'; and an indenture of April 2, 1586. But beyond such trifling mention his name does not occur until April 27, 1586, when he was admitted to Gray's Inn, possibly with the object of following, like his father, some legal or semi-legal profession.

He seems at once to have entered into the life and fellowship of the Inn. The collegiate character of the Inns of Court was far more marked during the Elizabethan age than it ever has been since; and, if Campion made few friends at Cambridge, he made plenty here. Of the names mentioned in his pages which we can identify, by far the greater number were connected with the Inn, and nearly all those of whom he speaks in the language of affection were his actual contemporaries; as, for example, Edmund Bracy, Francis Manby, John Stanford, William Hattecliffe, George Gervis, Robert Castell, Thomas Michelborne, James Huishe, and others. He appears, indeed, to have been one of those persons in whom friendship rises almost to the level of a passion. Himself an orphan from an early age, with a stepfather and stepmother who may have been unsympathetic (we never get a line about Steward in the 1595 *Poemata,* so full of other personalities), it is natural that he may have turned to the solace of friendship with an ardency unusual in those not deprived of other spheres of affection. That is at any rate the impression derived from reading his more personal Latin poems, such as those written to Francis Manby or upon his death, or the half pathetic lines *Ad amicos cum ægrotaret.*

The social activities of the Inns of Court were at this time put forward mainly in the direction of plays and masques, written and acted by members upon occasions of rejoicing. On such occasions the honoured guest was usually Queen Elizabeth, who, dearly as she loved such revels, was best pleased when they were paid for by others; and on one occasion expressed herself ' much beholden'

[1] Eg. MS. 2599, f. 75.   [2] Ib. f. 107.

to Gray's Inn, 'for that it did always study for some sports to present unto her.'[1] Soon after Campion was admitted, the famous *Misfortunes of Arthur*, written by various of the elder members, was produced. The poet may have taken part in this, but we have documentary evidence of his participation in some subsequent revels which took place in January, 1588. Lans. MS. 55 (f. 4) contains, in Lord Burghley's own hand, the following cast, endorsed :—

> xvii Janv. 1587
> The Names of yᵉ Gĕtillmĕ
> of Gray's In yᵗ played ther
> a Coṁedy
> befor Ye L. Burghley
> Er. of lec.
> Er. of warr.
> Erl. of Ọrmŏd.
> & Grey of Wilt.
> etc.

The cast itself runs as follows :—

Dominus de purpoole : Hatclyff[2]

The prologue	: Ellis [3]
Hidaspes ye sonn	: Campion
Manilius madd	: Anderton [4]
Pvso	: Farnley [5]
Lucius	: Astley [6]
Mummius old man	: Toppham [7]
Byrrhia parasite	: Stauerton [8]
Flamantia curtizan	: Sandfort [9]
Sr Delicate	: Sr Peter Shackerley [10]

[1] Nichols's *Progresses of Queen Elizabeth*, iii. 319.

[2] William Hatcliffe, son and heir of Thomas Hatcliffe, of Hatcliffe, Co. Lincoln, was admitted November 4, 1586. See also p. 339.

[3] Barnard Ellis, of Warmell, parish of Sebberam, Co. Cumberland, gent., was admitted May 26, 1587. He played the part of 'Master of the wards and Idiots' in the *Gesta Graiorum*.

[4] William Anderton, of Euxton, Co. Lancaster, and of Barnard's Inn, was admitted February 2, 158⅘.

[5] This must be John Fernley, son of Thomas Fernley, of Cretyng, Suffolk, admitted May 29, 1584.

[6] Is this Andrew Ashley, of London, who was admitted on June 20, 1586, at the request of Sir Francis Walsingham ?

[7] Of Barnard's Inn ; admitted to Gray's Inn in 1582.

[8] Either Francis Stafferton, of Barnard's Inn, admitted in 1578, or Patrick Stafferton, admitted January 23, 158⅞.

[9] 'Thomas Sandforthe, of Howgill, Westmoreland, gent.' was admitted in 1586.

[10] See Notes, p. 376.

Catelyne		: Rhodes [1]
Clodius		: Stanfort [2]
Salust		: Crwe [3]
Cato	} Censors	: Hutton [4]
Crassus		: Williamson [5]
Scilla Dictator		: Montfort [6]
Cinna 1 consull		: Davenport [7]
„ 2 consull		: Starkey [8]
Tribunus plebis		: Smyth [9]
Melancholy		: Campion
Epilogue		: Ellis

Masquers

Rhodes [10]	Ross [13]
Luttrell [11]	Peniston
Champnes [12]	Daye [14]

[1] Either Js. or Francis Roodes, specially admitted in 1577, or, more likely, Geoffrey Rhodes, fourth son of Francis Rhodes, one of the Judges of the Common Bench; admitted May 11, 1587, *absque fine* as his father was of the Inn.

[2] See Notes, p. 376.

[3] Of Nantwich, Co. Chester; admitted in 1585.

[4] Probably Richard Hutton, admitted 1580; afterwards a Judge.

[5] Richard Williamson, of Barnard's Inn, and Gainsborough, Co. York., admitted February 8, 1581-2.

[6] Thomas Mountford, of Gainsborough, late of Staple Inn, admitted November 15, 1585. There was a Momford or Montford at Peterhouse in Campion's time; and the latter was associated with a Dr. Mountfort in attendance upon Sir Thomas Monson (p. xlv). But this Dr. Mountfort, who is mentioned in the poem 'Of London Phisicons', is in the notes thereto stated to be the younger son of Sir Edmund Mountford, Kt., of Feltwell, Co. Norfolk. [Ed. J. P. Collier.]

[7] It is impossible to identify this Davenport among the three of the name who were at the Inn at this time. Two 'Damportes' took part in the *Gesta Graiorum*, one playing 'Lord Chief Baron of the Common Pleas', the other 'Lord Warden of the Four Ports'.

[8] Peter Starkey of Staple Inn, admitted November 1, 1587. He played 'Recorder' in the *Gesta Graiorum*.

[9] There were too many Smiths at this time to allow of identification. Two of that name took part in the *Gesta*; and see p. 376.

[10] See 1 above.

[11] Either Andrew Luttrell, admitted in 1580, or Thomas or George Luttrell, admitted October 26 of the same year.

[12] Justinian Champneys, son and heir of Justinian Champneys of Bexley, Kent, Esq., admitted January 24, 158¾.

[13] Thomas Ross, admitted 1585.

[14] Either Robert Day, of Clavering, Essex, admitted June 21, 1582, or Henry Day, of Oxborough, Norfolk (ex relatione Christopher Yelverton, reader), admitted May 25, 1582.

This ' Comedy' cannot be identified, but as to its nature I am indebted to an acute criticism of Mr. Daniel, who suggests that the cast involves a confusion of two plays, one on the model of the ordinary Terentine comedy, the other an historical drama, similar to Lodge's *Wounds of Civil War*, based upon Roman history. It will be noted, however, that the historical characters introduced are not all contemporary, and I am inclined to think that the play may really be one, and that it may have contained a review or procession of great Romans.

In the meantime Campion's financial affairs were put straight with Augustine Steward. It is presumed that his assent was necessary to confirm his mother's disposition of her real estate ; and accordingly by a deed[1] of March 2, 1587 (in which he is referred to as ' Thomas Campion de Grayes Ynne '), he releases Steward of all claims whatsoever which he might have had against him in respect of his mother's property, excepting in respect of the sum of £260 secured by the condition of an obligation delivered to Thomas Hall, gent., and others. Upon the poet's coming of age, a further deed[2] was executed to the same effect on October 20, 1588, and witnessed by Rose Campion. Business matters were also cleared up about the same time with Thomas Sisley, who had been entered at Staple Inn some time after he attained his majority, but who migrated thence to Gray's Inn in 159⅔. These arrangements were, however, more lengthy, as involving a considerable amount of property.

Campion was not called to the Bar, and it is evident from his Latin epigrams that legal studies were very little to his taste. It is tolerably clear, however, that he was already writing the Latin epigrams which afterwards figured in the 1595 *Poemata*, and he had also turned his attention to English verse.[3] From our knowledge of his acquaintance, it is certain that, whether in residence or not, he continued his connexion with the Inn until at least 1595, for early in that year the friend whom he laments in his 1619 edition of epigrams, James Huishe, was admitted, while he had written verses for the *Gesta Graiorum*, performed in 1594.

Our knowledge of the next episode in the poet's life is based on inference only from internal evidence, an inference which I have in vain endeavoured to confirm from other sources. In 1591 the Queen levied 4,000 men and a small body of horse for

[1] Eg. MS. 2599, f. 30.   [2] Ib. f. 33.   [3] *v. infra*, p. li.

the assistance of Henri IV; this expedition, commanded by the Earl of Essex, arrived at Dieppe on the 2nd August; and, though nominally dispatched as a reinforcement against the Spanish invaders of Brittany, was employed by the King, much to his royal sister's disgust, in the reduction of his refractory Catholic subjects, who were refusing to recognize his accession. With this object Rouen, then in the hands of the League under their able general, Villars, was invested on the 11th November, but without success, and the siege was finally raised on the 20th April following, at the approach of the Spanish troops under Parma. I believe that Campion accompanied this expedition from its dispatch until, at any rate, the following winter or spring, for the following reasons which I give in their natural sequence:—

My attention was first called to the likelihood of the poet having at one time undergone military service, by the epigram in the 1595 *Poemata*, entitled *De Se* [1]—

> Vsus et hoc natura mihi concedit vtrinque,
> Vt sim pacis amans, militiæ patiens.

It should be remembered that these *Poemata* are clearly a collection of scattered epigrams and poems composed at different times, and it seems natural to conclude from this distich that at some time prior to 1595 the poet had served as a soldier and had written the epigram in humorous depreciation of his military qualifications. On casting about further for indications of the precise campaign to which allusion is made, one cannot but be struck with the epigram *In obitum fratris clariss. comitis Essexii* (p. 340) in the 1595 *Poemata*, reprinted as Ep. 9, Book II, of the 1619 edition. The language of this poem and the accuracy of the description of the incident, suggest that it was written by an eyewitness.

According to State Papers in the Record Office (S. P. For. France, xxv. 290) Villars, in command of Rouen, made an expedition with the object of surprising Pont de Mer,[2] which was in the King's hands. Essex, seeing an opportunity of 'fleshing' his hitherto untried English levies, made a reconnaissance in force on Sept. 8, 1591, from his quarters at Pavilly against the enemy's position, with 250 French horse, 200 English horse, and 1500 picked English foot. These troops occupied a hill close to the walls, whence they threatened the town of Rouen, insomuch that the garrison, in great alarm, sent to recall Villars, and made

---

[1] *v.* p. 345.   [2] Now Pont-Audemer.

several sallies which were defeated and driven back. In the course of one of these skirmishes, however, a soldier, in ambush behind a hedge, fired his piece at Walter Devereux, Essex's brother, and captain of the cavalry squadron; and the ball, entering his jaw, passed up into his head and slew him. A Homeric struggle for the body ensued, in which several captains, notably Gerard, John Wotton, and Sir Conyers Clifford, after great efforts, finally succeeded in effecting a rescue. The reconnaissance then drew off victorious, but in universal mourning for the death of Devereux, whose noble qualities had made him generally beloved.

If this account be compared with Campion's, the latter will appear very close to the facts. His description of the disaster and of the topography is correct, and his reference to Devereux dropping from his horse reminds us that, whereas the captains of infantry must have fought on foot, Devereux, as captain of the cavalry, was certainly mounted. The vivid style of the narrative also, in my opinion, strongly suggests the eyewitness.

From the concluding lines of the epigram, 'Peribit ergo Rhona,' &c., I think it may be fairly inferred that it was written *before* the siege was raised. If, therefore, the poet was writing Latin epigrams during his actual military service, it is most likely that the epigram *De Se* was written at the same time.

There is more evidence of a similar character. There is the epigram in the 1595 *Poemata*, *De Th. Grimstono et Io. Goringo* (p. 341). In the 1591 expedition Captain Thomas Grimston commanded 150 Suffolk men, and Captain John Goring 180 men of York and Rutland; they served through the siege until December, when, among others, their bands were 'cast', i.e. the remnants were absorbed into other companies. In the following February Captain Grimston figures in the musters held in England as commanding a fresh draft of 150 Hertford-shire men, and Captain Goring, in joint command with Captain Sir Thomas Baskerville, of a draft of 350 London men, both drafts forming part of a reinforcement of 1600.

A stronger piece of evidence is the epigram *Ad Rob. Caræum Equitem Auratum nobilissimum* (46, Book I, 1619 edition). Now in the original expedition Sir Robert Carey (he was knighted by Essex during the campaign) commanded 100 London men and 50 Surrey men. The second line of the poem makes it clear that the reference is to these times of civil war in France, and Carey's own Memoirs show that his only French military service was on this expedition until shortly before Christmas, 1591, when he returned to England with Essex. Further, the word *cernebam* must, I think, be regarded as strong evidence of Campion's actual presence at these wars.

If so much is conceded, it may be seen with sufficient probability in what capacity the poet joined the expedition. The musters from which the above figures are extracted refer only to the men compulsorily levied by the several counties, but in addition to these there must have been a considerable number of 'Gentlemen Adventurers', or volunteers. Campion was in all likelihood attached to Carey's London company, and this, as we know, was particularly rich in volunteers, doubtless owing to the gallant and chivalrous personality of its young captain. In a muster held at Mont de Malades on December 17, 1591, Carey's band, which originally, be it remembered, numbered 150, figures as—

$$\left.\begin{array}{ll} \tilde{p}\text{sent} & 36 \\ \text{sick} & 17 \\ \text{for forag(e)} & 5 \end{array}\right\} 58$$

and is pronounced 'verry wek but for gentlemen Adventurers' (S. P. For. France, xxvii, 953). Carey himself states in his Memoirs that Essex had 200 horse and 4,000 foot, 'besides volunteers which were many,' and relates further that during his own command he kept 'a table all the while I was there that cost me thirty pounds a week'. Doubtless the guests entertained were gentlemen volunteers, with, very possibly, Campion among them. Coningsby, in his rather disjointed account of the siege (*Camden Misc.* I) refers to gentlemen adventurers to the number of about forty horse, who were in attendance upon the Earl of Essex, but from the muster above quoted it seems that there were other volunteers serving on foot in Carey's company, doubtless those who could not afford to mount themselves.

I think we may fairly conclude from the foregoing that Campion joined the expedition which reached Dieppe on August 2, 1591, as a Gentleman Adventurer probably attached to Carey's London contingent; witnessed the death of Walter Devereux, became intimate with Goring and Grimston, and finally, perhaps conceiving a distaste for warfare, withdrew himself from the campaign some time before its termination: I say, before its termination, inasmuch as the terms of the epigram to Grimston and Goring suggest that at the time it was written they were on active service in France, and he was separated from them.

Campion's foreign service is indicated by yet another piece of evidence, the epigram *In Barnum* in the 1595 collection (p. 344), reprinted as Ep. 80 Book II of the 1619 volume. Now the epigram as it stands might have been written by any one who resented Barnes's bragging, on mere suspicion, and without any knowledge of the facts. But this was not the impression it gave his contemporaries. Nashe, at any rate, seems to have believed that Campion was 'showing up' Barnes with a first-hand knowledge of his real cowardice. In *Have with you to Saffron Walden* Nashe says of Barnes that, 'hauing followed the Campe for a weeke or two . . . to the Generall he went and told him he did not like of this quarrelling kinde of life, . . . wherefore hee desir'd license to depart, for hee stood euerie howre in feare and dread of his person, and it was alwais his praier *from suddain death, good Lord, deliuer vs* . . . One of the best Articles against *Barnes* I haue ouerslipt, which is that he is in Print for a Braggart in that vniversall applauded Latine Poem of Master *Campions*; wherein an Epigram entituled *In Barnum*, beginning thus :—

Mortales decem tela inter Gallica cæsos,

he shewes how hee bragd, when he was in *France*, he slue ten men, when (fearfull cowbaby) he neuer heard peice shot off but hee fell flat on his face. *To this effect it is, though the words somwhat varie.*'

The words certainly do vary considerably (the italics of the last sentence are mine), but the point is that, whatever the actual words, Nashe construed them as a first-hand refutation of Barnes's claims to prowess. It is clear that Barnes served on the 1591 expedition, from Nashe's sneering allusion in *Have with you*, &c. (published in 1596), to 'his doughtie service in France *five* yeares agoe'. From another passage in the same book, it appears that Barnes served under Sir Thomas Baskerville, who was captain of a Gloucester company in the original expedition, and later, in February, 1592, in joint command with Goring of a fresh draft of London men. Barnes, therefore, possibly joined this latter draft, and if Campion's term of service for any period overlapped that of Barnes, the former cannot have returned until some date in or after February, 1592.

The connexion with Gray's Inn temporarily broken off by Campion's association with this expedition was resumed on his return, for his interests in that institution continued for some time after this date. Further, while, as we have seen, he had written Latin verse by this time, it is clear that he had also written

English poetry, for in 1591 his first printed poems, the set of five anonymous ' Cantos' included in the *Poems and Sonets of Sundry other Noblemen and Gentlemen* appended to Newman's surreptitious edition of Sidney's *Astrophel and Stella*, appeared. It is clear, moreover, that he must have written a considerable amount of English verse by this time, for Peele refers to it in his *Honour of the Garter*, published in 1593, in the lines

Why goest not thou

That richly cloth'st conceite with well made words,

Campion ?

and his poems were already appearing in the commonplace-books of the time. For example, Newman's 1591 edition of *Astrophel and Stella* contains the poems on pp. 349–51 ; the common-place-book of John Sanderson (Lans. MS. 241) contains the verses ' What if a day' under an entry apparently made in 1592, while in 1596, the date of Harl. MS. 6910, three of his poems were transcribed. According to the usage of the time, to which there are numerous references in contemporary literature, these verses passed from hand to hand in MS.: it was even a fashion with some to despise anything which had been given to the public in print, as we gather from the preface *To the Reader*, prefixed to *Two Bookes*.

The first entire book that Campion published was, however, a collection of Latin poems, entered in the Stationers' Register on December 2, 1594, ' RICHARD FEILD Entred for his copie vnder the wardens hands in court, a booke intituled THOMA CAMPIANE *Poema* . . . vj^d,' and published in 1595. This book won him a considerable reputation almost immediately. The same year appeared William Covell's *Polimanteia*, in which, after exhorting the University of Oxford, and adducing the many shining lights in literature which that seat of learning had brought forth, the author thus addresses himself to the sister University : ' I know, *Cambridge*, howsoeuer now old, thou hast some young, bid them be chast, yet suffer them to be wittie ; let them be soundly learned, yet suffer them to be gentlemanlike qualified,' and the marginal note to the passage is ' Sweet Master Campiõ '. His allusion is usually held to relate to Campion's English poems, but I am inclined to believe that, if the words contain, as they seem to do, any suggestion of criticism or gentle rebuke, it is the Latin poems at which the writer levels. In the *Poemata*, Campion, in imitation of the licence assumed by his models, the classical epigrammatists, frequently resorts to degrees of obscenity unusual even in that age, while the allusion to sound learning would not be likely to refer to poems composed in the vernacular. Further instance of Campion's recognition as a Latin poet is to be found in Meres's *Palladis Tamia* (1598) (which consists of a series of euphuistically balanced parallels between past and contemporary authors, to the glorification of English letters), and Fitzgeffrey's *Affaniæ* (1601). The passage in the first book runs :—

As these Neoterickes, Iouianus Pontanus, Politianus, Marullus Tarchaniota, the two Strozae, the father and the son, Palingenius, Mantuanus, Philelphus, Quintianus Stoa, and Germanus Brixius have obtained renown and good place among the ancient Latine poets : so also these Englishmen, being Latine poets, Gualter Haddon, Nicholas Car, Gabriel Haruey, Christopher Ocland, Thomas Newton with his *Leyland*, Thomas Watson, Thomas Campion, Brunswerd and Willey have attained good report and honourable advancement in the Latin empyre.

The epigrams of Fitzgeffrey, who was, by the way, a close friend of Campion and addressed other epigrams to him, are as follows : —

> Primus apud Britones Latiis Epigrammata verbis
>   More tuo scripsit nomine notus Eques.
> Huic ætate quidem sed non tamen arte secunda
>   Cui Campus nomen Delius ingenium.
> Ultimus his ego sum, quem quamvis mille sequantur
>   Præcipiet vereor hunc mihi nemo locum.

Here it will be seen that Campion is regarded as the second English writer of Latin epigrams, Sir Thomas More having been the first with his *Epigrammata*, published at Basle in 1520. As a Latin elegist, however, Campion arrogates to himself the first place in Elegeia I of this 1595 collection. The other epigram of Fitzgeffrey alludes directly to Campion as a Latin elegist, in support of his claim.

> O cuius genio Romana elegeia debet
>   Quantum Nasoni debuit arte suo,—
> Ille sed inuitus Latiis deduxit ab oris
>   In Scythicos fines barbaricosque Getas,—
> Te duce cæruleos inuisit prima Britannos
>   Quamque potest urbem dicere iure suam.
> (Magnus enim domitor late, dominator et orbis
>   Viribus effractis, Cassiuelane, tuis,
> Iulius Ausonium populum Latiosque penates
>   Victor in hac olim iusserat urbe coli.)
> Ergo relegatas Nasonis crimine Musas
>   In patriam reuocas restituisque suis.

To Dowland's *First Booke of Songs and Ayres* which appeared in 1597, Campion contributed a Latin epigram, and in 1601 he published with Philip Rosseter[1] his first English book, *A Booke of Ayres,* in two parts, the music of the first of which was composed by him, that of the second by Rosseter, while we may for the present assume[2] that all the words were written by the former. In the following year, 1602, he published a work of considerable academic importance, the *Obseruations in the Art of English Poesie,* discussed below, to which Daniel in the same year published a complete and overwhelming counterblast in his *Defence of Ryme.* We should note in passing that Daniel refers to Campion as 'a man of faire parts and good reputation', and as one 'whose commendable rymes, albeit now himself an enemy to ryme, have given heretofore to the world the best notice of his worth', a direct and accurate estimate of the relatively greater value of his English verse, which he was always disposed to regard as the 'superfluous blossoms of his deeper studies', as compared with his Latin verse, of which he seems to have been extremely proud. Drummond of Hawthornden tells us that Jonson wrote a *Discourse of Poesy* both against Campion and Daniel; but this has not survived.

In Camden's *Remaines of a Greater Worke concerning Britaine,* published in 1605, occurs a mention of Campion among the most celebrated men of the day, which argues that he had already attained considerable reputation and popularity. The passage runs: 'These may suffice for some Poeticall descriptions of our auncient Poets: if I would come to our time, what a world could I present to you out of Sir *Philipp Sidney, Ed. Spencer, Samuel Daniel, Hugh Holland, Ben. Ionson, Th. Campion, Mich. Drayton, George Chapman, Iohn Marston, William Shakespeare,* and other most pregnant witts of these our times, whom succeeding ages may iustly admire.' To be ranked among these giants was high praise, the more so when we consider how small a portion of his English poetry had by this time appeared.

---

[1] Philip Rosseter was one of the patentees and manager of the Queen's Revels Company in January, 1610. This Company was amalgamated with Henslowe's in March 161⅔ (Dulwich MS. i. 106); when Henslow bought apparel from Rosseter to the value of £63, which suggests that Rosseter was retiring from management. He was owner of the new Blackfriars house in 1615. He published *Lessons for Consort* in 1609; he was universal legatee under Campion's will (p. xlvii); died himself on the May 5, 1623, and was buried at St. Dunstan's in the West two days later.

[2] *v. infra,* p. lii.

Despite this significant mention, for a period of four years reckoned from the production of the *Obseruations* until the appearance of Barnabe Barnes's *Foure Bookes of Offices* in 1606 with Campion's prefatory Latin verses, we are met with a total silence on his part.   This may, however, be explained by his description in connexion with these verses as ' Doctor in Physic '.   After this date allusions to that degree are frequent, though there is no extant previous mention of it ; and it is natural to infer that during this lacuna in his literary output he studied for and obtained it.   It is clear that he left Cambridge without a degree ; and a comparison between his 1595 and 1619 editions of Latin poems, from the total absence of medical allusions in the former and the abundance in the latter, will assure us that he had not studied medicine before 1595.   Ep. 2, Book II, of the later edition contains, moreover, a curiously definite statement on the subject in the lines [1]

> Lusus si mollis, iocus aut leuis, hic tibi, Lector,
>   Occurrit, vitae prodita vere scias,
> Dum regnat Cytheræa : ex illo musa quieuit
>   Nostra diu, Cereris curaque maior erat :
> In medicos vbi me campos deduxit Apollo,
>   Aptare et docuit verba Britanna sonis.

I think it tolerably clear from all these indications that some time after 1595 Campion had exhausted his small patrimony and any other means he may have had, and found himself face to face with the necessity of adopting some profession.   He accordingly qualified as a physician, proceeding to his degree at a date which we are obliged to fix some time between 1602 and 1606.

It remains to inquire at what University this degree was conferred, and to this query it is to be regretted that we have no definite answer.   It is worthy of notice in passing that the study of medicine was fostered at Peterhouse, which possessed at this time an unusually full library of works upon medicine and its current substitute, astrology, while there were contemporary with Campion several medical fellows, including Professor Lorkin, Bartholomew Heath, Thomas Laker, and others.   But the evidence is, on the whole, against the poet having proceeded to his degree at Cambridge.   The records of degrees were not kept at all between the years 1589 and 1602, as appears from Fuller's *History*, in which we find that ' Stokys was made Register

---

[1] These lines are an apology for the levity of Book II, which is in the main a reprint of the 1595 epigrams : hence *ex illo* means since 1595.

by grace 1558 and appears to have been a very good Register, but he was strangely mistaken in his deputy and successor Tho. Smith, who was so very false to his trust . . . accordingly we find no graces at all entered, but a perfect and total neglect of everything from 1589 till 1601 when Tabor came into office.' As we have seen, however, it is not likely that Campion had obtained his degree by 1602, and as it was not conferred at Oxford, it seems necessary to conclude that the poet studied at one of the continental Universities. Here, again, the usage at Peterhouse is interesting as bearing upon this point. The college definitely sought to foster study at the foreign Universities, and throughout the Tudor period leave was frequently granted to Fellows to absent themselves for two, three, four, or even ten years for study at some approved *generale studium in partibus transmarinis.*

It seems probable, therefore, that Campion studied medicine abroad, though at which university the paucity of records and their difficulty of access makes it hard to decide. There are no indications in his Latin poems of his having travelled in any particular country, saving bare references to 'lingua Gallica' and 'litterae Gallicae'[1] which suggest that he was acquainted with the French language and literature. It is clear that he was well known as a practising physician. He is referred to in the satirical poem *Of London Physicons*[2] found in the MS. poetical commonplace-book of a Cambridge student (date about 1611), the allusion running :—

> How now Doctor Champion, musicks and poesies stout
> Champion,
> Will you nere leave prating?

while about the same time (viz. 1610–11) the following appeared among the verses addressed *To Worthy Persons*, appended to John Davies of Hereford's *Scourge of Folly.*

> *To the most iuditious and excellent* Lyrick-Poet,
> Doctor Campion.
>
> Vpon my selfe I should *iust* vengeance take
> Should I omitt thy mention in my *Rimes*,
> Whose *Lines* and *Notes* do lullaby (awake)
> In Heau'ns of pleasure, these vnpleasant *Times.*

---

[1] *Epigrams*, Book I. 168 (p. 259), Book II. 186 (p. 300). See also the reference to French orthography in the *Obseruations* (p. 54). I have ascertained that Campion did not enter Montpellier : Paris would have been a likely choice, but I can get no information as to this.   [2] Ed. J. P. Collier.

Neuer did Lyricks more then happie *straines,*
(Straind out of *Arte* by *nature,* so with ease,)
So purely hitt the *moods* and various *Vaines*
Of musick and her Hearers as do These.
So thou canst cure the *Body* and the *minde,*
(Rare *Doctor,*) with thy twofold soundest *Arte* ;
Hipocrates hath taught thee the one kinde,
Apollo and the *Muse* the other Part :
    And both so well that thou with both dost please
    The Minde, *with* pleasure ; *and the* Corps, *with ease.*

Further, as we shall see hereafter, Campion attended Sir
Thomas Monson in the Tower.

In 1607 his masque for the marriage of Lord Hayes was per-
formed and published, and in 1609 appeared Ferrabosco's *Ayres,*
with his verses prefixed. In 1611 appeared Coryate's *Crudities*
with his prefatory Latin epigram. His output during this period
was indeed slender, but the lean years were atoned for by his
subsequent fecundity. In 1613 he published the *Songs of
Mourning* for Prince Henry, whose universally regretted death
took place on November 6, 1612, brought about, as was generally
believed, by the sweating sickness : and in the same year he wrote
and published three other masques—the *Lords Maske* for the
wedding of the Princess Elizabeth to the Count Palatine on
April 14; the masque-entertainment for the amusement of the
Queen during her stay at Caversham House as the guest of Lord
Knowles on April 28 and 29, and a third for the Earl of
Somerset's marriage to Frances Howard, Countess of Essex,
on December 26. To this *annus mirabilis* of the poet's,
moreover, is attributed with some probability his second col-
lection of English songs, *Two Bookes of Ayres.* This bears no
date, but it contains allusions to the death of Prince Henry, and
must accordingly be later than 1612. While, however, on the
whole it seems likely that it was published in 1613, I do not think
the evidence of these allusions very satisfactory, having regard to
the fact that the book is a collection of occasional songs which
may have been written some time before their publication.

Of the masques proper performed in this year, the *Lords
Maske,* and the masque at the marriage of the Earl of Somerset,
some unfavourable criticism is reported in Chamberlain's cor-
respondence. Of the former [1] he wrote, 'Of the Lords Maske
I hear no great commendation save only for riches, their devices

---

[1] Winwood's *Memorials,* iii. 435.

being long and tedious, and more like a play than a masque.'
But whatever this masque may have been, it can hardly be called
long, and, as Nichols suggests, Chamberlain, who was not present,
may have confused it with Chapman's production for the same
occasion, which its author himself confessed to be unduly lengthy.
Of the latter[1] Chamberlain wrote to Mrs. Alice Carleton on
December 30, 1613: 'I hear little or no commendation of the
masque made by the Lords that night, either for device or dancing,
only it was rich and costly.'

To this masque, considerable personal interest attaches by
reason of its connexion and that of its author with the famous
Overbury murder case. For the complete comprehension of
Campion's share in this sordid conspiracy it will be necessary
briefly to recount the course of events.[2] Frances Howard,
Countess of Essex, was enamoured of Robert Car, Viscount
Rochester (afterwards Earl of Somerset), and on 25 Sept., 1613, she
succeeded in getting her marriage annulled. But Car's friends,
including Sir Thomas Overbury, exerted their private influence to
prevent the consequent marriage, which Car and the Countess
were eager to contract, from taking place. Overbury's remon-
strances brought him to an open rupture with Car during an
interview in the gallery at Whitehall, in the course of which
he said: 'Well, my lord, if you do marry that filthy base woman,
you will utterly ruin your self; you shall never do it by mine
advice or consent; and if you do, you had best to stand fast.'
Roused to a violent passion, Car replied: 'My own legs are
straight and strong enough to bear me up, but in faith I will
be even with you for this,' and so parted from him in a fit of rage.
A hollow reconciliation was afterwards effected, but Car concealed
his hatred, and neither he nor the Countess ever forgave the
insult. They accordingly resolved upon the death of the unfor-
tunate Overbury, who with extreme credulity believed that the
incident had been forgotten.

The plot was laid with devilish cunning, each link in the long
chain of crime being contrived with careful forethought. Prepara-
tions being ready, Car, who was in high favour at Court, arranged
that Overbury should be offered the post of ambassador to Russia.
The office was an honourable one, and Overbury's own in-
clinations would have caused him to accept, but in private con-

---

[1] Nichols's *Progresses of King James*, ii, 725.

[2] This account is in the main derived from MSS. Add. 15476 and Sloane
1002.

ference Car, who concealed the fact that he was prime mover in the appointment, dissuaded him from accepting, adding the promise of his protection in the event of any displeasure occasioned by the refusal. Overbury, who appears to have acted throughout with suicidal credulity, refused the offer, and was promptly committed to the Tower on April 6, 1613.

Matters had been in the meantime arranged in this quarter. The Lieutenant of the Tower at this time was Sir William Wade, and the Keeper in charge of Overbury one Cary, but Car had made plans for the replacement of these persons by more convenient tools, and Sir Jervis Elwes was fixed upon to succeed Wade. The transaction was carried out with all the circumstances of an ordinary venal traffic in office, Sir Thomas Monson acting as intermediary. As afterwards transpired from Elwes's evidence on trial (reported in Add. MS. 15476) Monson 'told him that Wade was to be removed, and that if he succeeded Sir William Wade, he was to bleed, that is, give 2,000^{li}'. The prophetically sinister nature of this language was remarked upon at the trial; and the prophecy was indeed fulfilled with Elwes's execution. The evidence continues : 'And ten days after Wade was removed, he (Elwes) came into the place, and payd 1400^{li} of the money at his unkle alderman Helvash his house to Doctor Campian.' Wade was removed on the 27th April, and Elwes took his place on the 6th May following.

The next step was the appointment of the keeper. The man selected was one Weston ; and at the Countess's request Monson recommended him to Elwes, who gave him the post. The train was now complete. Between Weston and Anne Turner, the infamous serving-woman of the Countess and the accomplice of all her guilt, an understanding existed that the former should administer to Overbury whatever was sent him. Elwes's connivance was already secured.

On the 6th May, the first day of Weston's keepership, rosacre, or blue vitriol, was sent him and duly administered to Overbury, who grew very sick, but did not die. Then Car sent the prisoner a powder to be taken as a specific for his ailment, which Overbury accordingly took. The powder was white arsenic ; and he grew exceedingly ill. At this point his suspicions were aroused, and he wrote to Car taxing him with treachery. But his fears were allayed by Car's reply, and on the latter's offer to provide him with any food he might fancy, he asked for tarts and jellies, which were duly supplied poisoned with corrosive sublimate. These, how-

ever, do not appear to have been consumed. Overbury was by
this time seriously ill, but his progress was not sufficiently rapid
for those who were plotting his destruction; and after he had
lingered on to the 6th September, they procured his final dispatch
by means of a poisoned glyster. His body, covered with
enormous and repulsive sores, was wrapped in a single sheet and
hastily buried in a pit dug in a mean place in the Tower pre-
cincts.

Overbury removed, the wedding took place on the 26th
December following, when Campion's beautiful masque was
produced. Donne wrote an *Epithalamium* for the occasion, and
Jonson, who had written his *Masque of Hymen* for Frances
Howard's first ill-starred marriage, now contributed a set of verses.
In 1615, however, Car fell into disfavour, and rumours of the
crime, previously whispered, now began to be openly reported.
A series of prosecutions ensued, in the course of which the matter
was thoroughly investigated. Elwes, Ann Turner,[1] and Weston
were executed. The Earl and the Countess were arraigned and
condemned; then reprieved, and confined to the Tower until
1622, when they were released and permitted to live in retire-
ment.

But it is, of course, the share of Campion and his patron,
Monson, in this business which we desire to assess. As already
seen, Campion had acted as agent for Monson in the sale of the
Lieutenancy to Elwes, and on October 26, 1615, his depositions
were taken, the original minute of which in the Record Office,
signed in autograph by the poet and those sitting to hear evidence,
(S. P. Dom. James I. 82) is reproduced as a frontispiece to this
volume. It runs as follows :—

The exãiation of Thom̃s Campion docter of phisicke taken
this 26 of Oct. 1615.

He confesseth that he receiued of alderman Helwys for the vse
of Sʳ Thom̃s Mounson fourten hundred pounds wᶜʰ Sʳ gervis
Elwis left or provided for him there,[2] and this event was about the
midsommer after Sʳ gervis became lievetenant of the tower, and
that pt of that 1400ˡⁱ was in gold, and pt in white money and the
gold Sʳ Thom̃s Mounson took wᵗʰ him and the white money
being in Bagge, Darwyn Sʳ Thom̃s Mounson's man caused to be

---

[1] She is said to have killed the fashion for yellow starch by being hanged in
a ruff starched yellow.

[2] 'there' is preceded in the MS. by the word 'at' which has been erased.

caried to Sr Thoṁs Mouns. as he taketh it, And for what con-
sideration it was payd this exãĩate saith he knoweth not.

(signed)

Tho: Campion.

J. Ellesmere, Canc.

Lenox.

E. Zouch.

The same month Monson was arrested, and after having been
detained in somewhat privileged confinement in the house of an
alderman, was brought before the Court on the 4th December;
and, no substantial evidence against him being forthcoming, was
remanded to the Tower. Here his health seems to have failed,
for on January 24, 1616, a warrant,[1] signed by 'J. Ellesmere,
canc.', 'Lenox', and 'Edw. Coke', was issued to the then
Lieutenant of the Tower, Sir George More, 'to allow Dr.
Montford and Dr. Campian, physicians, to have access to Sir
Thomas Munson, Knt., a prisoner in the Tower, to confer
with the said Sir Thomas on matters relating to his health in the
presence of the said Lieutenant.'

On February 13, 1617, Sir Thomas Monson pleaded at the
Court of King's Bench for a pardon, but, as he was careful to
make clear, it was not the ordinary pardon implying guilt which
he sought. He still reiterated his innocence, and in this attitude
the Lord Chief Justice supported him, finally stating that the
pardon was granted 'tam pietatis quam iustitia(e) motu.'

Monson admittedly acted as go-between in the sale of the
Tower Lieutenancy, recommended Weston at the Countess's
request, and charged Elwes (on whose authority does not appear,
but probably on Car's) to keep Overbury close without com-
munication with the exterior world. Further, it was a dependant
of Monson's, a musician named Marston or Marson, who actually
carried the poisoned tarts and jellies. But all this does not
necessarily imply a guilty cognizance of the intended crime. He
protested his entire innocence from first to last, and, in spite of
the threatening attitude of the court at his arraignment on the 4th
December, nothing was elicited against him. Elwes himself,
during his examination on October 3, 1615, stated that he thought
Monson innocent, while it transpired during the examination of
John Lepton on February 2, 1616, that the King also, on perusing
the evidence against Monson, thought that there was not one
count which was unanswerable. We may justly conclude that

[1] VII. Rep. Comm. Hist. MSS. p. 671.

the utmost guilt that can be laid to his charge in this affair is a reprehensible carelessness and complaisance in putting himself and his protégés at the service of the great, incurious of what vile ends he might thereby be furthering. So much for Sir Thomas Monson. As to Campion, the case stands thus : If Monson had been guilty, Campion might possibly, though not necessarily, have been also guilty. But if Monson was innocent, *a fortiori* Campion's innocence is established, and his fair fame is un-challenged by the least suspicion. At his patron's request he attended to receive a sum of money due to the former ; and, as he declared in his evidence, ' he knew not for what consideration the money was paid.' We may turn the pages of Campion's beautiful masque with relief that its very beauties are not rendered a hideous mockery by our sense of an underlying consciousness of guilt, and we may give ourselves up to the enjoyment of its rapturous bridal songs, untroubled by the suspicion that the hand that penned them was, by however slight participation, sullied with innocent blood.

In 1614 appeared Ravenscroft's *Brief Discourse*, with Campion's prefatory verses ; and shortly after Monson's pardon in February, 1617, the *Third and Fourth Booke of Ayres*, dedicated to the latter and offering congratulations upon his recent enlargement. The next year (1618) was published the *Ayres that were svng and played at Brougham Castle* for the entertainment of King James at that seat by the Earl of Cumberland on the former's return from Scotland in August, 1617. The music of these songs was composed by George Mason and John Earsden, while the author of the words is not stated, but it is tolerably certain that they were written by Campion. To this time possibly also belongs the undated *New Way of making Fowre Parts in Counter-point*, a technical work on music which was for many years a standard textbook ; while in 1619 he published his last work, the enlarged edition of his Latin poems, entitled *Epigrammatum Libri II. Vmbra. Elegiarum liber vnus.* This volume contains the epigrams of the 1595 edition in Book II, a further collection as Book I, nearly all the elegies and the *Fragmentum Vmbrae* of the earlier book in a finished condition, the whole being revised and added to.

He died on March 1, 1620 (16$\frac{19}{20}$), and was buried on the same day at St. Dunstan's in the West, Fleet Street, the entry in the register under that date being : 'Thomas Campion, doctor of Phisicke, was buried.' From the fact that his will was made in the article of death, and that he was buried on the same day, it has been suggested that he died of the plague, or some such sudden malady. But it seems to have been a tolerably frequent custom at this period to bury soon after the event of death. This was done in the case of Simon Forman's father, as we learn from the former's *Autobiography*, while there is even a closer parallel in the case of Tarlton, the famous actor, who, like Dr. Campion, made his will and was buried upon one day.

Campion's will, a nuncupatory one, was proved in the Commissary Court of London on August 3, 1620, the Probate Act Book showing his estate to be of the value of £22. The instrument admitted to Probate runs as follows :—

'MEMORANDUM that THOMAS CAMPION, late of the parishe of St. Dunstons in the West, Doctor of Phisicke, being in p̄fect mynde and memory, did with an intent to make and declare his last will and testament vpon the first of March, 1619, and not longe before his death saie that he did giue all that he had vnto Mr. Phillip Rosseter and wished that his estate had bin farr more, or he vsed words to that effecte, being then and there present divers credible witnesses.'

Philip Rosseter was, of course, his old friend and collaborator in *A Booke of Ayres*. There is no evidence as to Campion having ever married, but if he did, I think it may be safely inferred from the above bequest that he left neither wife nor children surviving him.

Of Campion's personality we know nothing beside what can be gleaned from his works. We learn from a Latin epigram,[1] included in the 1619 edition only, that he was of a spare condition of body, and envied his brethren cast in a stouter mould. His character seems to have been warm, sensitive, and impetuous ; and, during the earlier period, to use his own language, *dum regnat Cytherœa*, he seems to have sowed wild oats with the thoroughness of an inflammable disposition unchecked by home interests or parental influence. Orphaned at the age of ten, and thrust forth in his minority to sink or swim in the midst of the manifold seductions which Elizabethan London had for a youth of good standing, means, and attractive parts, it requires no violent effort of imagination to realize that the lines among his Latin poems, *Ignarum iuvenem nudum cur trudis in urbem?* were written by him when looking back in the maturity of ripe experience upon the follies of his early plunge into the world. Often as the battle has been fought between those who search for personalities in erotic

---

[1] Book II. 23 : p. 275.

D

poetry, and those who ignore them as immaterial, I have little hesitation in saying that the divinities addressed in the Latin poems were no creatures of the imagination. That is sufficiently clear from the whole tone and nature of the elegies and epigrams; their peculiarly intimate and real atmosphere; their allusion to obviously real occurrences, passions, and disappointments permitting of little doubt on the point. In particular he seems to have had 'two loves', who appear and reappear in his pages as *Caspia* and *Mellea*; and, though not 'of comfort and despair', vexed him with tortures arising from causes opposed; the latter being too free of her favours, the former not sufficiently free.

This same intimacy and reality extends to the relations of pure friendship mirrored in the Latin poems. As already stated, Campion seems to have thrown himself into friendship with the same abandonment and devotion with which he made the pilgrimage to Paphos. His passionate regrets for the dead Manby, and his complaints at the inevitable separation from the friends addressed in the elegy *Ad amicos cum ægrotaret*, give us a clear insight into his generous and affectionate nature. From that poem, too, we may infer in passing that, prior to 1595, and probably during his sojourn at Gray's Inn, he was afflicted with a severe illness, involving insomnia varied by bad dreams resembling delirium. To this illness there are several other references.

A brief account of the friends who played so large a part in Campion's early life may be of interest. First, the Mychelburnes, three brothers named Edward, Laurence, and Thomas. Anthony Wood called Edward Mychelburne 'a most noted Latin poet of his time'; but, saving two copies of verses prefixed to Bales's *Art of Brachygraphy*, nothing of his is extant. He was a member of St. Mary Hall, Oxford, whence he migrated to Gloucester Hall. He died at Oxford in 1626, and was buried in the Church of St. Thomas the Martyr. Campion and Fitzgeffrey both strove to break his resolution not to publish, but apparently in vain.

Laurence was also a poet. I find little of him except what is told us in the curious sidelight thrown upon his death by a letter from Dudley Carleton (Stowe MS. 171, fol. 368b), which contains the following passage : 'There is one Laurence Michalborne lately drowned in the way betwixt Genoa and Millan as he was riding through a current which fell frõ the mountains : his horse escaped, and he had ill luck, for he was a Poett and a passing good fellow, and men of that sort doe commonly end theyre dayes with better luck. From Venice this 5th day of Mc͞h 1620'

(162$\frac{0}{1}$). The *Dictionary of National Biography* gives no clue to
the parentage of these brothers, but I am inclined to believe that
they were the children[1] of Thomas Mychelburne of Gray's Inn,
and Alice, daughter of William Lawrence of Winchester. Their
father was admitted to the Inn in 1555, and Thomas the younger
in 1580. If these brothers are the sons of Thomas Mychelburne,
we may notice that Edward, Laurence, and another brother, John,
(not mentioned by Campion) died without issue, while Thomas
married Dorothy, daughter of Benjamin Shoyswell, of Shoyswell
in Sussex. Of the sister whose death is referred to in Campion's
elegy, I can find no trace. The family adhered to Roman
Catholicism ; and, for reasons of faith, Edward Mychelburne
abstained from proceeding to a degree.

Fitzgeffrey was another intimate member of the poet's circle.
He was the author of *Sir Francis Drake, His Honorable Life's
Commendation*, which appeared in 1596, and *Affaniæ*, a collection
of Latin epigrams published in 1601, already referred to, several[2]
of which were addressed to Campion and Mychelburne. William
Percy was another, the son of Henry Percy, Earl of Northumber-
land, and author of *Cœlia* (1595). Percy is known to have been
a member of Gloucester Hall, Oxford ; but there were two Percys
at Peterhouse in Campion's time, through whom they might have
become acquainted. Of Grimston and Goring mention has
already been made ; while some account will be found else-
where of William Strachey,[3] Edmund Bracy,[4] Francis Manby,[5]
William Hattecliffe,[6] John Stanford,[7] James Thurbarne,[8] Thomas
Smith,[9] George Gervis,[10] James Huishe,[11] and Robert Castle,[12]
among the poet's more private friends. Among those better
known may be mentioned George, Earl of Cumberland, Thomas
Sackville, Earl of Dorset, Sir Thomas Monson, Lord Bacon, Sir
John Davies, Nashe, Camden, Ferrabosco, Dowland, and
Rossiter.

His early extravagances he outlived ; and if it were possible to
recall the time of his later years, we may imagine that we should
find a kindly gentleman, full of ripe experience and judgement,
yet cherishing the memories of old loves and friendships, and the
generous illusions of youth ; devoted to the studies of poetry,
music, and medicine, a true son of Apollo, as he was never tired

[1] Rawl. MS. B. 435ᵃ f. 143. [5] *v*. p. 373. [9] *v*. p. 376.
[2] *v*. p. xxxiii. [6] *v*. p. xxix. [10] *v*. p. 376.
[3] *v*. p. 373. [7] *v*. p. 376. [11] *v*. p. 372.
[4] *v*. p. 376. [8] *v*. p. 376. [12] *v*. p. 376.

of urging ; clothed with that finer tact and sympathy which comes to a good physician. And pervaded by the same kindly temper we may conceive his after life to have been spent until its latest day, when even in the hour of death his thoughts were occupied with the kindly wish that his worldly goods had been greater for his friend's behoof.

CHAPTER II. THE POETICAL WORKS.

Some of the poems in this volume have not been previously included in the canon of Campion's works ; the authenticity of these, therefore, and of some others I propose to consider before proceeding to discuss the verse itself. And to clear the way to some of my attributions, I would call attention to a frequent trick of the poet's, which can be used as a critical test of some value ; I mean his habit of versifying the same thoughts and ideas in both English and Latin. A list of the more patent examples will make this clear.

'It fell on a sommers day' (*A Booke*, I, viii, p. 10).
'In Lycium et Clytham' (1619 ed., II, 60, p. 281). 'De Thermanio et Glaia' (1595 ed., p. 343).

'Thou art not faire for all thy red and white' (*A Booke*, I, xii, p. 12).
'Ad Caspiam' (1619 ed., II, 53 ; 1595 ed., p. 343).

'I must complain yet doe enioye my Loue' (*Fourth Booke*, xvii, p. 183).

ll. 4–6.
'In Melleam' (1619 ed., II, 18).

ll. 11 and 12.
'Ad Cambricum' (1619 ed., II, 116).

'Why presumes thy pride on that that must so priuate be' (*Third Booke*, vi, p. 163).
'Ad Leam' (1619 ed., II, 117, p. 291).

'Kate can fancy only berdles husbands' (*Obseruations*, p. 45).
'In Laurentiam' (1619 ed., I, 56, p. 244).

There are other examples, but these will be sufficient. Now if an English poem can be found which is an equally close version of any of Campion's other Latin poems, I think that, in reliance upon the habit demonstrated above, we may assign it to him, provided that such other evidence as we possess is not hostile to the conclusion. At the weakest, the parallel would afford strong presumptive evidence of authorship.

The attribution of the set of five *Cantos* of 1591 (pp. 349–51) turns mainly upon this criterion. They occur among the *Poems and Sonets of Sundry Other Noblemen and Gentlemen* appended to Newman's surreptitious edition of Sidney's *Astrophel and Stella*, edited by Nashe, who, we know, was friendly with Campion. The poems are obviously a set of five, numbered in series, and written by one man, whose pseudonym, *Content*, is subscribed to the set. Now the first is 'Harke all you ladies', which we know to be Campion's. *Canto tertio*, 'My Loue bound me with a kisse,' is a poem which afterwards appeared in a more lengthy form in Jones's *Second Booke* (1601). On applying our test, we find a close parallel in Epigram 12 of Book II of the 1619 edition of Latin poems, 'In Melleam' (p. 273). Its application in the case of *Canto quarto*, 'Loue whets the dullest wittes,' provides us with an even closer example in Ep. 54 of Book II, 'Ad Amorem'; and I can find little reason to doubt that the whole set is Campion's.

One other important attribution should be mentioned, though the use of this critical test might perhaps be extended. The *Ayres that were svng and playd at Brougham Castle*, published in 1618, were composed by George Mason and John Earsden, the author of the words being unstated. There is already, however, external evidence for their connexion with Campion in a letter adduced by Nichols, quoted at length in Whittaker's *History of Craven* (p. 293). Concerning the festivities at which these *Ayres* were performed, the Earl of Cumberland writes to his son, Lord Clifford, as follows: 'Sonn, I have till now expected your lettres according to your promis at your departure; so did George Minson (Mason) your directions touching the musick, whereupon he mought the better have writt to Dr. Campion. He is now gone to my Lord Presidents at York, and will be ready to do as he heares from you,' &c. This is good evidence, as far as it goes; but the matter can be almost clinched. Applying our test, we shall find an interesting parallel between Stanza 2 of III, *The Kings Goodnight*, and Ep. 188, Book I of the 1619 edition, *De Regis reditu e Scotia*, written about the same event. Here we find the same conceit of the sun dawning from the north, and close verbal parallels to lines 4 and 7 of the English stanza. Campion's style may be traced in some of the verses, notably in VI, 'Robin is a louely Lad'; but they are not all up to his best level. It is, however, in accordance with the unfortunate custom which has left us in the dark as to the authorship of some of the most perfect gems in the songbooks that the names of the composers alone are given; and the assumption that Campion suppressed his connexion with these verses as unworthy of him is unwarrantable. The Elizabethans were seldom so self-critical.

The next matter which must be dealt with is the authenticity of *A Booke of Ayres*, which has always been taken for granted, but which should, I think, be examined. The chief evidence is to be found in the address to Sir Thomas Monson, where it is stated that 'the first ranke of songs are of his owne (Campion's) composition, made in his vacant houres, and priuately emparted to his friends, whereby they grew both publicke and (as coine crackt in exchange) corrupted: some of them, both words and notes, vnrespectively challenged by others'. By 'first ranke' is meant Part I; and though Campion is only stated to be the composer, it is clear from the reference to the words being claimed by others, that these were also his; the truth being that he paid little attention or regard to these 'superfluous blossoms of his deeper studies'. An examination of the poems themselves, besides, bears out the attribution: there are Latin versions of 'It fell on a sommers day', and 'Thou art not faire'; 'Mistris, since you so much desire', and 'Your faire lookes enflame my desire' reappear in a slightly different dress in the *Fourth Booke*; 'The man of life vpright' reappears in *Two Bookes*; while, as we have already seen, 'Harke, all you ladies' had already appeared in circumstances which leave us little or no doubt as to its authorship. But when we proceed to examine Part II, this abundance of evidence entirely fails. Rossiter's preface continues: 'Yet it hath pleased him, vpon my entreaty, to grant me the impression of part of them, to which I have added an equall number of mine owne.' This must mean that the songs in Part II were composed by Rossiter. Now while, having regard to the intimacy between Campion and Rossiter, it is extremely likely that the former supplied words for these songs, there is no certainty that he necessarily supplied them all. I have no knowledge of Rossiter ever having written verse, but he might have had recourse to the general sources whence the other songbooks were compiled. The songs themselves afford no such evidence as that adduced in the case of Part I, save the one straw at which, perhaps, we may clutch, that the name *Laura*, a favourite one with Campion, occurs

in two of them. On considerations of style I am disposed to
assign most, if not all, of them to Campion ; but a personal sense
of style is a slippery thing ; and while we may for the present
include these songs among his works, I do not think that their ap-
pearance in *A Booke* should be regarded as a rebuttal of any other
attribution of which good evidence may hereafter present itself.

There are no similar doubts in the case of his other songbooks.
The reference in the prefatory verses to the *Diuine and Morall
Songs* to 'Graue words', and the sense of 'read them, or else
hear', are clear enough. The gift of verses for perusal would be a
sorry one if they were not the giver's. The reference in the
prefatory verses to the *Light Conceits* to 'my Notes and Rime'
is even clearer. And, finally, the whole tenor of the address in
the *Third and Fourth Bookes, To The Reader*, implies that the
words in these books are Campion's.

The inclusion of the rest of the works in this volume needs no
explanation, except, perhaps, as regards 'What if a day', the
authenticity of which has been questioned. But the doubt ex-
pressed by Mr. Swaen in his excellent monograph [1] arises from
incorrect information as to the date of one MS. ; and, as I have
shown in my note upon that poem, no reliance can be placed upon
this evidence. It is certain that there are numerous poems of
Campion's scattered about the songbooks of the time and as yet
unclaimed for him : some few suggested attributions will be found
in the notes ; while from contemporary commonplace-books I have
gleaned a few interesting versions of poems which appear in my
text. Two other poems, in quitting this subject, I must mention
as appearing, on grounds of style alone, to be Dr. Campion's : the
one (an attribution of Mr. Bullen) the charming song, ' The hower
of sleepy night decayes apace ',[2] which occurs at the end of

---

[1] *v. infra*, p. 378.

[2] The hower of sleepy night decayes apace,
   And now warme beds are fitter than this place;
   All time is longe that is unwilling(ly) spent
   But howers are minitts when they yeld content :
   The gathered flowers wee love, that breathe sweet sent,
   But loathe them, there sweet odours being spente :
       It is a life is never ill
       To lye and sleep in roses still.

   The rarer pleasure is, it is more sweet ;
   And friends are kindest when they seldome meet.
   Who would not heare the nightingale still singe ;
   Or who grew ever weary of the Springe ?

Nichols's transcript of the *Mountebanks Masque*; and the other, the lines "Do not, oh do not prize thy beauty at too high a rate"[1] from Robert Jones's *Vltimum Vale*. The *Mountebanks Masque* formed part of the second part of the *Gesta Graiorum* in which we know Campion had a hand. Mr. Bullen, while assigning this song to him, attributes the masque itself to Marston and includes it in his edition of Marston's works (vol. iii), but I am almost inclined to go further and to attribute nearly all the lyrics, except the comic ones, to Campion on mere grounds of style. For the same reason I think the song from *Vltimum Vale* to be Campion's: it seems to me to have the very ring and lilt which we are accustomed to find in his verse; and there is some similarity in the language. But in neither case have I been able to find any objective evidence. *The Masque of Flowers*, performed by the gentlemen of Gray's Inn on Twelfth Night, 161¾, has been attributed to our poet, but, I think, without justification. It is little better than doggerel.

Of the Latin poems it is not necessary to say much; for their literary value for the present generation is but slender. Their chief interest is in the information which they afford concerning the poet's loves and friendships, and in the clear presentment of his real

> The day must have her nighte, the Springe her fall;
> All is divided, none is lorde of all.
> > It were a most delightful thinge
> > To live in a perpetuall Springe.

Mr. Bullen's text reads 'sweety night' in l. 1; 'are better' in l. 2. The above text is that of Nichols (*Progresses of Queen Elizabeth*, vol. iii).

[1]   Do not, O do not prize thy beauty at too high a rate:
  Love to be loved whilst thou art lovely, lest thou love too late;
    Frowns print wrinkles in thy brows,
      At which spiteful age doth smile,
    Women in their froward vows
      Glorying to beguile.

  Wert thou the only world's admired thou canst love but one,
  But many have before been loved, thou art not loved alone:
    Couldst thou speak with heavenly grace,
      Sappho might with thee compare;
    Blush the roses in thy face,
      Rosamond was as fair.

  Pride is the canker that consumeth beauty in her prime,
  They that delight in long debating feel the curse of time.
    All things with the time do change
      That will not the time obey;
    Some even to themselves seem strange
      Through their own delay.

self which he did not hesitate to commit to the discretion of a dead language. Critically, they afford the test mentioned above, which has already proved useful, and may do so again. In style purely imitative, they are nevertheless graceful and elegant, and often neatly turned ; showing considerable control of the Latin lyric metres. In the earlier book, published when his youth got the better of his discretion, he pressed the obscenity without which no imitation of the classical epigrammatists would have been deemed complete, to unusual lengths ; and, as we have seen, received a gentle rebuke from William Covell. But these indiscretions were toned down considerably in the subsequent edition, revised in the light of riper judgement. Besides revision with this object, however, Campion had another purpose which is responsible for much alteration. The more usual scheme of hendecasyllabic, or Phalaecian, verse commences, as is well known, with a spondee ; but there was an alternative[1] employed by Catullus of which Campion made much use in his first collection, viz. of commencing with a trochee, or, more rarely, with an iambus. Some time, however, between the first and second editions he seems to have become doubtful as to the propriety of this practice, for in the latter every instance is expunged, in numerous cases the only purpose of the revision being the elimination of this foot.

But it is Campion's English verse with which we are mainly concerned, despite its author's low estimate, real or feigned, of its importance. Not only was he writing good verse at an early age— his first poem appearing when he was 24—but its appearance is all the more striking by its unlikeness to the poetry of the day, which with few exceptions was heavy and lumbering. Breton, Lodge, and the rest of the men on Campion's level, were not as yet emancipated from the trammels of laborious versification ; but Campion's verse was from the beginning free and musical. This musical quality is indeed the one which distinguishes the whole of his poetry ; it is undoubtedly connected with the practice of musical composition and due to a feeling for musical effect, to which, with his trained musical ear, he was peculiarly susceptible.

Among the earliest poems, and itself one of the freest and most charming, is ' Harke, all you ladies '. It will be noticed that this song has a somewhat curious scheme of dactyls and anapaests : the first three lines of each stanza follow the usual iambic or trochaic rhythm ; but the final quatrain changes, its first two lines being anapaestic, the third dactylic, and the fourth an Adonic (except in

---

[1] Campion refers himself to this practice in the *Obseruations* (p. 43).

the last stanza, where dactyls take the place of anapaests through-
out). I am inclined to think that this poem foreshadows Campion's
subsequent experiments in classical metres; while *Canto Secundo*
in the same set most certainly does. These curious lines are an
attempt at composition in an accentual version of the Latin First
Asclepiad, the metre of Horace's ' Maecenas atavis edite regibus ';
and the effect is certainly extraordinary. As far as the individual
lines are concerned, the result is sometimes fairly melodious,
sometimes almost doggerel; while an occasional deviation from
the strict scheme may perhaps be put down to textual corruption.
But it will be noticed that in such an accentual scheme the last
accent must fall on the antepenultimate syllable; and unless the
poet makes use of *versi sdruccioli* or antepenultimate rhymes
(which he never does) the rhymes will be unaccented and almost
unheard. This is, in fact, what actually happens; for the rhymes are
submerged, except in so far as it is possible to get a slight secon-
dary accent on the last : and it is quite easy to read the poem at
least once without perceiving that it is actually rhymed. Perhaps,
indeed, this may have marked a second stage in the poet's progress
towards unrhymed verse, as involving the discovery that, in some
forms of 'classical' prosody, rhyme became a negligible quantity.
The further course of Campion's infection with the prevailing
hostility to rhyme I shall discuss more fully in the next chapter :
suffice it to say here that in the whole of his English works, ex-
cluding the examples in the *Obseruations*, we only get one complete
specimen of his 'classical' metres, the abominable Sapphics at the
end of Part I of *A Booke of Ayres*. His musical and artistic sense
was too strong for his neoterizing tendencies.

One other aspect of Campion's verse should be noticed, the
extraordinary fluidity and lack of stability in his rhythms. This
again is referable to the purpose of musical composition with which
they were written. The marriage of music to Campion's verse was
no casual or one-sided union; nor was music a mistress with whom
his poetry dallied, while possessed of more serious interest. Words
and music were born for each other, and in their wedding was
consummated the only object of their existence. Hence, to-day,
in the divorce resulting from the verdict of time that the
poetry is worthy of immortality, while the music is not, we are
guilty of treating the former to some extent as *in vacuo*, and apart
from its usual environment. It would be exceedingly instructive if
an account could be obtained from a good composer-poet of the
mental processes necessary to the writing of both words and music

for the same song. In many instances the nature of the air would suggest the rhythm of the verse; and conversely a half-phrase or casual line would suggest a musical theme; with the result that both words and music might have assumed some form before either had been fully worked out or committed to writing. This must have occurred in most of Campion's lyrics. On some occasions he even wrote words to music, thus reversing the usual practice; for we find two pairs of songs written to the same music, where one poem in each pair must have been written subsequently. And this close interdependence between his words and his music is the quality for which above all others he took chief credit, and received it from his contemporaries. He says himself: 'In these English Ayres I haue chiefely aymed to couple my Words and Notes louingly together, which will be much for him to doe that hath not power over both'; from which it seems that the result proceeded not only from spontaneous causes, but also from conscious effort. Again, it is to this quality that Davies alludes in the lines already quoted:—

> Neuer did Lyricks more then happie *straines*
> (Straind out of *Arte* by *nature*, so with ease,)
> So purely hitt the *moods* and various *Vaines*
> Of *Musick* and her Hearers as do These.

While, however, the cause and object of these fluid rhythms was the musical setting, we are left with nothing of which to complain in their artificial separation. Campion's verse is always fresh and melodious, and agreeably varied with subtle cadences.

Campion was one of the last of the Euphuists; and to his position among those, as one who embroidered thought with a tissue of rich diction, Peele alludes in the reference above quoted.[1] This Euphuism was not, however, of the grosser variety, but of a refined and sublimated type; which upon ultimate analysis may be reduced merely to an unemphatic balance, or antithesis, in the structure of his sentences; a very rare illustration from natural objects; and an occasional flavour of moral sentiment. But in many of his poems even this degree of Euphuism is totally absent, as, for example, in 'Turn back, you wanton flyer', 'Harke, all you ladies', 'If thou long'st so much to view', and several others.

Attention should also be drawn to the unlyrical quality of some of Campion's songs, which are in reality little monologue sketches;

---

[1] *v. supra,* p. xxxvi.

consisting, not of the lover's prayer or praise in the detached atmosphere of his contemplation, but in an actual scene of life, a dramatic dialogue where one voice is not heard. Instances will be found in 'Come, you pretty false eied wanton', 'Your fair lookes urge my desire', and a few others.

Campion's gift is mainly lyrical, and the value which his masques have for us is solely lyrical. He served no apprenticeship in dramatic construction; and where the practised hand of Ben Jonson knew just the necessary degree of coherence that a masque would admit of with advantage, Campion's plots strike me as either slightly invertebrate or slightly complicated; the best being his first, that for the marriage of Lord Hayes. But as to the poetical quality of these masques there can be no dissentient voice. They abound with the most perfect lyrical gems, while the whole web of verse is of a very high order of beauty.

His work supplies a link between two periods of different inspiration: he was acquainted with the veteran Sackville, Lord Dorset, with whose *Induction* came the first promise of light for English poetry; and, during his declining years, he was contemporary with John Donne, whose influence was already pervading the world of letters. Campion escaped that influence because his style was fixed in the earlier school. His fame, which was so deservedly great in his own time, was soon extinguished. This is entirely due to historical events, and their effect upon the ephemeral media in which he worked. The masque was at all times too expensive an entertainment to be produced by any but rich nobles and prosperous institutions; and with the establishment of the Commonwealth it disappeared, never to return. In the same way the Puritan ascendancy, with its hatred of music, especially secular music, slew the short-lived vogue of the songbooks: some hint of the trend of opinion towards distaste for the madrigal and madrigal poetry may be seen in the *Theatrum Poetarum* of Edward Phillips, Milton's nephew, who only refers to Campion on account of his mention by Camden, and expresses the opinion that he was 'a writer of no extraordinary fame'. As might have been expected, the only song that can be traced as having survived any considerable time is a sacred one, 'Neuer weather-beaten Saile,' rightly held up to admiration by Mr. Bullen as an example of rare lyrical beauty united with sincere religious fervour. This song occurs in a commonplace-book of 1707 in circumstances which suggest that it was still living at that date as a hymn.[1]   But

---

[1] *v.* p. 363.

after his long oblivion it was Mr. Bullen who acted as a pioneer of his works, and who restored him, as he has restored so much else that is good in Elizabethan literature, to a grateful and appreciative generation, to the occupation of a seat among the immortals, and to the permanent enjoyment of mankind.

CHAPTER III. THE PROSE WORKS.

Of Campion's prose works, by far the more important is, of course, his *Obseruations in the Art of English Poesie*, which requires careful examination. Its value for literary history consists in the fact that it was a final statement of the craze against rhyming formulated by one of its best equipped and sanest partisans ; and that, the controversy thus coming to a head, the movement was finally demolished by Daniel's reply. It is difficult at this distance to appreciate or to account for the Renaissance objection to rhyme ; but it was clearly regarded as a relic of barbarism and the dark ages, the offspring of the monkish leonine hexameters, and of no greater literary value.

The movement itself, whatever its origin, seems to have gathered strength first in Italy, with Claudio Tolomei's *Versi e Regoli della Nuova Poesia*, and to have spread thence to other countries, taking root according to the predisposition of the soil. In Italy itself it did not flourish long : the unchallenged supremacy of the Sonnet, Canzone, Ottava, and Terza Rima was too strong for the innovating influence, and put the position of rhyme beyond danger. In France there were experiments in *vers mesurés*, but the character of the language made even a semblance of quantitative verse impossible ; while Spain was content to follow the lead of Italy. But in England the soil was predisposed, and the new poesy found many adherents. There was, in fact, no one settled system of prosody which held the field without question ; no fewer than three competing schemes were struggling for the upper hand : the Chaucerian, or blended system, resulting in a kind of syllabic equivalence ; a revival of alliterative verse represented by Poulter's measure and the ballad metres, and strengthened by the alliterative tendencies of Euphuism ; and the forms newly introduced from Italy by Wyat and Surrey, who were poets of promise rather than performance, and did outrage in many ways to the mother tongue. None of these schemes had won complete recognition ; and the Renaissance enthusiasts, with their extraordinary veneration for the classics, turned with eager expectation to the classical models of prosody.

Campion affords an interesting example of the fact that the movement, so far as we can trace it in England, appears to have been set on foot and maintained in the courts of Cambridge. When it originated cannot be stated, but it was no new thing in the time of Ascham, who says: 'This misliking of rhyming beginneth not now of any new fangle singularity, but hath been long misliked, and that of men of greatest learning and deepest judgment.' Its earliest champions were a little group at St. John's, comprising the Master, Thomas Watson, Bishop of Lincoln; Ascham, one of the fellows; and Drant, then an undergraduate; and the Cambridge tradition in this respect was maintained by Gascoigne, Spenser, Harvey, Sidney, Dyer, and Webbe. It was not, therefore, surprising that Campion should have been enlisted in the crusade against rhyme.

Campion seeks to set aside rhyme altogether as unworthy of serious notice, and to substitute for rhymed verse certain metres classified according to the terminology of Greek and Latin prosody, which he sought to make, and believed to be, imitations of classical quantitative verse. Now the fallacy of Campion and all those who seek to harmonize quantitative verse with the *natural* structure of the English language, is due to a confusion between quantitative and accentual prosody, and a misapprehension of their respective natures; quantitative being, of course, that based upon the distribution of syllables bearing a proportion to one another of actual time in enunciation; accentual being based upon the distribution of stresses. In Campion's time, the nature of quantity was not fully understood: classical verse was scanned, as it has always been until recently in our schools, on an accentual system; by substituting a thesis for every long syllable and an arsis for every short. I do not believe that Campion fully understood the difference between quantitative and accentual prosody: I am inclined to think that he had some perception of the nature of quantity, as a necessary outcome of his studies in music; but it was his very connexion with the art of music, to which he is always appealing by way of example, that vitiated and coloured his pronouncements on prosody. When he set one of his ordinary English songs to music, he naturally fitted the stronger accents to the longer notes, for, as he says himself in this book: In ioyning of words to harmony there is nothing more offensive to the eare than to place a long sillable with a short note, or a short sillable with a long note, though in the last the vowell often beares it out.' By 'long' and 'short' he means 'accented' and 'unaccented'; and the practice is, of course, quite in accordance with the rules of good musical composition. Now, the song having been duly composed, Campion finds his confusion confirmed: what was accentual verse when *read*, becomes quantitative verse when *sung*, the words being held out in the singing voice to the length of the notes, which, of course, bear a time-proportion to one another; and Campion's purpose in writing verse was so purely musical that he was unable to regard his words apart from their musical setting.

It would seem, therefore, that he had some perception of quantity, though I do not think he appreciated the nature of accent. But the essential difference between quantitative and accentual prosody he certainly did not understand; and the key to the *Observations*, difficult as they are to follow, is to be found in his confusion of the two systems. An example will make this clearer. Tennyson has written verses on classical models, but without confusion as to their real basis; for he drew himself a clear distinction between his really quantitative verse ('Hexameters no worse', &c.), and other verse, in 'classical' metres such as that of Coleridge, in which the longs and shorts of the true classical metre are simply translated by accented and unaccented. In the first, the true quantitative verse, there is no paltering with accent: all considerations of English accent go by the board, and the words are given a new pronunciation in strict accordance with quantity. For example, the usual pronunciation of 'hexámeters' becomes quantitatively 'héxămĕtérs'. The accent is ancillary in the great majority of cases to the long syllable, but this is no concern of the poet, who has regard only to the quantity arising from the two considerations of nature and position; even pushing this entirely logical position so far as to treat 'the' in 'the state' as long before *st*, and to pronounce it accordingly. This verse is therefore strictly quantitative; but Tennyson is not deluded with the conviction that it is also English poetry: it is a 'barbarous experiment' which does violence to the natural structure of the language and its current literary pronunciation: it makes English a foreign tongue.

Neither is he subject to the illusion that 'In the hexameter rises the fountain's silvery column' is an example of classical prosody. It is rhymeless accentual verse composed according to an arrangement of theses and arses corresponding to the arrangement of longs and shorts in the classical hexameter. The former kind is true quantitative verse which does not purport to be English poetry, the latter English poetry which no one can admit to be quantitative.

Logically, all had been well if Campion had taken either of these positions. Whether productive of good or bad verse, neither scheme involves the confusion which is everywhere patent in this book. He saw that quantity proper did enter into his songs when set to music, out of which condition he could hardly conceive of them ; and he also saw that it was possible to write English verse according to the so-called classical metres, replacing long with thesis, as in the hexameters of Clough, Kingsley, and Coleridge. He was possibly further misled by the fact that the enunciation of a strong accent does involve a slightly increased time period, so that to an almost imperceptible degree the relation of accented and unaccented is accompanied by a relation of longer time to shorter time. But (with the rest of his partisans, and probably the whole of his contemporaries) he entirely failed to see that accentual verse is that constructed around the natural and inherent distribution of accents in the language, while quantitative poetry is that constructed around the equally natural distribution of quantities, the incidental or ancillary accent or quantity, which may arise in each case, being entirely secondary, and not the primary cause of the grouping and selection of words which constitute verse.

So Campion is constantly sinning against the light ; rationalizing on quantitative principles, and making feeble compromises with his conscience where the absurdity of his conclusions is too patent. He begins : ' But above all the accent of one word is diligently to be observed, for chiefly by the accent in any language the true value of the sillables is to be measured. Neither can I remember any impediment except position that can alter the accent of any sillable of our English verse. For though we accent the second of *Trumpington* short, yet is it naturally long, and so of necessity must be held of every composer. Wherefore the first rule that is to be observed is the nature of the accent, which we must ever follow.' It is clear that confusion has already crept in. But he proceeds : ' The next rule is position, which makes euery sillable long, whether the position happens in one or two words.' There is nothing about vowels being long by nature [1] here, and I imagine that ' accent ', above

[1] Professor Saintsbury interprets *naturally long* above as meaning *long by*

referred to, takes the place of 'nature' in Campion's metrical scheme. However, realizing that this rule of position is plainly at variance with actual facts, he attempts a compromise which knocks the bottom out of the theory. He continues: 'Also because our English orthography (as the French) differs from our common pronunciation, we must esteeme our sillables as we speake, not as we write; for the sound of them in a verse is to be censured and not their letters.' No one can quarrel with this dictum as exemplified by the words immediately following, as 'dangerous' which is to be reckoned as 'dangerus', but Campion is forced to a wider extension of the principle, which of course reduces the rule of position to a nullity. Naturally, if the words 'appear', 'attend', 'oppose', are spelt 'apear', 'atend', 'opose', the first syllable of each becomes 'short' by position; and Campion does not realize that it is the absence of accent which renders these syllables 'short', irrespective of their position, real or notional. The whole procedure resembles nothing less absurd than the practice charged by Macaulay against Gladstone, of bringing forward a forged bond endorsed with a forged release, of setting up a fallacious principle, and excusing its application by an irrelevant exception. The whole of the rest of the treatise consists in a series of empirical rules and examples demonstrating what syllables are really 'long' or 'short', to avoid the application of the rule of position, which, once formulated, has got entirely out of its author's control.

But in spite of the hopeless confusion of all this, we are indebted to Campion for several striking and acute observations. In some cases his very perception and delicacy of ear plunged him yet deeper into the slough. He notes the undoubted fact that some sounds take relatively longer to pronounce, but in the case of some of the longer ones, 'warre, barre, starre, farre, marre,' his rationalizing instinct drives him to conclude that these sounds are lengthened in position by the double consonants! Take again the curious passage where he asserts that the Latin hexameter of six feet and the English verse of five feet are equal, in that they both *quinque perficiunt tempora*, 'fill up the quantity (as it were)

---

nature; but this does not make the passage any clearer. 'Nature,' as understood in classical prosody, is nowhere explained or referred to; and is, further, entirely *de trop* in Campion's system. According to him, there are two rules only: first, 'the nature of the accent,' and, next, 'position'. On the other hand, the second of *Trumpington* being accented short, by what reckoning is it 'naturally long'? By position, or how?

of five sem'briefs,' a passage of considerable difficulty. Campion means that, in a recitation of equal quickness, such Latin and English lines would take the same length of absolute time by the stop watch.[1] There is no question here of the number of accents, or proportion in time : the meaning is simply that whereas in Latin a short syllable can be pronounced in a short time because it is by definition unhampered with consonants, a 'short' syllable in English frequently requires changes of position in the organs of speech involving a hiatus of vocal preparation, and the whole line takes longer to say. This is a rationalization based upon the old erroneous practice of reading quantitative verse ; but its real importance is Campion's appreciation of the fact that English poetry will not have long lines ; and its purpose in his argument is to prove the unnatural character of English hexameters and the validity of his own shorter verse lengths.

Campion also shows himself a pioneer of metrical equivalence, which was not thoroughly established until Milton ; and, in his undoubtedly justifiable admission of the tribrach to English prosody, was more advanced than even recent critics. His remarks in connexion with his own unrhymed examples betray an accurate perception and a delicate ear, which, as he says, 'Poets Orators and Musitians of all men ought to have most excellent.' Setting aside the confusion and vitiation which proceed from his incomplete comprehension of classical prosody, what is the effect of his book? It proves that some sort of poetry can be written without rhyme. But, as Daniel points out, there must be some considerable inducement before we can make such a momentous change, and Campion's specimens are hardly sufficient earnest of a change for the better. 'Rose cheekt Lawra' and 'Iust beguiler' are certainly most charming, but how much more charming they would have been in rhyme ! Except in the case of heroic blank verse, which, as Daniel pointed out, was no innovation, no advantage is to be gained by getting rid of rhyme. Why, then, get rid of rhyme?

To this very pertinent question Campion only replies with an expression of prejudice, thinly veiled beneath rationalization.

[1] By proving verses to time with the hand Campion does not mean merely beating time, but beating *standard* time, such as is afforded nowadays by the metronome. The practice of singing part music unaccompanied was so popular that doubtless most persons of any skill in music could beat a standard time for the bar, which would in itself conform to a uniform period of absolute time, and thus serve as a metronome would for the purpose of the above-mentioned test.

But after this date we have no more of these follies : his practice was always better than his precept; and I, for one, believe that he was converted, either by Daniel or by his own good sense.

Little need be said in a book of this character concerning Campion's pretensions as a musical theorist. The main value, however, of the 'New Way', is, as I have shown with more detail in the Notes, that it affords a rule of thumb for the harmonization of a tune with simple concords. Its only originality is that of the dress in which he presents his rule, a Table of the use of the Fifth, Third and Octave, which is nothing more than an arithmetical formula of the use of the common chord. Instead of terming this the triad and its inversions, he calls his notes 5, 3, and 8. There is little enough in this to warrant his claim that he had effected more in Counterpoint than any man before him had ever attempted.

But even this small measure of originality may be doubted, if not denied outright. It is pretty evident that he was well acquainted with Morley's famous 'Plaine and easie Introduction to Practical Musick', first published in 1597, the Third Part of which treats of the Composing and Setting of Songs. At p. 143 Morley gives a Table of proper progressions in three parts ; while at pp. 146–7 he gives a table containing the usual chords for the composition of four or more parts profusely illustrated with examples in score. Campion's rule is a modification of these tables, very possibly derived from them ; the difference being that he uses the figures instead of setting down the notes of the common chord. There are considerable traces in the 'Tones of Musicke' also that Campion was not free from obligation to Morley in respect of this portion of the work ; while 'Of the taking of all Concords' is probably little more than a translation from the Latin of Sethus Calvisius, whose works were not unknown in England prior to this date.

But while we are unable to concede his claims in anything like their entirety touching 'A New Way', we must at least admit that his own compositions possess considerable merit. Many of the *Ayres* are arch, dainty little things ; full of charm and lighthearted grace.

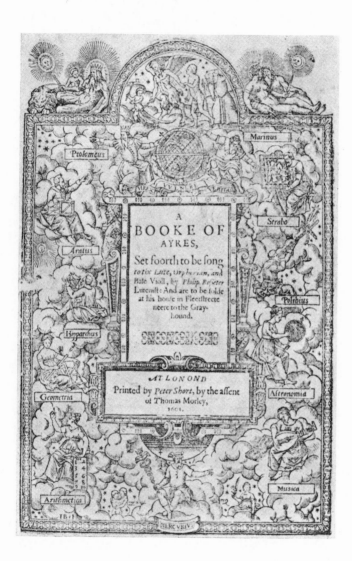

A
BOOKE OF
AYRES,

Set foorth to be song
to the Lute, Orpherian, and
Bale Violl, by Philip Roseter
Lutenist: And are to be folde
at his houfe in Fleetftreete
neere to the Gray-
hound.

AT LONDON
Printed by *Peter Short*, by the affent
of Thomas Morley,
1601.

To face p. lxvi

44
5   10
106

TO THE RIGHT VERTVOVS
AND WORTHY KNIGHT, SIR
THOMAS MOVNSON.

SIR,

The generall voice of your worthines, and the manie particular
fauours which I haue heard Master *Campion*, with dutifull
respect, often acknowledge himselfe to haue receiued from you,
haue emboldned mee to present this Booke of Ayres to your
fauourable iudgement and gracious protection ; especially because
the first ranke of songs are of his owne composition, made at his
vacant houres, and priuately emparted to his friends, whereby
they grew both publicke, and (as coine crackt in exchange)
corrupted : some of them both words and notes vnrespectiuely
challenged by others. In regard of which wronges, though his
selfe neglects these light fruits as superfluous blossomes of his
deeper Studies, yet hath it pleased him, vpon my entreaty, to
grant me the impression of part of them, to which I haue added
an equall number of mine owne. And this two-faced *Ianus* thus
in one bodie vnited, I humbly entreate you to entertaine and
defend, chiefely in respect of the affection which I suppose you
beare him, who I am assured doth aboue all others loue and
honour you. And for my part, I shall thinke my self happie if in
anie seruice I may deserue this fauour.

Your Worships humbly deuoted,

PHILIP ROSSETER.

TO THE READER.

WHAT Epigrams are in Poetrie, the same are Ayres in musicke, then in their chiefe perfection when they are short and well seasoned. But to clogg a light song with a long Præludium, is to corrupt the nature of it. Manie rests in Musicke were inuented either for necessitie of the fuge, or granted as an harmonicall licence in songs of many parts: but in Ayres I find no vse they haue, vnlesse it be to make a vulgar and triuiall modulation seeme to the ignorant strange, and to the iudiciall tedious. A naked Ayre without guide, or prop, or colour but his owne, is easily censured of euerie eare, and requires so much the more inuention to make it please. And as MARTIALL *speakes in defence of his short Epigrams, so may I say in th' apologie of Ayres, that where there is a full volume, there can be no imputation of shortnes. The Lyricke Poets among the Greekes and Latines were first inuenters of Ayres, tying themselues strictly to the number, and value of their sillables, of which sort, you shall find here onely one song in Saphicke verse; the rest are after the fascion of the time, eare-pleasing rimes without Arte. The subiect of them is for the most part, amorous, and why not amorous songs, as well as amorous attires? Or why not new Ayres, as well as new fascions? For the Note and Tableture, if they satisfie the most, we haue our desire, let expert masters please themselues with better. And if anie light error hath escaped vs, the skilfull may easily correct it, the vnskilfull will hardly perceiue it. But there are some, who to appeare the more deepe, and singular in their iudgement, will admit no Musicke but that which is long, intricate, bated with fuge, chaind with sincopation, and where the nature of euerie word is precisely exprest in the Note, like the old exploded action in Comedies, when if they did pronounce* Memeni, *they would point to the hinder part of their heads, if* Video, *put their finger in their eye. But such childish obseruing of words is altogether ridiculous, and we ought to maintaine as well in Notes, as in action a manly cariage, gracing no word, but that which is eminent, and emphaticall. Neuertheles, as in Poesie we giue the preheminence to the Heroicall Poeme so in Musicke we yeeld the chiefe place to the graue, and well inuented Motet, but not to euery harsh and dull confused Fantasie, where in multitude of points the Harmonie is quite drowned. Ayres haue both their Art and pleasure, and I will conclude of them, as the Poet did in his censure, of* CATVLLVS *the Lyricke, and* VERGIL *the Heroicke writer:*

Tantum magna suo debet Verona Catullo:
Quantum parua suo Mantua Vergilio.

A Table of halfe the Songs contained

in this Booke, by T. C.

I.

My sweetest Lesbia let vs liue and loue,
And though the sager sort our deedes reproue,
Let vs not way them : heau'ns great lampes doe diue
Into their west, and strait againe reuiue,
But soone as once set is our little light,
Then must we sleepe one euer-during night.

If all would lead their liues in loue like mee,
Then bloudie swords and armour should not be,
No drum nor trumpet peaceful sleepes should moue,
Vnles alar'me came from the campe of loue :   10
But fooles do liue, and wast their little light,
And seeke with paine their euer-during night.

When timely death my life and fortune ends,
Let not my hearse be vext with mourning friends,
But let all louers rich in triumph come,
And with sweet pastimes grace my happie tombe ;
And Lesbia close vp thou my little light,
And crowne with loue my euer-during night.

II.

Though you are yoong and I am olde,
Though your vaines hot, and my bloud colde,
Though youth is moist, and age is drie,
Yet embers liue, when flames doe die.

The tender graft is easely broke,
But who shall shake the sturdie Oke?
You are more fresh and faire then I,
Yet stubs do liue when flowers doe die.

Thou that thy youth doest vainely boast,
Know buds are soonest nipt with frost,   10
Thinke that thy fortune still doth crie,
Thou foole, to-morrow thou must die.

III.

I care not for these Ladies,
That must be woode and praide,
Giue me kind Amarillis
The wanton countrey maide;
Nature art disdaineth,
Her beautie is her owne;
  Her when we court and kisse,
  She cries, forsooth, let go.
  But when we come where comfort is,
  She neuer will say no.   10

If I loue Amarillis,
She giues me fruit and flowers,
But if we loue these Ladies,
We must giue golden showers,
Giue them gold that sell loue,
Giue me the Nutbrowne lasse,
  Who when we court and kiss,
  She cries, forsooth, let go.
  But when we come where comfort is,
  She neuer will say no.   20

These Ladies must haue pillowes,
And beds by strangers wrought,
Giue me a Bower of willowes,
Of mosse and leaues vnbought,
And fresh Amarillis,
With milke and honie fed,
  Who, when we court and kiss,
  She cries, forsooth, let go.
  But when we come where comfort is,
  She neuer will say no.   30

IIII.

Followe thy faire sunne, vnhappy shadowe,
Though thou be blacke as night,
And she made all of light,
Yet follow thy faire sun, vnhappie shadowe.

Follow her whose light thy light depriueth,
Though here thou liu'st disgrac't,
And she in heauen is plac't,
Yet follow her whose light the world reuiueth.

Follow those pure beames whose beautie burneth,
That so haue scorched thee,   10
As thou still blacke must bee,
Til her kind beames thy black to brightnes turneth.

Follow her while yet her glorie shineth :
There comes a luckles night,
That will dim all her light;
And this the black vnhappie shade deuineth.

Follow still since so thy fates ordained :
The Sunne must haue his shade,
Till both at once doe fade,
The Sun still proud, the shadow still disdained.   20

V.

My loue hath vowd hee will forsake mee,
And I am alreadie sped.
Far other promise he did make me
When he had my maidenhead.
If such danger be in playing,
And sport must to earnest turne,
I will go no more a-maying.

Had I foreseene what is ensued,
And what now with paine I proue,
Vnhappie then I had eschewed   10
This vnkind euent of loue:
Maides foreknow their own vndooing,
But feare naught till all is done,
When a man alone is wooing.

Dissembling wretch, to gaine thy pleasure,
What didst thou not vow and sweare?
So didst thou rob me of the treasure,
Which so long I held so deare,
Now thou prou'st to me a stranger,
Such is the vile guise of men   20
When a woman is in danger.

That hart is neerest to misfortune
That will trust a fained toong,
When flattring men our loues importune,
They entend vs deepest wrong,
If this shame of loues betraying
But this once I cleanely shun,
I will go no more a-maying.

VI.

When to her lute Corrina sings,
Her voice reuiues the leaden stringes,
And doth in highest noates appeare,
As any challeng'd eccho cleere;
But when she doth of mourning speake,
Eu'n with her sighes the strings do breake.

And as her lute doth liue or die,
Led by her passion, so must I,
For when of pleasure she doth sing,
My thoughts enioy a sodaine spring,   10
But if she doth of sorrow speake,
Eu'n from my hart the strings doe breake.

VII.

Turne backe, you wanton flyer,
And answere my desire
With mutuall greeting,
Yet bende a little neerer,
True beauty stil shines cleerer
In closer meeting.
Harts with harts delighted
Should striue to be vnited
Either others armes with armes enchayning;
Harts with a thought,   10
Rosie lips with a kisse still entertaining.

What haruest halfe so sweete is
As still to reape the kisses
Growne ripe in sowing,
And straight to be receiuer
Of that which thou art giuer,
Rich in bestowing?
There's no strickt obseruing
Of times or seasons sweruing,
There is euer one fresh spring abiding;   20
Then what we sow,
With our lips let vs reape, loues gaines deuiding.

VIII.

It fell on a sommers day,
While sweete Bessie sleeping laie
In her bowre, on her bed,
Light with curtaines shadowed,
Iamy came: shee him spies,
Opning halfe her heauie eies.

Iamy stole in through the dore,
She lay slumbring as before;
Softly to her he drew neere,
She heard him, yet would not heare,   10
Bessie vow'd not to speake,
He resolu'd that dumpe to breake.

First a soft kisse he doth take,
She lay still, and would not wake;
Then his hands learn'd to woo,
She dreamp't not what he would doo,
But still slept, while he smild
To see loue by sleepe beguild.

Iamy then began to play,
Bessie as one buried lay,   20
Gladly still through this sleight
Deceiu'd in her owne deceit,
And since this traunce begoon,
She sleepes eu'rie afternoone.

IX.

The Sypres curten of the night is spread,
And ouer all a silent dewe is cast.
The weaker cares by sleepe are conquered :
But I alone, with hidious griefe, agast,
In spite of Morpheus charmes, a watch doe keepe
Ouer mine eies, to banish carelesse sleepe.

Yet oft my trembling eyes through faintnes close,
And then the Mappe of hell before me stands,
Which Ghosts doe see, and I am one of those
Ordain'd to pine in sorrowes endles bands,   10
Since from my wretched soule all hopes are reft
And now no cause of life to me is left.

Griefe, ceaze my soule, for that will still endure,
When my cras'd bodie is consum'd and gone,
Bear it to thy blacke denne, there keepe it sure,
Where thou ten thousand soules doest tyre vpon.
But all doe not affoord such foode to thee
As this poore one, the worser part of mee.

X.

Follow your Saint, follow with accents sweet ;
Haste you, sad noates, fall at her flying feete :
There, wrapt in cloud of sorrowe pitie moue,
And tell the rauisher of my soule I perish for her loue.
But if she scorns my neuer-ceasing paine,
Then burst with sighing in her sight and nere returne againe.

All that I soong still to her praise did tend,
Still she was first ; still she my songs did end.
Yet she my loue and Musicke both doeth flie,
The Musicke that her Eccho is and beauties simpathie; 10
Then let my Noates pursue her scornfull flight :
It shall suffice that they were breath'd and dyed for her delight.

XI.

Faire, if you expect admiring,
Sweet, if you prouoke desiring,
Grace deere loue with kind requiting.
Fond, but if thy sight be blindnes,
False, if thou affect vnkindnes,
Flie both loue and loues delighting.
Then when hope is lost and loue is scorned,
Ile bury my desires, and quench the fires that euer yet in
    vaine haue burned.

Fates, if you rule louers fortune,
Stars, if men your powers importune,   10
Yield reliefe by your relenting :
Time, if sorrow be not endles,
Hope made vaine, and pittie friendles,
Helpe to ease my long lamenting.
But if griefes remaine still vnredressed,
I'le flie to her againe, and sue for pitie to renue my hopes
    distressed.

XII.

Thou art not faire for all thy red and white,
For all those rosie ornaments in thee,
Thou art not sweet, though made of meer delight,
Nor faire nor sweet, vnlesse thou pitie mee.
I will not sooth thy fancies : thou shalt proue
That beauty is no beautie without loue.

Yet loue not me, nor seeke thou to allure
My thoughts with beautie, were it more deuine,
Thy smiles and kisses I cannot endure,
I'le not be wrapt vp in those armes of thine,   10
Now shew it, if thou be a woman right,—
Embrace, and kisse, and loue me, in despight.

XIII.

See where she flies enrag'd from me,
View her when she intends despite,
The winde is not more swift then shee,
Her furie mou'd such terror makes,
As to a fearfull guiltie sprite
The voice of heau'ns huge thunder cracks:
But when her appeased minde yeelds to delight,
All her thoughts are made of ioies,
Millions of delights inuenting;
Other pleasures are but toies   10
To her beauties sweete contenting.

My fortune hangs vpon her brow,
For as she smiles or frownes on mee,
So must my blowne affections bow;
And her proude thoughts too well do find
With what vnequal tyrannie,
Her beauties doe command my mind.
Though, when her sad planet raignes,
Froward she bee,
She alone can pleasure moue,   20
And displeasing sorrow banish.
May I but still hold her loue,
Let all other comforts vanish.

XIIII.

Blame not my cheeks, though pale with loue they be;
The kindly heate vnto my heart is flowne,
To cherish it that is dismaid by thee,
Who art so cruell and vnsteadfast growne:
For nature, cald for by distressed harts,
Neglects and quite forsakes the outward partes.

But they whose cheekes with careles blood are stain'd,
Nurse not one sparke of loue within their harts,
And, when they woe, they speake with passion fain'd,
For their fat loue lyes in their outward parts: 10
But in their brests, where loue his court should hold,
Poore Cupid sits and blowes his nailes for cold.

F

XV.

When the God of merrie loue
As yet in his cradle lay,
Thus his wither'd nurse did say:
Thou a wanton boy wilt proue
To deceiue the powers aboue;
For by thy continuall smiling
I see thy power of beguiling.

Therewith she the babe did kisse;
When a sodaine fire out came
From those burning lips of his,   10
That did her with loue enflame,
But none would regard the same,
So that, to her daie of dying,
The old wretch liu'd euer crying.

XVI.

Mistris, since you so much desire
To know the place of Cupids fire,
In your faire shrine that flame doth rest,
Yet neuer harbourd in your brest,
It bides not in your lips so sweete,
Nor where the rose and lillies meete
But a little higher, but a little higher;
There, there, O there lies Cupids fire.

Euen in those starrie pearcing eyes,
There Cupids sacred fire lyes.   10
Those eyes I striue not to enioy,
For they haue power to destroy.
Nor woe I for a smile, or kisse,
So meanely triumphs not my blisse,
But a little higher, but a little higher,
I climbe to crowne my chast desire.

XVII.

Your faire lookes enflame my desire:
  Quench it againe with loue.
Stay, O striue not still to retire:
  Doe not inhumane proue.
If loue may perswade,
  Loues pleasures, deere, denie not.
Heere is a silent grouie shade;
  O tarrie then, and flie not.

Haue I seaz'd my heauenly delight
  In this vnhaunted groue?   10
Time shall now her furie requite
  With the reuenge of loue.
Then come, sweetest, come,
  My lips with kisses gracing;
Here let vs harbour all alone,
  Die, die in sweete embracing.

Will you now so timely depart,
  And not returne againe?
Your sight lends such life to my hart
  That to depart is paine.   20
Feare yeelds no delay,
  Securenes helpeth pleasure:
Then, till the time giues safer stay,
  O farewell, my liues treasure.

XVIII.

The man of life vpright,
  Whose guiltlesse hart is free
From all dishonest deedes,
  Or thought of vanitie,

The man whose silent dayes,
  In harmeles ioys are spent,
Whome hopes cannot delude,
  Nor sorrow discontent;

That man needs neither towers
　Nor armour for defence,   10
Nor secret vautes to flie
　From thunders violence.

Hee onely can behold
　With vnafrighted eyes
The horrours of the deepe
　And terrours of the Skies.

Thus, scorning all the cares
　That fate, or fortune brings,
He makes the heau'n his booke,
　His wisedome heeu'nly things,   20

Good thoughts his onely friendes,
　His wealth a well-spent age,
The earth his sober Inne
　And quiet Pilgrimage.

XIX.

Harke, al you ladies that do sleep;
　The fayry queen Proserpina
Bids you awake and pitie them that weep.
　You may doe in the darke
What the day doth forbid;
　Feare not the dogs that barke,
　　Night will haue all hid.

But if you let your louers mone,
　The Fairie Queene Proserpina
Will send abroad her Fairies eu'ry one,   10
　That shall pinch blacke and blew
Your white hands and faire armes
　That did not kindly rue
　　Your Paramours harmes.

In Myrtle Arbours on the downes
　The Fairie Queene Proserpina,
This night by moone-shine leading merrie rounds
　Holds a watch with sweet loue,
Downe the dale, vp the hill;
　No plaints or groanes may moue   20
　　Their holy vigill.

All you that will hold watch with loue,
  The Fairie Queene Proserpina
Will make you fairer then Diones doue;
  Roses red, Lillies white,
And the cleare damaske hue,
  Shall on your cheekes alight:
    Loue will adorne you.

All you that loue, or lou'd before,
  The Fairie Queene Proserpina   30
Bids you encrease that louing humour more:
  They that yet haue not fed
On delight amorous,
  She vowes that they shall lead
    Apes in Auernus.

XX.

When thou must home to shades of vnder ground,
And there ariu'd, a newe admired guest,
The beauteous spirits do ingirt thee round,
White Iope, blith Hellen, and the rest,
To heare the stories of thy finisht loue
From that smoothe toong whose musicke hell can moue;

Then wilt thou speake of banqueting delights,
Of masks and reuels which sweete youth did make,
Of Turnies and great challenges of knights,
And all these triumphes for thy beauties sake: 10
When thou hast told these honours done to thee,
Then tell, O tell, how thou didst murther me.

XXI.

Come, let vs sound with melody, the praises
Of the kings king, th' omnipotent creator,
Author of number, that hath all the world in
                Harmonie framed.

Heau'n is His throne perpetually shining,
His deuine power and glorie, thence he thunders,
One in all, and all still in one abiding,
                Both Father and Sonne

O sacred sprite, inuisible, eternall
Eu'ry where, yet vnlimited, that all things   10
Canst in one moment penetrate, reuiue me,
          O holy Spirit.

Rescue, O rescue me from earthly darknes,
Banish hence all these elementall obiects,
Guide my soule that thirsts to the liuely Fountaine
          Of thy deuinenes.

Cleanse my soule, O God, thy bespotted Image,
Altered with sinne so that heau'nly purenes
Cannot acknowledge me, but in thy mercies,
          O Father of grace.   20

But when once thy beames do remoue my darknes,
O then I'le shine forth as an Angell of light,
And record, with more than an earthly voice, thy
          Infinite honours.

FINIS.

I.

Sweete, come againe;
  Your happie sight, so much desir'd,
Since you from hence are now retir'd,
  I seeke in vaine.
Stil must I mourn
  And pine in longing paine,
Till you, my liues delight, againe
  Vouchsafe your wisht returne.

If true desire,
  Or faithfull vow of endles loue,   10
Thy heart enflam'd may kindly moue
  With equall fire;
O then my ioies,
  So long destraught, shall rest,
Reposed soft in thy chast brest,
  Exempt from all annoies.

You had the power
  My wandring thoughts first to restraine,
You first did heare my loue speake plaine,
  A child before: 20
Now it is growne
  Confirm'd, do you it keepe,
And let it safe in your bosome sleepe,
  There euer made your owne.

And till we meete,
  Teach absence inward art to find,
Both to disturbe and please the mind.
  Such thoughts are sweete
And such remaine
  In hearts whose flames are true;   30
Then such will I retaine, till you
  To me returne againe.

II.

And would you see my Mistris face?
  It is a flowrie garden place,
Where knots of beauties haue such grace
  That all is worke and nowhere space.

  It is a sweete delicious morne,
    Where day is breeding, neuer borne,
  It is a Meadow yet vnshorne,
    Whome thousand flowers do adorne.

It is the heauens bright reflexe,
  Weake eies to dazle and to vexe,   10
It is th' Idæa of her sexe,
  Enuie of whome doth world perplexe.

It is a face of death that smiles,
  Pleasing, though it killes the whiles,
Where death and loue in pretie wiles
  Each other mutuallie beguiles.

It is faire beauties freshest youth,
  It is the fain'd Eliziums truth:
The spring that winter'd harts renu'th;
  And this is that my soule pursu'th.   20

III.

No graue for woe, yet earth my watrie teares deuoures;
Sighes want ayre, and burnt desires kind pitties showres:
Stars hold their fatal course, my ioies preuenting:
The earth, the sea, the aire, the fire, the heau'ns vow my
    tormenting.

Yet still I liue, and waste my wearie daies in grones,
And with wofull tunes adorne dispayring mones.
Night still prepares a more displeasing morrow;
My day is night, my life my death, and all but sence of
    sorrow.

IIII.

If I vrge my kinde desires,
She vnkind doth them reiect;
Womens hearts are painted fires
To deceiue them that affect.
I alone loues fires include;
Shee alone doth them delude.

Shee hath often vow'd her loue;
But, alas, no fruit I finde.
That her fires are false I proue,
Yet in her no fault I finde :   10
I was thus vnhappy borne,
And ordain'd to be her scorne.

Yet if humane care or paine,
May the heau'nly order change,
She will hate her owne disdaine
And repent she was so strange :
For a truer heart then I,
Neuer liu'd, or lou'd to die.

V.

What harts content can he finde,
  What happy sleepes can his eies embrace,
That beares a guiltie minde ?
  His tast sweet wines will abhorre :
No musicks sounde can appease the thoughts
  That wicked deeds deplore.
The passion of a present feare
  Stil makes his restles motion there ;
And all the day hee dreads the night,
  And all the night, as one agast, he feares the morning light. 10

But he that loues to be lou'd,
  And in his deedes doth adore heauens power,
And is with pitie mou'd ;
  The night giues rest to his heart,
The cheerefull beames do awake his soule,
  Reuiu'd in euerie part.
He liues a comfort to his friendes,
  And heauen to him such blessing sendes
That feare of hell cannot dismaie
  His stedfast hart that is enurd the truth still to obey. 20

VI.

Let him that will be free and keep his hart from care,
Retir'd alone, remaine where no discomforts are.
For when the eie doth view his griefe, or haplesse eare his
    sorrow heares,
Th' impression still in him abides, and euer in one shape
    appeares.

Forget thy griefes betimes; long sorrow breedes long paine,
For ioie farre fled from men, will not returne againe;
O happie is the soule which heauen ordained to liue in endles
    peace ;
His life is a pleasing dreame, and euerie houre his ioyes encrease.

You heauie sprites, that loue in seuer'd shades to dwell,
'That nurse despaire, and dreame of vnrelenting hell,   10
Come sing this happie song, and learne of me the Arte of true
    content,
Loade not your guiltie soules with wrong, and heauen then will
    soone relent.

VII.

Reproue not loue, though fondly thou hast lost
    Greater hopes by louing :
Loue calms ambicious spirits, from their brests
    Danger oft remouing :
Let lofty humors mount vp on high,
    Down againe like to the wind,
While priuat thoghts, vow'd to loue,
    More peace and plesure find.

Loue and sweete beautie makes the stubborne milde,
    And the coward fearelesse ;   10
The wretched misers care to bountie turnes,
    Cheering all thinges cheerlesse.
Loue chaines the earth and heauen,
    Turnes the Spheares, guides the yeares in endles peace ;
The flourie earth through his power
    Receiu's her due encrease.

VIII.

And would you faine the reason know
Why my sad eies so often flow?
My heart ebs ioy, when they doe so,
And loues the moone by whom they go.

And will you aske why pale I looke?
'Tis not with poring on my booke:
My Mistris cheeke, my bloud hath tooke,
For her mine owne hath me forsooke.

Doe not demaund why I am mute:
Loues silence doth all speech confute.   10
They set the noat, then tune the Lute;
Harts frame their thoughts, then toongs their suit.

Doe not admire why I admire:
My feuer is no others fire:
Each seuerall heart hath his desire;
Els proofe is false, and truth a lier.

If why I loue you should see cause:
Loue should haue forme like other lawes,
But fancie pleads not by the clawes:
'Tis as the sea, still vext with flawes.   20

No fault vpon my loue espie:
For you perceiue not with my eie;
My pallate to your tast may lie,
Yet please it selfe deliciously.

Then let my sufferance be mine owne:
Sufficeth it these reasons showne;
Reason and loue are euer knowne
To fight till both be ouerthrowne.

IX.

When Laura smiles her sight reuiues both night and day:
The earth and heauen viewes with delight her wanton play:
And her speech with euer-flowing musicke doth repaire
The cruell wounds of sorrow and vntam'd despaire.

The sprites that remaine in fleeting aire
Affect for pastime to vntwine her tressed haire,
And the birds thinke sweete Aurora, mornings Queene doth shine
From her bright sphere, when Laura shewes her lookes deuine.

Dianas eyes are not adorn'd with greater power
Then Lauras, when she lists awhile for sport to loure :   10
But when she her eyes encloseth, blindnes doth appeare
The chiefest grace of beautie, sweetelie seated there.

Loue hath no fire but what he steales from her bright eyes ;
Time hath no power but that which in her pleasure lyes :
For she with her deuine beauties all the world subdues,
And fils with heau'nly spirits my humble muse.

X.

Long haue mine eies gaz'd with delight,
Conueying hopes vnto my soule ;
In nothing happy, but in sight
Of her, that doth my sight controule :
But now mine eies must loose their light.

My obiect now must be the aire,
To write in water words of fire,
And teach sad thoughts how to despaire :
Desert must quarrell with desire.
All were appeas'd were she not faire.   10

For all my comfort, this I proue,
That Venus on the Sea was borne :
If Seas be calme, then doth she loue ;
If stormes arise, I am forlorne ;
My doubtfull hopes, like wind doe moue.

XI.

Though far from ioy, my sorrowes are as far,
And I both betweene ;
Not too low, nor yet too high
Aboue my reach, would I bee seene.
Happy is he that so is placed,
Not to be enui'd nor to bee disdain'd or disgraced.

The higher trees, the more stormes they endure ;
Shrubs be troden downe :
But the meane, the golden meane,
Doth onely all our fortunes crowne :   10
Like to a streame that sweetely slideth
Through the flourie banks, and still in the midst his course guideth.

XII.

Shall I come, if I swim? wide are the waues, you see :
Shall I come, if I flie, my deere loue, to thee?
Streames Venus will appease ;   Cupid giues me winges ;
All the powers assist my desire
Saue you alone, that set my wofull heart on fire.

You are faire, so was Hero that in Sestos dwelt ;
She a priest, yet the heate of loue truly felt.
A greater streame then this did her loue deuide ;
But she was his guide with a light :
So through the streames Leander did enioy her sight.   10

XIII.

Aye me ! that loue should natures workes accuse :
   Where cruell Laura still her beautie viewes,
Riuer, or cloudie iet, or christal bright,
   Are all but seruants of her selfe-delight.

Yet her deformed thoughts, she cannot see ;
   And thats the cause she is so sterne to mee.
Vertue and duetie can no fauour gaine :
   A griefe, O death, to liue and loue in vaine.

XIIII.

Shall then a traiterous kis or a smile
   All my delights vnhappily beguile?
Shall the vow of fayned loue receiue so ritch regard,
   When true seruice dies neglected, and wants his due reward ?

Deedes meritorious soone be forgot,
  But one offence no time can euer blot;
Euery day it is renu'd, and euery night it bleedes,
  And with bloudy streames of sorrow drownes all our better deedes.

Beautie is not by desert to be woon;
  Fortune hath all that is beneath the Sunne.   10
Fortune is the guide of loue, and both of them be blind;
  All their waies are full of errors, which no true feete can find.

XV.

If I hope, I pine; if I feare, I faint and die;
  So betweene hope and feare, I desp'rat lie,
Looking for ioy to heauen, whence it should come:
  But hope is blinde; ioy, deafe; and I am dumbe.

Yet I speake and crie; but, alas, with words of wo:
  And ioy conceiues not them that murmure so.
He that the eares of ioy will euer pearse,
  Must sing glad noates, or speak in happier verse.

XVI.

Vnlesse there were consent twixt hell and heauen
That grace and wickednes should be combind,
I cannot make thee and thy beauties euen;
Thy face is heauen, and torture in thy minde;
For more then worldly blisse is in thy eie
And hellish torture in thy minde doth lie.

A thousand Cherubins flie in her lookes,
And hearts in legions melt vpon their view:
But gorgeos couers wall vp filthie bookes;
Be it sinne to saie, that so your eyes do you: 10
But sure your mind adheres not with your eies,
For what they promise, that your heart denies.

But, O, least I religion should misuse,
Inspire me thou, that ought'st thy selfe to know,
Since skillesse readers reading do abuse,
What inward meaning outward sence doth show:
For by thy eies and heart, chose and contem'd,
I wauer, whether saued or condemn'd.

XVII.

If she forsake me, I must die :
    Shall I tell her so ?
Alas, then strait she will replie,
    No, no, no, no, no.
If I disclose my desp'rat state,
She will but make sport thereat,
    And more vnrelenting grow.

What heart can long such paines abide ?
    Fie vppon this loue.
I would aduenture farre and wide,   10
    If it would remoue.
But loue will still my steppes pursue,
I cannot his wayes eschew :
    Thus still helpeles hopes I proue.

I doe my loue in lines commend,
    But, alas, in vaine ;
The costly gifts, that I doe send,
    She returnes againe :
Thus still is my despaire procur'd,
And her malice more assur'd :   20
    Then come, death, and end my paine.

XVIII.

What is a day, what is a yeere
    Of vaine delight and pleasure ?
Like to a dreame it endlesse dies,
    And from vs like a vapour flies :
And this is all the fruit that we finde,
    Which glorie in worldly treasure.

He that will hope for true delight,
    With vertue must be graced ;
Sweete follie yeelds a bitter tast,
    Which euer will appeare at last :   10
But if we still in vertue delight,
    Our soules are in heauen placed.

XIX.

Kinde in vnkindnesse, when will you relent
And cease with faint loue true loue to torment?
Still entertain'd, excluded still I stand;
Her gloue stil holde, but cannot touch the hand.

In her faire hand my hopes and comforts rest:
O might my fortunes with that hand be blest,
No enuious breaths then my deserts could shake,
For they are good whom such true loue doth make.

O let not beautie so forget her birth,
That it should fruitles home returne to earth.   10
Loue is the fruite of beautie, then loue one;
Not your sweete selfe, for such selfe loue is none.

Loue one that onely liues in louing you;
Whose wrong'd deserts would you with pity view,
This strange distast which your affections swaies
Would relish loue, and you find better daies.

Thus till my happie sight your beautie viewes,
Whose sweet remembrance stil my hope renewes,
Let these poore lines sollicite loue for mee,
And place my ioys where my desires would bee.   20

XX.

What then is loue but mourning?
    What desire, but a selfe-burning?
Till shee that hates doth loue returne,
Thus will I mourne, thus will I sing,
    Come away, come away, my darling.

Beautie is but a blooming,
    Youth in his glorie entombing;
Time hath a while, which none can stay:
Then come away, while thus I sing,
    Come away, come away, my darling.   10

Sommer in winter fadeth;
    Gloomie night heau'nly light shadeth:
Like to the morne are Venus flowers;
Such are her howers: then will I sing,
    Come away, come away, my darling.

G

XXI.

Whether men doe laugh or weepe,
Whether they doe wake or sleepe,
Whether they die yoong or olde,
Whether they feele heate or colde;
There is, vnderneath the sunne,
Nothing in true earnest done.

All our pride is but a iest;
None are worst, and none are best;
Griefe, and ioy, and hope, and feare,
Play their Pageants euery where: 10
Vaine opinion all doth sway,
And the world is but a play.

Powers aboue in cloudes doe sit,
Mocking our poore apish wit;
That so lamely, with such state,
Their high glorie imitate:
No ill can be felt but paine,
And that happie men disdaine.

FINIS.

OBSERVATIONS
in the Art of English
Poesie.

By *Thomas Campion*.

Wherein it is demonstra-
tiuely prooued, and *by example*
confirmed, that the English toong
will receiue eight seuerall kinds of num-
bers, proper to it selfe, which are all
in this booke set forth, and were
neuer before this time by any
man attempted.

Printed at London by RICHARD FIELD
for *Andrew Wise.* 1602.

To the Right Noble and
worthily honourd, the Lord
Buckhurst, Lord high Trea-
surer of England.

In two things (right honorable) it is generally agreed that man excels all other creatures, in reason and speech : and in them by how much one man surpasseth an other, by so much the neerer he aspires to a celestiall essence.

Poesy in all kind of speaking is the chiefe beginner, and maintayner of eloquence, not only helping the eare with the acquaintance of sweet numbers, but also raysing the minde to a more high and lofty conceite. For this end haue I studyed to induce a true forme of versefying into our language : for the vulgar and vnarteficiall custome of riming hath, I know, deter'd many excellent wits from the exercise of English Poesy. The obseruations which I haue gathered for this purpose I humbly present to your Lordship, as to the noblest iudge of Poesy, and the most honorable protector of all industrious learning ; which if your Honour shall vouchsafe to receiue, who both in your publick and priuate Poemes haue so deuinely crowned your fame, what man will dare to repine? or not striue to imitate them? Wherefore with all humility I subiect my selfe and them to your gratious fauour, beseeching you in the noblenes of your mind to take in worth so simple a present, which by some worke drawne from my more serious studies I will hereafter endeuour to excuse.

Your Lordships humbly deuoted,

Thomas Campion.

The Writer to his Booke.

Whether thus hasts my little booke so fast?
To Paules Churchyard. What? in those cels to stand,
With one leafe like a riders cloke put vp
To catch a termer? or lye mustie there
With rimes a terme set out, or two, before?
Some will redeeme me. Fewe. Yes, reade me too.
Fewer. Nay loue me. Now thou dot'st, I see.
Will not our English *Athens* arte defend?
Perhaps. Will lofty courtly wits not ayme
Still at perfection? If I graunt? I flye.
Whether? To Pawles. Alas, poore booke, I rue
Thy rash selfe-loue; goe, spread thy pap'ry wings:
‧Thy lightnes can not helpe or hurt my fame.

Obseruations in the Art

of English Poesy, by *Thomas* Campion.

The first Chapter, intreating of numbers in Generall.

THERE is no writing too breefe that, without obscuritie, com-
prehends the intent of the writer. These my late obseruations in
English Poesy I haue thus briefely gathered, that they might
proue the lesse troublesome in perusing, and the more apt to be
retayn'd in memorie. And I will first generally handle the nature
of Numbers. Number is *discreta quantitas ;* so that when we 10
speake simply of number, we intend only the disseuer'd quantity ;
but when we speake of a Poeme written in number, we consider
not only the distinct number of the sillables, but also their value,
which is contained in the length or shortnes of their sound. As
in Musick we do not say a straine of so many notes, but so many
sem'briefes (though sometimes there are no more notes then sem'-
briefes), so in a verse the numeration of the sillables is not so much
to be obserued, as their waite and due proportion. In ioyning
of words to harmony there is nothing more offensiue to the eare then
to place a long sillable with a short note, or a short sillable with a 20
long note, though in the last the vowell often beares it out. The
world is made by Simmetry and proportion, and is in that respect
compared to Musick, and Musick to Poetry : for *Terence* saith,
speaking of Poets, *artem qui tractant musicam*, confounding musick
and Poesy together. What musick can there be where there is no
proportion obserued ? Learning first flourished in *Greece* ; from
thence it was deriued vnto the *Romaines*, both diligent obseruers
of the number and quantity of sillables, not in their verses only
but likewise in their prose. Learning, after the declining of the
Romaine Empire and the pollution of their language through the 30
conquest of the *Barbarians*, lay most pitifully deformed till the
time of *Erasmus, Rewcline,* Sir *Thomas More,* and other learned
men of that age, who brought the Latine toong again to light,
redeeming it with much labour out of the hands of the illiterate
Monks and Friers : as a scoffing booke, entituled *Epistolæ*

obscurorum virorum, may sufficiently testifie. In those lack-learning
times, and in barbarized *Italy*, began that vulgar and easie kind
of Poesie which is now in vse throughout most parts of Christen-
dome, which we abusiuely call Rime, and Meeter, of *Rithmus* and
Metrum, of which I will now discourse.

The second Chapter, declaring the vnaptnesse
of Rime in Poesie.

I am not ignorant that whosoeuer shall by way of reprehension
examine the imperfections of Rime must encounter with many
10 glorious enemies, and those very expert and ready at their weapon,
that can if neede be extempore (as they say) rime a man to death.
Besides there is growne a kind of prescription in the vse of Rime, to
forestall the right of true numbers, as also the consent of many
nations, against all which it may seeme a thing almost impossible
and vaine to contend.   All this and more can not yet deterre me
from a lawful defence of perfection, or make me any whit the sooner
adheare to that which is lame and vnbeseeming.   For custome I
alleage that ill vses are to be abolisht, and that things naturally im-
perfect can not be perfected by vse.   Old customes, if they be better,
20 why should they not be recald, as the yet florishing custome of
numerous poesy vsed among the *Romanes* and *Grecians*?   But the
vnaptnes of our toongs and the difficultie of imitation dishartens
vs: againe, the facilitie and popularitie of Rime creates as many
Poets as a hot sommer flies.   But let me now examine the nature
of that which we call Rime.   By Rime is vnderstoode that which
ends in the like sound, so that verses in such maner composed
yeeld but a continual repetition of that Rhetoricall figure which
we tearme *similiter desinentia*, and that, being but *figura verbi*,
ought (as *Tully* and all other Rhetoritians have iudicially obseru'd)
30 sparingly to be vs'd, least it should offend the eare with tedious
affectation.   Such was that absurd following of the letter amongst
our English so much of late affected, but now hist out of Paules
Church-yard: which foolish figuratiue repetition crept also into
the Latine toong, as it is manifest in the booke of Pˢ cald *prælia*
porcorum, and another pamphlet all of Fˢ which I haue seene im-
printed: but I will leaue these follies to their owne ruine, and
returne to the matter intended.   The eare is a rationall sence and
a chiefe iudge of proportion; but in our kind of riming what
proportion is there kept where there remaines such a confusd
40 inequalitie of sillables?   *Iambick* and *Trochaick* feete, which are

opposd by nature, are by all Rimers confounded ; nay, oftentimes
they place instead of an *Iambick* the foot *Pyrrychius*, consisting of
two short sillables, curtalling their verse, which they supply in
reading with a ridiculous and vnapt drawing of their speech.   As
for example :

> *Was it my desteny, or dismall chaunce?*

In this verse the two last sillables of the word *Desteny*, being both
short, and standing for a whole foote in the verse, cause the line
to fall out shorter then it ought by nature.   The like impure errors
haue in time of rudenesse bene vsed in the Latine toong, as the   10
Carmina prouerbialia can witnesse, and many other such reuerend
bables.   But the noble *Grecians* and *Romaines*, whose skilfull
monuments outliue barbarisme, tyed themselues to the strict
obseruation of poeticall numbers, so abandoning the childish
titillation of riming that it was imputed a great error to *Ouid* for
setting forth this one riming verse,

> *Quot cælum stellas tot habet tua Roma puellas.*

For the establishment of this argument, what better confirmation
can be had then that of Sir *Thomas Moore* in his booke of Epi-
grams, where he makes two sundry Epitaphs vpon the death of   20
a singing-man at *Westminster*, the one in learned numbers and
dislik't, the other in rude rime and highly extold : so that he con-
cludes, *tales lactucas talia labra petunt*, like lips, like lettuce.
   But there is yet another fault in Rime altogether intollerable,
which is, that it inforceth a man oftentimes to abiure his matter
and extend a short conceit beyond all bounds of arte ; for in
Quatorzens me thinks the Poet handles his subiect as tyrannically
as *Procrustes* the thiefe his prisoners, whom, when he had taken,
he vsed to cast vpon a bed, which if they were too short to fill, he
would stretch them longer, if too long, he would cut them shorter.   30
Bring before me now any the most selfe-lou'd Rimer, and let me see
if without blushing he be able to reade his lame halting rimes.
Is there not a curse of Nature laid vpon such rude Poesie, when
the Writer is himself asham'd of it, and the hearers in contempt
call it Riming and Ballating?   What Deuine in his Sermon, or
graue Counsellor in his Oration, will alleage the testimonie of
a rime?   But the deuinity of the *Romaines* and *Gretians* was all
written in verse : and *Aristotle*, *Galene*, and the bookes of all the
excellent Philosophers are full of the testimonies of the old Poets.
By them was laid the foundation of all humane wisedome, and from   40
them the knowledge of all antiquitie is deriued.   I will propound

but one question, and so conclude this point.   If the *Italians,*
Frenchmen and *Spanyards,* that with commendation haue written
in Rime, were demaunded whether they had rather the bookes
they haue publisht (if their toong would beare it) should remaine as
they are in Rime, or be translated into the auncient numbers of
the *Greekes* and *Romaines,* would they not answere into numbers?
What honour were it then for our English language to be the first
that after so many yeares of barbarisme could second the per-
fection of the industrious *Greekes* and *Romaines?* which how it
10 may be effected I will now proceede to demonstrate.

The third Chapter: of our English numbers in generall.

   There are but three feete, which generally distinguish the Greeke
and Latine verses, the *Dactil,* consisting of one long sillable and
two short, as *viŭĕrĕ*; the *Trochy,* of one long and one short, as
vītă ; and the *Iambick* of one short and one long, as *ămōr*.   The
Spondee of two long, the *Tribrach* of three short, the *Anapæstick* of
two short and a long, are but as seruants to the first.   Diuers
other feete I know are by the Grammarians cited, but to little
purpose.   The *Heroical* verse that is distinguisht by the *Dactile*
20 hath bene oftentimes attempted in our English toong, but with
passing pitifull successe ; and no wonder, seeing it is an attempt
altogether against the nature of our language.   For both the
concurse of our monasillables make our verses vnapt to slide, and
also if we examine our polysillables, we shall find few of them by
reason of their heauinesse, willing to serue in place of a *Dactile.*
Thence it is, that the writers of English heroicks do so often repeate
Amyntas, Olympus, Auernus, Erinnis, and such like borrowed
words, to supply the defect of our hardly intreated *Dactile.*   I could
in this place set downe many ridiculous kinds of *Dactils* which they
30 vse, but that it is not my purpose here to incite men to laughter.
If we therefore reiect the *Dactil* as vnfit for our vse (which of
necessity we are enforst to do), there remayne only the *Iambick*
foote, of which the *Iambick* verse is fram'd, and the *Trochee,* from
which the *Trochaick* numbers haue their originall.   Let vs now
then examine the property of these two feete, and try if they con-
sent with the nature of our English sillables.   And first for the
Iambicks, they fall out so naturally in our toong, that, if we examine
our owne writers, we shall find they vnawares hit oftentimes vpon
the true *Iambick* numbers, but alwayes ayme at them as far as their
40 eare without the guidance of arte can attain vnto, as it shall here-
after more euidently appeare.   The *Trochaick* foote, which is but

an *Iambick* turn'd ouer and ouer, must of force in like manner
accord in proportion with our Brittish sillables, and so produce
an English *Trochaicall* verse. Then hauing these two principall
kinds of verses, we may easily out of them deriue other formes, as
the Latines and Greekes before vs haue done: whereof I will make
plaine demonstration, beginning at the *Iambick* verse.

The fourth Chapter: of the Iambick verse.

I haue obserued, and so may any one that is either practis'd
in singing, or hath a naturall eare able to time a song, that the
Latine verses of sixe feete, as the *Heroick* and *Iambick*, or of fiue
feete, as the *Trochaick*, are in nature all of the same length of
sound with our English verses of fiue feete; for either of them
being tim'd with the hand, *quinque perficiunt tempora*, they fill vp
the quantity (as it were) of fiue sem'briefs; as for example, if any
man will proue to time these verses with his hand.

A pure *Iambick.*
Suis et ipsa Roma viribus ruit.

A licentiate *Iambick.*
Ducunt volentes fata, nolentes trahunt.

An *Heroick* verse.
Tytere, tu patulæ recubans sub tegmine fagi.

A *Trochaick* verse.
Nox est perpetua vna dormienda.

English *Iambicks* pure.
The more secure, the more the stroke we feele
Of vnpreuented harms; so gloomy stormes
Appeare the sterner, if the day be cleere.

Th' English *Iambick* licentiate.
Harke how these winds do murmur at thy flight.

The English *Trochee.*
Still where Enuy leaues, remorse doth enter.

The cause why these verses differing in feete yeeld the same length
of sound, is by reason of some rests which either the necessity of
the numbers or the heauiness of the sillables do beget. For we find
in musick that oftentimes the straines of a song cannot be reduct

to true number without some rests prefixt in the beginning and
middle, as also at the close if need requires.   Besides, our English
monasillables enforce many breathings which no doubt greatly
lengthen a verse, so that it is no wonder if for these reasons our
English verses of fiue feete hold pace with the *Latines* of sixe.
The pure *Iambick* in English needes small demonstration, because
it consists simply of *Iambick* feete; but our *Iambick licentiate* offers
itselfe to a farther consideration, for in the third and fift place we
must of force hold the *Iambick* foote, in the first, second, and fourth
10 place we may vse a *Spondee* or *Iambick* and sometime a *Tribrack* or
Dactile, but rarely an *Anapestick* foote, and that in the second or
fourth place.   But why an *Iambick* in the third place?   I answere,
that the forepart of the verse may the gentlier slide into his
Dimeter, as, for example sake, deuide this verse:

> *Harke how these winds do murmure at thy flight.*

Harke how these winds, there the voice naturally affects a rest;
then *murmur at thy flight*, that is of itselfe a perfect number, as
I will declare in the next Chapter; and therefore the other odde
sillable betweene them ought to be short, least the verse should
20 hang too much betweene the naturall pause of the verse and the
Dimeter following; the which *Dimeter* though it be naturally
Trochaical, yet it seemes to haue his originall out of the *Iambick*
verse.   But the better to confirme and expresse these rules, I will
set downe a short Poeme in *Licentiate Iambicks*, which may giue
more light to them that shall hereafter imitate these numbers.

> *Goe, numbers, boldly passe, stay not for ayde*
> *Of shifting rime, that easie flatterer,*
> *Whose witchcraft can the ruder eares beguile.*
> *Let your smooth feete, enur'd to purer arte,*
> 30 *True measures tread.   What if your pace be slow,*
> *And hops not like the Grecian elegies?*
> *It is yet gracefull, and well fits the state*
> *Of words ill-breathed and not shap't to runne.*
> *Goe then, but slowly, till your steps be firme;*
> *Tell them that pitty or peruersely skorne*
> *Poore English Poesie as the slaue to rime,*
> *You are those loftie numbers that reuiue*
> *Triumphs of Princes and sterne tragedies:*
> *And learne henceforth t'attend those happy sprights*
> 40 *Whose bounding fury, height, and waight affects.*
> *Assist their labour, and sit close to them,*

Neuer to part away till for desert
Their browes with great Apollos *bayes are hid.*
He first taught number and true harmonye ;
Nor is the lawrell his for rime bequeath'd.
Call him with numerous accents paisd by arte,
He'le turne his glory from the sunny clymes
The North-bred wits alone to patronise.
Let France their Bartas, *Italy* Tasso *prayse ;*
Phœbus *shuns none but in their flight from him.*

Though, as I said before, the naturall breathing-place of our English *Iambick* verse is in the last sillable of the second foote, as our *Trochy* after the manner of the Latine *Heroick* and *Iambick* rests naturally in the first of the third foote, yet no man is tyed altogether to obserue this rule, but he may alter it, after the iudgment of his eare, which Poets, Orators, and Musitions of all men ought to haue most excellent. Againe, though I said peremtorily before that the third and fift place of our licentiate *Iambick* must alwayes hold an *Iambick* foote, yet I will shew you example in both places where a *Tribrack* may be very formally taken, and first in the third place :

> *Some trade in* Barbary, *some in* Turky *trade.*

An other example :
> *Men that do fall to misery, quickly fall.*

If you doubt whether the first of *misery* be naturally short or no, you may iudge it by the easie sliding of these two verses following :
The first :
> *Whome misery can not alter, time deuours.*

The second :
> *What more vnhappy life, what misery more ?*

Example of the *Tribrack* in the fift place, as you may perceiue in the last foote of the fourth verse :
> *Some from the starry throne his fame deriues,*
> *Some from the mynes beneath, from trees or herbs :*
> *Each hath his glory, each his sundry gift,*
> *Renown'd in eu'ry art there liues not any.*

To proceede farther, I see no reason why the English *Iambick* in his first place may not as well borrow a foote of the *Trochy* as our

Trochy, or the Latine *Hendicasillable*, may in the like case make
bold with the *Iambick* : but it must be done euer with this caueat,
which is, that a *Sponde, Dactile,* or *Tribrack* do supply the next
place ; for an *Iambick* beginning with a single short sillable, and
the other ending before with the like, would too much drinke vp
the verse if they came immediatly together.

The example of the *Sponde* after the *Trochy* :

As the faire sonne the lightsome heau'n adorns.

The example of the *Dactil* :

10　　　　*Noble, ingenious, and discreetly wise.*

The example of the *Tribrack* :

Beawty to ielosie brings ioy, sorrow, feare.

Though I haue set downe these second licenses as good and
ayreable enough, yet for the most part my first rules are generall.

These are those numbers which Nature in our English destinates
to the Tragick and Heroik Poeme : for the subiect of them both
being all one, I see no impediment why one verse may not serue
for them both, as it appeares more plainly in the old comparison
of the two Greeke writers, when they say, *Homerus est Sophocles*
20 *heroicus*, and againe, *Sophocles est Homerus tragicus*, intimating that
both Sophocles and Homer are the same in height and subiect,
and differ onely in the kinde of their numbers.

The Iambick verse in like manner being yet made a little more
licentiate, that it might thereby the neerer imitate our common
talke, will excellently serue for Comedies ; and then may we vse
a *Sponde* in the fift place, and in the third place any foote except
a *Trochy*, which neuer enters into our Iambick verse but in the
first place, and then with his caueat of the other feete which must
of necessitie follow.

30　*The fift Chapter : of the Iambick Dimeter, or English march.*

The *Dimeter* (so called in the former Chapter) I intend next of
all to handle, because it seems to be a part of the *Iambick*, which
is our most naturall and auncient English verse. We may terme
this our English march, because the verse answers our warlick
forme of march in similitude of number. But call it what you
please, for I will not wrangle about names, only intending to set
down the nature of it and true structure. It consists of two feete
and one odde sillable. The first foote may be made either a

Trochy, or a *Spondee*, or an *Iambick*, at the pleasure of the com-
poser, though most naturally that place affects a *Trochy* or *Spondee*;
yet, by the example of *Catullus* in his *Hendicasillables*, I adde in
the first place sometimes an *Iambick* foote. In the second place
we must euer insert a *Trochy* or *Tribrack*, and so leaue the last
sillable (as in the end of a verse it is alwaies held) common. Of
this kinde I will subscribe three examples, the first being a peece
of a *Chorus* in a Tragedy.

> *Rauing warre, begot*
> *In the thirstye sands*   10
> *Of the* Lybian *Iles,*
> *Wasts our emptye fields;*
> *What the greedye rage*
> *Of fell wintrye stormes*
> *Could not turne to spoile,*
> *Fierce* Bellona *now*
> *Hath laid desolate,*
> *Voyd of fruit, or hope.*
> *Th' eger thriftye hinde,*
> *Whose rude toyle reuiu'd* 20
> *Our skie-blasted earth,*
> *Himselfe is but earth,*
> *Left a skorne to fate*
> *Through seditious armes:*
> *And that soile, aliue*
> *Which he duly nurst,*
> *Which him duly fed,*
> *Dead his body feeds:*
> *Yet not all the glebe*
> *His tuffe hands manur'd* 30
> *Now one turfe affords*
> *His poore funerall.*
> *Thus still needy liues,*
> *Thus still needy dyes*
> *Th' vnknowne multitude.*

An example *Lyrical.*

> *Greatest in thy wars,*
> *Greater in thy peace,*
> *Dread* Elizabeth;
> *Our muse only Truth,* 40

Figments cannot vse,
Thy ritch name to deck
That it selfe adornes:
But should now this age
Let all poesye fayne,
Fayning poesye could
Nothing faine at all
Worthy halfe thv fame.

An example *Epigrammaticall.*

10
Kind in euery kinde
This, deare Ned, resolue.
Neuer of thy prayse
Be too prodigall;
He that prayseth all
Can praise truly none.

The sixt Chapter: of the English Trochaick verse.

Next in course to be intreated of is the English *Trochaick*, being a verse simple, and of it selfe depending. It consists, as the Latine *Trochaick*, of fiue feete, the first whereof may be a *Trochy*,
20 a *Spondee*, or an *Iambick*, the other foure of necessity all *Trochyes*; still holding this rule authenticall, that the last sillable of a verse is always common. The spirit of this verse most of all delights in *Epigrams*, but it may be diuersly vsed, as shall hereafter be declared. I haue written diuers light Poems in this kinde, which for the better satisfaction of the reader I thought conuenient here in way of example to publish. In which though sometimes vnder a knowne name I haue shadowed a fain'd conceit, yet it is done without reference or offence to any person, and only to make the stile appeare the more English.

30
The first *Epigramme.*

Lockly spits apace, the rhewme he cals it,
But no drop (though often vrgd) he straineth
From his thirstie iawes, yet all the morning
And all day he spits, in eu'ry corner;
At his meales he spits, at eu'ry meeting;
At the barre he spits before the Fathers;
In the Court he spits before the Graces;
In the Church he spits, thus all prophaning

With that rude disease, that empty spitting :
Yet no cost he spares, he sees the Doctors,
Keeps a strickt diet, precisely vseth
Drinks and bathes drying, yet all preuailes not,
'Tis not China (Lockly), Salsa Guacum,
Nor dry Sassafras *can help, or ease thee ;*
'Tis no humor hurts, it is thy humor.

The second *Epigramme.*

Cease, fond wretch, to loue, so oft deluded,
Still made ritch with hopes, still vnrelieued.   10
Now fly her delaies ; she that debateth
Feeles not true desire ; he that, deferred,
Others times attends, his owne betrayeth :
Learne t'affect thy selfe ; thy cheekes deformed
With pale care reuiue by timely pleasure,
Or with skarlet heate them, or by paintings
Make thee louely ; for such arte she vseth
Whome in vayne so long thy folly loued.

The third *Epigramme.*

Kate *can fancy only berdles husbands,*   20
Thats the cause she shakes off eu'ry suter,
Thats the cause she liues so stale a virgin,
For, before her heart can heate her answer,
Her smooth youths she finds all hugely berded.

The fourth *Epigramme.*

All in sattin Oteny *will be suted,*
Beaten sattin (as by chaunce he cals it) ;
Oteny *sure will haue the bastinado.*

The fift *Epigramme.*

Tosts as snakes or as the mortall Henbane   30
Hunks *detests when huffcap ale he tipples,*
Yet the bread he graunts the fumes abateth ;
Therefore apt in ale, true, and he graunts it ;
But it drinks vp ale, that Hunks *detesteth.*

The sixt *Epigramme.*

What though Harry *braggs, let him be noble ;*
Noble Harry *hath not halfe a noble.*

The seauenth *Epigramme.*

Phœbe *all the rights* Elisa *claymeth,*
Mighty riuall, in this only diff'ring
That shees only true, thou only fayned.

The eight *Epigramme.*

Barnzy *stiffly vows that hees no Cuckold,*
Yet the vulgar eu'rywhere salutes him,
With strange signes of hornes, from eu'ry corner;
Wheresoere he commes, a sundry Cucco
10   *Still frequents his eares; yet hees no Cuccold.*
But this Barnzy *knowes that his* Matilda,
Skorning him, with Haruy *playes the wanton.*
Knowes it? nay desires it, and by prayers
Dayly begs of heau'n, that it for euer
May stand firme for him; yet hees no Cuccold.
And 'tis true, for Haruy *keeps* Matilda,
Fosters Barnzy, *and relieues his housbold,*
Buyes the Cradle, and begets the children,
Payes the Nurces, eu'ry charge defraying,
20   *And thus truly playes* Matildas *husband:*
So that Barnzy *now becomes a cypher,*
And himselfe th' adultrer of Matilda.
Mock not him with hornes, the case is altered;
Haruy *beares the wrong, he proues the Cuccold.*

The ninth *Epigramme.*

Buffe *loues fat vians, fat ale, fat all things,*
Keepes fat whores, fat offices, yet all men
Him fat only wish to feast the gallous.

The tenth *Epigramme.*

30   Smith, *by sute diuorst, the knowne adultres*
Freshly weds againe; what ayles the mad-cap
By this fury? euen so theeues by frailty
Of their hemp reseru'd, againe the dismall
Tree embrace, againe the fatall halter.

The eleuenth *Epigramme.*

His late losse the Wiueless Higs *in order*
Eu'rywere bewailes to friends, to strangers;

Tels them how by night a yongster armed
Saught his Wife (as hand in hand he held her)
With drawne sword to force; she cryed; he mainely
Roring ran for ayde, but (ah) returning
Fled was with the prize the beawty-forcer,
Whome in vain he seeks, he threats, he followes.
Chang'd is Hellen, Hellen *hugs the stranger,*
Safe as Paris *in the Greeke triumphing.*
Therewith his reports to teares he turneth,
Peirst through with the louely Dames remembrance;   10
Straight he sighes, he raues, his haire he teareth,
Forcing pitty still by fresh lamenting.
Cease vnworthy, worthy of thy fortunes,
Thou that couldst so faire a prize deliuer,
For feare vnregarded, vndefended,
Hadst no heart I thinke, I know no liuer.

The twelfth *Epigramme.*

Why droopst thou, Trefeild? *Will* Hurst *the Banker*
Make dice of thy bones? By heau'n he can not.
Can not? What's the reason? Ile declare it: 20
Th'ar all growne so pockie and so rotten.

The seauenth Chapter: of the English Elegeick verse.

The *Elegeick* verses challenge the next place, as being of all compound verses the simplest. They are deriu'd out of our owne naturall numbers as neere the imitation of the *Greekes* and *Latines* as our heauy sillables will permit. The first verse is a meere licentiate *Iambick*; the second is fram'd of two vnited *Dimeters.* In the first *Dimeter* we are tyed to make the first foote either a *Trochy* or a *Spondee*, the second a *Trochy*, and the odde sillable of it alwaies long. The second *Dimeter* consists of two Trochyes 30 (because it requires more swiftnes then the first) and an odde sillable, which, being last, is euer common. I will giue you example both of *Elegye* and *Epigramme*, in this kinde.

An *Elegye.*

Constant to none, but euer false to me,
Traiter still to loue through thy faint desires,
Not hope of pittie now nor vaine redresse
Turns my griefs to teares and renu'd laments.

Too well thy empty vowes and hollow thoughts
  Witnes both thy wrongs and remorseles hart.
Rue not my sorrow, but blush at my name;
  Let thy bloudy cheeks guilty thoughts betray.
My flames did truly burne, thine made a shew,
  As fires painted are which no heate retayne,
Or as the glossy Pirop *faines to blaze,*
  But toucht cold appeares, and an earthy stone.
True cullours deck thy cheeks, false foiles thy brest,
10 *Frailer then thy light beawty is thy minde.*
None canst thou long refuse, nor long affect,
  But turn'st feare with hopes, sorrow with delight,
Delaying, and deluding eu'ry way
  Those whose eyes are once with thy beawty chain'd.
Thrice happy man that entring first thy loue
  Can so guide the straight raynes of his desires,
That both he can regard thee and refraine:
  If grac't, firme he stands, if not, easely falls.

Example of *Epigrams,* in Elegeick verse.

The first *Epigramme.*
20

Arthure *brooks only those that brooke not him,*
  Those he most regards, and deuoutly serues:
But them that grace him his great brau'ry skornes,
  Counting kindnesse all duty, not desert:
Arthure *wants forty pounds, tyres eu'ry friend,*
  But finds none that holds twenty due for him.

The second *Epigramme.*

If fancy can not erre which vertue guides,
  In thee, Laura, *then fancy can not erre.*

The third *Epigramme.*
30

Drue *feasts no Puritans; the churles, he saith,*
  Thanke no men, but eate, praise God, and depart

The fourth *Epigramme.*

A wiseman wary liues, yet most secure,
  Sorrowes moue not him greatly, nor delights:
Fortune and death he skorning, only makes
  Th' earth his sober Inne; but still heau'n his home.

The fifth *Epigramme.*

Thou telst me, Barnzy, Dawson *hath a wife:*
Thine he hath, I graunt; Dawson *hath a wife.*

The sixt *Epigramme.*

Drue *giues thee money, yet thou thankst not him,*
But thankst God for him, like a godly man.
Suppose, rude Puritan, thou begst of him,
And he saith God help, who's the godly man?

The seauenth *Epigramme.*

All wonders Barnzy *speakes, all grosely faind:*   10
Speake some wonder once, Barnzy, *speake the truth.*

The eight *Epigramme.*

None then should through thy beawty, Lawra, *pine,*
Might sweet words alone ease a loue-sick heart:
But your sweet words alone, that quit so well
Hope of friendly deeds, kill the loue-sick heart.

The ninth *Epigramme.*

At all thou frankly throwst, while Frank *thy wife,*
Bars not Luke *the mayn;* Oteny *barre the bye.*

The eight Chapter: of DITTIES *and* ODES.   20

To descend orderly from the more simple numbers to them that
are more compounded, it is now time to handle such verses as are
fit for *Ditties* or *Odes* ; which we may call *Lyricall,* because they
are apt to be soong to an instrument, if they were adorn'd with
conuenient notes.   Of that kind I will demonstrate three in this
Chapter, and in the first we will proceede after the manner of the
Saphick, which is a *Trochaicall* verse as well as the *Hendicasillable*
in Latine.   The first three verses therefore in our English *Saphick*
are meerely those *Trochaicks* which I handled in the sixt Chapter,
excepting only that the first foote of either of them must euer of 30
necessity be a *Spondee,* to make the number more graue.   The
fourth and last closing verse is compounded of three *Trochyes*
together, to giue a more smooth farewell, as you may easily obserue
in this Poeme made vpon a Triumph at *Whitehall,* whose glory
was dasht with an vnwelcome showre, hindring the people from
the desired sight of her Maiestie.

The English *Sapphick.*

Faiths pure shield, the Christian Diana,
Englands *glory crownd with all deuinenesse,*
Liue long with triumphs to blesse thy people
At thy sight triumphing.

Loe, they sound; the Knights in order armed
Entring threat the list, adrest to combat
For their courtly loues; he, hees the wonder
Whome Eliza *graceth.*

10 *Their plum'd pomp the vulgar heaps detaineth,*
And rough steeds; let vs the still deuices
Close obserue, the speeches and the musicks
Peacefull arms adorning.

But whence showres so fast this angry tempest,
Clowding dimme the place? Behold, Eliza
This day shines not here; this heard, the launces
And thick heads do vanish.

The second kinde consists of *Dimeter,* whose first foote may
either be a *Sponde* or a *Trochy.* The two verses following are
20 both of them *Trochaical,* and consist of foure feete, the first of
either of them being a *Spondee* or *Trochy,* the other three only
Trochyes. The fourth and last verse is made of two *Trochyes.*
The number is voluble, and fit to expresse any amorous conceit.

The Example.

Rose-cheekt Lawra, *come*
Sing thou smoothly with thy beawties
Silent musick, either other
Sweetely gracing.

Louely formes do flowe
30 *From concent deuinely framed;*
Heau'n is musick, and thy beawties
Birth is heauenly.

These dull notes we sing
Discords neede for helps to grace them;
Only beawty purely louing
Knowes no discord,

But still mooues delight,
Like cleare springs renu'd by flowing,
Euer perfet, euer in them-
                selues eternall.

The third kind begins as the second kind ended, with a verse consisting of two *Trochy* feete, and then as the second kind had in the middle two *Trochaick* verses of foure feete, so this hath three of the same nature, and ends in a *Dimeter* as the second began.   The *Dimeter* may allow in the first place a *Trochy* or a *Spondee*, but no *Iambick*.   10

The Example.

Iust beguiler,
Kindest loue, yet only chastest,
Royall in thy smooth denyals,
Frowning or demurely smiling,
            Still my pure delight.

Let me view thee
With thoughts and with eyes affected,
And if then the flames do murmur,
Quench them with thy vertue, charme them   20
            With thy stormy browes.

Heau'n so cheerefull
Laughs not euer, hory winter
Knowes his season, euen the freshest
Sommer mornes from angry thunder
            Iet not still secure.

The ninth Chapter, of the Anacreontick *Verse.*

If any shall demaund the reason why this number, being in it selfe simple, is plac't after so many compounded numbers, I answere, because I hold it a number too licentiate for a higher place, and in 30 respect of the rest imperfect ; yet is it passing gracefull in our English toong, and will excellently fit the subiect of a *Madrigall*, or any other lofty or tragicall matter.   It consists of two feete : the first may be either a *Sponde* or *Trochy*, the other must euer represent the nature of a *Trochy*, as for example :

Follow, followe,
Though with mischiefe
Arm'd, like whirlewind
Now she flyes thee ;

Time can conquer
Loues vnkindnes ;
Loue can alter
Times disgraces ;
Till death faint not
Then but followe.
Could I catch that
Nimble trayter,
Skornefull Lawra,
10   *Swift foote* Lawra,
Soone then would I
Seeke auengement.
Whats th' auengement ?
Euen submissely
Prostrate then to
Beg for mercye.

Thus haue I briefely described eight seueral kinds of English
numbers simple or compound. The first was our *Iambick* pure
and licentiate. The second, that which I call our *Dimeter,* being
20 deriued either from the end of our *Iambick* or from the beginning
of our *Trochaick.* The third which I deliuered was our English
Trochaick verse. The fourth our English *Elegeick.* The fift, sixt,
and seauenth were our English *Sapphick,* and two other *Lyricall*
numbers, the one beginning with that verse which I call our
Dimeter, the other ending with the same. The eight and last
was a kind of *Anacreontick* verse, handled in this Chapter. These
numbers which by my long obseruation I have found agreeable
with the nature of our sillables, I haue set forth for the benefit of
our language, which I presume the learned will not only imitate
30 but also polish and amplifie with their owne inuentions. Some
eares accustomed altogether to the fatnes of rime may perhaps
except against the cadences of these numbers ; but let any man
iudicially examine them, and he shall finde they close of themselues
so perfectly that the help of rime were not only in them superfluous
but also absurd. Moreouer, that they agree with the nature of
our English it is manifest, because they entertaine so willingly
our owne British names, which the writers in English Heroicks
could neuer aspire vnto, and euen our Rimers themselues haue
rather delighted in borrowed names than in their owne, though
40 much more apt and necessary. But it is now time that I proceede
to the censure of our sillables, and that I set such lawes vpon

them as by imitation, reason, or experience I can confirme. Yet
before I enter into that discourse, I will briefely recite and dispose
in order all such feete as are necessary for composition of the
verses before described. They are sixe in number, three whereof
consist of two sillables, and as many of three.

Feete of two sillables.

Iambick: ⎫   ⎧ *rĕuēnge*
Trochaick: ⎬ as ⎨ *Bēawtĭe*
Sponde: ⎭   ⎩ *cōnstānt*

Feete of three sillables.   10

Tribrack: ⎫   ⎧ *mĭsĕrĭe*
Anapestick: ⎬ as ⎨ *mĭsērīes*
Dactile: ⎭   ⎩ *Dēstĕnĭĕ*

The tenth Chapter: of the quantity of English sillables.

The *Greekes* in the quantity of their sillables were farre more
licentious then the *Latines,* as *Martiall* in his Epigramme of
Earinon witnesseth, saying, *Musas qui colimus seueriores.* But the
English may very well challenge much more licence then either of
them, by reason it stands chiefely vpon monasillables, which, in
expressing with the voyce, are of a heauy cariage, and for that 20
cause the *Dactil, Trybrack,* and *Anapestick* are not greatly mist in our
verses. But aboue all the accent of our words is diligently to be
obseru'd, for chiefely by the accent in any language the true value
of the sillables is to be measured. Neither can I remember any
impediment except position that can alter the accent of any
sillable in our English verse. For though we accent the second
of *Trumpington* short, yet is it naturally long, and so of necessity
must be held of euery composer. Wherefore the first rule that is
to be obserued is the nature of the accent, which we must euer
follow.   30

The next rule is position, which makes euery sillable long,
whether the position happens in one or in two words, according to
the manner of the *Latines,* wherein is to be noted that *h* is no
letter.

Position is when a vowell comes before two consonants, either
in one or two words. In one, as in *best, e* before *st* makes the
word *best* long by position. In two words, as in *setled loue,*
e before *d* in the last sillable of the first word and *l* in the
beginning of the second makes *led* in *setlēd* long by position.

A vowell before a vowell is alwaies short, as *flīing, dīing, gŏing*, vnlesse the accent alter it, in *dĕnīing*.

The diphthong in the midst of a word is alwaies long, as *plaīing, decēiuing*.

The *Synalæphas* or *Elisions* in our toong are either necessary to auoid the hollownes and gaping in our verse, as *to* and *the*, *t'inchaunt, th' inchaunter*, or may be vsd at pleasure, as for *let vs* to say *let's*; for *we will, wee'l*; for *euery, eu'ry*; for *they are, th'ar*; for *he is, hee's*; for *admired, admir'd*; and such like.

Also, because our English Orthography (as the French) differs from our common pronunciation, we must esteeme our sillables as we speake, not as we write; for the sound of them in a verse is to be valued, and not their letters, as for *follow* we pronounce *follo*; for *perfect, perfet*; for *little, littel*; for *loue-sick, loue-sik*; for *honour, honor*; for *money, mony*; for *dangerous, dangerus*; for *raunsome, raunsum*; for *though, tho*; and their like.

Deriuatiues hold the quantities of their primatiues, as *dĕuōut, dĕuōutelĭe*; *prŏphāne, prŏphānelĭe;* and so do the compositiues, as *dĕsĕru'd, ūndĕsĕru'd*.

In words of two sillables, if the last haue a full and rising accent that sticks long vpon the voyce, the first sillable is always short, vnlesse position, or the diphthong, doth make it long, as *dĕsīre, prĕsērue, dĕfīne, prŏphāne, rĕgārd, mănūre*, and such like.

If the like dissillables at the beginning haue double consonants of the same kind, we may vse the first sillable as common, but more naturally short, because in their pronunciation we touch but one of those double letters, as *ătĕnd, ăpēare, ŏpōse*. The like we may say when silent and melting consonants meete together, as *ădrēst, rĕdrēst, ŏprēst, rĕprēst, rĕtrĭu'd*, and such like.

Words of two sillables that in their last sillable mayntayne a flat or falling accent, ought to hold their first sillable long, as *rĭgŏr, glōrie, spĭrĭt, fūrie, lăboŭr*, and the like: *ăny, măny, prĕty, hŏly*, and their like are excepted.

One obseruation which leades me to iudge of the difference of these dissillables whereof I last spake, I take from the originall monasillable; which if it be graue, as *shāde*, I hold that the first of *shādie* must be long; so *trūe, trūlie*; *hāue, hāuĭng*; *tīre, tīrĭng*.

Words of three sillables for the most part are deriued from words of two sillables, and from them take the quantity of their first sillable, as *flŏrĭsh, flŏrĭshing* long; *hŏlie, hŏlĭnes* short; but *mi* in *mīser* being long hinders not the first of *mĭsery* to be short, because the sound of the *i* is a little altred.

De, di, and *pro* in trisillables (the second being short) are long, as *dēsŏlāte, dĭlĭgēnt, prōdĭgāll.*

Re is euer short, as *rĕmĕdie, rĕfĕrēnce, rĕdŏlēnt, rĕuĕrēnd.*

Likewise the first of these trisillables is short, as the first of *bĕnĕfit, gĕnĕrall, hĭdĕous, mĕmŏrie, nŭmĕrous, pĕnĕtrāte, sĕpărat, tĭmĕrous, vărĭant, vărĭous;* and so may we esteeme of all that yeeld the like quicknes of sound.

In words of three sillables the quantity of the middle sillable is lightly taken from the last sillable of the originall dissillable, as the last of *dĕuine,* ending in a graue or long accent, makes the second of *dĕuīning* also long, and so *ēspīe, ēspūing, dĕnīe, dĕnūing:* contrarywise it falles out if the last of the dissillable beares a flat or falling accent, as *glŏrĭe, glŏrĭing, ēnuĭe, ēnuĭing,* and so forth.

Words of more sillables are eyther borrowed and hold their owne nature, or are likewise deriu'd and so follow the quantity of their primatiues, or are knowne by their proper accents, or may be easily censured by a iudiciall eare.

All words of two or more sillables ending with a falling accent in *y* or *ye,* as *fairelĭe, dĕmurelĭe, beawtĭe, pittĭe,* or in *ue,* as *vertuĕ, rēscuĕ,* or in *ow,* as *follŏw, hŏllŏw,* or in *e,* as *parlĕ, Daphnĕ,* or in *a,* as *Mannă,* are naturally short in their last sillables; neither let any man cauill at this licentiate abbreuiating of sillables, contrary to the custome of the Latines, which made all their last sillables that ended in *u* long, but let him consider that our verse of fiue feete, and for the most part but of ten sillables, must equall theirs of six feete and of many sillables, and therefore may with sufficient reason aduenture vpon this allowance. Besides, euery man may obserue what an infinite number of sillables both among the *Greekes* and *Romaines* are held as common. But words of two sillables ending with a rising accent in *y* or *ye,* as *denye, descrye,* or in *ue,* as *ensue,* or in *ee,* as *foresee,* or in *oe,* as *forgoe,* are long in their last sillables, vnlesse a vowell begins the next word.

All monasillables that end in a graue accent are euer long, as *wrāth, hāth, thēse, thōse, tōoth, sōoth, thrōugh, dāy, plāy, feāte, speēde, strīfe, flōw, grōw, shēw.*

The like rule is to be obserued in the last of dissillables bearing a graue rising sound, as *deuine, delaie, retire, refuse, manure,* or a graue falling sound, as *fortune, pleasure, vampire.*

All such as haue a double consonant lengthning them, as *wārre, bārre, stārre, fūrre, mūrre,* appear to me rather long then any way short.

There are of these kinds other, but of a lighter sound, that, if

the word following do begin with a vowell, are short, as *doth,*
though, thou, now, they, two, too, flye, dye, true, due, see, are, far,
you, thee, and the like.

These monasillables are alwayes short, as *ă, thĕ, thĭ, shĕ, wĕ, bĕ,*
hĕ, nŏ, tŏ, gŏ, sŏ, dŏ, and the like.

But if *i* or *y* are ioyn'd at the beginning of a word with any
vowell, it is not then held as a vowell, but as a consonant, as *ielosy,*
iewce, iade, ioy, Iudas, ye, yet, yel, youth, yoke. The like is to be
obseru'd in *w,* as *winde, wide, wood :* and in all words that begin
10 with *va, ve, vi, vo,* or *vu,* as *vacant, vew, vine, voide,* and *vulture.*

All Monasillables or Polysillables that end in single con-
sonants, either written or sounded with single consonants, hauing
a sharp liuely accent and standing without position of the word
following, are short in their last sillable, as *scăb, flĕd, pārtĕd, Gŏd,*
ŏf, ĭf, bāndŏg, ānguĭsh, sĭck, quĭck, rĭuăl, wĭll, pēoplĕ, sĭmplĕ, cŏme,
sŏme, hĭm, thĕm, frŏm, sūmmŏn, thĕn, prŏp, prōspĕr, hōnoŭr, lāboŭr,
thĭs, hĭs, spēchĕs, gōddĕsse, pērfĕct, bŭt, whăt, thăt, and their like.

The last sillable of all words in the plurall number that haue
two or more vowells before *s* are long, as *vertūes, dutĭes, miserīes,*
20 *fellowēs.*

These rules concerning the quantity of our English sillables
I haue disposed as they came next into my memory ; others
more methodicall, time and practise may produce.   In
the meane season, as the Grammarians leaue many
sillables to the authority of Poets, so do I
likewise leaue many to their iudgments ;
and withall thus conclude, that
there is no Art begun and
perfected at one
30   enterprise.

F I N I S

THE
DISCRIPTION OF
A
MASKE,

Prefented before the Kinges Maieftie
at *White-Hall,* on *Twelfth Night*
laft, in honour of the Lord HAYES, and
his Bride, Daughter and ·Heire to the
Honourable the Lord DENNYE, *their*
Marriage hauing been the fame Day
at Court folemnized.

To this by occafion other fmall Poemes
are adioyned.

Inuented and fet forth by THOMA.
CAMPION *Doctor of Phificke.*

LONDON
Imprinted by IOHN WINDET for IOHN BROVVN
and are to be folde at his fhop in S. Dunftones
Churchyeard in Fleetftreet. 1607.

To the most puisant and
Gratious IAMES *King of great*
Britaine.

The disvnited Scithians when they sought
To gather strength by parties, and combine
That perfect league of freends which once beeing wrought
No turne of time or fortune could vntwine,
This rite they held : a massie bowle was brought,
And eu'ry right arme shot his seuerall blood
Into the mazar till 'twas fully fraught.   10
Then hauing stird it to an equall floud
They quaft to th' vnion, which till death should last,
In spite of priuate foe, cr forraine feare,
And this blood sacrament being knowne t' haue past,
Their names grew dreadfull to all far and neere.
O then, great Monarch, with how wise a care
Do you these bloods deuided mixe in one,
And with like consanguinities prepare
The high, and euerliuing Vnion
   Tweene Scots and English : who can wonder then   20
   If he that marries kingdomes, marries men ?

An Epigram.

Merlin, the great King Arthur *being slaine,*
Foretould that he should come to life againe,
And long time after weild great Brittaines state
More powerfull ten-fould, and more fortunate.
   Prophet, 'tis true, and well we find the same,
   Saue onely that thou didst mistake the name.

Ad Inuictissimum,

Serenissimumque IACOBVM
Magnæ Britanniæ Regem.

Angliæ, et vnanimis Scotiæ pater, anne maritus
  Sis dubito, an neuter, (Rex) vel vterque simul.
Vxores pariter binas sibi iungat vt vnus,
  Credimus hoc, ipso te prohibente, nephas.
Atque, maritali natas violare parentem
  Complexu, quis non cogitat esse scelus?
At tibi diuinis successibus vtraque nubit;   10
  Vna tamen coniux, coniugis vnus amor.
Connubium O mirum, binas qui ducere, et vnam
  Possis! tu solus sic, Iacobe, *potes:*
Diuisas leuiter terras componis in vnam
  Atque vnam æternum nomine, ˋreque facis:
Natisque, et nuptis, pater et vir factus vtrisque es;
  Vnitis coniux vere, et amore parens.

To the Right Noble and Vertu-
ous *Theophilus Howard*, Lorde of
Walden, sonne and Heire to the right Hono-
rable the Earle of Suffolke.

If to be sprong of high and princely blood,
If to inherite vertue, honour, grace,
If to be great in all things, and yet good,
If to be facill, yet t' haue power and place,
  If to be iust, and bountifull, may get
  The loue of men, your right may chalenge it.   10

The course of forraine manners far and wide,
The courts, the countries, Cities, townes ˋand state,
The blossome of your springing youth hath tried,
Honourd in eu'ry place and fortunate,
  Which now grown fairer doth adorne our Court
  With princelie reuelling, and timely sport.

But if th' admired vertues of your youth
Breede such despairing to my daunted muse,
That it can scarcely vtter naked truth,
How shall it mount as rauisht spirits vse   20
    Vnder the burden of your riper dayes,
    Or hope to reach the so far distant bayes?

My slender Muse shall yet my loue expresse,
And by the fair Thames side of you sheele sing;
The double streames shall beare her willing verse
Far hence with murmur of their ebbe and spring.
    But if you fauour her light tunes, ere long
    Sheele striue to raise you with a loftier song.

To the Right Vertuous, and Hono- rable, the Lord and Lady HAYES.

Should I presume to separate you now,
That were so lately ioyn'de by holy vow,
For whome this golden dreame which I report
Begot so many waking eyes at Court,
And for whose grace so many nobles chang'd,
Their names and habites, from themselues estrang'd?
Accept together, and together view
This little worke which all belongs to you,   10
And liue together many blessed dayes,
To propagate the honour'd name of *HAYES.*

Epigramma.

Hæredem (vt spes est) pariet noua nupta Scot' Anglum;
    Quem gignet posthac ille, Britannus erit:
Sic noua posteritas, ex regnis orta duobus,
    Vtrinque egregios nobilitabit auos.

THE

Description of a Maske presented

*before the Kinges Maiestie at White
Hall, on twelft night last, in honour*
of the Lord *HAYES*, and his Bride, daugh-
*ter and heire to the Honourable the Lord
DENNYE, their mariage hauing been
the same day at Court solemnized.*

As in battailes, so in all other actions that are to bee reported,
10 the first, and most necessary part is the discription of the place,
with his oportunities, and properties, whether they be naturall or
artificiall.   The greate hall (wherein the Maske was presented)
receiued this diuision, and order: The vpper part where the cloth
and chaire of State were plac't, had scaffoldes and seates on eyther
side continued to the skreene; right before it was made a partition
for the daucing place; on the right hand whereof were consorted
ten Musitions, with Basse and Meane lutes, a Bandora, a double
Sack-bott, and an Harpsicord, with two treble Violins; on the
other side somewhat neerer the skreene were plac't 9 Violins and
20 three Lutes, and to answere both the Consorts (as it were in a
triangle) sixe Cornets, and sixe Chappell voyces, were seated almost
right against them, in a place raised higher in respect of the
pearcing sound of those Instruments; eighteen foote from the
skreen, an other Stage was raised higher by a yearde then that
which was prepared for dancing: This higher Stage was all en-
closed with a double vale, so artificially painted, that it seemed as
if darke cloudes had hung before it: within that shrowde was con-
cealed a greene valley, with greene trees round about it, and in the
midst of them nine golden trees of fifteene foote high, with armes
30 and braunches very glorious to behold: From the which groue
toward the State was made a broade descent to the daucing place,
iust in the midst of it; on either hand were two ascents, like the
sides of two hilles, drest with shrubbes and trees; that on the
right hand leading to the bowre of *Flora*: the other to the
house of *Night*; which bowre and house were plac't opposite at

(Page 63, line 37)

To face page 63.

either end of the skreene, and betweene them both was raised a hill, hanging like a cliffe ouer the groue belowe, and on the top of it a goodly large tree was set, supposed to be the tree of *Diana*; behind the which toward the window was a small descent, with an other spreading hill that climed vp to the toppe of the window, with many trees on the height of it, whereby those that played on the Hoboyes at the Kings entrance into the hall were shadowed: The bowre of *Flora* was very spacious, garnisht with all kind of flowers, and flowrie branches with lights in them; the house of *Night* ample and stately, with blacke pillors, whereon many starres 10 of gold were fixt: within it, when it was emptie, appeared nothing but cloudes and starres, and on the top of it stood three Turrets vnderpropt with small blacke starred pillers, the middlemost being highest and greatest, the other two of equall proportion: about it were plac't on wyer artificial Battes and Owles, continually mouing; with many other inuentions, the which for breuitie sake I passe by with silence.

Thus much for the place, and now from thence let vs come to the persons.

The Maskers names were these (whom both for order and 20 honour I mention in the first place).

1 *Lord Walden.*
2 *Sir Thomas Howard.*
3 *Sir Henrie Carey, Master of the Iewell house.*
4 *Sir Richard Preston* ⎫ *Gent. of the K. priuie Chamber.*
5 *Sir Iohn Ashley*   ⎭
6 *Sir Thomas Iarret, Pentioner.*
7 *Sir Iohn Digby, one of the King's Caruers.*
8 *Sir Thomas Badger, Master of the King's Hariers.*
9 *Maister Goringe.* 30

Their number Nine, the best and amplest of numbers, for as in Musicke seuen notes containe all varietie, the eight being in nature the same with the first, so in numbring after the ninth we begin again, the tenth beeing as it were the Diappason in Arithmetick. The number of 9 is framed by the Muses and Worthies, and it is of all the most apt for chaunge and diuersitie of proportion. The chiefe habit which the Maskers did vse is set forth to your view in the first leafe: they presented in their fayned persons the Knights of *Apollo*, who is the father of heat and youth, and consequently of amorous affections. 40

FLORA the Queene of Flowers, attired in a changeable Taffatie Gowne, with a large vale embrodered with flowers, a Crowne of flowers, and white buskins painted with flowers.

ZEPHYRVS in a white loose robe of sky coloured Taffatie, with a mantle of white silke, prop't with wyre, stil wauing behind him as he moued; on his head hee wore a wreath of Palme deckt with Primmeroses and Violets, the hayre of his head and beard were flaxen, and his buskins white, and painted with flowers.

10   *NIGHT* in a close robe of blacke silke and gold, a blacke mantle embrodered with starres, a crowne of starres on her head, her haire blacke and spangled with gold, her face blacke, her buskins blacke, and painted with starres; in her hand shee bore a blacke wand, wreathed with gold.

HESPERVS in a close robe of a deep crimson Taffatie mingled with skye colour, and ouer that a large loose robe of a lighter crimson taffatie; on his head he wore a wreathed band of gold, with a starre in the front thereof, his haire and beard red, and buskins yellow.

20   These are the principall persons that beare sway in this inuention, others that are but secunders to these, I will describe in their proper places, discoursing the Maske in order as it was performed.

As soone as the King was entred the great Hall, the Hoboyes (out of the wood on the top of the hil) entertained the time till his Maiestie and his trayne were placed, and then after a little expectation the consort of ten began to play an Ayre, at the sound whereof the vale on the right hand was withdrawne, and the ascent of the hill with the bower of *Flora* were discouered, where *Flora* and *Zepherus* were busily plucking flowers from the

30   Bower, and throwing them into two baskets, which two *Siluans* held, who were attired in changeable Taffatie, with wreathes of flowers on their heads. As soone as the baskets were filled, they came downe in this order; First *Zepherus* and *Flora*, then the two *Siluans* with baskets after them; Foure *Siluans* in greene taffatie and wreathes, two bearing meane Lutes, the third, a base Lute, and the fourth a deepe Bandora.

As soone as they came to the discent toward the dauncing place, the consort of tenne ceac't, and the foure *Siluans* playd the same Ayre, to which *Zepherus* and the two other *Siluans* did

40   sing these words in a base, Tenor, and treble voyce, and going vp and downe as they song, they strowed flowers all about the place.

Song.

Now hath Flora *rob'd her bowers*
To befrend this place with flowers :
   Strowe aboute, strowe aboute.
The Skye rayn'd neuer kindlyer Showers.
Flowers with Bridalls well agree,
Fresh as Brides, and Bridgromes be :
   Strowe aboute, strowe aboute ;
And mixe them with fit melodie.
   Earth hath no Princelier flowers
Then Roses white, and Roses red,   10
But they must still be mingled :
And as a Rose new pluckt from Venus *thorne,*
So doth a Bride her Bride-groomes bed adorne.

Diuers diuers Flowers affect
For some priuate deare respect :
   Strowe about, strowe about.
Let euery one his owne protect ;
But hees none of Floras *friend*
That will not the Rose *commend.*
   Strow about, strow about ;   20
Let Princes Princely flowers defend :
   Roses, the Gardens pride,
Are flowers for loue and flowers for Kinges,
In courts desir'd and Weddings :
And as a Rose in Venus *bosome worne,*
So doth a Bridegroome his Brides bed adorne.

The Musique ceaseth, and
Flora speaks.

Flora.   *Flowers and good wishes* Flora *doth present,*
Sweete flowers, the ceremonious ornament   30
Of maiden mariage, Beautie figuring,
And blooming youth ; which though we careles fling
About this sacred place, let none prophane
Think that these fruits from common hils are tane,
Or Vulgar vallies which do subiect lie
To winters wrath and cold mortalitie.
But these are hallowed and immortall flowers
With Floras *hands gather'd from* Floras *bowres.*
Such are her presents, endles, as her loue,
And such for euer may this nights ioy proue.   40

Zephyrus,
the
westerne
wind, of all
the most
mild and
pleasant,
who with
Venus, the
Queene of
loue, is said
to bring in
the spring,
when
naturall
heate and
appetite
reuiueth,
and the
glad earth
begins to be
beautified
with
flowers.

Zeph. *For euer endles may this nights ioy proue,*
So eccoes Zephyrus *the friend of loue,*
Whose aide Venus *implores when she doth bring*
Into the naked world the greene-leau'd spring.
When of the Sunnes warme beames the Nets we weaue
That can the stubborn'st heart with loue deceiue.
That Queene of beauty, and desire by me
Breaths gently forth this Bridall prophecie:
Faithfull and fruitfull shall these Bedmates proue,
Blest in their fortunes, honoured in their loue.

Flor. *All grace this night, and,* Siluans, *so must you,*
Off'ring your mariage song with changes new.

The song in forme of a Dialogue.

Can. *Who is the happier of the two,*
    A maide, or wife?
Ten. *Which is more to be desired,*
    Peace or strife?
Can. *What strife can be where two are one,*
    Or what delight to pine alone?
20 Bas. *None such true freendes, none so sweet life,*
    As that betweene the man and wife.
Ten. *A maide is free, a wife is tyed.*
Can. *No maide but faine would be a Bride.*
Ten. *Why liue so many single then?*
    'Tis not I hope for want of men.
Can. *The bow and arrow both may fit,*
    And yet 'tis hard the marke to hit.
Bas. *He leuels faire that by his side*
    Laies at night his louely Bride.
30 Cho. *Sing Io; Hymen, Io; Io; Hymen.*

This song being ended the whole veil is sodainly drawne, the groue
and trees of gold, and the hill with *Dianas* tree are at once discouered.

Night appeares in her house with her 9 houres, apparrelled in large
robes of black taffatie, painted thicke with starres, their haires long,
blacke, and spangled with gold, on their heads coronets of stars, and
their faces blacke. Euery houre bore in his hand a blacke torch,
painted with starres, and lighted. Night presently descending from
her house spake as followeth.

Night. *Vanish, darke vales ; let night in glory shine*
As she doth burn in rage: come leaue our shrine
You black-hair'd hours, and guide vs with your lights,
Flora *hath wakened wide our drowsy sprights :*
See where she triumphs, see her flowers are throwne,
And all about the seedes of malice sowne.
Despightful Flora, *ist not enough of griefe*
That Cynthia's *robd, but thou must grace the theefe ?*
Or didst not hear Nights soueraigne Queen complaine
Hymen *had stolne a Nimph out of her traine,*
And matcht her here, plighted henceforth to be
Loues *friend, and stranger to Virginitie ?*
And mak'st thou sport for this ?

Flora. *Bee mild, sterne night ;*
Flora *doth honour* Cinthia, *and her right.*
Virginitie is a voluntary powre,
Free from constraint, euen like an vntoucht flower
Meete to be gather'd when 'tis throughly blowne.
The Nimph was Cinthias *while she was her owne,*
But now another claimes in her a right,   20
By fate reseru'd thereto and wise foresight.

Zeph. *Can* Cynthia *one kind virgins loss bemone ?*
How if perhaps she brings her tenne for one ?
Or can shee misse one in so full a traine ?
Your Goddesse doth of too much store complaine.
If all her Nimphes would aske aduise of me
There should be fewer virgins then there be.
Nature ordaind not Men to liue alone,
Where there are two a Woman should be one.

Night. *Thou breath'st sweet poison, wanton* Zephyrus,   30
But Cynthia *must not be deluded thus.*
Her holy Forrests are by theeues prophan'd,
Her Virgins frighted, and loe, where they stand
That late were Phœbus *Knights, turnd now to trees*
By Cynthias *vengement for their iniuries*
In seeking to seduce her Nymphes with loue :
Here they are fixt, and neuer may remoue
But by Dianaes *power that stucke them here.*
Apollos *loue to them doth yet appeare,*

Diana, *the Moone and Queene of Virginitie, is saide to be regent and Empresse of Night, and is therefore by night defended, as in her quarrel for the losse of the Bride, her virgin.*

In that his beames hath guilt them as they grow,
To make their miserie yeeld the greater show.
But they shall tremble when sad Night *doth speake,*
And at her stormy words their boughes shall breake.

Toward the end of this speech *Hesperus* begins to descend by the house of *Night*, and by that time the speech was finisht he was readie to speake.

Hesperus, *the Euening starre, foreshews that the wisht marriage-night is at hand, and for that cause is supposed to be the friend of Bridegroomes and Brides.*

Hesp.   *Hayle reuerend angrie* Night, *haile Queene of Flowers,*
Mild sprited Zephyrus, *haile,* Siluans *and* Howers.
Hesperus *brings peace, cease then your needlesse iarres*
Here in this little firmament of starres.
Cynthia *is now by* Phœbus *pacified,*
And well content her Nymph is made a Bride,
Since the faire match was by that Phœbus *grac't*
Which in this happie Westerne Ile is plac't
As he in heauen, one lampe enlightning all
That vnder his benigne aspect doth fall.
Deepe Oracles he speakes, and he alone
For artes and wisedomes meete for Phœbus *throne.*
20 *The Nymph is honour'd, and* Diana *pleas'd :*
Night, *be you then, and your blacke howers appeas'd :*
And friendly listen what your Queene by me
Farther commaunds : let this my credence be,
View it, and know it for the highest gemme
That hung on her imperiall Diadem.

Night.   *I know, and honour it, louely* Hesperus,
Speake then your message, both are welcome to vs.

Hesp.   *Your Soueraigne from the vertuous gem she sends*
Bids you take power to retransforme the frends
30 *Of* Phœbus, *metamorphos'd here to trees,*
And giue them straight the shapes which they did leese.
This is her pleasure.

Night.   Hesperus, *I obey,*
Night *must needs yeeld when* Phœbus *gets the day.*

Flo.   *Honor'd be* Cynthia *for this generous deede.*
Zep.   *Pitie grows onely from celestiall seede.*

Night.   *If all seeme glad, why should we onely lowre ?*
Since t'expresse gladnes we haue now most power.

Frolike, grac't Captiues, we present you here
This glasse, wherein your liberties appeare:
Cynthia *is pacified, and now blithe* Night
Begins to shake off melancholy quite.

    Zeph.   *Who shold grace mirth and reuels but the night?*
Next loue she should be goddesse of delight.

    Night.   *Tis now a time when* (Zephyrus) *all with dancing*
Honor me, aboue day my state aduancing.
Ile now be frolicke, all is full of hart,
And eu'n these trees for ioy shall beare a part: 10
Zephyrus, *they shall dance.*

    Zeph.   *Daunce, Goddesse? how?*

    Night.   *Seemes that so full of strangenes to you now?*
Did not the Thracian harpe long since the same?
And (if we ripp the ould records of fame)
Did not Amphions *lyre the deafe stones call,*
When they came dancing to the Theban wall?
Can musicke then ioye? ioy mountaines moues
And why not trees? ioyes powerful when it loues.
Could the religious Oake speake Oracle   20
Like to the Gods? and the tree wounded tell
T'Æneas his sad storie? haue trees therefore
The instruments of speech and hearing more
Then th' haue of pacing, and to whom but Night
Belong enchantments? who can more affright
The eie with magick wonders? Night alone
Is fit for miracles, and this shalbe one
Apt for this Nuptiall daunsing iollitie.
Earth, then be soft and passable to free
These fettered roots: ioy, trees! the time drawes neere   30
When in your better formes you shall appeare.
Daunsing and musicke must prepare the way,
Ther's little tedious time in such delay.

    This spoken, the foure *Siluans* played on their instruments the first
straine of this song following: and at the repetition thereof the voices
fell in with the instrumentes which were thus deuided; a treble and
a base were placed neere his Maiestie, and an other treble and base
`neere the groue, that the words of the song might be heard of all,
because the trees of gould instantly at the first sound of their voices
began to moue and dance according to the measure of the time which 40

the musitians kept in singing, and the nature of the wordes which they
deliuered.

Song.

Moue now with measured sound,
You charmed groue of gould,
Trace forth the sacred ground
That shall your formes vnfold.

Diana *and the starry* Night *for your* Apollos *sake*
Endue your Siluan *shapes with powre this strange delight to make.*
Much ioy must needs the place betide where trees for gladnes moue :
10 *A fairer sight was nere beheld, or more expressing loue.*

Yet neerer Phœbus *throne*
Mete on your winding waies,
Your Brydall mirth make knowne
In your high-graced Hayes.

Let Hymen *lead your sliding rounds, and guide them with his light,*
While we do Io Hymen *sing in honour of this night,*
Ioyne three by three, for so the night by triple spel decrees,
Now to release Apollos *knights from these enchanted trees.*

20 This dancing-song being ended, the goulden trees stood in rankes
three by three, and Night ascended vp to the groue, and spake thus,
touching the first three seuerally with her wand.

Night. *By vertue of this wand, and touch deuine,*
These Siluan *shadowes back to earth resigne:*
Your natiue formes resume, with habite faire,
While solemne musick shall enchant the aire.

Presently the *Siluans* with their four instruments, and fiue voices,
began to play, and sing together the song following, at the beginning
whereof that part of the stage whereon the first three trees stoode
began to yeeld, and the three formost trees gently to sincke, and this
was effected by an Ingin plac't vnder the stage. When the trees had
sunke a yarde they cleft in three parts, and the Maskers appeared out
of the tops of them, the trees were sodainly conuayed away, and the
first three Maskers were raysed againe by the Ingin. They appeared
then in a false habit, yet very faire, and in forme not much vnlike their
principall, and true robe. It was made of greene taffatie cut into leaues,
and laid vpon cloth of siluer, and their hats were sutable to the same.

Night and Diana *charge,*
       And th'Earth obayes,
Opening large
       Her secret waies,

Songe of
transformation.

While Apollos *charmed men*
       Their formes receiue againe.
Giue gratious Phœbus *honour then,*
And so fall downe, and rest behinde the traine,
Giue gratious Phœbus *honour then*
And so fall, etc.

and the 9 *trees beeing left vnsett together euen to the same night.*

When those wordes were sung, the three maskers made an honour to the King, and so falling backe the other sixe trees, three by three, came forward, and when they were in their appointed places, Night spake againe thus: 10

     Night.   *Thus can celestials work in humane fate,*
Transforme and forme as they do loue or hate;
Like touch and change receiue: The Gods agree
The best of numbers is contained in three.

         The song of transformation againe.

           Night and Diana, &c.

Then Night toucht the second three trees and the stage suncke with them as before: and in breefe the second three did in all points as the first. Then Night spake againe.

     Night.   *The last, and third of nine, touch, magick wand,*   20
And giue them back their formes at nights command.

Night toucht the third 3. trees, and the same charme of Night and Diana was sung the third time; the last three trees were transformed, and the Maskers raisd. When presently the first Musique began his full *Chorus.*

       Againe this song reuiue and sound it hie:
       Long liue Apollo, *Brittaines glorious eye.*

This *Chorus* was in manner of an Eccho seconded by the Cornets, then by the consort of ten, then by the consort of twelue, and by a double *Chorus* of voices standing on either side, the one against the 30 other, bearing fiue voices a peece, and sometime euery *Chorus* was heard seuerally, somtime mixt, but in the end all together: which kinde of harmony so distinguisht by the place, and by the seuerall nature of instruments, and changeable conueyance of the song, and performed by so many excellent masters as were actors in that musicke, (their number in all amounting to fortie two voyces and instruments) could not but yeeld great satisfaction to the hearers.

While this *Chorus* was repeated twice ouer, the Nine maskers in their greene habitts solemnely descended to the dauncing place, in such order as they were to begin their daunce, and as soone as the 40 *Chorus* ended, the violins, or consorte of twelue began to play the

second new daunce, which was taken in form of an Eccho by the
cornetts, and then catch't in like manner by the consort of ten, some-
time they mingled two musickes together ; sometime plaid all at once ;
which kind of ecchoing musicke rarely became their *Siluan* attire, and
was so truely mixed together, that no daunce could euer bee better
grac't then that, as (in such distraction of musicke) it was performed
by the maskers. After this daunce *Night* descended from the groue,
and addreste her speech to the maskers, as followeth.

> Night. Phœbus *is pleas'd, and all reioice to see*
> 10 *His seruants from their golden prison free.*
> *But yet since* Cinthia *hath so freendly smilde,*
> *And to you tree-borne Knights is reconcild,*
> *First ere you any more worke vndertake,*
> *About her tree solemne procession make,*
> Dianas *tree, the tree of Chastitie,*
> *That plac't alone on yonder hill you see.*
> *These greene leaued robes, wherein disguisde you made*
> *Stelths to her Nimphes through the thicke forrests shade,*
> *There to the goddesse offer thankfully,*
> 20 *That she may not in vaine appeased be.*
> *The Night shall guide you, and her howres attend you*
> *That no ill eyes, or spirits shall offend you.*

At the end of this speech Night began to leade the way alone, and
after her an Houre with his torch, and after the Houre a masker ; and
so in order one by one, a torch-bearer and a masker, they march on
towards *Dianas* tree. When the Maskers came by the house of
Night, euery one by his Houre receiued his helmet, and had his false
robe pluckt off, and, bearing it in his hand, with a low honour offred
it at the tree of Chastitie, and so in his glorious habit, with his Houre
30 before him march't to the bowre of *Flora*. The shape of their habit
the picture before discouers, the stuffe was of Carnation saten layed
thicke with broad siluer lace, their helmets beeing made of the same
stuffe. So through the bowre of *Flora* they came, where they ioyned
two torch-bearers, and two Maskers, and when they past downe to the
groue, the Houres parted on either side, and made way betweene
them for the Maskers, who descended to the dauncing place in such
order as they were to begin their third new dance. All this time
of procession the sixe Cornets, and sixe Chappell voices sung a
sollemne motet of sixe parts made vpon these wordes.

> 40 *With spotles mindes now mount we to the tree*
> *Of single chastitie.*
> *The roote is temperance grounded deepe,*
> *Which the coldiewc't earth doth steepe :*

> Water it desires alone,
> Other drinke it thirsts for none:
> Therewith the sober branches it doth feede,
> Which though they fruitlesse be,
> Yet comely leaues they breede,
> To beautifie the tree.

> Cynthia *protectresse is, and for her sake*
> *We this graue procession make.*
> *Chast eies and eares, pure heartes and voices,*
> *Are graces wherein* Phœbe *most reioyces.*   10

The motet beeing ended, the Violins began the third new dance, which was liuely performed by the Maskers, after which they tooke forth the Ladies, and danc't the measures with them; which being finisht, the Maskers brought the Ladies back againe to their places: and *Hesperus* with the rest descended from the groue into the dauncing place, and spake to the Maskers as followeth.

Hesperus. *Knights of* Apollo, *proude of your new birth,*
Pursue your triumphs still with ioy and mirth:
Your changed fortunes, and redeemed estate,
Hesperus *to your Soueraigne will relate.*   20
Tis now high time he were far hence retir'd,
Th'ould Bridall friend, that vshers Night desir'd
Through the dimme euening shades, then taking flight
Giues place and honour to the nuptiall Night.
I, that wish't euening starre, must now make way
To Hymens *rights much wrong'd by my delay.*
But on Nights princely state you ought t' attend,
And t' honour your new reconciled frind.

Night. Hesperus *as you with concord came, eu'n so*
Tis meet that you with concord hence shold go.   30
Then ioyne you, that in voice and art excell,
To giue this starre a musicall farewell.

A Diologue of foure voices, two Bases and two trebles.

1   *Of all the starres which is the kindest*
        To a louing Bride?
2   Hesperus *when in the west*
        He doth the day from night deuide.
1   *What message can be more respected*
        Then that which tells wish't ioyes shalbe effected?

2 *Do not Brides watch the euening starre?*
1 *O they can discerne it farre.*
2 *Loue Bridegroomes reuels?*
          1 *But for fashion.*
2 *And why?*   1 *They hinder wisht occasion.*
2 *Longing hearts and new delights,*
   Loue short dayes and long nights.

Chorus. Hesperus, *since you all starres excell*
          In Bridall kindnes, kindly farewell, farewell.

10   While these words of the *Chorus* (*kindly farewell, farewell*) were in
singing often repeated, *Hesperus* tooke his leaue seuerally of *Night*,
Flora, and *Zephyrus*, the *Howers* and *Siluans*, and so while the
Chorus was sung ouer the second time, hee was got vp to the groue,
where turning againe to the singers, and they to him, *Hesperus* took a
second farwel of them, and so past away by the house of *Night*.
Then *Night* spake theis two lines, and therewith all retired to the
groue where they stoode before.

    Night. *Come,* Flora, *let vs now withdraw our traine*
    That th'ecclipst reuels maie shine forth againe.

20   Now the Maskers began their lighter daunces as Currantoes,
Leualtas and galliards, wherein when they had spent as much time as
they thought fit, *night* spake thus from the groue, and in her speech
descended a little into the dauncing place.

    N. *Here stay: Night leaden-eied and sprighted growes,*
    And her late houres begin to hang their browes.
    Hymen *long since the Bridal bed hath drest,*
    And longs to bring the turtles to their nest.
    Then with one quick dence sound vp your delight,
    And with one song weele bid you all god-Night.

30   At the end of these words, the violins began the 4. new dance,
which was excellently discharged by the Maskers, and it ended with
a light change of musick and mesure. After the dance followed this
dialogue of 2 voices, a base and tenor sung by a *Siluan* and an
Howre.

    Ten. Siluan. *Tell me gentle howre of night,*
          Wherein dost thou most delight?
    Bas. Howre. *Not in sleepe.* Sil. *Wherein then?*
    Howre. *In the frolicke vew of men.*
    Sil. *Louest thou musicke?* Howre. *O 'tis sweet.*
40   Sil. *Whats dauncing?* Howre. *Eu'n the mirth of feete.*
    Sil. *Ioy you in Fayries and in elues?*

How. *We are of that sort our selues.*
    But, Siluan, *say why do you loue*
    Onely to frequent the groue?
  Sil. *Life is fullest of content,*
    Where delight is innocent.
How. *Pleasure must varie, not be long.*
    Come then lets close, and end our song.
Chorus. *Yet, ere we vanish from this princely sight,*
    Let vs bid Phœbus *and his states god-night.*

This *Chorus* was performed with seuerall Ecchoes of musicke, and [10]
voices, in manner as the great *Chorus* before. At the end whereof the
Maskers, putting off their visards and helmets, made a low honour
to the King, and attended his Ma: to the banquetting place.

To the Reader.

Neither buskin now, nor bayes
Challenge I: a Ladies prayse
Shall content my proudest hope.
Their applause was all my scope ;
And to their shrines properly
Reuels dedicated be :   [20]
Whose soft eares none ought to pierce
But with smooth and gentle verse.
Let the tragicke Poeme swell,
Raysing raging feendes from hell ;
And let Epicke Dactils range
Swelling seas and Countries strange :
Little roome small things containes ;
Easy prayse quites easy paines.
Suffer them whose browes do sweat
To gaine honour by the great :   [30]
Its enough if men me name
A Retailer of such fame.

Epigramma.

Quid tu te numeris immisces? anne medentem
  Metra cathedratum ludicra scripta decent?
Musicus et medicus, celebris quoque, Phœbe, Poeta es,
  Et lepor ægrotos, arte rogante, iuuat.
Crede mihi doctum qui carmen non sapit, idem
  Non habet ingenuum, nec genium medici.

FINIS.

K

III.

Shewes and nightly reuels, signes of ioy and peace,
Fill royall Britaines court while cruell warre farre off doth rage,
    for euer hence exiled.
Faire and princely branches with strong arms encrease
From that deepe rooted tree whose sacred strength and glory forren
    malice hath beguiled.
Our deuided kingdomes now in frendly kindred meet
And old debate to loue and kindnes turns, our power with double
    force vniting ;
Truly reconciled, griefe appeares at last more sweet
Both to our selues and faithful friends, our vndermining foes
    affrighting.

IIII.

Triumph now with Ioy and mirth ;
    The God of Peace hath blest our land :
Wee enioy the fruites of earth
    Through fauour of his bounteous hand.
We throgh his most louing grace
    A King and kingly seed beholde,
Like a son with lesser stars
    Or carefull shepheard to his fold :
Triumph then, and yeelde him praise
That giues vs blest and ioyfull dayes.

V.

Time, that leads the fatall round,
Hath made his center in our ground,
    With swelling seas embraced ;
And there at one stay he rests,
And with the fates keepes holy feasts,
    With pomp and pastime graced.
Light Cupids there do daunce and Venus sweetly singes
With heauenly notes tun'd to sound of siluer strings :
Their songs are al of ioy, no signe of sorrow there,
But all as starres glistring faire and blith appeare.

These Songes were vsed in the Maske, whereof the first two
Ayres were made by M. Campion, the third and last by M. Lupo,
the fourth by M. Tho. Giles, and though the last three Ayres
were deuised onely for dauncing, yet they are here set forth with
words that they may be sung to the Lute or Violl.

[Songs I and II are respectively ' Now hath *Flora*' on p. 65, and
' Moue now with measured sound ' on p. 70. It has not been
thought worth while reprinting those songs in this place. All five are
given with their music.]

A
RELATION
OF THE LATE ROY
ALL ENTERTAINMENT
GIVEN BY THE RIGHT HONO.

RABLE THE LORD KNOVVLES, AT
Cawsome-House neere Reddmg: to our most
Gracious Queene, Queene ANNE, in her
Progresse toward the Bathe, vpon
the seuen and eight and twentie
dayes of Aprill.
1613.

Whereunto is annexed the Description,
Speeches and Songs of the Lords Maske, presented in the
Banquetting-house on the Mariage night of the High
and Mightie, COVNT PALATINE, and the
Royally descended the Ladie
ELIZABETH.

Written by THOMAS CAMPION.

LONDON,
Printed for Iohn Budge, and are to be sold at his Shop
at the South-doore of S. Pauls, and at Bri-
taines Bursse. 1613.

A RELATION OF
THE LATE ROYALL
ENTERTAINMENT GIVEN BY

the Right Honorable, the Lord KNOWLES,

at *Cawsome*-House neere *Redding* : to our

most gracious Queen, Queene ANNE,

in her Progresse toward the *Bathe*

vpon the seuen and eight and

twentie dayes of Aprill.

10   1613.

For as much as this late Entertainment hath beene much desired in
writing, both of such as were present at the performance thereof, as
also of many which are yet strangers both to the busines and place ; it
shall be conuenient, in this generall publication, a little to touch at the
description and situation of Cawsome *seate.   The house is fairely built*
of bricke, mounted on the hillside of a Parke, within view of Redding,
they being seuered about the space of two miles.   Before the Parke-gate,
directly opposite to the House, a new passage was forced through
earable-land, that was lately paled in, it being from the Parke about
20 *two flight-shots in length; at the further en.l whereof, vpon the*
Queenes approach, a Cynick *appeared out of a Bower, drest in a skin-*
coate, with Bases, of greene Calico, set thicke with leaues and boughes :
his nakednesse being also artificially shadowed with leaues; on his
head he wore a false haire, blacke and disordered, stucke carelessely
with flowers.

The speech of the Cynick *to the Queene and her Traine.*

Cynick. Stay ; whether you humane be or diuine, here is no
passage ; see you not the earth furrowed ? the region solitarie ?
Cities and Courts fit tumultuous multitudes : this is a place of
30 silence ; heere a kingdome I enioy without people ; my selfe
commands, my self obeyes ; Host, Cooke, and Guest my selfe ;
I reape without sowing, owe all to Nature, to none other
beholding : my skinne is my coate, my ornaments these boughes

and flowers, this Bower my house, the earth my bed, herbes my food, water my drinke; I want no sleepe, nor health ; I enuie none, nor am enuied, neither feare I nor hope, nor ioy, nor grieue : if this be happinesse, I haue it; which you all that depend on others seruice, or command, want : will you be happy? be priuate, turn Pallaces to Hermitages, noies to silence, outward felicitie to inward content.

A stranger on horse-back was purposely thrust into the troupe disguised, and wrapt in a cloake that he might passe vnknowne, who at the conclusion of this speech beganne to discouer himselfe as a fan- 10 *tastick Traueller in a silken sute of strange Checker-worke, made vp after the Italian cut, with an Italian hat, a band of gold and silke, answering the colours of his sute, with a Courtly feather, long guilt spurres, and all things answerable.*

The Trauellers speech on horseback.

Trauell. Whither trauels thy tongue, ill nurtur'd man? thy manners shew madnesse, thy nakednesse pouertie, thy resolution folly. Since none will vndertake thy presumption, let mee descend, that I may make thy ignorance know how much it hath injured sacred eares.   20

The Traueller then dismounts and giues his cloake and horse to his Foot-man : in the meane time the Cynick *speakes.*

Cyn. Naked I am, and so is truth ; plaine, and so is honestie ; I feare no mans encounter, since my cause deserues neither excuse nor blame.

Trau. Shall I now chide or pitie thee? thou art as miserable in life, as foolish in thy opinion. Answere me ; doest thou thinke that all happinesse consists in solitarinesse?

Cyn. I doe.

Trau. And are they vnhappy that abide in societie?   30

Cyn. They are.

Trau. Doest thou esteeme it a good thing to liue?

Cyn. The best of things.

Trau. Hadst thou not a Father and Mother?

Cyn. Yes.

Trau. Did they not liue in societie?

Cyn. They did.

Trau. And wert not thou one of their societie when they bred thee, instructing thee to goe and speake?

Cyn. True.   40

Trau. Thy birth then and speech in spite of thy splene

make thee sociable, goe, thou art but a vaine-glorious counterfait, and wanting that which should make thee happie, contemnest the meanes; view but the heau'ns : is there not aboue vs a Sunne and Moone, giuing and receiuing light? are there not millions of Starres that participate their glorious beames? is there any Element simple? is there not a mixture of all things? and wouldst thou only be singular? action is the end of life, vertue the crowne of action, society the subject of vertue, friendship the band of societie, solitarinesse the breach. Thou art yet yong,
10 and faire enough, wert thou not barbarous; thy soule, poore wretch, is farre out of tune, make it musicall; come, follow me, and learn to liue.

Cyn. I am conquered by reason, and humbly aske pardon for my error, henceforth my heart shall honour greatnesse, and loue societie; leade now, and I will follow, as good a fellow as the best.

The Traueller *and* Cynick *instantly mount on horse-backe, and hasten to the Parke-gate, where they are receiue.l by two Keepers, formally attired in green* Perpetuana, *with ierkins and long hose, all*
20 *things else being in colour sutable, hauing either of them a horne hanging formally at their backes, and on their heads they had greene* Mommoth-*caps, with greene feathers, the one of them in his hand bearing a hooke-bill, and the other a long pike-staffe, both painted greene: with them stood two* Robin-Hood *men in sutes of greene striped with blacke, drest in doublets with great bellies and wide sleeues, shaped fardingale-wise at the shoulders, without wings; their hose were round, with long greene stockings; on their heads they wore broad flat caps with greene feathers crosse quite ouer them, carrying greene Bowes in their hands, and greene Arrowes by their sides.*

30 *In this space* Cornets *at sundrie places entertaine the time, till the Queene with her traine is entred into the Parke : and then one of the Keepers presents her with this short speech.*

Keeper. More then most welcome, renowned and gracious Queene, since your presence vouchsafes to beautifie these woods, whereof I am Keeper, be it your pleasure to accept such rude intertainment, as a rough Wood-man can yeeld. This is to vs a high holy-day, and henceforth yearly shall bee kept and celebrated with our Countrie sports, in honour of so Royall a guest; come, friends and fellowes, now prepare your voices, and present your
40 ioys in a Siluan dance.

Here standing on a smooth greene, and enuironed with the Horse-men, they present a Song of fiue Parts, and withall a liuely Siluan-dance of sixe persons : the Robin-Hood-*men fune two Trebles; one of*

the Keepers with the Cynick *sing two Counter-tenors, the other Keeper*
the Base; but the Traueller being not able to sing, gapes in silence,
and expresseth his humour in Antike gestures.

A Song and Dance of sixe, two Keepers, two *Robin-*
hood-men, the fantastick Traueller, and
the *Cynick.*

1

Dance now and sing; the ioy and loue we owe
Let chearfull voices and glad gestures showe:
   The Queene of grace is shee whom we receiue: 10
   Honour and State are her guides,
   Her presence they can neuer leaue.
Then in a stately Siluan forme salute
   Her euer flowing grace;
Fill all the Woods with Ecchoed welcomes,
   And strew with flowers this place;
Let eu'ry bow and plant fresh blossomes yeeld,
   And all the aire refine:
Let pleasure striue to please our Goddesse,
   For shee is all diuine.   20

2

Yet once againe, let vs our measures moue,
And with sweet notes record our ioyfull loue.
   An obiect more diuine none euer had:
   Beautie, and heau'n-borne worth,
   Mixt in perfection neuer fade.
Then with a dance triumphant let vs sing
   Her high aduanced praise,
And eu'n to heau'n our gladsome welcomes
   With wings of musick raise;   30
Welcome, O welcome, euer-honoured Queene,
   To this now-blessed place,
That groue, that bowre, that house is happy
   Which you vouchsafe to grace.

This song being sung and danced twice ouer, they fall instantly into
a kind of *Curranta*, with these wordes following:—

   No longer delay her,
    'Twere sinne now to stay her
     From her ease with tedious sport;
   Then welcome still crying   40
   And swiftly hence flying,
    Let vs to our homes resort.

In the end whereof the two Keepers carrie away the Cynick *; and the two* Robin-Hood-*men the Traueller; when presently Cornets begin againe to sound in seuerall places, and so continue with varietie, while the Queen passeth through a long smooth greene way, set on each side with Trees in equall distance; all this while her Maiestie being carried in her Caroch.*

But because some wet had fallen that day in the forenoone (though the Garden-walks were made artificially smooth and drie) yet all her foot-way was spred with broad cloth, and so soone as her Maiestie
10 *with her traine were all entred into the Lower Garden, a Gardiner, with his Man and Boy, issued out of an Arbour to give her Highnesse entertainment: The Gardener was suted in gray with a ierkin double iagged all about the wings and skirts, he had a paire of great slops with a cod-peece, and buttoned Gamachios all of the same stuffe: on his head he had a strawne hat, pibaldly drest with flowers, and in his hand a siluered spade: His man was also suted in gray with a great buttoned flap on his ierkin, hauing large wings and skirts, with a paire of great slops and Gamachios of the same, on his head he had a strawne hat, and in his hand a siluered Mattox: The Gardiners Boy*
20 *was in a prettie sute of flowrie stuffe, with a siluered Rake in his hand: when they approched neere the Queene, they all valed Bonet; and lowting low, the Gardner began after his anticke fashion this speech.*

Gard. Most Magnificent and peerelesse Diety, loe, I the surueyer of Lady *Floras* workes, welcome your grace with fragrant phrases into her Bowers, beseeching your greatnesse to beare with the late woodden entertainment of the Wood-men; for Woods are more full of weeds then wits, but gardens are weeded, and Gardners witty, as may appeare by me. I haue flowers for
3⁰ all fancies. Tyme for truth, Rosemary for remembrance, Roses for loue, Hartsease for ioy, and thousands more, which all harmoniously reioyce at your presence; but my selfe, with these my Paradisians heere, will make you such musick as the wilde Wooddists shall bee ashamed to heare the report of it. Come, sirs, prune your pipes, and tune your strings, and agree together like birds of a feather.

A Song of a treble and bass, sung by the Gardiners boy and man, to musicke of Instruments, that was readie to second them in the Arbour.

I

40   Welcome to this flowrie place,
         Faire Goddesse and sole Queene of grace:
            All eyes triumph in your sight,
         Which through all this emptie space
         Casts such glorious beames of light.

2

Paradise were meeter farre
To entertain so bright a Starre:
  But why erres my folly so?
Paradise is where you are:
Heau'n above, and heau'n below.

3

Could our powers and wishes meete,
How well would they your graces greete.
  Yet accept of our desire: 10
Roses, of all flowers most sweete,
Spring out of the silly brier.

After this song, the Gardiner speakes againe.

Gard. Wonder not (great Goddesse) at the sweetnesse of our Garden-aire (though passing sweet it be). *Flora* hath perfumed it for you (*Flora* our mistresse, and your seruant) who enuites you yet further into her Paradise; shee inuisibly will leade your grace the way, and we (as our duetie is) visibly stay behinde.

From thence the Queene ascends by a few steps into the vpper Garden, at the end whereof, neere the house, this Song was sung by an 20 *excellent counter-tenor voice, with rare varietie of diuision vnto two vnusuall instruments, all being concealed within the Arbour.*

1

O Ioyes exceeding,
From loue, from power of your wisht sight proceeding.
  As a faire morne shines diuinely,
  Such is your view, appearing more diuinely.

2

Your steppes ascending,
Raise high your thoughts for your content contending;   30
  All our hearts of this grace vaunting,
  Now leape as they were moued by inchaunting.

So ended the entertainment without the House for that time; and the Queenes pleasure being that night to suppe priuately, the Kings Violins attended her with their sollemnest musick, as an excellent consort in like manner did the next day at dinner.

¶Supper being ended, her Maiestie, ac-
companied with many Lords and Ladies, *came
into the Hall, and rested Her selfe in Her Chaire of State,
the Scaffoldes of the Hall being on all partes filled with beholders
of worth.* Suddainely forth came the *Traueller, Gardiner,
Cynicke, with the rest of their crue, and others furnished with
their Instruments, and in maner following entertaine the time.*

Traueller.

A hall; a hall; for men of moment, Rationals and Irrationals,
10 but yet not all of one breeding. For I an Academicke am,
refined by trauel, that haue learn'd what to Courtship belongs,
and so deuine a presence as this; if we presse past good manners,
laugh at our follies, for you cannot shew vs more fauour then to
laugh at vs. If we proue ridiculous in your sights, we are
gracious; and therefore wee beseech you to laugh at vs. For
mine owne part (I thank my Starres for it) I haue beene laught
at in most parts of Christendome.

Gardiner. I can neither bragge of my Trauels, nor yet am
ashamed of my profession; I make sweet walkes for faire Ladies;
20 Flowers I prepare to adorne them; close Arbours I build wherein
their Loues vnseene may court them; and who can doe Ladies
better seruice, or more acceptable? When I was a Child and
lay in my Cradle, (a very pretie Child) I remember well that
Lady *Venus* appeared vnto me, and setting a Siluer Spade and
Rake by my Pillow, bade me proue a Gardiner; I told my
Mother of it (as became the duetie of a good Child) whereupon
shee prouided straight for me two great Platters full of Pappe;
which hauing duetifully deuoured, I grew to this portrature you
see, sprung sodainely out of my Cabine, and fell to my pro-
30 fession.

Trau. Verily by thy discourse thou hast Trauelled much, and
I am asham'd of my selfe that I come so farre behind thee, as
not once to haue yet mentioned *Venus* or *Cupid*, or any other
of the gods to haue appeared to mee. But I will henceforth boast
truely, that I haue now seen a Dietie as farre beyond theirs, as
the beautie of light is beyond darknesse, or this Feast, whereof
we haue had our share, is beyond thy Sallets.

Cynick. Sure I am, it hath stir'd vp strange thoughts in me;
neuer knew I the difference betweene Wine and Water before.
40 *Bacchus* hath opened mine eyes; I now see brauerie and admire

it, beautie and adore it. I find my Armes naked, my discourse
rude, but my heart soft as Waxe, ready to melt with the least
beame of a faire eye; which (till this time) was as vntractable
as Iron.

Gard. I much ioy in thy conuersion, thou hast long beene
a mad fellow, and now prouest a good fellow; let vs all there-
fore ioyne together sociably in a Song, to the honour of good
fellowship.

Cyn. A very Musicall motion, and I agree to it.

Trau. Sing that sing can, for my part I will onely, while you 10
sing, keepe time with my gestures, *A la mode de France.*

A Song of three Voyces with diuers Instruments.

1

Night as well as brightest day hath her delight.
Let vs then with mirth and Musicke decke the night,
   Neuer did glad day such store
    Of ioy to night bequeath:
   Her Starres then adore,
    Both in Heau'n, and here beneath.

2   20

Loue and beautie, mirth and Musicke yeeld true ioyes,
Though the *Cynickes* in their folly count them toyes,
   Raise your spirits nere so high,
    They will be apt to fall:
   None braue thoughts enuie,
    Who had ere braue thought at all.

3

Ioy is the sweete friend of life, the nurse of blood,
Patron of all health, and fountaine of all good.
   Neuer may ioy hence depart,   30
    But all your thoughts attend;
   Nought can hurt the heart,
    That retaines so sweete a friend.

At the end of this Song enters Siluanus, *shapt after the description
of the ancient Writers; his lower parts like a Goate, and his vpper
parts in an anticke habit of rich Taffatie, cut into Leaues, and on his
head he had a false Haire, with a wreath of long Boughs and Lillies,
that hung dangling about his necke, and in his hand a Cypresse branch,
in memorie of his loue* Cyparissus. *The Gardiner, espying him,
speakes thus.*   40

Gard. Silence, sirs, here comes *Siluanus*, god of these Woods, whose presence is rare, and importes some noueltie.

Trau. Let vs giue place, for this place is fitter for Dieties then vs.

They all vanish and leaue Siluanus *alone, who comming nearer to the State, and making a low Congee, speakes.*

SILVANVS.

That health which harbours in the fresh-air'd groues,
Those pleasures which greene hill and valley moues,
10   *Siluanus,* the commander of them all,
Here offers to this State Emperiall;
Which as a homager he visites now,
And to a greater power his power doth bow.
With all, thus much his duetie signifies:
That there are certaine Semideities,
Belonging to his Siluan walkes, who come
Led with the Musicke of a Spritely drome,
To keepe the night awake and honour you,
(Great Queene) to whom all Honours they hold due.
20   So rest you full of ioy and wisht content,
Which though it be not giuen, 'tis fairely ment.

At the end of this speech there is suddainly heard a great noise of drums and phifes, and way being made, eight Pages first enter, with greene torches in their hands lighted; their sutes were of greene Satten, with cloakes and caps of the same, richly and strangely set forth. Presently after them the eight Maskers came, in rich imbrodered sutes of greene Satten, with high hats of the same, and all their acoutrements answerable to such Noble and Princely personages, as they concealed vnder their visards, and so they instantly fell into
30   *a new dance: at the end whereof they tooke forth the Ladies, and danced with them; and so well was the Queene pleased with her intertainment, that shee vouchsafed to make her selfe the head of their Reuels, and graciously to adorne the place with her personall dancing: much of the night being thus spent with varietie of dances, the Maskers made a conclusion with a second new dance.*

At the Queenes parting on wednesday in the afternoone, *the Gardiner with his Man and Boy and three handsome Countrie Maides, the one bearing a rich bagge with linnen in it, the second a rich apron, and the third a rich mantle, appeare all out of an Arbour in the*
40   *lower Garden, and meeting the Queene, the Gardiner presents this speech.*

GARDINER.

Stay, Goddess, stay a little space,
Our poore Countrie loue to grace ;
Since we dare not too long stay you,
Accept at our hands, we pray you,
These meane presents, to expresse
Greater loue then we professe,
Or can vtter now for woe
Of your parting hast'ned so.
Gifts these are, such as were wrought   10
By their hands that them haue brought,
Home-bred things, which they presumed,
After I had them perfumed
With my flowrie incantation,
To giue you in presentation
At your parting. Come, feate Lasses,
With fine cursies, and smooth faces,
Offer vp your simple toyes
To the Mistris of our ioyes;
While we the sad time prolong   20
With a mournefull parting song.

*A Song of three voices continuing while the presents
are deliuered and receiued.*

I

Can you, the Author of our ioy,
    So soone depart ?
Will you reuiue, and straight destroy,
New mirth to teares conuert ?
    O that euer cause of gladnesse
    Should so swiftly turne to sadnesse.   30

2

Now as we droupe, so will these flowers,
    Bard of your sight,
Nothing auaile them heau'nly showres
Without your heau'nly light.
    When the glorious Sunne forsakes vs,
    Winter quickly ouer-takes vs.

3

Yet shall our praiers your waies attend,
  When you are gone;
And we the tedious time will spend,
  Remembring you alone.
    Welcome here shall you heare euer
    But the word of parting neuer.

Thus ends this ample intertainment, which as it was most nobly performed by the right honourable the Lord and Ladie of the house, and fortunately executed by all that any way were Actors in it, so was it as graciously receiued of her Maiestie, and celebrated with her most royall applause.

THE DESCRIPTION,
SPEECHES, AND SONGS, OF
The Lords Maske, Presented In
the Banquetting-house on the mariage night
of the high and mightie Count Palatine,
and the royally descended the Ladie
Elisabeth.

(***)

*I haue now taken occasion to satisfie many, who long since were
desirous that the Lords maske should be published, which, but for
some priuate lets, had in due time come forth. The* Scene *was* 10
*diuided into two parts from the roofe to the floore, the lower part
being first discouered (vpon the sound of a double consort, exprest by
seuerall instruments, plac't on either side of the roome) there appeared
a Wood in prospectiue, the innermost part being of releaue or whole
round, the rest painted. On the left hand from the seate was a Caue,
and on the right a thicket, out of which came* Orpheus, *who was attired
after the old Greeke manner, his haire curled and long, a lawrell
wreath on his head, and in his hand hee bare a siluer bird; about him
tamely placed seuerall wild beasts: and vpon the ceasing of the
Consort* Orpheus *spake.* 20

Orphevs.

Agen, agen, fresh kindle *Phœbus* sounds,
T'exhale *Mania* from her earthie den;
Allay the furie that her sense confounds,
And call her gently forth; sound, sound agen.

The Consorts both sound againe, and Mania, *the Goddesse of
madnesse, appears wildly out of her caue. Her habit was confused
and strange, but yet gracefull; shee as one amazed speaks.*

Mania. What powerfull noise is this importunes me,
T'abandon darkenesse which my humour fits? 30
Ioues hand in it I feele, and euer he
Must be obai'd eu'n of the franticst wits.
Orpheus. Mania!
Mania. Hah.

Orpheus. Braine-sick, why start'st thou so?
Approch yet nearer, and thou then shall know
The will of *Ioue*, which he will breath from me.
Mania. Who art thou? if my dazeled eyes can see,
Thou art the sweet Enchanter heau'nly *Orpheus*.
Orpheus. The same, *Mania*, and *Ioue* greets thee thus:
Though seuerall power to thee and charge he gaue
T'enclose in thy Dominions such as raue
Through blouds distemper, how durst thou attempt
10 T'imprison *Entheus* whose rage is exempt
From vulgar censure? it is all diuine,
Full of celestiall rapture, that can shine
Through darkest shadowes: therefore *Ioue* by me
Commands thy power strait to set *Entheus* free.
Mania. How can I? Franticks with him many more
In one caue are lockt vp; ope once the dore,
All will flie out, and through the world disturbe
The peace of *Ioue*; for what power then can curbe
Their rainelesse furie?——
20 *Orpheus.* Let not feare in vaine
Trouble thy crazed fancie; all againe,
Save *Entheus*, to thy safeguard shall retire,
For *Ioue* into our musick will inspire
The power of passion, that their thoughts shall bend
To any forme or motion we intend.
Obey *Ioues* will then; go, set *Entheus* free.
Mania. I willing go, so *Ioue* obey'd must bee.
Orph. Let Musicke put on *Protean* changes now;
Wilde beasts it once tam'd, now let Franticks bow.

30 *At the sound of a strange musicke twelue Franticks enter, six men
and six women, all presented in sundry habits and humours: there
was the Louer, the Selfe-louer, the melancholicke-man full of feare,
the Schoole-man ouer-come with phantasie, the ouer-watched Vsurer,
with others that made an absolute medly of madnesse; in middest
of whom Entheus (or Poeticke furie) was hurried forth, and tost
vp and downe, till by vertue of a new change in the musicke, the
Lunatickes fell into a madde measure, fitted to a loud phantasticke
tune; but in the end thereof the musick changed into a very solemne
ayre, which they softly played, while Orphues spake.*

40 *Orph.* Through these soft and calme sounds, *Mania*, passe
With thy Phantasticks hence; heere is no place

Longer for them or thee ; *Entheus* alone
Must do *Ioues* bidding now, all else be gone.

During this speech Mania *with her Franticks depart, leauing*
Entheus *behind them, who was attired in a close Curace of the
Anticke fashion, Bases with labels, a Roabe fastned to his shoulders,
and hanging downe behind; on his head a wreath of Lawrell, out of
which grew a paire of wings ; in the one hand he held a booke, and in
the other a pen.*

    Enth. Diuinest *Orpheus,* ô how all from thee
Proceed with wondrous sweetnesse ! Am I free ?   10
Is my affliction vanisht ?
    Orph. Too too long,
Alas, good *Entheus,* hast thou brook't this wrong.
What ! number thee with madmen ! ô mad age,
Sencelesse of thee, and thy celestiall rage.
For thy excelling rapture, eu'n through things
That seems most light, is borne with sacred wings :
Nor are these Musicks, Showes, or Reuels vaine,
When thou adorn'st them with thy *Phœbean* braine.
Th'are pallate sick of much more vanitie,   20
That cannot taste them in their dignitie.
Ioue therefore lets thy prison'd spright obtaine
Her libertie and fiery scope againe ;
And heere by me commands thee to create
Inuentions rare, this night to celebrate,
Such as become a nuptiall by his will
Begun and ended.—
    Enth. Ioue I honor still,
And must obey. *Orpheus,* I feele the fires
Are reddy in my braine, which *Ioue* enspires.   30
Loe, through that vaile I see *Prometheus* stand
Before those glorious lights which his false hand
Stole out of heau'n, the dull earth to enflame
With the affects of Loue and honor'd Fame.
I view them plaine in pompe and maiestie
Such as being seene might hold riualitie
With the best triumphes. *Orpheus,* giue a call
With thy charm'd musicke, and discouer all.
    Orph. Flie, cheerfull voices, through the ayre, and clear
These clouds, that yon hid beautie may appeare.   40

A Song.

1

Come away; bring thy golden theft,
 Bring, bright *Prometheus*, all thy lights;
Thy fires from Heau'n bereft
 Shew now to humane sights.
Come quickly, come: thy stars to our stars straight present,
For pleasure being too much defer'd loseth her best content.
What fair dames wish, should swift as their own thoughts
 appeare,
10 To louing and to longing harts euery houre seemes a yeare.

2

See how faire, O how faire, they shine;
 What yeelds more pompe beneath the skies?
Their birth is yet diuine,
 And such their forme implies.
Large grow their beames, their nere approch afford them so;
By nature sights that pleasing are, cannot too amply show.
O might these flames in humane shapes descend this place,
How louely would their presence be, how full of grace!

20 *In the end of the first part of this Song, the vpper part of the Scene*
was discouered by the sodaine fall of a curtaine; then in clowdes
of seuerall colours (the vpper part of them being fierie, and the middle
heightned with siluer) appeared eight Starres of extraordinarie
bignesse, which so were placed, as that they seemed to be fixed betweene
the Firmament and the Earth; in the front of the Scene stood
Prometheus, *attyred as one of the ancient Heroes.*

 Enth. Patron of mankinde, powerfull, and bounteous,
Rich in thy flames, reuerend *Prometheus*,
In *Hymens* place aide vs to solempnize
30 These royall Nuptials; fill the lookers eyes
With admiration of thy fire and light,
And from thy hand let wonders flow tonight.
 Prom. Entheus and *Orpheus*, names both deare to me,
In equall ballance I your Third will be
In this nights honour. View these heau'n borne Starres,
Who by my stealth are become Sublunars;
How well their natiue beauties fit this place,
Which with a chorall dance they first shall grace;
Then shall their formes to humane figures turne,
40 And these bright fires within their bosomes burne.

Orpheus, apply thy musick, for it well
Helps to induce a Courtly miracle.
  Orp. Sound, best of Musicks, raise yet higher our sprights,
While we admire *Prometheus* dancing lights.

A Song.

1

Aduance your Chorall motions now,
  You musick-louing lights :
This night concludes the nuptiall vow,
  Make this the best of nights :   10
So brauely Crowne it with your beames
  That it may liue in fame
As long as *Rhenus* or the *Thames*
  Are knowne by either name.

2

Once moue againe, yet nearer moue
  Your formes at willing view ;
Such faire effects of ioy and loue
  None can expresse but you.
Then reuel midst your ayrie Bowres   20
  Till all the clouds doe sweat,
That pleasure may be powr'd in showres
  On this triumphant Seat.

3

Long since hath louely *Flora* throwne
  Her Flowers and Garlands here ;
Rich *Ceres* all her wealth hath showne,
  Prowde of her daintie cheare.
Chang'd then to humane shape, descend,
  Clad in familiar weede,   30
That euery eye may here commend
  The kinde delights you breede.

*According to the humour of this Song, the Starres mooued in an
exceeding strange and delightfull maner, and I suppose fewe haue
euer seene more* neate artifice, then *Master* Innigoe Iones *shewed
in contriuing their Motion, who in all the rest of the workmanship
which belong'd to the whole inuention shewed extraordinarie industrie
and skill, which if it be not as liuely exprest in writing as it appeared
in view, robbe not him of his due, but lay the blame on my want
of right apprehending his instructions for the adoring of his Arte.* 40

But to returne to our purpose; about the end of this Song, the Starres suddainely vanished, as if they had been drowned amongst the Cloudes, and the eight Maskers appeared in their habits, which were infinitly rich, befitting States (such as indeede they all were) as also a time so farre heightned the day before, with all the richest shew of solemnitie that could be inuented. The ground of their attires was massie Cloth of Siluer, embossed with flames of Embroidery; on their heads, they had Crownes, Flames made all of Gold-plate Enameled, and on the top a Feather of Silke, representing a cloude of
10 *smoake. Vpon their new transformation, the whole Scœne being Cloudes dispersed, and there appeared an Element of artificiall fires, with seuerall circles of lights, in continuall motion, representing the house of* Prometheus, *who then thus applies his speech to the Maskers.*

They are transformed.

Prometh. So pause awhile, and come, yee fiery spirits,
Breake forth the earth like sparks t'attend these knights.

Sixteene Pages, like fierie spirits, all their attires being alike composed of flames, with fierie Wings and Bases, bearing in either
20 *hand a Torch of Virgine Waxe, come forth below dauncing a liuely measure, and the Daunce being ended,* Prometheus *speakes to them from aboue.*

The Torch-bearers Daunce.

Pro. Wait, spirits, wait, while through the clouds we pace,
And by descending gaine a hier place.

The Pages returne toward the Scœne, to giue their attendance to the Maskers with their lights: from the side of the Scœne appeared a bright and transparant cloud, which reached from the top of the heauens to the earth: on this cloud the Maskers led by Prometheus *descended*
30 *with the musicke of a full song; and at the end of their descent, the cloud brake in twaine, and one part of it (as with a winde) was blown ouerthwart the Scœne.*

While this cloud was vanishing, the wood being the vnder-part of the Scœne, was insensibly changed, and in place thereof appeared foure Noble women-statues of siluer, standing in seuerall nices, accompanied with ornaments of Architecture, which filled all the end of the house, and seemed to be all of gold-smithes work. The first order consisted of Pillasters all of gold, set with Rubies, Saphyrs, Emeralds, Opals, and such like. The Capitels were composed, and of
40 *a new ·inuention. Over this was a bastard order with Cartouses reuersed, comming from the Capitels of euery Pillaster, which made the vpper part rich and full of ornament. Ouer euery statue was placed a history in gold, which seemed to be of base releaue; the*

conceits which were figured in them were these. In the first was Prometheus, *embossing in clay the figure of a woman, in the second he was represented stealing fire from the chariot-wheele of the Sunne; in the third he is exprest putting life with this fire into his figure of clay; and in the fourth square* Iupiter, *enraged, turns these new made women into statues. Aboue all, for finishing, ran a Cornish, which returned ouer euery Pillaster, seeming all of gold and richly carued.*

A full Song.

Supported now by Clouds descend,
Diuine *Prometheus, Hymens* friend: 10
Leade downe the new transformed fires
And fill their breasts with loues desires;
That they may reuell with delight,
And celebrate this nuptiall night.
So celebrate this nuptiall night
  That all which see may say
They neuer viewed so faire a sight
  Euen on the cleerest day.

While this song is sung, and the Maskers court the fowre new transformed Ladies, foure other Statues appeare in their places. 20

Entheus. See, see, *Prometheus,* four of these first dames
Which thou long since out of thy purchac't flames,
Did'st forge with heau'nly fire, as they were then
By *Ioue* transformed to Statues, so agen
They suddenly appeare by his command
At thy arriuall; Loe, how fixt they stand;
So did *Ioues* wrath too long, but now at last,
It by degrees relents, and he hath plac't
These Statues, that we might his ayde implore,
First for the life of these, and then for more.   30
Prom. Entheus, thy councels are diuine and iust,
Let *Orpheus* decke thy Hymne, since pray we must.

The first Inuocation in a full Song.

Powerfull *Ioue,* that of bright starres,
Now hast made men fit for warres,
Thy power in these Statues proue
And make them women fit for loue.
Orpheus. See, *Ioue* is pleas'd; Statues haue life and moue:
Go, new-borne men, and entertaine with loue

These new-borne women, though your number yet
Exceedes theirs double, they are arm'd with wit
To beare your best encounters; Court them faire:
When words and Musicke speake, let none despaire.

The Song.

1

Wooe her, and win her, he that can:
    Each woman hath two louers,
So shee must take and leaue a man,
10   Till time more grace discouers.
This doth *Ioue* to shew that want
    Makes beautie most respected;
If faire women were more skant,
    They would be more affected.

2

Courtship and Musicke suite with loue,
    They both are workes of passion;
Happie is he whose words can moue,
    Yet sweete notes helpe perswasion.
20 Mixe your words with Musicke then,
    That they the more may enter;
Bold assaults are fit for men,
    That on strange beauties venture.

Promet. Cease, cease your woing strife; see, *Ioue* intends
To fill your number vp, and make all friends.
Orpheus and *Entheus*, ioyne your skils once more,
And with a Hymne the Dietie implore.

The second Inuocation to the tune of the first.

Powerfull *Ioue*, that hast giuen fower,
30   Raise this number but once more,
That complete, their numerous feet
May aptly in iust measures meet.

The other foure statues are transformed into women, in the time of this inuocation.

Enth. The number's now complete, thanks be to *Ioue*:
No man needs fear a Riuall in his loue;
For all are sped, and now begins delight
To fill with glorie this triumphant night.

The Maskers, hauing euery one entertained his Lady, begin their first new entring dance: after it, while they breath, the time is entertained with a dialogue song.

Breath you now, while Io Hymen
  To the Bride we sing:
O how many ioyes and honors,
  From this match will spring!
Euer firme the league will proue,
Where only goodnesse causeth loue.
Some for profit seeke   10
What their fancies most disleeke:
These loue for vertues sake alone:
Beautie and youth vnite them both in one.

Chorvs.

Liue with thy Bridegroome happy, sacred Bride;
How blest is he that is for loue enui'd.

The Maskers second dance.

Breathe againe, while we with musicke
  Fill the emptie space:
O but do not in your dances   20
  Your selues only grace.
Eu'ry one fetch out your *Pheare*,
Whom chiefely you will honor heere.
Sights most pleasure breed,
When their numbers most exceed:
Chuse then, for choice to all is free;
Taken or left, none discontent must bee.

Chorvs.

Now in thy Reuels frolicke-faire delight,
To heap Ioy on this euer honored night.   30

The Maskers during this Dialogue take out others to daunce with them, men women, and women men, and first of all the Princely Bridegroome and Bride were drawne into these solemne Reuels, which continued a long space, but in the end were broken off with this short Song.

A Song.

Cease, cease you Reuels, rest a space;
New pleasures presse into this place,
Full of beautie and of grace.

The whole scœne was now againe changed, and became a prospectiue
with Porticoes on each side, which seemed to go in a great way; in
the middle was erected an Obeliske, all of siluer, and in it lights
of seuerall colours; on the side of this Obeliske, standing on Pedestals,
were the statues of Bridegroome and Bride, all of gold in gratious
postures. This Obeliske was of that height, that the toppe thereof
touched the highest cloudes, and yet Sybilla did draw it forth with
a threed of gold. The graue Sage was in a Roabe of gold tuckt vp
before to her girdle, a Kirtle gathered full, and of siluer; with a vaile
10 on her head, being bare neckt, and bearing in her hand a scrole of
Parchment.

Entheus. Make cleare the passage to *Sibillas* sight,
Who with her Trophee comes, to crowne this night;
And, as her selfe with Musicke shall be led,
So shall shee pull on with a golden thread
A high vast *Obeliske*, dedicate to fame,
Which immortalitie it selfe did frame.
Raise high your voices now; like Trumpets fill
The roome with sounds of Triumph, sweete and shrill.

20   A Song.

Come triumphing, come with state,
    Old *Sibilla*, reuerend Dame;
Thou keep'st the secret key of fate,
    Preuenting swiftest fame.
This night breathe onely words of ioy,
And speake them plaine, now be not coy.

                               S i b.

Debetur alto iure Principium Ioui,
Votis det ipse vim meis, dictis fidem.
30   *Vtrinque decoris splendet egregium Iubar;*
Medio triumphus mole stat dignus sua,
Cælumque summo Capite dilectum petit.
Quam pulchra pulchro sponsa respondet viro!
Quam plena numinis! Patrem vultu exprimit,
Parens futura masculæ prolis, Parens
Regum, imperatorum: Additur Germaniæ
Robur Britannicum: ecquid esse par potest?
Vtramque iunget vna mens gentem, fides.
Deique Cultus vnus, et simplex amor.
40   *Idem erit vtrique hostis, sodalis idem, idem*
Votum periclitantium, atque eadem manus.

Fauebit illis Pax, fauebit bellica
Fortuna, semper aderit Adiutor Deus.
Sic, sic Sibilla ; vocibus nec his deest
Pondus, nec hoc inane monumentum trahit.
Et aureum est, et quale nec flammas timet,
Nec fulgura, ipsi quippe sacratur Ioui.

Pro. The good old *Sage* is silenc't, her free tongue
That made such melodie, is now vnstrung :
Then grace her Trophee with a dance triumphant ;
Where *Orpheus* is none can fit musick want.   10

A Song and dance triumphant of the Maskers.

1

Dance, dance, and visit now the shadowes of our ioy,
All in height, and pleasing state, your changed formes imploy.
And as the bird of *Ioue* salutes, with loftie wing, the morn,
So mount, so flie, these Trophees to adorne.
Grace them with all the sounds and motions of delight,
Since all the earth cannot expresse a louelier sight.
View them with triumph, and in shades the truth adore :
No pompe or sacrifice can please *Ioues* greatnesse more.   20

2

Turne, turne, and honor now the life these figures beare :
Loe, how heau'nly natures farre aboue all art appeare :
Let their aspects reuiue in you the fire that shin'd so late,
Still mount and still retaine your heauenly state.
Gods were with dance and with musick seru'd of old,
Those happy daies deriu'd their glorious stile from gold :
This pair, by *Hymen* ioyn'd, grace you with measures then,
Since they are both diuine and you are more then men.

Orph. Let here *Sybillas* Trophee stand,   30
Leade her now by either hand,
That shee may approch yet nearer,
And the Bride and Bridegroome heare her
Blesse them in her natiue tongue,
Wherein old prophesies shee sung,
Which time to light hath brought :
Shee speakes that which *Ioue* hath taught :
Well may he inspire her now,
To make a ioyfull and true vow.

Syb. *Sponsam sponse toro tene pudicam,*
Sponsum sponsa tene toro pudicum.
Non hæc vnica nox datur beatis,
At vos perpetuo hæc beabit vna
Prole multiplici, parique amore.
Læta, ac vera refert Sybilla; ab alto
Ipse Iuppiter annuit loquenti.

    Pro. So be it euer, ioy and peace,
And mutuall loue giue you increase,
10   That your posteritie may grow
In fame, as long as Seas doe flow.
    Enth. Liue you long to see your ioyes,
In faire Nymphs and Princely Boyes;
Breeding like the Garden flowers,
Which kinde heau'n drawes with her warme showers.
    Orph. Enough of blessing, though too much
Neuer can be said to such;
But night doth wast, and *Hymen* chides,
Kinde to Bridegroomes and to Brides.
20   Then, singing, the last dance induce,
So let good night preuent excuse.

The Song.

No longer wrong the night
Of her *Hymenæan* right;
A thousand *Cupids* call away,
Fearing the approching day;
The Cocks alreadie crow:
    Dance then and goe.

The last new Dance of the Maskers, which concludes
30   *all with a liuely straine at their go-*
ing out.

FINIS.

Songs of Mourning:

BEVVAILING
the vntimely death of
Prince *Henry*.

VVorded by THO. CAMPION.

And set forth to bee sung with one voyce
to the Lute, or Violl :

By JOHN COPRARIO.

LONDON,
Printed for *Iohn Browne*, and
are to be sould in S. dunstons
Churchyard, 1613.

To face p. 100

ILLVSTRISSIMO,

POTENTISSIMOQVE PRIN-

CIPI, *FREDRICO* QVINTO, RHENI

COMITI PALATINO, DVCI BAVARIÆ, &C.

Cogimur; inuitis (Clarissime) parce querelis
  Te saluo; lætis non sinit esse Deus:
Nec speratus Hymen procedit lumine claro;
  Principis extincti nubila fata vetant.
Illius inferias mæsto iam Musica cantu
  Prosequitur, miseros hæc Dea sola iuuat.
Illa suos tibi summittit (Dux inclite) quæstus,
  Fraternus fleto quem sociauit amor:
Sed noua gaudia, sed tam dulcia fœdera rupit
  Fati infœlicis liuor, et hora nocens.   10
Quod superest, nimios nobis omni arte dolores
  Est mollire animus, spes meliora dabit:
Cunctatosque olim cantabimus ipsi Hymenæos,
  Læta simul fas sit reddere vota Deo.

AN ELEGIE
vpon the vntimely death of
Prince *Henry*

Reade, you that haue some teares left yet vnspent,
Now weepe your selues hart sicke, and nere repent:
For I will open to your free accesse
The sanctuary of all heauinesse,
Where men their fill may mourne, and neuer sinne:
And I their humble Priest thus first beginne.
   Fly from the Skies, yee blessed beames of light;
Rise vp in horrid vapours, vgly night,
And fetter'd bring that rauenous monster Fate,
The fellon and the traytour to our state.   10
Law-Eloquence wee neede not to conuince
His guilt; all know it, 'tis hee stole our Prince,
The Prince of men, the Prince of all that bore
Euer that princely name: O now no more
Shall his perfections, like the Sunne-beames, dare
The purblinde world: in heau'n those glories are.
What could the greatest artist, Nature, adde
T'encrease his graces? deuine forme hee had,
Striuing in all his parts which should surpasse;
And like a well tun'd chime his carriage was   20
Full of cœlestiall witchcraft, winning all
To admiration and loue personall.
His Launce appear'd to the beholders eyes,
When his faire hand aduanc't it to the skyes,
Larger then truth, for well could hee it wield,
And make it promise honour in the field.
When Court and Musicke cal'd him, off fell armes,
And as hee had beene shap't for loues alarmes,
In harmony hee spake, and trod the ground
In more proportion then the measur'd sound.   30
How fit for peace was hee, and rosie beds!
How fit to stand in troopes of iron heads,

When time had with his circles made complete
His charmed rounds! All things in time grow great.
  This feare, euen like a commet that hangs high,
And shootes his threatning flashes through the skye,
Held all the eyes of Christendome intent
Vpon his youthfull hopes, casting th' euent
Of what was in his power, not in his will:
For that was close conceal'd, and must lye still,   40
As deeply hid as that designe which late
With the French Lyon died. O earthly state,
How doth thy greatnesse in a moment fall,
And feastes in highest pompe turn funerall!
  But our young *Henry* arm'd with all the arts
That sute with Empire, and the gaine of harts,
Bearing before him fortune, power, and loue,
Appear'd first in perfection, fit to moue
Fixt admiration: though his yeeres were greene
Their fruit was yet mature: his care had beene   50
Suruaying India, and implanting there
The knowledge of that God which hee did feare:
And eu'n now, though hee breathlesse lyes, his sayles
Are strugling with the windes, for our auayles
T' explore a passage hid from humane tract,
Will fame him in the enterprise or fact.
O Spirit full of hope, why art thou fled
From deedes of honour? why's that vertue dead
Which dwelt so well in thee? a bowre more sweet,
If Paradise were found, it could not meete.   60
  Curst then bee Fate that stole our blessing so,
And had for vs now nothing left but woe,
Had not th' All-seeing prouidence yet kept
Another ioy safe, that in silence slept:
And that same Royall workeman, who could frame
A Prince so worthy of immortall fame,
Liues; and long may hee liue, to forme the other
His exprest image, and grace of his brother,
To whose eternall peace wee offer now
Guifts which hee lou'd, and fed; Musicks that flow   70
Out of a sowre and melancholike vayne,
Which best sort with the sorrowes wee sustaine.

TO THE MOST SACRED
King *Iames.*

1

O Griefe, how diuers are thy shapes wherein men languish!
    The face sometime with teares thou fil'st,
    Sometime the hart thou kill'st
            With vnseene anguish.
Sometime thou smil'st to view how Fate
        Playes with our humane state:
So farre from suretie here
        Are all our earthly ioys,
That what our strong hope buildes, when least we feare,
    A stronger power destroyes.   10

2

O Fate, why shouldst thou take from KINGS their ioy and
    treasure?
    Their Image if men should deface
    'Twere death, which thou dost race
            Euen at thy pleasure.
Wisedome of holy Kings yet knowes
        Both what it hath, and owes.
Heau'ns hostage, which you bredd
        And nurst with such choyce care,
Is rauisht now, great KING, and from vs ledd
    When wee were least aware.   20

TO THE MOST SACRED
Queene *Anne.*

1

Tis now dead night, and not a light on earth,
    Or starre in heauen, doth shine:
Let now a mother mourne the noblest birth
    That euer was both mortall and diuine.
    O sweetnesse peerelesse! more then humane grace!
    O flowry beauty! O vntimely death!
        Now, Musicke, fill this place
        With thy most dolefull breath:
    O singing wayle a fate more truely funerall
    Then when with all his sonnes the sire of Troy did fall. 10

2

Sleepe, Ioy, dye, Mirth, and not a smile be seene,
    Or shew of harts content:
For neuer sorrow neerer touch't a QVEENE,
    Nor were there euer teares more duely spent.
O deare remembrance, full of ruefull woe!
O ceacelesse passion! O vnhumane hower!
       No pleasure now can grow,
       For wither'd is her flower.
O anguish doe thy worst and fury Tragicall,
Since fate in taking one hath thus disorder'd all.   20

TO THE MOST HIGH AND MIGHTY
Prince Charles.

1

Fortune and Glory may be lost and woone,
But when the worke of Nature is vndone
    That losse flyes past returning;
    No helpe is left but mourning.
What can to kinde youth more despightfull proue
    Than to be rob'd of one sole Brother?
       Father and Mother
Ask reuerence, a Brother onely loue.
Like age and birth, like thoughts and pleasures moue:
  What gayne can he heape vp, though showers of Crownes
    descend,   10
Who for that good must change a brother and a friend?

2

Follow, O follow yet thy Brothers fame,
But not his fate: lets onely change the name,
    And finde his worth presented
    In thee, by him preuented.
Or past example of the dead be great,
    Out of thy selfe begin thy storie:
       Vertue and glorie
Are eminent being plac't in princely seate.
Oh, heauen, his age prolong with sacred heate,   20
  And on his honoured head let all the blessings light
  Which to his brothers life men wish't, and wish't them right.

M

TO THE MOST PRINCELY AND VERTVOVS
the Lady *Elizabeth.*

I

So parted you as if the world for euer
  Had lost with him her light:
Now could your teares hard flint to ruth excite,
    Yet may you neuer
  Your loues againe partake in humane sight:
O why should fate such two kind harts disseuer
As nature neuer knit more faire or firme together?

2

So loued you as sister should a brother
  Not in a common straine,
For Princely blood doeth vulgar fire disdaine: 10
    But you each other
  On earth embrac't in a celestiall chaine.
Alasse for loue, that heau'nly borne affection
To change should subiect be and suffer earths infection.

TO THE MOST ILLVSTRIOVS AND MIGHTY
Fredericke *the fift,* Count Palatine of the Rhein.

I

How like a golden dreame you met and parted,
  That pleasing straight doth vanish:
  O who can euer banish
The thought of one so princely and free-harted!
But hee was pul'd vp in his prime by fate,
And loue for him must mourne though all too late.
  Teares to the dead are due, let none forbid
  Sad harts to sigh: true griefe cannot be hid.

2

Yet the most bitter storme to height encreased
  By heau'n againe is ceased: 10
  O time, that all things mouest,
In griefe and ioy thou equall measure louest:
Such the condition is of humane life,
Care must with pleasure mixe and peace with strife:
  Thoughts with the dayes must change; as tapers waste,
  So must our griefes; day breakes when night is past.

To the most disconsolate
Great Brittaine.

1

When pale famine fed on thee,
　　With her vnsatiate iawes;
When ciuill broyles set murder free
　　Contemning all thy lawes;
When heau'n enrag'd consum'd thee so
With plagues that none thy face could know,
　　　Yet in thy lookes affliction then shew'd lesse
　　　Then now for ones fate all thy parts expresse.

2

Now thy highest States lament
　　A sonne, and Brothers losse;　　　　　　10
Thy nobles mourne in discontent,
　　And rue this fatall crosse;
Thy Commons are with passion sad
To thinke how braue a Prince they had:
　　　If all thy rockes from white to blacke should turne
　　　Yet couldst thou not in shew more amply mourne.

To the World.

1

O poore distracted world partly a slaue
　　To Pagans sinnefull rage, partly obscur'd
With ignorance of all the meanes that saue!
　　　And eu'n those parts of thee that liue assur'd
　　　Of heau'nly grace, Oh how they are deuided
　　　With doubts late by a Kingly penne decided!
O happy world, if what the Sire begunne
Had beene clos'd vp by his religious Sonne!

2

Mourne all you soules opprest vnder the yoake
　　Of Christian-hating Thrace: neuer appeared　　10
More likelyhood to haue that blacke league broke,
　　　For such a heauenly Prince might well be fear'd
　　　Of earthly fiends. Oh how is Zeale inflamed
With power, when truth wanting defence is shamed!
　　O princely soule, rest thou in peace, while wee
　　In thine expect the hopes were ripe in thee.

A Table of all the Songs contayned in
this Booke.

FINIS.

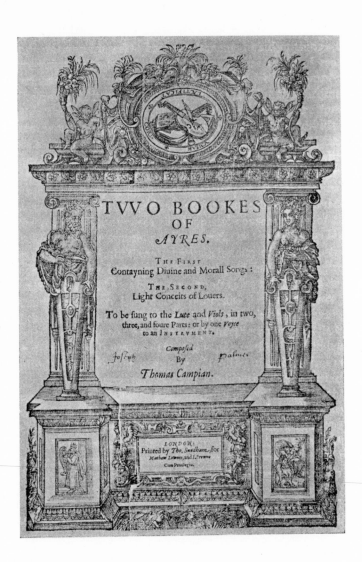

TVVO BOOKES
OF
AYRES.

THE FIRST
Contayning Diuine and Morall Songs:
THE SECOND,
Light Conceits of Louers.

To be sung to the *Lute* and *Viols*, in two,
three, and foure Parts: or by one *Voyce*
to an INSTRVMENT.

Ioseph   Composed   Palmer
By
Thomas Campian.

LONDON:
Printed by *Tho. Snodham*, for
Mathew Lownes, and I. *Browne*
Cum Priuilegio.

To face p. 110

TO THE RIGHT
HONOVRABLE, BOTH
IN BIRTH AND VERTVE, FRANCIS, EARLE
OF CVMBERLAND.

What patron could I chuse, great *Lord*, but you?
  Graue words your years may challenge as their owne,
And eu'ry note of Musicke is your due,
  Whose House the *Muses* pallace I haue knowne.

To loue and cherish them, though it descends
  With many honours more on you, in vaine
Preceding fame herein with you contends,
  Who haue both fed the *Muses*, and their trayne.

These Leaues I offer you, Deuotion might
  Her selfe lay open, read them, or else heare   10
How grauely, with their tunes they yeeld delight
  To any vertuous and not curious eare.
Such as they are, accept them, Noble *Lord*;
If better, better could my zeale afford.

Your Honors,

THOMAS CAMPIAN.

TO THE Reader.

Ovt of many Songs which, partly at the request of friends, partly for my owne recreation, were by mee long since composed, I haue now enfranchised a few, sending them forth diuided, according to their different subiect, into seuerall Bookes. The first are graue and pious ; the second, amorous and light. For hee that in publishing any worke, hath a desire to content all palates, must cater for them accordingly.

——————Non omnibus vnum est
Quod placet, hic Spinas colligit, ille Rosas.

These Ayres were for the most part framed at first for one voyce with the Lute, or Violl, but vpon occasion, they haue since beene filled with more parts, which who so please may vse, who like not may leaue. Yet doe wee daily obserue, that when any shall sing a Treble to an Instrument, the standers by will be offring at an inward part out of their owne nature ; and, true or false, out it must, though to the peruerting of the whole harmonie. Also, if we consider well, the Treble tunes, which are with vs commonly called Ayres, are but Tenors mounted eight Notes higher, and therefore an inward part must nedes well become them, such as may take vp the whole distance of the Diapason, and fill vp the gaping betweene the two extreame parts ; whereby though they are not three parts in perfection, yet they yeeld a sweetnesse and content both to the eare and minde, which is the ayme and perfection of Musicke. Short Ayres, if they be skilfully framed, and naturally exprest, are like quicke and good Epigrammes in Poesie, many of them shewing as much artifice, and breeding as great difficultie as a larger Poeme. Non omnia possumus omnes, said the Romane Epick Poet. But some there are who admit onely French or Italian Ayres, as if euery Country had not his proper

Ayre, which the people thereof naturally vsurpe in their Musicke. Others taste nothing that comes forth in Print, *as if* Catullus *or* Martials *Epigrammes were the worse for being published. In these* English *Ayres, I haue chiefely aymed to couple my Words and Notes louingly together, which will be much for him to doe that hath not power ouer both. The light of this will best appeare to him who hath paysd our Monasyllables and Syllables combined, both of which, are so loaded with Consonants, as that they will hardly keepe company with swift Notes, or giue the Vowell conuenient liberty. To conclude ; mine owne opinion of these Songs I deliuer thus :*

Omnia nec nostris bona sunt, sed nec mala libris ;
Si placet hac cantes, hac quoque lege legas.

Farewell.

A TABLE OF ALL THE SONGS

contayned in these BOOKES.

I.

Author of light, reuiue my dying spright;
Redeeme it from the snares of all-confounding night.
      Lord, light me to thy blessed way:
For blinde with worldly vaine desires, I wander as a stray.
      Sunne and Moone, Starres and vnderlights I see,
But all their glorious beames are mists and darknes, being
      compar'd to thee.

Fountaine of health, my soules deepe wounds recure,
Sweet showres of pitty raine, wash my vncleannesse pure.
      One drop of thy desired grace
The faint and fading hart can raise, and in ioyes bosome
      place.   10
      Sinne and Death, Hell and tempting Fiends may rage;
But God his owne will guard, and their sharp paines and
      griefe in time asswage.

II.

      The man of life vpright,
        Whose chearfull minde is free
      From waight of impious deedes
        And yoake of vanitee;

      The man whose silent dayes
        In harmelesse ioyes are spent,
      Whom hopes cannot delude
        Nor sorrowes discontent;

      That man needes neyther towres,
        Nor armour for defence: 10
      Nor vaults his guilt to shrowd
        From thunders violence;

      Hee onely can behold
        With vnaffrighted eyes
      The horrors of the deepe
        And terrors of the Skies.

Thus, scorning all the cares
  That fate or fortune brings,
His Booke the Heau'ns hee makes,
  His wisedome heau'nly things;   20

Good thoughts his surest friends,
  His wealth a well-spent age,
The earth his sober Inne,
  And quiet pilgrimage.

III.

Where are all thy beauties now, all harts enchayning?
Whither are thy flatt'rers gone with all their fayning?
All fled; and thou alone still here remayning.

Thy rich state of twisted gold to Bayes is turned;
Cold, as thou art, are thy loues, that so much burned:
Who dye in flatt'rers armes are seldome mourned.

Yet, in spight of enuie, this be still proclaymed,
That none worthyer then thy selfe thy worth hath blamed;
When their poore names are lost, thou shalt liue famed.

When thy story, long time hence, shall be perused,   10
Let the blemish of thy rule be thus excused,
None euer liu'd more iust, none more abused.

IIII.

Out of my soules deapth to thee my cryes haue sounded:
Let thine eares my plaints receiue, on iust feare grounded.
Lord, should'st thou weigh our faults, who 's not confounded?

But with grace thou censur'st thine when they haue erred,
Therefore shall thy blessed name be lou'd and feared.
Eu'n to thy throne my thoughts and eyes are reared.

Thee alone my hopes attend, on thee relying;
In thy sacred word I'le trust, to thee fast flying,
Long ere the Watch shall breake, the morne descrying.

In the mercies of our God who liue secured,   10
May of full redemption rest in him assured,
Their sinne-sicke soules by him shall be recured.

V.

View mee, Lord, a worke of thine :
Shall I then lye drown'd in night ?
Might thy grace in mee but shine,
I should seeme made all of light.

But my soule still surfets so
On the poysoned baytes of sinne,
That I strange and vgly growe,
All is darke and foule within.

Clense mee, Lord, that I may kneele
At thine Altar, pure and white :   10
They that once thy Mercies feele,
Gaze no more on earths delight.

Worldly ioyes like shadowes fade,
When the heau'nly light appeares ;
But the cou'nants thou hast made,
Endlesse, know nor dayes, nor yeares.

In thy word, Lord, is my trust,
To thy mercies fast I flye ;
Though I am but clay and dust,
Yet thy grace can lift me high.   20

VI.

Brauely deckt, come forth, bright day,
Thine houres with Roses strew thy way,
      As they well remember.
Thou receiu'd shalt be with feasts :
Come, chiefest of the *British* ghests,
      Thou fift of *Nouember.*
Thou with triumph shalt exceede
      In the strictest ember ;
For by thy returne the Lord records his blessed deede.

Britaines, frolicke at your bourd ;   10
But first sing praises to the Lord
      In your Congregations.

Hee preserued your state alone,
His louing grace hath made you one
    Of his chosen Nations.
But this light must hallowed be
    With your best Oblations;
Prayse the Lord, for onely great and mercifull is hee.

Death had enter'd in the gate,
And ruine was crept neare the State;   20
    But heau'n all reuealed.
Fi'ry Powder hell did make,
Which, ready long, the flame to take,
    Lay in shade concealed.
God vs helped, of his free grace:
    None to him appealed;
For none was so bad to feare the treason or the place.

God his peacefull Monarch chose,
To him the mist he did disclose,
    To him, and none other: 30
This hee did, O King, for thee,
That thou thine owne renowne might'st see,
    Which no time can smother.
May blest *Charles*, thy comfort be,
    Firmer then his Brother:
May his heart the loue of peace and wisedome learne from
    thee.

VII.

To Musicke bent is my retyred minde,
And faine would I some song of pleasure sing;
But in vaine ioys no comfort now I finde,
From heau'nly thoughts all true delight doth spring.
Thy power, O God, thy mercies, to record,
Will sweeten eu'ry note and eu'ry word.

All earthly pompe or beauty to expresse,
Is but to carue in snow, on waues to write.
Celestiall things, though men conceiue them lesse,
Yet fullest are they in themselues of light: 10
Such beames they yeeld as know no meanes to dye,
Such heate they cast as lifts the Spirit high.

VIII.

Tune thy Musicke to thy hart,
Sing thy ioy with thankes, and so thy sorrow :
  Though Deuotion needes not Art,
Sometimes of the poore the rich may borrow.

  Striue not yet for curious wayes :
Concord pleaseth more, the lesse 'tis strained ;
  Zeale affects not outward prayse,
Onely striues to show a loue vnfained.

  Loue can wondrous things affect,
Sweetest Sacrifice, all wrath appeasing ;   10
  Loue the highest doth respect ;
Loue alone to him is euer pleasing.

IX.

Most sweet and pleasing are thy wayes, O God,
Like Meadowes deckt with Christall streames and flowers :
Thy paths no foote prophane hath euer trod :
Nor hath the proud man rested in thy Bowers :
There liues no Vultur, no deuouring Beare,
But onely Doues and Lambs are harbor'd there.

The Wolfe his young ones to their prey doth guide ;
The Foxe his Cubbs with false deceit endues ;
The Lyons Whelpe suckes from his Damme his pride ;
In hers the Serpent malice doth infuse :   10
The darksome Desart all such beasts contaynes,
Not one of them in Paradice remaynes.

X.

Wise men patience neuer want ;
Good men pitty cannot hide ;
Feeble spirits onely vant
Of reuenge, the poorest pride :
Hee alone, forgiue that can,
Beares the true soule of a man.

Some there are, debate that seeke,
Making trouble their content,
Happy if they wrong the meeke,
Vexe them that to peace are bent: 10
Such vndooe the common tye
Of mankinde, societie.

Kindnesse growne is, lately, colde;
Conscience hath forgot her part;
Blessed times were knowne of old,
Long ere Law became an Art:
Shame deterr'd, not Statutes then,
Honest loue was law to men.

Deeds from loue, and words, that flowe,
Foster like kinde *Aprill* showres;   20
In the warme Sunne all things grow,
Wholsome fruits and pleasant flowres;
All so thriues his gentle rayes,
Where on humane loue displayes.

XI.

Neuer weather-beaten Saile more willing bent to shore,
Neuer tyred Pilgrims limbs affected slumber more,
Than my wearied spright now longs to flye out of my troubled
    brest.
    O come quickly, sweetest Lord, and take my soule to rest.

Euer-blooming are the ioys of Heau'ns high paradice,
Cold age deafes not there our eares, nor vapour dims our eyes:
Glory there the Sun outshines, whose beames the blessed
    onely see;
    O come quickly, glorious Lord, and raise my spright to thee.

XII.

Lift vp to heau'n, sad wretch, thy heauy spright,
What though thy sinnes, thy due destruction threat?
The Lord exceedes in mercy as in might;
His ruth is greater, though thy crimes be great.
Repentance needes not feare the heau'ns iust rod,
It stayes eu'n thunder in the hand of God.

With chearefull voyce to him then cry for grace,
Thy Faith and fainting Hope with Prayer reuiue;
Remorce for all that truely mourne hath place;
Not God, but men of him themselues depriue: 10
Striue then, and hee will help; call him he'll heare:
The Sonne needes not the Fathers fury feare.

XIII.

Loe, when backe mine eye,
  Pilgrim-like, I cast,
What fearefull wayes I spye,
Which, blinded, I securely past?

But now heau'n hath drawne
  From my browes that night;
As when the day doth dawne,
So cleares my long imprison'd sight.

Straight the caues of hell,
  Drest with flowres I see: 10
Wherein false pleasures dwell,
That, winning most, most deadly be.

Throngs of masked Feinds,
  Wing'd like Angels flye,
Euen in the gates of Friends
In faire disguise blacke dangers lye.

Straight to Heau'n I rais'd
  My restored sight,
And with loud voyce I prais'd
The Lord of euer-during light.   20

And since I had stray'd
  From his wayes so wide,
His grace I humble pray'd
Hence-forth to be my guard and guide.

XIIII.

As by the streames of *Babilon*
Farre from our natiue soyle we sat,
Sweet *Sion*, thee we thought vpon,
And eu'ry thought a teare begat.

N

Aloft the trees, that spring vp there,
Our silent Harps wee pensiue hung:
Said they that captiu'd us, Let's heare
Some song, which you in *Sion* sung.

Is then the song of our God fit
To be prophaned in forraine land?   10
O *Salem*, thee when I forget,
Forget his skill may my right hand!

Fast to the roofe cleaue may my tongue,
If mindelesse I of thee be found:
Or if, when all my ioys are sung,
Ierusalem be not the ground.

Remember, Lord, how *Edoms* race
Cryed in *Ierusalems* sad day,
Hurle downe her wals, her towres deface,
And, stone by stone, all leuell lay.   20

Curst *Babels* seede! for *Salems* sake
Iust ruine yet for thee remaines!
Blest shall they be thy babes that take
And 'gainst the stones dash out their braines.

XV.

  Sing a song of ioy
    Prayse our God with mirth:
His flocke who can destroy?
Is hee not Lord of heau'n and earth?

  Sing wee then secure,
    Tuning well our strings:
With voyce, as Eccho pure,
Let vs renowne the King of Kings.

  First who taught the day
    From the East to rise?   10
Whom doth the Sunne obey
When in the Seas his glory dyes?

  Hee the Starres directs
    That in order stand:
Who heau'n and earth protects
But hee that fram'd them with his hand?

Angels round attend,
  Wayting on his will;
Arm'd millions hee doth send
To ayde the good or plague the ill.   20

All that dread his Name,
  And his Hests obserue,
His arme will shield from shame:
Their steps from truth shall neuer swerue.

Let us then reioyce,
  Sounding loud his prayse:
So will hee heare our voyce
And blesse on earth our peacefull dayes.

XVI.

Awake, awake, thou heauy spright,
That sleep'st the deadly sleepe of sinne,
  Rise now and walke the waies of light;
'Tis not too late yet to begin.
    Seeke heauen earely, seeke it late:
    True faith still findes an open gate.

Get vp, get vp, thou leaden man:
Thy tracks to endlesse ioy or paine
  Yeelds but the modell of a span;
Yet burnes out thy lifes lampe in vaine.   10
    One minute bounds thy bane, or blisse,
    Then watch and labour, while time is.

XVII.

Come, chearfull day, part of my life, to mee:
For while thou view'st me with thy fading light,
Part of my life doth still depart with thee,
And I still onward haste to my last night.
  Times fatall wings doe euer forward flye,
  Soe eu'ry day we liue a day wee dye.

But, O yee nights, ordain'd for barren rest,
How are my dayes depriu'd of life in you,
When heauy sleepe my soule hath dispossest,
By fayned death life sweetly to renew!   10
  Part of my life in that, you life denye:
  So eu'ry day we liue a day wee dye.

XVIII.

Seeke the Lord, and in his wayes perseuer.
　O faint not, but as Eagles flye;
　For his steepe hill is high;
Then striuing gaine the top, and triumph euer.

When with glory there thy browes are crowned,
　New ioys so shall abound in thee,
　Such sights thy soule shall see,
That worldly thoughts shall by their beames be drowned.

Farewell, World, thou masse of meere confusion,
　False light, with many shadowes dimm'd,　　　　　10
　Old Witch, with new foyles trimm'd,
Thou deadly sleepe of soule, and charm'd illusion.

I the King will seek, of Kings adored;
　Spring of light, tree of grace and blisse,
　Whose fruit so sou'raigne is
That all who taste it are from death restored.

XIX.

Lighten, heauy hart, thy spright,
　The ioyes recall that thence are fled;
Yeeld thy brest some liuing light;
　The man that nothing doth is dead.
Tune thy temper to these sounds,
　And quicken so thy ioylesse minde;
Sloth the worst and best confounds:
　It is the ruine of mankinde.

From her caue rise all distasts,
　Which vnresolu'd Despaire pursues;　　　　　10
Whom soone after, Violence hasts,
　Her selfe vngratefull to abuse.
Skies are clear'd with stirring windes,
　Th' vnmoued water moorish growes;
Eu'ry eye much pleasure findes
　To view a streame that brightly flowes.

XX.

Iacke and *Ione* they thinke no ill,
But louing liue, and merry still;
Doe their weeke dayes worke, and pray
Deuotely on the holy day:
Skip and trip it on the greene,
And help to chuse the Summer Queene:
Lash out, at a Country Feast,
Their siluer penny with the best.

Well can they iudge of nappy Ale,
And tell at large a Winter tale;   10
Climbe vp to the Apple loft,
And turne the Crabs till they be soft.
Tib is all the fathers ioy,
And little *Tom* the mothers boy.
All their pleasure is content;
And care, to pay their yearely rent.

Ione can call by name her Cowes,
And decke her windowes with greene boughs;
Shee can wreathes and tuttyes make,
And trimme with plums a Bridall Cake.   20
Iacke knowes what brings gaine or losse;
And his long Flaile can stoutly tosse:
Make the hedge, which others breake,
And euer thinkes what he doth speake.

Now, you Courtly Dames and Knights,
That study onely strange delights;
Though you scorne the home-spun gray,
And reuell in your rich array:
Though your tongues dissemble deepe,
And can your heads from danger keepe;   30
Yet, for all your pompe and traine,
Securer liues the silly Swaine.

XXI.

All lookes be pale, harts cold as stone,
For *Hally* now is dead, and gone,
    Hally, in whose sight,
      Most sweet sight,
        All the earth late tooke delight.
Eu'ry eye, weepe with mee.
Ioyes drown'd in teares must be.

His Iu'ry skin, his comely hayre,
His Rosie cheekes, so cleare and faire,
    Eyes that once did grace   10
      His bright face,
        Now in him all want their place.
Eyes and hearts weepe with mee!
For who so kinde as hee?

His youth was like an *Aprill* flowre,
Adorn'd with beauty, loue, and powre.
    Glory strow'd his way,
      Whose wreaths gay
        Now are all turn'd to decay.
Then againe weepe with mee   20
None feele more cause then wee.

No more may his wisht sight returne,
His golden Lampe no more can burne.
    Quencht is all his flame;
      His hop't fame
        Now hath left him nought but name.
For him all weepe with mee
Since more him none shall see.

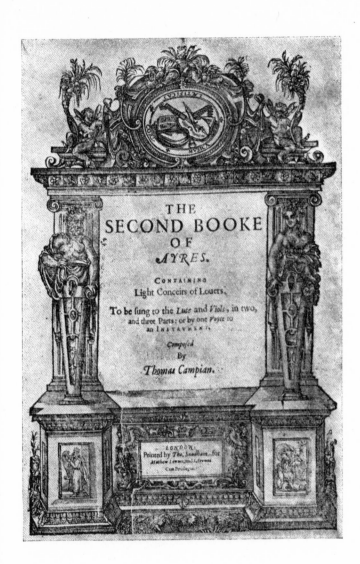

THE
SECOND BOOKE
OF
AYRES.

CONTAINING
Light Conceits of Louers.

To be sung to the *Lute* and *Viols*, in two,
and three Parts: or by one *Voyce* to
an INSTRVMENT.

Composed
By
Thomas Campian.

LONDON,
Printed by *Tho. Snodham*, for
Mathew Lownes, and *I. Browne*
Cum Priuilegio.

TO THE RIGHT
NOBLE, AND VERTVOVS
HENRY Lord CLIFFORD, Son and Heyre to

the Right Honourable, FRANCIS, Earle of

CVMBERLAND.

Such dayes as weare the badge of holy red
  Are for deuotion markt and sage delight;
The vulgar Low-dayes, vndistinguished,
  Are left for labour, games, and sportfull sights.

This seu'rall and so diff'ring vse of Time,
  Within th'enclosure of one weeke wee finde;
Which I resemble in my Notes and Rime,
  Expressing both in their peculiar kinde.

Pure Hymnes, such as the seauenth day loues, doe leade;
  Graue age did iustly chalenge those of mee: 10
These weeke-day workes, in order that succeede,
  Your youth best fits, and yours, yong Lord, they be,
As hee is who to them their beeing gaue:
If th' one, the other you of force must haue.

Your Honors,
THOMAS CAMPIAN.

To the READER.

That holy Hymnes with Louers cares are knit
Both in one Quire here, thou maist think't vnfit.
Why do'st not blame the Stationer as well,
Who in the same Shop sets all sorts to sell?
Diuine with stiles prophane, graue shelu'd with vaine,
And some matcht worse; yet none of him complaine.

I.

Vaine men, whose follies make a God of Loue,
Whose blindnesse beauty doth immortall deeme ;
Prayse not what you desire, but what you proue,
Count those things good that are, not those that seeme :
I cannot call her true that's false to me,
Nor make of women more then women be.

How faire an entrance breakes the way to loue !
How rich of golden hope and gay delight !
What hart cannot a modest beauty moue?
Who, seeing cleare day once, will dreame of night?   10
Shee seem'd a Saint, that brake her faith with mee,
But prou'd a woman as all other be.

So bitter is their sweet, that true content
Vnhappy men in them may neuer finde :
Ah, but without them none ; both must consent,
Else vncouth are the ioys of eyther kinde.
Let vs then prayse their good, forget their ill :
Men must be men, and women women still.

II.

How eas'ly wert thou chained,
Fond hart, by fauours fained !
Why liu'd thy hopes in grace,
Straight to dye disdained?
But since th' art now beguiled
By Loue that falsely smiled,
In some lesse happy place
Mourne alone exiled !
My loue still here increaseth,
And with my loue my griefe,   10
While her sweet bounty ceaseth,
That gaue my woes reliefe.
Yet 'tis no woman leaues me,
For such may proue uniust ;
A Goddesse thus deceiues me,
Whose faith who could mistrust ?

A Goddesse so much graced,
That Paradice is placed
In her most heau'nly brest,
Once by loue embraced :   20
But loue, that so kinde proued,
Is now from her remoued,
Nor will he longer rest
Where no faith is loued.
If Powres Celestiall wound vs
And will not yeeld reliefe,
Woe then must needs confound vs,
For none can cure our griefe.
No wonder if I languish
Through burden of my smart ;   30
It is no common anguish
From Paradice to part.

III.

Harden now thy tyred hart, with more then flinty rage ;
Ne'er let her false teares henceforth thy constant griefe asswage.
Once true happy dayes thou saw'st when shee stood firme and
    kinde,
Both as one then liu'd and held one eare, one tongue, one
    minde :
But now those bright houres be fled, and neuer may returne ;
What then remaines but her vntruths to mourne ?

Silly Traytresse, who shall now thy carelesse tresses place ?
Who thy pretty talke supply, whose eare thy musicke grace ?
Who shall thy bright eyes admire ? what lips triumph with thine ?
Day by day who'll visit thee and say 'th'art onely mine' ?   10
Such a time there was, God wot, but such shall neuer be :
Too oft, I feare, thou wilt remember me.

IIII.

O what vnhop't for sweet supply !
    O what ioyes exceeding !
What an affecting charme feele I,
    From delight proceeding !
That which I long despair'd to be,
    To her I am, and shee to mee.

Shee that alone in cloudy griefe
    Long to mee appeared,
Shee now alone with bright reliefe
    All those clouds hath cleared.   10
Both are immortall and diuine :
    Since I am hers, and she is mine.

V.

Where shee her sacred bowre adornes,
    The Riuers clearely flow ;
The groues and medowes swell with flowres,
    The windes all gently blow.
Her Sunne-like beauty shines so fayre,
    Her Spring can neuer fade :
Who then can blame the life that striues
    To harbour in her shade ?

Her grace I sought, her loue I wooed ;
    Her loue though I obtaine,   10
No time, no toyle, no vow, no faith,
    Her wished grace can gaine.
Yet truth can tell my heart is hers,
    And her will I adore ;
And from that loue when I depart,
    Let heau'n view me no more.

Her roses with my prayers shall spring ;
    And when her trees I praise,
Their boughs shall blossome, mellow fruit
    Shall straw her pleasant wayes.   20
The words of harty zeale haue powre
    High wonders to effect ;
O why should then her Princely eare
    My words, or zeale neglect ?

If shee my faith misdeemes, or worth,
    Woe-worth my haplesse fate :
For though time can my truth reueale,
    That time will come too late.
And who can glory in the worth,
    That cannot yeeld him grace ?   30
Content in eu'rything is not,
    Nor ioy in eu'ry place.

But from her bowre of Ioy since I
  Must now excluded be,
And shee will not relieue my cares,
  Which none can helpe but shee;
My comfort in her loue shall dwell,
  Her loue lodge in my brest,
And though not in her bowre, yet I
  Shall in her temple rest.   40

VI.

Faine would I my loue disclose,
Ask what honour might denye;
But both loue and her I lose,
From my motion if shee flye.
Worse then paine is feare to mee:
Then hold in fancy though it burne
If not happy, safe Ile be,
And to my clostred cares returne.

Yet, ô yet, in vaine I striue
To represse my school'd desire;   10
More and more the flames reuiue,
I consume in mine owne fire.
She would pitty, might shee know
The harmes that I for her endure:
Speak then, and get comfort so;
A wound long hid growes past recure.

Wise shee is, and needs must know
All th' attempts that beauty moues:
Fayre she is, and honour'd so
That she, sure, hath tryed some loues.   20
If with loue I tempt her then,
'Tis but her due to be desir'd:
What would women thinke of men
If their deserts were not admir'd?

Women, courted, haue the hand
To discard what they distaste:
But those Dames whom none demand
Want oft what their wils imbrac't.

Could their firmnesse iron excell,
As they are faire, they should be sought: 30
When true theeues use falsehood well,
As they are wise they will be caught.

VII.

Giue beauty all her right,
Shee's not to one forme tyed;
Each shape yeelds faire delight,
Where her perfections 'bide.
Hellen, I grant, might pleasing be;
And *Ros'mond* was as sweet as shee.

Some the quicke eye commends;
Some swelling lips and red;
Pale lookes haue many friends,
Through sacred sweetnesse bred.   10
Medowes haue flowres that pleasure moue,
Though Roses are the flowres of loue.

Free beauty is not bound
To one vnmoued clime:
She visits eu'ry ground,
And fauours eu'ry time.
Let the old loues with mine compare,
My sou'raigne is as sweet, and fayre.

VIII.

O deare that I with thee might liue,
From humane trace remoued:
Where iealous care might neither grieue,
Yet each dote on their loued.
While fond feare may colour finde, Loue's seldome pleased;
But much like a sicke mans rest, it's soone diseased.

Why should our mindes not mingle so,
When loue and faith is plighted,
That eyther might the others know,
Alike in all delighted?   10
Why should frailtie breed suspect, when hearts are fixed?
Must all humane ioyes of force with griefe be mixed?

How oft haue wee eu'n smilde in teares,
 Our fond mistrust repenting?
As snow when heauenly fire appeares,
 So melts loues hate relenting.
Vexed kindnesse soone fals off and soone returneth:
Such a flame the more you quench the more it burneth.

IX.

Good men, shew, if you can tell,
Where doth humane pittie dwell?
Farre and neere her I would seeke,
So vext with sorrow is my brest.
She, (they say) to all, is meeke,
And onely makes th' vnhappie blest.

Oh! if such a Saint there be,
Some hope yet remaines for me:
Prayer or sacrifice may gaine
From her implored grace reliefe;   10
To release mee of my paine,
Or at the least to ease my griefe.

Young am I, and farre from guile,
The more is my woe the while:
Falshood with a smooth disguise
My simple meaning hath abus'd:
Casting mists before mine eyes,
By which my senses are confus'd.

Fair he is, who vow'd to me
That he onely mine would be;   20
But, alas, his minde is caught
With eu'ry gaudie bait he sees:
And too late my flame is taught
That too much kindnesse makes men freese.

From me all my friends are gone,
While I pine for him alone;
And not one will rue my case,
But rather my distresse deride:
That I thinke there is no place
Where pittie euer yet did bide.   30

X.

What haruest halfe so sweet is
As still to reape the kisses
   Grown ripe in sowing?
And straight to be receiuer
Of that which thou art giuer,
   Rich in bestowing?
Kiss then, my haruest Queene,
   Full garners heaping;
Kisses, ripest when th' are greene,
   Want onely reaping.   10

The Doue alone expresses
Her feruencie in kisses,
   Of all most louing:
A creature as offencelesse
As those things that are sencelesse
   And void of mouing.
Let vs so loue and kisse,
   Though all enuie vs:
That which kinde, and harmlesse is,
   None can denie vs.   20

XI.

Sweet, exclude mee not, nor be divided
  From him that ere long must bed thee:
All thy maiden doubts Law hath decided;
  Sure wee are, and I must wed thee.
  Presume then yet a little more:
    Here's the way, barre not the dore.

Tenants, to fulfill their Land-lords pleasure,
  Pay their rent before the quarter:
'Tis my case, if you it rightly measure;
  Put mee not then off with laughter.   10
  Consider then a little more:
    Here's the way to all my store.

Why were dores in loues despight deuised?
  Are not Lawes enough restrayning?
Women are most apt to be surprised
  Sleeping, or sleepe wisely fayning.
  Then grace me yet a little more:
    Here's the way, barre not the dore.

XII.

The peacefull westerne winde
The winter stormes hath tam'd,
And nature in each kinde
The kinde heat hath inflam'd :
The forward buds so sweetly breathe
Out of their earthy bowers,
That heau'n which viewes their pompe beneath
Would faine be deckt with flowers.

See how the morning smiles
On her bright easterne hill,   10
And with soft steps beguiles
Them that lie slumbring still.
The musicke-louing birds are come
From cliffes and rocks vnknowne,
To see the trees and briers blome
That late were ouerflowne.

What Saturne did destroy,
Loues Queene reuiues againe ;
And now her naked boy
Doth in the fields remaine,   20
Where he such pleasing change doth view
In eu'ry liuing thing,
As if the world were borne anew
To gratifie the Spring.

If all things life present,
Why die my comforts then ?
Why suffers my content ?
Am I the worst of men ?
O, beautie, be not thou accus'd
Too iustly in this case :   30
Vnkindly if true loue be vs'd,
'Twill yeeld thee little grace.

XIII.

There is none, O none but you,
That from mee estrange your sight,
Whom mine eyes affect to view
Or chained eares heare with delight.

Other beauties others moue,
   In you I all graces finde;
Such is the effect of loue,
   To make them happy that are kinde.

Women in fraile beauty trust,
   Onely seeme you faire to mee;   10
Yet proue truely kinde and iust,
   For that may not dissembled be.

Sweet, afford mee then your sight,
   That, suruaying all your lookes,
Endlesse volumes I may write
   And fill the world with enuyed bookes:

Which when after ages view,
   All shall wonder and despaire,
Woman to finde man so true,
   Or man a woman halfe so faire.   20

XIIII.

Pin'd I am and like to die,
And all for lacke of that which I
   Doe eu'ry day refuse.
If I musing sit or stand,
Some puts it daily in my hand,
   To interrupt my muse:
The same thing I seeke and flie,
And want that which none would denie.

In my bed, when I should rest,
It breeds such trouble in my brest   10
   That scarce mine eyes will close;
If I sleepe it seemes to be
Oft playing in the bed with me,
   But, wak't, away it goes.
'Tis some spirit sure, I weene,
And yet it may be felt and seene.

Would I had the heart and wit
To make it stand and coniure it,
   That haunts me thus with feare.
Doubtlesse 'tis some harmlesse spright,   20

For it by day as well as night
  Is ready to appeare.
Be it friend, or be it foe,
  Ere long Ile trie what it will doe.

XV.

So many loues haue I neglected
  Whose good parts might moue mee,
That now I liue of all reiected;
  There is none will loue me.
Why is mayden heate so coy?
  It freezeth when it burneth,
Looseth what it might inioy,
  And, hauing lost it, mourneth.

Should I then wooe, that haue beene wooed,
  Seeking them that flye mee?   10
When I my faith with teares haue vowed,
  And when all denye mee,
Who will pitty my disgrace,
  Which loue might haue preuented?
There is no submission base
  Where error is repented.

O happy men, whose hopes are licenc'd
  To discourse their passion,
While women are confin'd to silence,
  Loosing wisht occasion.   20
Yet our tongues then theirs, men say,
  Are apter to be mouing:
Women are more dumbe then they,
  But in their thoughts more rouing.

When I compare my former strangenesse
  With my present doting,
I pitty men that speake in plainenesse,
  Their true hearts deuoting;
While wee with repentance iest
  At their submissiue passion.   30
Maydes, I see, are neuer blest
  That strange be but for fashion.

XVI.

Though your strangenesse frets my hart,
Yet may not I complaine:
You perswade me, 'tis but Art,
That secret loue must faine.
If another you affect,
'Tis but a shew t'auoid suspect.
Is this faire excusing? O, no, all is abusing.

Your wisht sight if I desire,
Suspitions you pretend,
Causelesse you your selfe retire,   10
While I in vaine attend.
This a Louer whets, you say,
Still made more eager by delay.
Is this faire excusing? O, no, all is abusing.

When another holds your hand,
You sweare I hold your hart:
When my Riuals close doe stand,
And I sit farre apart,
I am neerer yet then they,
Hid in your bosome, as you say.   20
Is this faire excusing? O, no, all is abusing.

Would my Riual then I were,
Or els your secret friend:
So much lesser should I feare,
And not so much attend.
They enioy you, eu'ry one,
Yet I must seeme your friend alone.
Is this faire excusing? O, no, all is abusing.

XVII.

Come away, arm'd with loues delights,
  Thy spritefull graces bring with thee,
When loues longing fights,
  They must the sticklers be.
Come quickly, come, the promis'd houre is wel-nye spent,
And pleasure being too much deferr'd looseth her best content.

Is shee come? O, how neare is shee?
How farre yet from this friendly place?
How many steps from me?
When shall I her imbrace? 10
These armes Ile spred, which onely at her sight shall close,
Attending as the starry flowre that the Suns noone-tide knowes.

XVIII.

Come, you pretty false-ey'd wanton,
  Leaue your crafty smiling:
Thinke you to escape me now
  With slipp'ry words beguiling?
No; you mockt me th'other day;
  When you got loose, you fled away;
But, since I haue caught you now,
  Ile clip your wings for flying:
Smothring kisses fast Ile heape,
  And keepe you so from crying. 10

Sooner may you count the starres,
  And number hayle downe pouring,
Tell the Osiers of the *Temmes*,
  Or *Goodwins* Sands deuouring,
Then the thicke-showr'd kisses here
  Which now thy tyred lips must beare.
Such a haruest neuer was,
  So rich and full of pleasure,
But 'tis spent as soone as reapt,
  So trustlesse is loues treasure. 20

Would it were dumb midnight now,
  When all the world lyes sleeping:
Would this place some Desert were,
  Which no man hath in keeping.
My desires should then be safe,
  And when you cry'd then would I laugh:
But if ought might breed offence,
  Loue onely should be blamed:
I would liue your seruant still,
  And you my Saint vnnamed. 30

XIX.

A secret loue or two I must confesse
  I kindly welcome for change in close playing,
Yet my deare husband I loue ne'erthelesse,
  His desires, whole or halfe, quickly allaying,
At all times ready to offer redresse :
  His owne he neuer wants but hath it duely,
  Yet twits me I keepe not touch with him truly.

The more a spring is drawne the more it flowes,
  No Lampe lesse light retaines by lightning others :
Is hee a looser his losse that nere knowes?   10
  Or is he wealthy that wast treasure smothers?
My churl vowes no man shall sent his sweet Rose,
  His owne enough and more I giue him duely,
  Yet still he twits mee I keepe not touch truly.

Wise Archers beare more than one shaft to field,
  The Venturer loads not with one ware his shipping;
Should Warriers learn but one weapon to weilde,
  Or thriue faire plants e'er the worse for the slipping?
One dish cloyes, many fresh appetite yeeld :
  Mine own Ile vse, and his he shall haue duely,   20
  Iudge then what debter can keepe touch more truly.

XX.

Her rosie cheekes, her euer smiling eyes,
Are Spheares and beds where Loue in triumph lies :
Her rubine lips, when they their pearle vnlocke,
Make them seeme as they did rise
All out of one smooth Currall Rocke.
O that of other Creatures store I knew
More worthy, and more rare :
For these are old, and shee so new,
That her to them none should compare.

O could she loue, would shee but heare a friend;   10
Or that she only knew what sighs pretend.
Her lookes inflame, yet cold as Ice is shee.
Doe or speake, all's to one end,
For what shee is that will shee be.

Yet will I neuer cease her prayse to sing,
Though she giues no regard:
For they that grace a worthlesse thing
Are onely greedy of reward.

XXI.

Where shall I refuge seeke, if you refuse mee?
In you my hope, in you my fortune lyes,
In you my life, though you vniust accuse me,
My seruice scorn, and merit vnderprise:
    O bitter griefe, that exile is become
    Reward for faith, and pittie deafe and dumbe.

Why should my firmnesse finde a seate so wau'ring?
My simple vowes, my loue you entertain'd;
Without desert the same againe disfau'ring;
Yet I my word and passion hold vnstain'd.   10
    Oh wretched me, that my chiefe ioy should breede
    My onely griefe and kindnesse pitty neede!

FINIS.

THE
DESCRIPTION

of a Maske:

 # Presented in the

Banqueting roome at *Whitehall*, on
Saint Stephens night laſt, At the Mariage of
the Right Honourable the Earle of
Somerſet: And the right noble
the Lady F R A N C E S
Howard.

De dono
pretioſa
Emptor

Written by *Thomas Campion.*

Whereunto are annexed diuers choyſe *Ayres* compoſed
for this Maske that may be ſung with a ſingle voyce
to the Lute or Baſe-Viall.

LONDON
Printed by E. *A.* for *Laurence L'isle*, dwelling in Paules
Church-yard, at the ſigne of the *Tygers* head.
1 6 1 4.

Pulchro pulchra datur, sociali fœdere amanti
Tandem nubit amans; ecquid amabilius?

Veræ vt supersint nuptiæ
Præite duplici face:
Prætendat alteram necesse
Hymen, alteram par est Amor.

Vni ego mallem placuisse docto,
Candido, et fastu sine iudicanti,
Millium quam millibus imperitorum
Inque videntûm.

The description of a Masque, Presented in the Banqueting roome at *Whitehall*,

On St. *Stephens* night last : At the Mariage
of the right Honourable the Earle of
Somerset, & the right noble the
Lady *Frances Howard*.

In ancient times, when any man sought to shadowe or heighten his Inuention, he had store of feyned persons readie for his purpose ; as *Satyres*, *Nymphes*, and their like : such were then in request and beliefe among the vulgar. But in our dayes, although 10 they haue not vtterly lost their vse, yet finde they so little credit, that our moderne writers haue rather transferred their fictions to the persons of Enchaunters and Commaunders of spirits, as that excellent Poet *Torquato Tasso* hath done, and many others.

In imitation of them (having a presentation in hand for Persons of high State) I grounded my whole Inuention upon Inchauntmens and several transformations : The work-manship whereof was vndertaken by M. *Constantine*, an Italian, Architect to our late Prince *Henry* : but he being too much of him selfe, and no way to be drawne to impart his intentions, fayled so farre in the assurance 20 he gaue that the mayne inuention, euen at the last cast, was of force drawne into a farre narrower compasse then was from the beginning intended : The description whereof, as it was performed, I will as briefely as I can deliuer. The place wherein the Maske was presented, being the Banquetting house at White Hall : the vpper part, where the State is placed, was Theatred with Pillars, Scaffolds, and all things answerable to the sides of the Roome. At the lower end of the Hall, before the Sceane, was made an Arch Tryumphall, passing beautifull, which enclosed the whole Workes : The Sceane it selfe (the Curtaine being drawne) was in this manner 30 diuided.

On the vpper part there was formed a Skye of Clowdes very arteficially shadowed. On either side of the Sceane belowe was set a high Promontory, and on either of them stood three large pillars of golde : the one Promontory was bounded with a Rocke standing in the Sea, the other with a Wood ; In the midst betwene them apeared a Sea in perspectiue with ships, some cunningly painted, some arteficially sayling. On the front of the Sceane, on either side, was a beautifull garden, with sixe seates a peece to receaue the Maskers : behinde them the mayne Land, and in the middest a paire of stayres made exceeding curiously in the form of a Schalop shell. And in this manner was the eye first of all entertayned. After the King, Queene, and Prince were placed, 10 and preparation was made for the beginning of the Maske, there entred foure Squires, who as soone as they approached neare the Presence, humbly bowing themselues, spake as followeth.

The first Squire.

That fruite that neither dreads the *Syrian* heats,
Nor the sharp frosts which churlish *Boreas* threats,
The fruite of *Peace* and *Ioy* our wishes bring
To this high State, in a Perpetuall Spring.
Then pardon (Sacred Maiestie) our griefe
Vnseasonably that presseth for reliefe.
The ground whereof (if your blest eares can spare
20 A short space of Attention) we'le declare.

Great Honors Herrald, *Fame*, hauing Proclaym'd
This Nuptiall feast, and with it all enflam'd,
From euery quarter of the earth three Knights
(In Courtship seene, as well as Martiall fights)
Assembled in the Continent, and there
Decreed this night A solemne Seruice here.
For which, by sixe and sixe embarqu'd they were
In seuerall Keeles ; their Sayles for *Britaine* bent.
But (they that neuer fauour'd good intent)
30 Deformed *Errour*, that enchaunting fiend,
And wing-tongu'd *Rumor*, his infernall freind,
With *Curiositie* and *Credulitie*,
Both Sorceresses, all in hate agree
Our purpose to divert ; in vain they striue,
For we in spight of them came neere t'ariue,
When sodainly (as Heauen and hell had met)
A storme confus'd against our Tackle beat,
Seuering the Ships : but after what befell
Let these relate, my tongu's too weake to tell.

The second Squire.

A strange and sad Os'ent our Knights distrest;
For while the Tempests fierye rage increast,
About our Deckes and Hatches, loe, appeare
Serpents, as *Lerna* had been pour'd out there,
Crawling about vs; which feare to eschew,
The Knights the Tackle climb'd, and hung in view,
When violently a flash of lightning came,
And from our sights did beare them in the flame.
Which past, no Serpent there was to be seene,   10
And all was husht, as storme had neuer beene.

The third Squire.

At Sea their mischeifes grewe, but ours at Land,
For being by chance arriu'd, while our Knights stand
To view their storme-tost friends on two Cliffes neere,
Thence, loe, they vanish'd, and sixe Pillars were
Fixt in their footsteps; Pillars all of golde,
Faire to our eyes, but wofull to beholde.

The fourth Squire.

Thus with prodigious hate and crueltie,   20
Our good Knights for their loue afflicted be;
But, ô, protect vs now, Maiesticke Grace,
For see, those curst Enchanters presse in place
That our past sorrowes wrought: these, these alone
Turne all the world into confusion.

Towards the end of this speech, two Enchanters, and two Enchan-
teresses appeare: *Error* first, in a skin coate scaled like a Serpent,
and an antick habit painted with Snakes, a haire of curled Snakes,
and a deformed visard. With him *Rumor* in a skin coate full of
winged Tongues, and ouer it an antick robe; on his head a Cap like 30
a tongue, with a large paire of wings to it.

Curiosity in a skin coate full of eyes, and an antick habit ouer it,
a fantastick Cap full of Eyes.

Credulity in the like habit painted with eares, and an antick Cap
full of eares.

When they had whispered a while as if they had reioyced at the
wrongs which they had done to the Knights, the Musick and their
Daunce began: strait forth rusht the foure Windes confusedly, The
Easterne Winde in a skin coate of the colour of the Sun-rising, with
a yellow haire, and wings both on his shoulders and feete.   40

The Westerne Winde in a skin coate of darke crimson, with crimson
haire and wings.

The Southerne Winde in a darke russet skin coate, haire and wings sutable.

The Northern Winde in a grisled skin coate, with haire and wings accordingly.

After them in confusion came the foure Elements : *Earth*, in a skin coate of grasse greene, a mantle painted full of trees, plants and flowers, and on his head an oke growing.

Water, in a skin coate waved, with a mantle full of fishes, on his head a Dolphin.

10 *Ayre*, in a skye-coloured skin coate, with a mantle painted with Fowle, and on his head an Eagle.

Fire, in a skin coate, and a mantle painted with flames : on his head a cap of flames, with a Salamander in the midst thereof.

Then entred the foure parts of the earth in a confused measure.

Europe in the habit of an Empresse, with an Emperiall Crowne on her head.

Asia in a Persian Ladies habit, with a Crowne on her head.

Africa like a Queene of the Moores, with a crown.

America in a skin coate of the colour of the iuyce of Mulberies, on 20 her head large round brims of many coloured feathers, and in the midst of it a small Crowne.

All these hauing daunced together in a strange kind of confusion, past away, by foure and foure.

At which time, *Eternity* appeared in a long blew Taffata robe, painted with Starres, and on her head a Crowne.

Next, came the three Destinies, in long robes of white Taffata like aged women, with Garlands of *Narcissus* Flowers on their heads ; and in their left hands they carried distaffes according to the descriptions of *Plato* and *Catullus*, but in their right hands they carried altogether 30 a Tree of Golde.

After them, came Harmony with nine Musitians more, in long Taffata robes and caps of Tinsell, with Garlands guilt, playing and singing this Song.

Chorus.

Vanish, vanish hence, confusion;
Dimme not Hymens *goulden light*
　　With false illusion.
The Fates shall doe him right,
And faire Eternitie,
40　　*Who passe through all enchantements free.*

Eternitie singes alone.

Bring away this Sacred Tree,
The Tree of Grace and Bountie,
　　Set it in Bel-Annas *eye,*

For she, she, only she
  Can all Knotted spels vnty.
Pull'd from the Stocke, let her blest Hands conuay
  To any suppliant Hand, a bough,
   And let that Hand aduance it now
Against a Charme, that Charme shall fade away.

Toward the end of this Song the three destinies set the Tree of Golde
before the Queene.

Chorus.

Since Knightly valour rescues Dames distressed,   10
By Vertuous Dames let charm'd Knights be released.

 After this Chorus, one of the Squires speakes.

Since Knights by valour rescue Dames distrest,
Let them be by the Queene of Dames releast.
So sing the Destinyes, who neuer erre,
Fixing this Tree of Grace and Bountie heere,
From which for our enchaunted Knights we craue
A branche, pull'd by your Sacred Hand, to haue ;
That we may beare it as the Fates direct,
And manifest your glory in th' effect.   20
In vertues fauour then, and Pittie now,
(Great Queene) vouchsafe vs a diuine touch't bough.

At the end of this speech, the Queene puld a branch from the Tree
and gaue it to a Nobleman, who deliuered it to one of the Squires.

A Song while the Squires descend with the bough toward the Scene.

 Goe, happy man, like th' Euening Starre,
 Whose beames to Bride-groomes well-come are :
 May neither Hagge nor Feind withstand
 The pow're of thy Victorious Hand.
  The Vncharm'd Knights surrender now, 30
  By vertue of thy raised Bough.

 Away, Enchauntements, Vanish quite,
 No more delay our longing sight :
 'Tis fruitelesse to contend with Fate,
 Who giues vs pow're against your hate.
  Braue Knights, in Courtly pompe appeare
  For now are you long-look't for heere.

Then out of the ayre a cloude descends, discouering sixe of the Knights alike, in strange and sumptuous atires, and withall on either side of the Cloud, on the two Promontories, the other sixe Maskers are sodainly transformed out of the pillars of golde; at which time, while they all come forward to the dancing-place, this Chorus is sung, and on the sodaine the whole Sceane is changed: for whereas before all seemed to be done at the sea and sea coast, now the Promontories are sodainly remooued, and London with the Thames is very arteficially presented in their place.

10   The Squire lifts vp the Bough.

Chorus.

Vertue and Grace, in spight of Charmes,
Haue now redeem'd our men at Armes,
Ther's no inchauntement can withstand,
Where Fate directs the happy hand.

The Maskers first Daunce.

The third Song of three partes, with a Chorus of fiue partes,
sung after the first Daunce.

While dancing rests, fit place to musicke graunting,
20 *Good spe.'s the Fates shall breath, al enuy daunting,*
Kind eares with ioy enchaunting, chaunting.

Chorus.
Io, Io Hymen.

Like lookes, like hearts, like loues are linck't together:
So must the Fates be pleas'd, so come they hether,
To make this Ioy perseuer, euer.

Chorus.
Io, Io Hymen.

Loue decks the spring, her buds to th' ayre exposing,
30 *Such fire here in these bridall Breasts reposing,*
We leaue with charmes enclosing, closing.

Chorus.
Io, Io Hymen.

The Maskers second Daunce.

The fourth Song, a Dialogue of three, with a Chorus after the second Daunce.

1 Let vs now sing of Loues delight,
   For he alone is Lord to night.

2 Some friendship betweene man and man prefer,
   But I th' affection betweene man and wife.

3 What good can be in life,
   Whereof no fruites appeare?

1 Set is that Tree in ill houre,   10
   That yeilds neither fruite nor flowre.

2 How can man Perpetuall be,
   But in his owne Posteritie?

Chorus.

That pleasure is of all most bountifull and kinde,
That fades not straight, but leaues a liuing Ioy behinde.

After this Dialogue the Maskers daunce with the Ladies, wherein spending as much time as they held fitting, they returned to the seates prouided for them.

  Straight in the Thames appeared foure Barges with skippers in 20 them, and withall this song was sung.

> Come a shore, come, merrie mates,
> With your nimble heeles and pates:
> Summon eu'ry man his Knight,
> Enough honour'd is this night.
> Now, let your Sea-borne Goddesse come,
> Quench these lights, and make all dombe.
> Some sleepe; others let her call:
> And so Godnight to all, godnight to all.

At the conclusion of this song arriued twelue skippers in red capps, 30 with short cassocks and long slopps wide at the knees, of white canvas striped with crimson, white gloves and Pomps, and red stockins : these twelue daunced a braue and liuely daunce, shouting and tryumphing after their manner.

  After this followed the Maskers last daunce, wherewith they retyred.

  At the Embarking of the Knights, the Squires approach the state, and speake.

The first Squire.

All that was euer ask't, by vow of *Ioue*,
To blesse a state with, Plentie, Honor, Loue,
Power, Triumph, priuate pleasure, publique peace,
Sweete springs, and *Autumns* filld with due increase,
All these, and what good els thought can supplie,
Euer attend your Triple Maiestie.

The second Squire.

All blessings which the *Fates*, Propheticke, Sung,
10   At *Peleus* Nuptialls, and what euer tongue
Can figure more, this night, and aye betide,
The honour'd Bride-groome and the honour'd Bride.

All the Squires together.

Thus speakes in vs th' affection of our Knights,
Wishing your health, and Miriads of goodnights.

The Squires speeches being ended, this Song is Sung while the
Boates passe way.

20   *Hast aboord, hast now away;*
Hymen frownes at your delay:
Hymen doth long nights affect;
Yeild him then his due respect.
The Sea-borne Goddesse straight will come,
Quench these lights, and make all dombe.
Some Sleepe; others she will call:
And so godnight to all, godnight to all.

FINIS.

The Names of the Maskers.

1	The Duke of *Lennox.*	7	The Lord *Scroope.*
2	The Earle of *Pembrooke.*	8	The Lord *North.*
3	The Earle of *Dorset.*	9	The Lord *Hayes.*
4	The Earle of *Salisburie.*	10	Sir *Thomas Howard.*
5	The Earle of *Mountgomerie.*	11	Sir *Henry Howard.*
6	The Lord *Walden.*	12	Sir *Charles Howard.*

FINIS.

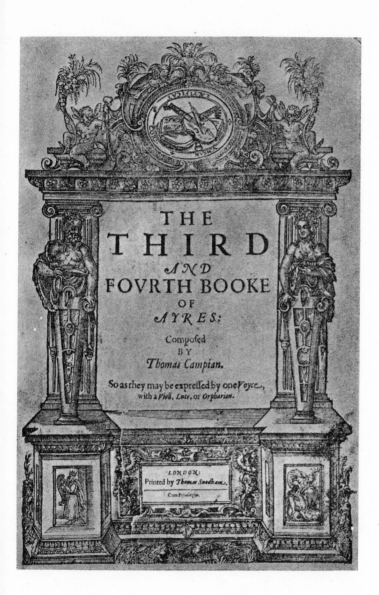

THE
THIRD
AND
FOVRTH BOOKE
OF
AYRES:

Compoſed
BY
Thomas Campian.

So as they may be expreſſed by one *Voyce*,
with a *Violl, Lute,* or *Orpharion.*

LONDON:
Printed by *Thomas Snodham,*
Cum Priuilegio.

To face p. 156

A Table of all the Songs contayned in
the two Bookes following.

FINIS.

TO MY HONOVRABLE FRIEND,

S^R THOMAS MOVNSON, *KNIGHT*

AND BARONET.

Since now those clouds, that lately ouer-cast
Your Fame and Fortune, are disperst at last:
And now since all to you fayre greetings make;
Some out of loue, and some for pitties sake:
Shall I but with a common stile salute
Your new enlargement? or stand onely mute?
I, to whose trust and care you durst commit
Your pined health, when Arte despayr'd of it?
I, that in your affliction often view'd
In you the fruits of manly fortitude,   10
Patience, and euen constancie of minde,
That Rocke-like stood, and scorn'd both waue, and winde?
Should I, for all your ancient loue to me,
Endow'd with waighty fauours, silent be?
Your merits and my gratitude forbid
That eyther should in *Lethean* Gulfe lye hid.
But how shall I this worke of fame expresse?
How can I better, after pensiuenesse,
Then with light straynes of Musicke, made to moue
Sweetly with the wide-spreading plumes of loue?   20
These youth-born *Ayres,* then, prisoned in this Booke,
Which in your Bowres much of their beeing tooke,
Accept as a kinde offring from that hand
Which, ioyn'd with heart, your vertue may command.
Who loue a sure friend, as all good men doe,
Since such you are, let these affect you to:
And may the ioyes of that Crowne neuer end,
That innocence doth pitty and defend.

Your deuoted,

THOMAS CAMPIAN.

I.

Oft haue I sigh'd for him that heares me not;
Who absent hath both loue and mee forgot.
O yet I languish still through his delay:
Dayes seeme as yeares when wisht friends breake their day.

Had hee but lou'd as common louers vse,
His faithlesse stay some kindnesse would excuse:
O yet I languish still, still constant mourne
For him that can breake vowes but not returne.

II.

Now let her change and spare not:
Since she proues strange I care not:
Fain'd loue charm'd so my delight
That still I doted on her sight.
But she is gone, new ioies imbracing
And my desires disgracing.

When did I erre in blindnesse?
Or vexe her with vnkindnesse?
If my cares seru'd her alone,
Why is shee thus vntimely gone?   10
True loue abides to th' houre of dying:
False loue is euer flying.

False, then farewell for euer:
Once false proues faithful neuer:
Hee that boasts now of thy loue,
Shall soone my present fortunes proue.
Were he as faire as bright *Adonis*,
Faith is not had, where none is.

III.

Were my hart as some mens are, thy errours would not moue me;
But thy faults I curious finde and speake because I loue thee:
Patience is a thing diuine and farre, I grant, aboue me.

Foes sometimes befriend vs more, our blacker deedes obiecting,
Then th' obsequious bosome guest, with false respect affecting,
Friendship is the glasse of Truth, our hidden staines detecting.

While I vse of eyes enioy and inward light of reason,
Thy obseruer will I be and censor, but in season :
Hidden mischiefe to conceale in State, and Loue is treason.

IIII.

Maydes are simple, some men say,
They, forsooth, will trust no men.
But should they mens wils obey,
Maides were very simple then.

Truth, a rare flower now is growne,
Few men weare it in their hearts ;
Louers are more easily knowne
By their follies, then deserts.

Safer may we credit giue
To a faithlesse wandring Iew   10
Then a young mans vowes beleeue
When he sweares his loue is true.

Loue they make a poore blinde childe,
But let none trust such as hee :
Rather then to be beguil'd,
Euer let me simple be.

V.

So tyr'd are all my thoughts, that, sence and spirits faile :
Mourning I pine, and know not what I ayle.
O what can yeeld ease to a minde
        Ioy in nothing that can finde?

How are my powres fore-spoke? What strange distaste is this?
Hence, cruell hate of that which sweetest is :
Come, come delight, make my dull braine
        Feele once heate of ioy againe.

The louers teares are sweet, their mouer makes them so ;
Proud of a wound the bleeding Souldiers grow.   10
Poore I alone, dreaming, endure
        Griefe that knowes nor cause, nor cure.

And whence can all this grow? euen from an idle minde,
That no delight in any good can finde.
Action alone makes the soule blest:
        Vertue dyes with too much rest.

VI.

Why presumes thy pride on that that must so priuate be,
Scarce that it can good be cal'd, though it seemes best to thee,
Best of all that Nature fram'd or curious eye can see?

'Tis thy beauty, foolish Maid, that, like a blossome, growes;
Which who viewes no more enioyes than on a bush a Rose,
That by manies handling fades; and thou art one of those.

If to one thou shalt proue true and all beside reiect,
Then art thou but one mans good; which yeelds a poore effect;
For the common'st good by farre deserues the best respect.

But if for this goodnesse thou thy selfe wilt common make, 10
Thou art then not good at all; so thou canst no way take
But to proue the meanest good, or else all good forsake.

Be not then of beauty proud, but so her colours beare
That they proue not staines to her that them for grace should
    weare:
So shalt thou to all more fayre than thou wert borne appeare.

VII.

    Kinde are her answeres,
      But her performance keeps no day;
Breaks time, as dancers
      From their own Musicke when they stray:
      All her free fauors and smooth words,
Wing my hopes in vaine.
O did euer voice so sweet but only fain?
      Can true loue yeeld such delay,
      Conuerting ioy to pain?

    Lost is our freedome,   10
      When we submit to women so:
Why doe wee neede them,
      When in their best they worke our woe?

There is no wisedome
Can alter ends, by Fate prefixt.
O why is the good of man with euill mixt?
Neuer were days yet cal'd two,
But one night went betwixt.

VIII.

O griefe, O spight, to see poore Vertue scorn'd,
Truth far exil'd, False arte lou'd, Vice ador'd,
Free Justice sold, worst causes best adorned,
Right cast by Powre, Pittie in vaine implor'd!
O who in such an age could wish to liue,
When none can haue or hold, but such as giue?

O times! O men! to Nature rebels growne,
Poore in desert, in name rich, proud of shame;
Wise, but in ill! Your stiles are not your owne,
Though dearely bought, honour is honest fame.   10
Old Stories onely, goodnesse now containe,
And the true wisedome that is iust, and plaine.

IX.

O neuer to be moued,
O beauty vnrelenting!
Hard hart, too dearely loued!
Fond loue, too late repenting!
Why did I dream of too much blisse?
Deceitfull hope was cause of this.
O heare mee speake this, and no more,
Liue you in ioy, while I my woes deplore!

All comforts despayred
Distaste your bitter scorning;   10
Great sorrows vnrepayred
Admit no meane in mourning:
Dye, wretch, since hope from thee is fled;
He that must dye is better dead.
O dear delight yet, ere I dye,
Some pitty shew, though you reliefe deny.

X.

Breake now, my heart, and dye! Oh no, she may relent.
Let my despaire preuayle! O stay, hope is not spent.
Should she now fixe one smile on thee, where were despaire?
  The losse is but easy, which smiles can repayre.
  A stranger would please thee, if she were as fayre.

Her must I loue or none, so sweet none breathes as shee;
The more is my despayre, alas, shee loues not mee:
But cannot time make way for loue through ribs of steele?
  The Grecian, inchanted all parts but the heele,
  At last a shaft daunted, which his hart did feele.   10

XI.

If Loue loues truth, then women doe not loue;
Their passions all are but dissembled shewes;
Now kinde and free of fauour if they proue,
Their kindnes straight a tempest ouerthrowes.
  Then as a Sea-man the poore louer fares;
  The storme drownes him ere hee can drowne his cares.

But why accuse I women that deceiue?
Blame then the Foxes for their subtile wile:
They first from Nature did their craft receiue:
It is a womans nature to beguile.   10
  Yet some, I grant, in louing stedfast grow;
  But such by vse are made, not nature, so.

O why had Nature power at once to frame
Deceit and Beauty, traitors both to Loue?
O would Deceit had dyed when Beauty came
With her diuinenesse eu'ry heart to moue!
  Yet doe we rather wish, what ere befall,
  To haue fayre women false then none at all.

XII.

  Now winter nights enlarge
  The number of their houres;
And clouds their stormes discharge
  Upon the ayrie towres.

Let now the chimneys blaze
　And cups o'erflow with wine,
Let well-tun'd words amaze
　With harmonie diuine.
Now yellow waxen lights
　Shall waite on hunny Loue　　　　　　　10
While youthfull Reuels, Masks, and Courtly sights,
　Sleepes leaden spels remoue.

This time doth well dispence
　With louers long discourse;
Much speech hath some defence,
　Though beauty no remorse.
All doe not all things well;
　Some measures comely tread;
Some knotted Ridles tell;
　Some Poems smoothly read.　　　　　　20
The Summer hath his ioyes,
　And Winter his delights;
Though Loue and all his pleasures are but toyes,
　They shorten tedious nights.

XIII.

Awake, thou spring of speaking grace, mute rest becomes not
　thee;
The fayrest women, while they sleepe, and Pictures, equall bee.
　O come and dwell in loues discourses,
　　Old renuing, new creating.
　The words which thy rich tongue discourses
　　Are not of the common rating.

Thy voyce is as an Eccho cleare which Musicke doth beget,
Thy speech is as an Oracle which none can counterfeit:
　For thou alone, without offending,
　　Hast obtain'd power of enchanting;　　　　10
　And I could heare thee without ending,
　　Other comfort neuer wanting.

Some little reason brutish liues with humane glory share;
But language is our proper grace, from which they seuer'd are.
　As brutes in reason man surpasses,
　　Men in speech excell each other:
　If speech be then the best of graces,
　　Doe it not in slumber smother.

XIIII.

What is it all that men possesse, among themselues conuersing?
Wealth or fame, or some such boast, scarce worthy the rehearsing.
Women onely are mens good, with them in loue conuersing.

If weary, they prepare vs rest; if sicke, their hand attends vs;
When with griefe our hearts are prest, their comfort best be-
    friends vs:
Sweet or sowre, they willing goe to share what fortune sends vs.

What pretty babes with paine they beare, our name and form
    presenting!
What we get, how wise they keepe! by sparing, wants pre-
    uenting;
Sorting all their houshold cares to our obseru'd contenting.

All this, of whose large vse I sing, in two words is expressed;
Good wife is the good I praise, if by good men possessed; 11
Bad with bad in ill sute well; but good with good liue blessed.

XV.

Fire that must flame is with apt fuell fed,
Flowers that will thriue in sunny soyle are bred;
How can a hart feele heate that no hope findes?
Or can hee loue on whom no comfort shines?

Fayre, I confesse there's pleasure in your sight:
Sweet, you haue powre, I grant, of all delight:
But what is all to mee, if I haue none?
Churle that you are, t'inioy such wealth alone.

Prayers moue the heau'ns but finde no grace with you;
Yet in your lookes a heauenly forme I view: 10
Then will I pray againe, hoping to finde,
As well as in your lookes, heau'n in your minde.

Saint of my heart, Queene of my life, and loue,
O let my vowes thy louing spirit moue:
Let me no longer mourne through thy disdaine,
But with one touch of grace cure all my paine.

XVI.

If thou long'st so much to learne (sweet boy) what 'tis to loue,
Doe but fixe thy thought on mee and thou shalt quickly proue.
    Little sute, at first, shal win
        Way to thy abasht desire,
    But then will I hedge thee in
        Salamander-like with fire.

With thee dance I will, and sing, and thy fond dalliance
    beare;
Wee the grouy hils will climbe, and play the wantons there;
    Other whiles wee'le gather flowres,
        Lying dalying on the grasse,   10
    And thus our delightfull howres
        Full of waking dreames shall passe.

When thy ioyes were thus at height, my loue should turne
    from thee;
Old acquaintance then should grow as strange as strange might
    be;
    Twenty riuals, thou should'st finde,
        Breaking all their hearts for mee,
    When to all Ile proue more kinde
        And more forward then to thee.

Thus thy silly youth enrag'd, would soone my loue defie;
But, alas, poore soule too late; clipt wings can neuer flye.   20
    Those sweet houres which wee had past,
        Cal'd to minde thy heart would burne;
    And could'st thou flye ne'er so fast,
        They would make thee straight returne.

XVII.

    Shall I come, sweet Loue, to thee,
        When the eu'ning beames are set?
    Shall I not excluded be?
        Will you finde no fained lett?
    Let me not, for pitty, more,
    Tell the long houres at your dore.

Who can tell what theefe or foe,
  In the couert of the night,
For his prey will worke my woe,
  Or through wicked foule despight :   10
So may I dye vnredrest,
Ere my long loue be possest.

But to let such dangers passe,
  Which a louers thoughts disdaine,
'Tis enough in such a place
  To attend loues ioyes in vaine.
Doe not mocke me in thy bed,
While these cold nights freeze me dead.

XVIII.

Thrice tosse these Oaken ashes in the ayre,
Thrice sit thou mute in this inchanted chayre ;
And thrice three times tye vp this true loues knot,
And murmur soft, shee will, or shee will not.

Goe burn these poys'nous weedes in yon blew fire,
These Screech-owles fethers and this prickling bryer ;
This Cypresse gathered at a dead mans graue ;
That all thy feares and cares, an end may haue.

Then come, you Fayries, dance with me a round ;
Melt her hard hart with your melodious sound :   10
In vaine are all the charms I can deuise :
She hath an Arte to breake them with her eyes.

XIX.

  Be thou then my beauty named,
Since thy will is to be mine :
  For by that am I enflamed,
Which on all alike doth shine.
  Others may the light admire,
  I onely truely feele the fire.

  But if lofty titles moue thee,
Challenge then a Sou'raignes place :
  Say I honour when I loue thee ;
Let me call thy kindnesse grace.   10
  State and Loue things diuers bee,
  Yet will we teach them to agree.

Or if this be not sufficing;
Be thou stil'd my Goddesse then:
I will loue thee sacrificing;
In thine honour, Hymnes Ile pen.
To be thine, what canst thou more?
Ile loue thee, serue thee, and adore.

XX.

Fire, fire, fire, fire.
Loe here I burne in such desire
That all the teares that I can straine
Out of mine idle empty braine
Cannot allay my scorching paine.
Come *Trent*, and *Humber*, and fayre *Thames*;
Dread Ocean, haste with all thy streames:
    And if you cannot quench my fire,
    O drowne both mee and my desire.

Fire, fire, fire, fire.   10
There is no hell to my desire.
See, all the Riuers backward flye,
And th' Ocean doth his waues deny,
For feare my heate should drink them dry.
Come, heau'nly showres, then, pouring downe;
Come you that once the world did drowne:
Some then you spar'd, but now saue all,
That else must burne, and with mee fall.

XXI.

O sweet delight, O more than humane blisse,
With her to liue that euer louing is;
To heare her speake, whose words so well are plac't,
That she by them, as they in her are grac't:
    Those lookes to view, that feast the viewers eye,
    How blest is he that may so liue and dye!

Such loue as this the golden times did know,
When all did reape, yet none tooke care to sow:
Such loue as this an endlesse Summer makes,
And all distaste from fraile affection takes.   10
    So lou'd, so blest, in my belou'd am I;
    Which till their eyes ake, let yron men enuy.

XXII.

Thus I resolue, and time hath taught me so;
Since she is fayre and euer kinde to me,
Though she be wilde and wanton-like in shew,
Those little staines in youth I will not see.
   That she be constant heauen I oft implore:
   If pray'rs preuaile not, I can doe no more.

Palme tree the more you presse, the more it growes:
Leaue it alone, it will not much exceede.
Free beauty if you striue to yoke, you lose,
And for affection strange distaste you breede.   10
   What Nature hath not taught, no Arte can frame:
   Wilde borne be wilde still, though by force made tame.

XXIII.

   Come, O come, my lifes delight,
Let me not in langour pine:
   Loue loues no delay; thy sight,
The more enioy'd, the more diuine:
     O come, and take from mee
     The paine of being depriu'd of thee.

   Thou all sweetnesse dost enclose,
Like a little world of blisse.
   Beauty guards thy lookes: the Rose
In them pure and eternall is.   10
     Come, then, and make thy flight
     As swift to me as heau'nly light.

XXIIII.

   Could my heart more tongues imploy
Than it harbors thoughts of griefe,
   It is now so farre from ioy,
That it scarce could aske reliefe.
     Truest hearts by deedes vnkinde
     To despayre are most enclin'd.

   Happy mindes that can redeeme
Their engagements how they please;
   That no ioyes, or hopes esteeme,
Halfe so pretious as their ease.   10
     Wisedom should prepare men so
     As if they did all foreknow.

Q

Yet no Art or Caution can
Growne affections easily change;
Vse is such a Lord of Man
That he brookes worst what is strange.
Better neuer to be blest
Than to loose all at the best.

XXV.

Sleepe, angry beauty, sleep, and feare not me.
For who a sleeping Lyon dares prouoke?
It shall suffice me here to sit and see
Those lips shut vp that neuer kindely spoke.
   What sight can more content a louers minde
   Then beauty seeming harmlesse, if not kinde?

My words haue charm'd her, for secure shee sleepes;
Though guilty much of wrong done to my loue;
And in her slumber, see, shee, close-ey'd, weepes:
Dreames often more then waking passions moue.   10
   Pleade, sleepe, my cause, and make her soft like thee,
   That shee in peace may wake and pitty mee.

XXVI.

Silly boy, 'tis ful Moone yet, thy night as day shines clearely;
Had thy youth but wit to feare, thou couldst not loue so dearely.
Shortly wilt thou mourne when all thy pleasures are bereaued;
Little knowes he how to loue that neuer was deceiued.

This is thy first mayden flame, that triumphes yet vnstayned;
All is artlesse now you speake, not one word yet is fayned;
All is heau'n that you behold, and all your thoughts are blessed;
But no Spring can want his Fall, each *Troylus* hath his *Cresseid.*

Thy well-order'd lockes ere long shall rudely hang neglected;
And thy liuely pleasant cheare reade griefe on earth deiected. 10
Much then wilt thou blame thy Saint, that made thy heart so
   holy,
And with sighs confesse, in loue, that too much faith is folly.

Yet be iust and constant still; Loue may beget a wonder,
Not vnlike a Summers frost, or Winters fatall thunder.
He that holds his Sweet-hart true vnto his day of dying,
Liues of all that euer breath'd most worthy the enuying.

XXVII.

Neuer loue vnlesse you can
Beare with all the faults of man:
Men sometimes will iealous bee,
Though but little cause they see;
   And hang the head, as discontent,
   And speake what straight they will repent.

Men that but one Saint adore,
Make a shew of loue to more:
Beauty must be scorn'd in none,
Though but truely seru'd in one: 10
   For what is courtship, but disguise?
   True hearts may haue dissembling eyes.

Men when their affaires require,
Must a while themselues retire:
Sometimes hunt, and sometimes hawke,
And not euer sit and talke.
   If these, and such like you can beare,
   Then like, and loue, and neuer fear.

XXVIII.

So quicke, so hot, so mad is thy fond sute,
So rude, so tedious growne, in vrging mee,
That faine I would with losse make thy tongue mute,
And yeeld some little grace to quiet thee:
   An houre with thee I care not to conuerse,
   For I would not be counted too peruerse,

But roofes too hot would proue for men all fire;
And hils too high for my vnused pace;
The groue is charg'd with thornes and the bold bryer;
Gray Snakes the meadowes shrowde in euery place: 10
   A yellow Frog, alas, will fright me so,
   As I should start and tremble as I goe.

Since then I can on earth no fit roome finde,
In heauen I am resolu'd with you to meete,
Till then, for Hopes sweet sake, rest your tir'd minde,
And not so much as see mee in the streete:
   A heauenly meeting one day wee shall haue,
   But neuer, as you dreame, in bed, or graue.

XXIX.

Shall I then hope when faith is fled?
Can I seeke loue when hope is gone?
Or can I liue when Loue is dead?
Poorely hee liues, that can loue none.
    Her vowes are broke, and I am free;
    Shee lost her faith in loosing mee.

When I compare mine owne euents,
When I weigh others like annoy;
All doe but heape vp discontents
That on a beauty build their ioy.   10
    Thus I of all complaine, since shee
    All faith hath lost in loosing mee.

So my deare freedome haue I gain'd,
Through her vnkindnesse and disgrace,
Yet could I euer liue enchain'd,
As shee my seruice did embrace.
    But shee is chang'd, and I am free:
    Faith failing her, Loue dyed in mee.

TO MY WORTHY FRIEND,

Mr Iohn Mounson, Sonne and Heyre to
Sir Thomas Mounson, Knight and Baronet.

On you th' affections of your Fathers Friends,
With his Inheritance by right descends;
But you your gracefull youth so wisely guide
That his you hold, and purchase much beside.
Loue is the fruit of Vertue, for whose sake
Men onely liking each to other take.
If sparkes of vertue shin'd not in you then,
So well how could you winne the hearts of men?
And since that honour and well-suted Prayse
Is Vertues Golden Spurre, let mee now rayse   10
Vnto an act mature your tender age;
This halfe commending to your Patronage,
Which from your Noble Fathers, but one side,
Ordain'd to doe you honour, doth diuide.
And so my loue betwixt you both I part,
On each side placing you as neare my heart

Yours euer,

THOMAS CAMPIAN.

TO THE READER.

*The Apothecaries haue Bookes of Gold, whose leaues being opened
are so light as that they are subiect to be shaken with the least breath,* 20
*yet rightly handled, they serue both for ornament and vse; such are
light Ayres.   But if any squeamish stomackes shall checke at two or
three vaine Ditties in the end of this Booke, let them powre off the clear-
est, and leaue those as dregs in the bottome.   Howsoeuer, if they be but
conferred with the* Canterbury Tales *of that venerable Poet* Chaucer,
*they will then appeare toothsome enough.   Some words are in these
Bookes, which haue beene cloathed in Musicke by others, and I am
content they then serued their turne: yet giue mee now leaue to make
vse of mine owne.   Likewise you may finde here some three or four
Songs that haue beene published before, but for them, I referre you* 30
to the Players Bill, that is stiled, Newly reuiued, with Additions, *for
you shall finde all of them reformed, eyther in Words or Notes.   To
be briefe, all these Songs are mine, if you expresse them well, otherwise
they are your owne.   Farewell.*

Yours, as you are his,

THOMAS CAMPIAN.

I.

Leaue prolonging thy distresse :
All delayes afflict the dying.
Many lost sighes long I spent, to her for mercy crying ;
    But now, vaine mourning, cease :
    Ile dye, and mine owne griefes release.

Thus departing from this light
To those shades that end all sorrow,
Yet a small time of complaint, a little breath Ile borrow,
    To tell my once delight
    I dye alone through her despight.   10

II.

Respect my faith, regard my seruice past ;
The hope you wing'd call home to you at last.
Great prise it is that I in you shall gaine,
So great for you hath been my losse and paine.
    My wits I spent and time for you alone,
    Obseruing you and loosing all for one.

Some rais'd to rich estates in this time are,
That held their hopes to mine inferiour farre :
Such, scoffing mee, or pittying me, say thus,
Had hee not lou'd, he might haue liu'd like vs.   10
    O then, deare sweet, for loue and pitties sake
    My faith reward, and from me scandall take.

III.

Thou ioy'st, fond boy, to be by many loued :
To haue thy beauty of most dames approued ;
For this dost thou thy natiue worth disguise
And play'st the Sycophant t' obserue their eyes ;
    Thy glass thou councel'st more t'adorne thy skin,
    That first should schoole thee to be fayre within.

'Tis childish to be caught with Pearle, or Amber,
And woman-like too much to cloy the chamber ;
Youths should the Field affect, heate their rough Steedes,
Their hardned nerues to fit for better deedes.   10
    Is 't not more ioy strong Holds to force with swords
    Than womens weakenesse take with lookes or words ?

Men that doe noble things all purchase glory:
One man for one braue Act haue prou'd a story:
But if that one tenne thousand Dames o'ercame,
Who would record it, if not to his shame?
    'Tis farre more conquest with one to liue true
    Then euery houre to triumph Lord of new.

IIII.

Vaile, loue, mine eyes; O hide from me
The plagues that charge the curious minde:
If beauty priuate will not be,
Suffice it yet that she proues kinde.
    Who can vsurp heau'ns light alone?
    Stars were not made to shine on one!

Griefes past recure fooles try to heale,
That greater harmes on lesse inflict,
The pure offend by too much zeale,
Affection should not be too strict.   10
    He that a true embrace will finde,
    To beauties faults must still be blinde.

V.

Eu'ry Dame affects good fame, what ere her doings be,
But true prayse is Vertues Bayes which none may weare but she.
Borrow'd guise fits not the wise, a simple look is best;
Natiue grace becomes a face, though ne'er so rudely drest.
    Now such new found toyes are sold, these women to disguise.
    That before the yeare growes old the newest fashion dyes.

Dames of yore contended more in goodnesse to exceede,
Then in pride to be enui'd, for that which least they neede:
Little Lawne then seru'd the Pawne, if Pawne at all there were;
Home-spun thread, and houshold bread then held out all the
    yeare.   10
    But th'attyres of women now weare out both house and land;
    That the wiues in silkes may flow, at ebbe the Good-men stand.

Once agen, *Astræa*, then, from heau'n to earth descend,
And vouchsafe in their behalf these errours to amend:
Aid from heau'n must make all eeu'n, things are so out of frame;
For let man striue all he can, hee needs must please his Dame.
    Happy man, content that giues and what hee giues, enioyes;
    Happy Dame, content that lives, and breakes no sleepe for
    toyes.

VI.

So sweet is thy discourse to me,
And so delightfull is thy sight,
As I taste nothing right but thee.
O why inuented Nature light?
Was it alone for beauties sake,
That her grac't words might better take?

No more can I old ioyes recall:
They now to me become vnknowne,
Not seeming to haue beene at all.
Alas, how soone is this loue growne   10
To such a spreading height in me
As with it all must shadowed be!

VII.

There is a Garden in her face,
Where Roses and white Lillies grow;
A heau'nly paradice is that place,
Wherein all pleasant fruits doe flow.
There Cherries grow, which none may buy
Till Cherry ripe themselues doe cry.

Those Cherries fayrely doe enclose
Of Orient Pearle a double row;
Which when her louely laughter showes,
They look like Rose-buds fill'd with snow.   10
Yet them nor Peere nor Prince can buy,
Till Cherry ripe themselues doe cry.

Her Eyes like Angels watch them still;
Her Browes like bended bowes doe stand,
Threatning with piercing frownes to kill
All that attempt with eye or hand
Those sacred Cherries to come nigh,
Till Cherry ripe themselues doe cry.

VIII.

To his sweet Lute *Apollo* sung the motions of the Spheares;
The wondrous order of the Stars, whose course diuides the yeares;
And all the Mysteries aboue:
But none of this could *Midas* moue,
Which purchast him his Asses eares.

Then *Pan* with his rude Pipe began the Country-wealth
    t'aduance ;
To boast of Cattle, flocks of Sheepe, and Goates, on hils that
    dance,
      With much more of this churlish kinde,
      That quite transported *Midas* minde,
      And held him rapt as in a trance.   10

This wrong the *God of Musicke* scorned from such a sottish
    Iudge,
And bent his angry bow at *Pan*, which made the Piper trudge :
      Then *Midas* head he so did trim
      That eu'ry age yet talkes of him
      And *Phœbus* right reuenged grudge.

IX.

    Young and simple though I am,
    I haue heard of *Cupids* name :
    Guesse I can what thing it is
    Men desire when they doe kisse.
      Smoake can neuer burne, they say,
      But the flames that follow may.

    I am not so foule or fayre
    To be proud, nor to despayre ;
    Yet my lips have oft obserued :
    Men that kiss them press them hard,   10
      As glad lovers vse to do
      When their new-met loves they woo.

    Faith, 'tis but a foolish minde,
    Yet me thinkes, a heate I finde,
    Like thirstlonging, that doth bide
    Euer on my weaker side,
      Where they say my heart doth moue.
      Venus, grant it be not loue.

    If it be, alas, what then ?
    Were not women made for men ?   20
    As good 'twere a thing were past,
    That must needes be done at last.
      Roses that are ouer-blowne,
      Growe lesse sweet, then fall alone.

Yet nor Churle, nor silken Gull,
Shall my Mayden blossome pull :
Who shall not I soone can tell ;
Who shall, would I could as well :
   This I know, who ere hee be,
   Loue hee must, or flatter me.   30

X.

Loue me or not, loue her I must or dye ;
Leaue me or not, follow her needs must I.
O that her grace would my wisht comforts giue.
How rich in her, how happy should I liue !

All my desire, all my delight should be,
Her to enioy, her to vnite to mee :
Enuy should cease, her would I loue alone :
Who loues by lookes, is seldome true to one.

Could I enchant, and that it lawfull were,
Her would I charme softly that none should heare. 10
But loue enforc'd rarely yeelds firme content ;
So would I loue that neyther should repent.

XI.

What meanes this folly, now to braue it so,
   And then to vse submission ?
Is that a friend that straight can play the foe ?
   Who loues on such condition ?

Though Bryers breed Roses, none the Bryer affect :
   But with the flowre are pleased.
Loue onely loues delight and soft respect :
   He must not be diseased.

These thorny passions spring from barren breasts,
   Or such as neede much weeding.   10
Loue only loues delight and soft respect ;
   But sends them not home bleeding.

Command thy humour, striue to giue content,
   And shame not loues profession.
Of kindnesse neuer any could repent
   That made choyce with discretion.

XII.

Deare if I with guile would guild a true intent
Heaping flattries that in heart were neuer meant:
      Easely could I then obtaine
        What now in vaine I force;
      Fals-hood much doth gaine,
        Truth yet holds the better course.

Loue forbid that through dissembling I should thriue,
Or in praysing you, my selfe of truth depriue:
      Let not your high thoughts debase
        A simple truth in me;   10
      Great is beauties grace,
        Truth is yet as fayre as shee.

Prayse is but the winde of pride, if it exceedes;
Wealth, pris'd in it selfe, no outward value needes.
      Fayre you are, and passing fayre;
        You know it, and 'tis true:
      Yet let none despayre
        But to finde as fayre as you.

XIII.

O Loue, where are thy Shafts, thy Quiuer, and thy Bow?
Shall my wounds onely weepe, and hee vngaged goe?
Be iust, and strike him, too, that dares contemne thee so.

No eyes are like to thine, though men suppose thee blinde,
So fayre they leuell when the marke they list to finde:
Then, strike, ô strike the heart that beares the cruell minde.

Is my fond sight deceiued? or do I *Cupid* spye,
Close ayming at his breast, by whom despis'd I dye?
Shoot home, sweet *Loue*, and wound him, that hee may not
    flye.

O then we both will sit in some vnhaunted shade,   10
And heale each others wound which *Loue* hath iustly made:
O hope, ô thought too vaine, how quickly dost thou fade!

At large he wanders still, his heart is free from paine,
While secret sighes I spend, and teares, but all in vaine:
Yet, *Loue*, thou know'st, by right, I should not thus complaine.

XIIII.

Beauty is but a painted hell:
    Aye me, aye me,
Shee wounds them that admire it,
Shee kils them that desire it.
    Giue her pride but fuell,
    No fire is more cruell.

Pittie from eu'ry heart is fled:
    Aye me, aye me,
Since false desire could borrow
Teares of dissembled sorrow,
    Constant vowes turn truthlesse,
    Loue cruele, Beauty ruthlesse.

Sorrow can laugh, and Fury sing:
    Aye me, aye me,
My rauing griefes discouer
I liu'd too true a louer:
    The first step to madnesse
    Is the excesse of sadnesse.

XV.

Are you, what your faire lookes expresse?
    O then be kinde:
From law of Nature they digresse
    Whose forme sutes not their minde:
Fairenesse seene in th' outward shape,
Is but th' inward beauties Ape.

Eyes that of earth are mortall made,
    What can they view?
All's but a colour or a shade,
    And neyther alwayes true.
Reasons sight, that is eterne.
Eu'n the substance can discerne.

Soule is the Man; for who will so
    The body name?
And to that power all grace we owe
    That deckes our liuing frame.
What, or how had housen bin,
But for them that dwell therein?

Loue in the bosome is begot,
    Not in the eyes;   20
No beauty makes the eye more hot,
    Her flames the spright surprise:
    Let our louing minds then meete,
    For pure meetings are most sweet.

XVI.

    Since she, eu'n she, for whom I liu'd,
Sweet she by Fate from me is torne,
    Why am not I of sence depriu'd,
Forgetting I was euer borne?
    Why should I languish, hating light?
    Better to sleepe an endlesse night.

    Be't eyther true, or aptly fain'd,
That some of *Lethes* water write,
    'Tis their best med'cine that are pain'd
All thought to loose of past delight.   10
    O would my anguish vanish so!
    Happy are they that neyther know.

XVII.

I must complain, yet doe enioy my Loue;
She is too faire, too rich in louely parts:
Thence is my grief, for Nature, while she stroue
With all her graces and diuinest Arts
    To form her too too beautifull of hue,
    Shee had no leasure left to make her true.

Should I, agrieu'd, then wish shee were lesse fayre?
That were repugnant to mine owne desires:
Shee is admir'd, new louers still repayre;
That kindles daily loues forgetfull fires.   10
    Rest, iealous thoughts, and thus resolue at last,
    Shee hath more beauty then becomes the chast.

XVIII.

Think'st thou to seduce me then with words that haue no
    meaning?
Parats so can learne to prate, our speech by pieces gleaning:
Nurces teach their children so about the time of weaning.

Learne to speake first, then to wooe: to wooing, much per-
tayneth :
Hee that courts vs, wanting Arte, soon falters when he fayneth,
Lookes a-squint on his discourse, and smiles, when hee com-
plaineth.

Skilfull Anglers hide their hookes, fit baytes for euery season ;
But with crooked pins fish thou, as babes doe that want reason ;
Gogions onely can be caught with such poore trickes of treason.

Ruth forgiue me, if 1 err'd, from humane hearts compassion, 10
When I laught sometimes too much to see thy foolish fashion :
But, alas, who lesse could doe that found so good occasion !

XIX.

Her fayre inflaming eyes,
   Chiefe authors of my cares,
I prai'd in humblest wise
   With grace to view my teares :
      They beheld me broad awake,
      But alasse, no ruth would take.

Her lips with kisses rich,
   And words of fayre delight,
I fayrely did beseech,
   To pitty my sad plight :   10
      But a voyce from them brake forth,
      As a whirle-winde from the North.

Then to her hands I fled,
   That can giue heart and all ;
To them I long did plead,
   And loud for pitty call :
      But, alas, they put mee off,
      With a touch worse then a scoffe.

So backe I straight return'd,
   And at her breast I knock'd ;   20
Where long in vaine I mourn'd,
   Her heart so fast was lock'd :
      Not a word could passage finde,
      For a Rocke inclos'd her minde.

Then downe my pray'rs made way
    To those most comely parts,
That make her flye or stay,
    As they affect deserts:
        But her angry feete, thus mou'd,
        Fled with all the parts I lou'd.   30

Yet fled they not so fast,
    As her enraged minde:
Still did I after haste,
    Still was I left behinde;
        Till I found 'twas to no end,
        With a Spirit to contend.

XX.

Turne all thy thoughts to eyes,
Turn al thy haires to eares,
Change all thy friends to spies,
And all thy ioyes to feares:
    True Loue will yet be free,
    In spite of Iealousie.

Turne darknesse into day,
Coniectures into truth,
Beleeue what th' enuious say,
Let age interpret youth: 10
    True loue will yet be free,
    In spite of Iealousie.

Wrest euery word and looke,
Racke eu'ry hidden thought,
Or fish with golden hooke;
True loue cannot be caught.
    For that will still be free,
    In spite of Iealousie.

XXI.

If any hath the heart to kill,
    Come rid me of this woefull paine.
For while I liue I suffer still
    This cruell torment all in vaine:
        Yet none aliue but one can guesse
        What is the cause of my distresse.

Thanks be to heau'n, no grieuous smart,
  No maladies my limbes annoy;
I beare a sound and sprightfull heart,
  Yet liue I quite depriu'd of ioy :   10
Since what I had in vaine I craue,
And what I had not now I haue.

A Loue I had, so fayre, so sweet,
  As euer wanton eye did see :
Once by appointment wee did meet :
  Shee would, but ah, it would not be :
She gaue her heart, her hand shee gaue;
All did I giue, shee nought could haue.

What Hagge did then my powers forespeake,
  That neuer yet such taint did feele !   20
Now shee reiects me as one weake,
  Yet am I all compos'd of steele.
Ah, this is it my heart doth grieue :
Now though shee sees, shee'le not belieue.

XXII.

Beauty, since you so much desire
To know the place of *Cupids* fire,
About you somewhere doth it rest,
Yet neuer harbour'd in your brest,
Nor gout-like in your heele or toe ;
What foole would seeke Loues flame so low ?
But a little higher, but a little higher,
There, there, ô there lyes *Cupids* fire.

Thinke not, when *Cupid* most you scorne,
Men iudge that you of Ice were borne ;   10
For though you cast loue at your heele,
His fury yet sometime you feele :
And where-abouts if you would know,
I tell you still not in your toe :
But a little higher, but a little higher,
There, there, ô there lyes *Cupids* fire.

XXIII.

  Your faire lookes vrge my desire :
    Calme it, sweet, with loue.
  Stay ; ô why will you retire ?
    Can you churlish proue ?

If loue may perswade,
  Loues pleasures, deare, deny not:
Here is a groue secur'd with shade:
  O then be wise, and flye not.

Harke, the Birds delighted sing,
  Yet our pleasure sleepes: 10
Wealth to none can profit bring,
  Which the miser keepes:
O come, while we may,
  Let's chayne Loue with embraces;
Wee haue not all times time to stay,
  Nor safety in all places.

What ill finde you now in this,
  Or who can complaine?
There is nothing done amisse
  That breedes no man payne.   20
'Tis now flow'ry *May*,
  But eu'n in cold *December*,
When all these leaues are blowne away,
  This place shall I remember.

XXIIII.

Faine would I wed a faire yong man that day and night could
  please mee,
When my mind or body grieued that had the powre to ease
  mee.
Maids are full of longing thoughts that breed a bloudlesse
  sickenesse,
And that, oft I heare men say, is onely cur'd by quicknesse.
Oft I haue beene woo'd and prai'd, but neuer could be moued;
Many for a day or so I haue most dearely loued,
But this foolish mind of mine straight loathes the thing resolued;
If to loue be sinne in mee that sinne is soone absolued.
Sure I thinke I shall at last flye to some holy Order;
When I once am setled there then can I flye no farther.   10
Yet I would not dye a maid, because I had a mother:
As I was by one brought forth I would bring forth another.

FINIS.

R

A NEVV VVAY
OF MAKING FOWRE
parts in *Counter-point*, by a
most familiar, and infallible
RVLE.

Secondly, a necessary discourse of *Keyes*,
and their proper *Closes*.

Thirdly, the allowed passages of all *Concords*
perfect, or imperfect, are declared.

*Also by way of Preface, the nature of the Scale is
expressed, with a briefe Method teaching to Sing.*

By THO: CAMPION.

LONDON:
Printed by *T. S.* for *Iohn Browne*, and are to be
sold at his shop in Saint *Dunstanes* Church-yard,
in Fleetstreet.

TO THE FLOWRE
OF PRINCES, CHARLES,
PRINCE OF GREAT
BRITTAINE.

The first inuentor of Musicke (most sacred Prince,) was by olde records *Apollo*, a King, who, for the benefit which Mortalls receiued from his so diuine inuention, was by them made a God.   *Dauid* a Prophet, and a King, excelled all men in the same excellent Art. What then can more adorne the greatnesse of a Prince, then the knowledge thereof?   But why should I, being by profession a Physition, offer a worke of Musicke to his Highnesse? *Galene* either first, or next the first of Physitions, became so expert a Musition, that he could not containe himselfe, but needes he must apply all the proportions of Musicke to the vncertaine motions of the pulse. 10 Such far-fetcht Doctrine dare I not attempt, contenting my selfe onely with a poore, and easie inuention ; yet new and certaine ; by which the skill of Musicke shall be redeemed from much dark-nesse, wherein enuious antiquitie of purpose did inuolue it.   To your gratious hands most humbly I present it, which if your Clemency will vouchsafe fauourably to behold, I haue then attained to the full estimate of all my labour.   Be all your daies euer musicall (most mighty Prince) and a sweet harmony guide the euents of all your royall actions.   So zealously wisheth

Your Highnesse   20
most humble seruant,
THO: CAMPION.

THE PREFACE.

There is nothing doth trouble, and disgrace our Traditionall
Musition more then the ambiguity of the termes of Musicke, if he
cannot rightly distinguish them, for they make him vncapable of any
rationall discourse in the art hee professeth: As if wee say a lesser
Third consists of a Tone, and a Semi-tone ; here by a Tone is ment
a perfect Second, or as they name it a whole note : But if wee aske in
what Tone is this or that song made, then by Tone we intend the key
which guides and ends the whole song. Likewise the word Note *is some-*
times vsed proprely, as when in respect of the forme of it, we name it
10 *a round or square Note ; in regard of the place we say, a Note in*
rule or a Note in space ; so for the·time, we call a Briefe or Sem-
briefe a long Note, a Crotchet or Quauer a short note. Sometime the
word Note *is otherwise to be understood, as when it is,* signum pro
signato, *the signe for the thing signified : so we say a Sharpe, or flat*
Note, meaning by the word Note, the sound it signifies ; also we terme
a Note high, or low, in respect of the sound. The word Note *simply*
produced hath yet another signification, as when we say this is
a sweet Note, or the Note I like, but not the words, wee then meane
by this word Note, the whole tune, putting the part for the whole : but
20 *this word* Note *with addition, is yet far otherwise to be vnderstood,*
as when we say a whole Note, or a halfe Note ; we meane a perfect
or imperfect Second, which are not Notes, but the seuerall distances
betweene two Notes, the one being double as much as the other ;
and although this kinde of calling them a whole and a halfe Note,
came in first by abusion, yet custome hath made that speech now
passable. In my discourse of Musicke, I haue therefore striued to
be plaine in my tearmes, without nice and vnprofitable distinctions, as
that is of tonus maior, *and* tonus minor, *and such like, whereof*
there can be made no vse.

30 *In like manner there can be no greater hinderance to him that*
desires to become a Musition, then the want of the true vnderstanding
of the Scale, which proceeds from the errour of the common Teacher,
who can doe nothing without the olde Gam-vt, *in which there is but*
one Cliffe, and one Note and yet in the same Cliffe he wil sing re *and*
sol. *It is most true that the first inuention of the* gam-vt *was*

a good inuention, but then the distance of Musicke was cancelled within the number of twenty Notes, so were the sixe Notes properly inuented to helpe youth in vowelling, but the liberty of the latter age hath giuen Musicke more space both aboue and below, altering thereby the former naming of the Notes : the curious obseruing whereof hath bred much vnnecessary difficultie to the learner, for the Scale may be more easily and plainely exprest by foure Notes, then by sixe, which is done by leauing out Vt *and* Re.

The substance of all Musicke, and the true knowledge of the scale, consists in the obseruations of the halfe note, which is expressed either by Mi Fa, *or* La Fa, *and they being knowne in their right places, the other Notes are easily applyed vnto them.* 10

To illustrate this I will take the common key which we call Gam-vt, *both sharpe in* Bemi *and flat, as also flat in* Elami, *and shew how with ease they may be expressed by these foure Notes, which are* Sol, La, Mi, Fa.

I shall neede no more then one eight for all, and that I haue chosen to be in the Base, because all the vpper eights depend vpon the lowest eight, and are the same with it in nature ; then thus first in the sharpe : 20

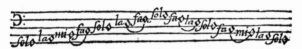

First obserue the places of the halfe Notes, which are marked with a halfe circle, and remember that if the lowest be Mi Fa, *the vpper halfe Note is* La Fa, *and contrariwise if the lowest halfe Note be* La Fa, *the vpper must be* Mi Fa.

It will giue great light to the vnderstanding of the Scale, if you trye it on a Lute, or Voyall, for there you shall plainely perceiue that there goe two frets to the raising of a whole Note, and but one to a halfe Note, as on the Lute in this manner the former eight may be expressed.

Here you may discerne that betweene A. *and* C. *and* C. *and* E. *is* 30 *interposed a fret, which makes it double as much as* E. *and* F. *which is markt for the halfe Note, so the whole Note you see containes in it*

the space of two halfe *Notes*, as A.C. *being the whole Note, containes in it these two halfe Notes,* A.B. *and* B.C.

Now for the naming of the *Notes, let this be a generall rule, aboue* Fa, *euer to sing* Sol, *and to sing* Sol *euer under* La.

Here in the flat Gam-vt, *you may finde* La Fa *below, and* Mi Fa *aboue ; which on the Lute take their places thus :*

The lower halfe Note is between C. *and* D. *the higher betweene* E. *and* A. *but next let vs examine this key as it is flat in* Elami, *which being properly to be set in* Are, *so is it to be sung with ease,* La
10 *instead of* Re, *being the right limits of this eight.*

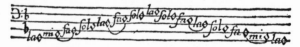

Mi Fa *here holds his place below, and* La Fa *aboue but yet remoued a Note lower: The same on the Lute.*

You shall here finde *the vpper halfe note placed a fret lower then it was in the example of the flat* Gam-vt *which was set downe next before, by reason of the flat in* Elami, *which makes that whole Note but halfe so much as it was being sharpe.*

This is an easie way for him that would eyther with ayde of *a teacher, or by his owne industrie learne to sing, and if hee shall well beare in minde the placing of the halfe Notes, it will helpe him much*
20 *in the knowledge of the cords, which haue all their variety from the halfe Note.*

Of Counterpoint.

THE parts of Musicke are in all but foure, howsoeuer some skilfull Musitions haue composed songs of twenty, thirty, and forty parts : for be the parts neuer so many, they are but one of these foure in nature. The names of those foure parts are these. The *Base* which is the lowest part and foundation of the whole song : The *Tenor*, placed next aboue the *Base* : next aboue the *Tenor* the *Meane* or *Counter-Tenor*, and in the highest place the *Treble*. These foure parts by the learned are said to resemble the foure Elements, the Base expresseth the true nature of the earth, who being the grauest and lowest of all the Elements, is as 10 a foundation to the rest. The Tenor is likened to the water, the Meane to the Aire, and the Treble to the Fire. Moreouer, by how much the water is more light then the earth, by so much is the Aire lighter then the water, and Fire then Aire : They haue also in their natiue property euery one place aboue the other, the lighter vppermost, the waightiest in the bottome. Hauing now demonstrated that there are in all but foure parts, and that the Base is the foundation of the other three, I assume that the true sight and iudgement of the vpper three must proceed from the lowest, which is the Base, and also I conclude that euery part in nature 20 doth affect his proper and naturall place as the elements doe.

True it is that the auncient Musitions who entended their Musicke onely for the Church, tooke their sight from the Tenor, which was rather done out of necessity then any respect to the true nature of Musicke : for it was vsuall with them to haue a Tenor as a Theame, to which they were compelled to adapt their other parts. But I will plainely conuince by demonstration that contrary to some opinions the Base containes in it both the Aire and true iudgement of the Key, expressing how any man at the first sight may view in it all the other parts in their originall 30 essence.

In respect of the variety in Musicke which is attained to by farther proceeding in the Arte, as when Notes are shifted out of their natiue places, the Base aboue the Tenor, or the Tenor aboue the Meane, and the Meane aboue the Treble, this kinde of Counterpoint, which I promise, may appeare simple and onely fit for young beginners (as indeede chiefly it is) yet the right speculation may giue much satisfaction, euen to the most skilfull, laying open vnto them, how manifest and certaine are the first grounds of Counterpoint.

First, it is in this case requisite that a formall Base, or at least part thereof be framed, the Notes, rising and falling according to the nature of that part, not so much by degrees as by leaps of a third, fourth, or fift, or eight, a sixt being seldome, a seauenth
10 neuer vsed, and neyther of both without the discretion of a skilfull Composer. Next wee must consider whether the Base doth rise or fall, for in that consists the mistery : That rising or that falling doth neuer exceed a fourth, for a fourth aboue, is the same that a fift is vnderneath, and a fourth vnderneath is as a fift aboue, for example, if a Base shall rise thus :

The first rising is said to be by degrees, because there is no Note betweene the two Notes, the second is by leaps, for *G.* skips ouer *A.* to *B.* and so leaps into a third, the third example also leaps two Notes into a fourth. Now for this fourth if the Base
20 had descended from *G.* aboue to *C.* vnderneath, that descending fift in sight and vse had beene all one with the fourth, as here you may discerne, for they both begin and end in the same keys : thus

This rule likewise holds if the Notes descend a second, third, or fourth ; for the fift ascending is all one with the fourth descending, example of the first Notes.

The third two Notes which make the distance of a fourth, are all one with this fift following

But let vs make our approach yet neerer. If the Base shall ascend either a second, third, or fourth, that part which stands in the third or tenth aboue the Base, shall fall into an eight, that which is a fift shall passe into a third, and that which is an eight shall remoue into a fift.

But that all this may appeare more plaine and easie, I haue drawne it all into these six figures.

8	3	5
3	5	8

Though you finde here onely mentioned and figured a third, fift and eight, yet not onely these single concords are ment, but by them also their compounds, as a tenth, a twelfth, a fifteenth, and so vpward, and also the vnison as well as the eight. 10

This being graunted, I will giue you example of those figures prefixed : When the Base riseth, beginning from the lowest figure, and rising to the vpper ; as if the Base should rise a second, in this manner.

Then if you will beginne with your third, you must set your Note in *Alamire*, which is a third to *Ffavt*, and so looke vpward, and that cord which you see next aboue it vse, and that is an 20 eight in *Gsolrevt*.

After that, if you will take a fift to the first Note, you must looke vpward and take the third you finde there for the second Note. Lastly if you take an eight for the first Note, you must take of the second Note the corde aboue it, which is the fift.

Example of all the three parts added to the Base.

What parts arise out of the rising of the second; the same answere in the rising of the third and fourth, thus:

This riseth a third, this riseth a fourth.

Albeit any man by the rising of parts, might of himselfe con-ceiue the same reason in the falling of them, yet that nothing may be thought obscure, I will also illustrate the descending Notes by example.

If the Base descends or falls, a second, third, or fourth, or riseth a fift (which is all one as if it had fallen a fourth, as has beene shewed before) then looke vpon the sixe figures, where in the first place you shall finde the eight which descends into the third, in the second place the third descending into the fift, and in the third and last place the fift which hath vnder it an eight.

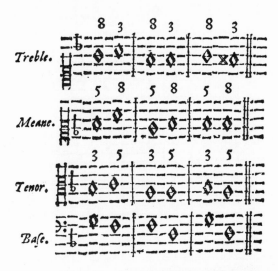

Thus much for the rising and falling of the Base in seuerall; now I will give you a briefe example of both of them mixed together in the plainest fashion, let this straine serue for the Base :

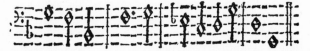

The first two Notes fall a second, the second and third Notes fall a fift, which you must call rising a forth, the third and forth Notes rise a fift which you must name the fourth falling, the fourth and fift Notes rise a second, the fift and sixt notes fall a third, the sixt and seauenth Notes also fall a third, the seauenth and eight rise a second, the eight and ninth Notes rise a fourth, the ninth and tenth fall a fourth, the tenth and eleuenth Notes fall a fift, which you must reckon rising a fourth.

Being thus prepared, you may chuse whether you will begin with an eight, a fift, or a third; for as soone as you haue taken any one of these, all the other Notes follow necessarily without respect of the rest of the parts, and euery one orderly without mixing, keeps his proper place aboue the other, as here you may easily discerne :

Let vs examine onely one of the parts, and let that be the Tenor, because it stands next to the Base. The first Note in *B.* is a third to the Base, which descends to the second Note of the
10 Base : now looke among the sixe figures, and when you haue found the third in the vpper place, you shall finde vnder it a fift, then take that fift which is *C.* : next from *F.* to *B.* below, is a fift descending, for which say ascending, and so you shall looke for the fift in the lowest row of the figures, aboue which stands a third which is to be taken ; that third stands in *D.* : then from *B.* to *F.* the Base rises a fift, but you must say falling, because a fift rising and a fourth falling is all one, as hath beene often declared before ; now a third when the Base falls requires a fift to follow it : But what needes farther demonstration when as he that knowes his
20 Cords cannot but conceiue the necessitie of consequence in all these with helpe of those sixe figures ?

But let them that haue not proceeded so farre, take this note with them concerning the placing of the parts ; if the vpper part or Treble be an eight, the Meane must take the next Cord vnder

it, which is a fift, and the Tenor the next Cord vnder that, which
is a third. But if the Treble be a third, then the Meane must
take the eight, and the Tenor the fift. Againe, if the vpper-
most part stands in the fift or twelfe, (for in respect of the learners
ease, in the simple Concord I conclude all his compounds) then
the Meane must be a tenth, and the Tenor a fift. Moreouer, all
these Cords are to be seene in the Base, and such Cords as stand
aboue the Notes of the Base are easily knowne, but such as in
sight are found vnder it, trouble the young beginner; let him
therefore know that a third vnder the Base, is a sixt aboue it, and
if it be a greater third, it yeelds the lesser sixt aboue; if the lesser
third, the greater sixt. A fourth vnderneath the Base is a fift
aboue, and a fift vnder the Base is a fourth aboue it. A sixt be-
neath the Base is a third aboue, and if it be the lesser sixt, then
is the third aboue the greater third, and if the greater sixt vnder-
neath, then is it the lesser third aboue; and thus far haue I
digressed for the Schollers sake.

If I should discouer no more then this already deciphered of
Counter-point, wherein the natiue order of foure parts with vse of
the Concords, is demonstratiuely expressed, might I be mine
owne Iudge, I had effected more in Counterpoint, then any man
before me hath euer attempted, but I will yet proceed a little
farther. And that you may perceiue how cunning and how cer-
taine nature is in all her operations, know that what Cords haue
held good in this ascending and descending of the Base answere
in the contrary by the very same rule, though not so formally as
the other, yet so, that much vse is and may be made of this sort
of Counter-point. To keepe the figures in your memorie, I will
here place them againe, and vnder them plaine examples.

In these last examples you may see what variety nature offers of her selfe; for if in the first Rule the Notes follow not in expected formality, this second way being quite contrary to the other, affords vs sufficient supply: the first and last two Notes rising and falling by degrees, are not so formall as the rest, yet thus they may be mollified, by breaking two of the first Notes.

How both the waies may be mixed together, you may perceiue by this next example, wherein the blacke Notes distinguish
10 the second way from the first.

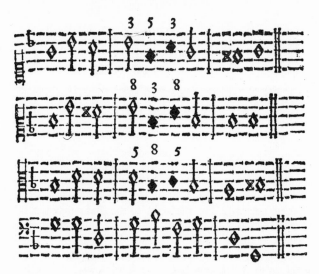

In this example the fift and sixt Notes of the three vpper parts are after the second way, for from the fourth Note of the Base, which is in from *G.* and goeth to *B.* is a third rising, so that according to the first rule, the eight should passe into a fift, the fift into a third, the third into an eight : but here contrariwise the eight goes into a third, the fift into an eight, and the third into a fift; and by these Notes you may censure the rest of that kinde.

Though I may now seeme to haue finished all that belongs to this sort of Counterpoint, yet there remaines one scruple, that is, how the sixt may take place here, which I will also declare. Know that whensoeuer a sixt is requisite, as in *B.* or in *E.* or *A.* the key being in *Gamvt,* you may take the sixt in stead of the fift, and vse the same Cord following which you would haue taken if the former cord had beene a fift example.

The sixt in both places (the Base rising) passes into a third, as it should haue done if the sixt had beene a fift. Moreouer if the Base shall vse a sharpe, as in *F.* sharpe; then must we take the sixt of necessity, but the eight to the Base may not be vsed, so that exception is to be taken against our rule of Counterpoint; To which I answere thus, first, such Bases are not true Bases, for where a sixt is to be taken, either in *F.* sharpe, or in *E.* sharpe, or in *B.* or in *A.* the true Base is a third lower, *F.* sharpe in *D.*, *E.* in *C.*, *B.* in *G.*, *A.* in *F.*, as for example.

10   In the first Base two sixes are to be taken, by reason of the imperfection of the Base, wanting due latitude, the one in *E.* the other in *F.* sharpe, but in the second Base the sixes are remoued away and the Musicke is fuller.

Neuerthelesse, if any be pleased to vse the Base sharpe, then in stead of the eight, to the Base hee may take the third to the Base, in this manner.

Here the Treble in the third Note, when it should haue past into the sharpe eight in *F.* takes for it a third to the Base in *A.* which causeth the Base and Treble to rise two thirds, whereof we will speake hereafter.

Note also that when the Base stands in *E.* flat, and the part that is an eight to it must passe into a sharpe or greater third, that this passage from the flat to the sharpe would be vnformall; and therefore it may be thus with small alteration auoided, by remouing the latter part of the Note into the third aboue, which though it meets in vnison with the vpper part, yet it is right good, 10 because it iumps not with the whole, but onely with the last halfe of it.

Example.

For the second example looke hereafter in the rule of thirds, but for the first example here: if in the Meane part the third Note that is diuided, had stood still a Minum (as by rule it should) and so had past into *F.* sharpe, as it must of force be made sharpe at a close, it had beene then passing vnformall.

But if the same Base had beene set in the sharpe key, the rest of the parts would haue falne out formall of themselues without any helpe, as thus :

But if the third Note of the Base in *E.* flat had been put in his place of perfection, that is in *C.* a third lower then the other parts would haue answered fitly, in this manner.

When the Base shall stand still in one key, as aboue it doth in the third Note, then the other parts may remoue at their pleasure.

Moreouer it is to be obserued that in composing of the Base, 10 you may break it at your pleasure, without altering any of the other parts : as for example.

One other obseruation more I will handle that doth arise out of this example, which according to the first rule may hold thus :

Herein are two errours, first in the second Notes of the Base and Treble, where the third to the Base ought to haue been sharpe, secondly in the second and third Notes of the same parts, where the third being a lesser third, holds while the Base falls into a fift which is vnelegant, but if the vpper third had beene the greater third, the fift had fitly followed, as you may see in the third and fourth Notes of the Tenor and the Base.

But that scruple may be taken away by making the second Note of the Treble sharpe, and in stead of a fift by remouing the third Note into a sixt:

Example.

There may yet be more variety afforded the Base, by ordering the fourth Notes of the vpper parts according to the second rule, thus :

But that I may (as neere as I can) leaue nothing vntoucht

concerning this kinde of Counterpoint, let vs now consider how two thirds being taken together betweene the Treble and the Base, may stand with our Rule. For sixes are not in this case to be mentioned, being distances so large that they can produce no formality: Besides the sixt is of it selfe very imperfect, being compounded of a third which is an imperfect Concord, and of a fourth which is a Discord: and this the cause is, that the sixes produce so many fourths in the inner parts. As for the third it being the least distance of any Concord, is therefore easily to be reduced into good order. For if the Base and Treble doe rise together in thirds, then the first Note of the Treble is regular with the other part, but the second of it is irregular; for by rule in stead of the rising third, it should fall into the eight. In like sort if the Base and Treble doe fall two thirds, the first Note of the Treble is irregular, and is to be brought into rule by being put into the eight, but the second Note is of it selfe regular. Yet whether those thirds be reduced into eights or no; you shall by supposition thereof finde out the other parts, which neuer vary from the rule but in the sharpe Base. But let mee explaine my selfe by example.

The first two Notes of the Treble are both thirds to the Base, but in the second stroke,[1] the first Note of the Treble is a third, and the second, which was before a third, is made an eight, onely to shew how you may finde out the right parts which are to be vsed when you take two thirds betweene the Treble and the Base:

---

[1] i. e. bar.

For according to the former rule, if the Base descends, the third then in the Treble is to passe into the eight, and the meane must first take an eight, then a fift, and the Tenor a fift, then a third, and these are also the right and proper parts if you returne the eight of the Treble into a third againe, as may appeare in the first example of the Base falling, and consequently in all the rest.

But let vs proceed yet farther, and suppose that the Base shall vse a sharpe, what is then to be done? as if thus:

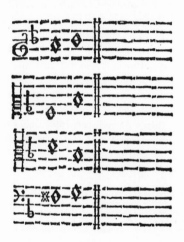

If you call to minde the rule before deliuered concerning the
10 sharpe Base, you shall here by helpe thereof see the right parts, though you cannot bring them vnder the rule: for if the first Note of the Base had been flat, the Meane part should haue taken that, and so haue descended to the fift; but being sharpe you take for it (according to the former obseruation) the third to the Base, and so rise vp into the fift. The Tenor that should take a fift, and so fall by degrees into a third, is heere forced by reason of the sharpe Base, for a fift to take a sixt and so leap downeward into the third. And so much for the thirds.

Lastly in fauour of young beginners let me also adde this, that
20 the Base intends a close as often as it riseth a fift, third or second and then immediately either falls a fift, or riseth a fourth. In like manner if the Base falls a fourth or second: and after falls a fift, the Base insinuates a close, and in all these cases the part must hold, that in holding can vse the fourth or eleauenth, and so passe eyther into the third or tenth.

In the examples before set downe I left out the closes, of purpose that the Cords might the better appeare in their proper places, but this short admonition will direct any young beginner to helpe that want at his pleasure. And thus I end my treatise of Counterpoint both briefe and certaine, such as will open an easie way to them that without helpe of a skilful Teacher endeauour to acquire the first grounds of this Arte.

A shorte Hymne, Composed after this forme of Counterpoint, to shew how well it will become any Diuine, *or graue* Subiect.

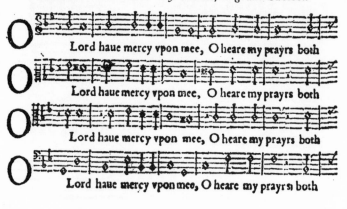

Lord haue mercy vpon mee, O heare my prayrs both

Lord haue mercy vpon mee, O heare my prayrs both

Lord haue mercy vpon mee, O heare my prayrs both

Lord haue mercy vpon mee, O heare my prayrs both

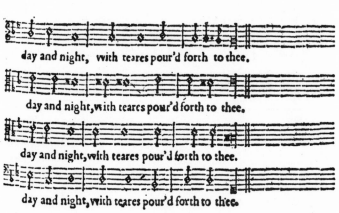

day and night, with teares pour'd forth to thee.

day and night, with teares pour'd forth to thee.

day and night, with teares pour'd forth to thee.

day and night, with teares pour'd forth to thee.

In this Aire the last Note onely is, for sweetnesse sake, altered from the rule, in the last Note of the Treble, where the eight being a perfect Concord, and better befitting an outward part at the Close, is taken for a third, and in the Tenor in stead of the fift, that third is taken descending, for in a middle part, imperfection is not so manifest as in the Treble at a close which is the perfection of a song.

Of the Tones of Musicke.

Of all things that belong to the making vp of a Musition, the most necessary and vsefull for him is the true knowledge of the Key or Moode, or Tone, for all signifie the same thing, with the closes belonging vnto it, for there is no tune that can haue any grace or sweetnesse, vnlesse it be bounded within a proper key, without running into strange keyes which haue no affinity with the aire of the song. I haue therefore thought good in an easie and briefe discourse to endeauour to expresse that, which many in large and obscure volumes haue made fearefull to the idle Reader.

The first thing to be herein considered is the eight which 10 is equally diuided into a fourth, and a fift as thus:

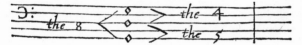

Here you see the fourth in the vpper place, and the fift in the lower place, which is called *Modus authentus*: but contrary thus:

This is called *Modus plagalij*, but howsoeuer the fourth in the eight is placed, wee must haue our eye on the fift, for that onely discouers the key, and all the closes pertaining properly thereunto. This fift is also diuided into two thirds, sometimes the lesser third hath the vpper place, and the greater third supports it below, sometimes the greater third is higher, and the lesser third rests in the lowest place, as for example: 20

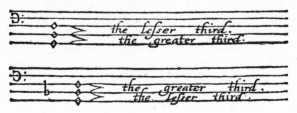

The lowest Note of this fift, beares the name of the Key, as if the eight be from *G.* to *G.* the fift from *G.* beneath to *D.* aboue, *G.* being the lowest Note of the fift, showes that *G.* is the key, and if one should demaund in what key your song is set, you must answere in *Gamvt,* or *Gsolrevt,* that is in *G.*

If the compasse of your song shall fall out thus:

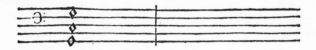

Respect not the fourth below, but looke to your fift aboue, and the lowest Note of that fift assume for your key, which is *C.* then diuide that fift into his two thirds, and so you shall finde out all
10 the closes that belong to that key.

The maine and fundamentall close is in the key it selfe, the second is in the vpper Note of the fift, the third is in the vpper Note of the lowest third, if it be the lesser third, as for example, if the key be in *G.* with *B.* flat, you may close in these three places.

The first close is that which maintaines the aire of the key, and may be vsed often, the second is next to be preferd, and the last, last.

But if the key should be in *G.* with *B.* sharpe, then the last
20 close being to be made in the greater or sharpe third is vnproper, and therfore for variety sometime the next key aboue is ioyned with it, which is *A.* and sometimes the fourth key, which is *C.* but these changes of keyes must be done with iudgement; yet haue I aptly closed in the vpper Note of the lowest third of the key, the

key being in *F.* and the vpper Note of the third standing in *A.* as
you may perceiue in this Aire :

In this aire the first close is in the vpper note of the fift, which
from *F.* is *C.* the second close is in the vpper Note of the
great third, which from *F.* is *A.*

But the last and finall close is in the key it selfe, which is *F.* as
it must euer be, wheresoeuer your key shall stand, either in *G.* or
C. or *F.* or elsewhere, the same rule of the fift is perpetuall, being
diuided into thirds, which can be but two waies, that is, eyther
when the vpper third is lesse by halfe a Note then the lower, or 10
when the lower third containes the halfe Note, which is *Mi Fa*, or
La Fa.

If the lower third containes the halfe Note it hath it eyther
aboue as *La Mi Fa* : *La Mi*, being the whole Note, and *Mi Fa*
but halfe so much, that is the halfe Note ; or else when the halfe
Note is vnderneath as in *Mi Fa Sol* : *Mi Fa*, is the halfe Note,
and *Fa Sol* is the whole Note ; but whether the halfe Note
be vppermost or lowermost, if the lowest third of the fift be
the lesser third, that key yeelds familiarly three closes ; example of
the halfe Note, standing in the vpper place was shewed before, 20
now I will set downe the other.

But for the other keyes that diuide the fift, so that it hath the lesse third aboue, and the greater vnderneath, they can challenge but two proper closes, one in the lowest Note of the fift which is the fundamentall key, and the other in the vppermost Note of the same wherin also you may close at pleasure. True it is that the key next aboue hath a great affinity with the right key, and may therefore as I said before be vsed, as also the fourth key aboue the finall key.

Examples of both in two beginnings of Songs.

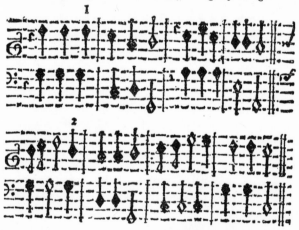

In the first example *A.* is mixt with *G.* and in the second *C.* is ioyned with *G.* as you may vnderstand by the second closes of both.

10   To make the key knowne is most necessary in the beginning of a song, and it is best exprest by the often vsing of his proper fift, and fourth, and thirds, rising or falling.

There is a tune ordinarily vsed, or rather abused, in our Churches, which is begun in one key and ended in another, quite contrary to nature ; which errour crept in first through the ignorance of some parish Clarks, who vnderstood better how to vse the keyes of their Church-doores, then the keyes of Musicke,

at which I doe not much meruaile, but that the same should passe
in the booke of Psalmes set forth in foure parts, and authorised by
so many Musitions, makes mee much amazed : This is the tune.

If one should request me to make a Base to the first halfe of
his aire, I am perswaded that I ought to make it in this manner :

Now if this be the right Base (as without doubt it is) what
a strange vnaireable change must the key then make from *F.* with
the first third sharp to *G.* with *B.* flat.

But they haue found a shift for it, and beginne the tune vpon
the vpper Note of the fift, making the third to it flat ; which is as
absurd as the other : For first they erre in rising from a flat
third into the vnison, or eight, which is condemned by the best
Musitions ; next the third to the fift, is the third which makes the
cadence of the key, and therefore affects to be sharpe by nature
as indeed the authour of the aire at the first intended it should
be. I will therefore so set it downe in foure parts according to
former Rule of Counterpoint.

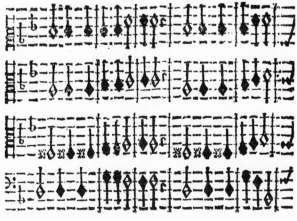

This was the Authors meaning, and thus it is lawfull to beginne a song in the fift, so that you maintaine the aire of the song, ioyning to it the proper parts, but for such dissonant and extrauagant errors as I haue iustly reprehended, I heartily wish they should be remedied, especially in deuine seruice, which is deuoted to the great authour of all harmony.   And briefly thus for the Tones.

Of the taking of all Concords,
perfect and imperfect.

OF all the latter writers in Musicke, whom I haue knowne, the best and most learned, is *Zethus Caluisius* a Germane; who out of the choisest Authors, hath drawne into a perspicuous method, the right and elegant manner of taking all Concords, perfect and imperfect, to whom I would referre our Musitions, but that his booke is scarce any where extant, and besides it is written in Latine, which language few or none of them vnderstand. I am therefore content for their sakes to become a Translator; yet so, 10 that somewhat I wil adde; and somewhat I will alter.

The consecution of perfect concords among themselues is easie; for who knowes not that two eights or two fifts are not to be taken rising or falling together, but a fift may eyther way passe into an eight, or an eight into a fift, yet most conueniently when the one of them moues by degrees, and the other by leaps, for when both skip together the passage is lesse pleasant: The waies by degrees are these.

The fourth way is onely excepted against, where the fift riseth into the eight, and in few parts it cannot well be admitted, but in 20 songs of many voices it is oftentimes necessary.

The passage also of perfect Concords into imperfect, eyther rising or falling, by degrees or leaps, is easie, and so an vnison may passe into a lesser third, or a greater third; also into the lesser sixt, but seldome into the greater sixt. A fift passeth into the greater sixt, and into the lesser sixt; as also into the greater or lesser third; and so you must judge of their eights;

T

for *de octauis idem est iudicium,* and therfore when you reade an vnison, or a fift, or a third, or a sixt, know that by the simple Concords, the Compounds also are meant.

Note here that it is not good to fall with the Base, being sharpe in *F.* from an eight vnto a sixt.

As thus.

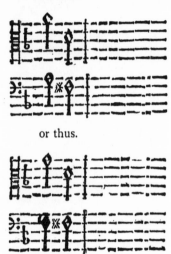

or thus.

But concerning imperfect cords, because they obserue not all one way in their passages, we will speake of them seuerally, first
10 declaring what Relation not harmonicall doth signifie, whereof mention will be made hereafter.

Relation or reference, or respect not harmonicall is *Mi* against *Fa* in a crosse forme, and it is in foure Notes, when the one being considered crosse with the other doth produce in the Musicke a strange discord. Example will yeeld it more plaine.

The first Note of the vpper part is in *Elami* sharpe, which being considered, or referred to the second Note of the lower part, which

is *Elami*, made flat by the cromaticke flat signe, begets a false
second, which is a harsh discorde, and though these Notes sound
not both together, yet in few parts they leaue an offence in the
eare.   The second example is the same descending, the third
is from *Elami* sharpe in the first Note of the lower part, to the
second note in the vpper part, it being flat by reason of the flat
signe, and so betweene them they mix in the Musicke a false fift,
the same doth the fourth example, but the fift example yeelds
a false fourth, and the sixt a false fift.

There are two kindes of imperfect concords, thirds or sixes, and 10
the sixes wholy participate of the nature of the thirds ; for to the
lesser third which consists but of a whole Note and halfe, adde
a fourth, and you haue the lesser sixt ; in like manner to the
greater third that consists of two whole Notes, adde a fourth, and
it makes vp the greater sixt ; so that all the difference is stil in the
halfe note according to that only saying, *Mi Et Fa sunt tota
Musica*.   Of these foure we wil now discourse proceeding in order
from the lesse to the greater.

Of the lesser or imperfect third.

The lesser third passeth into an vnison, first by degrees when 20
both parts meete, then by leaps ascending or descending when
one of the parts stand still, but when both the parts leap or fall
together, the passage is not allowed.

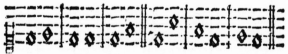

The lesser 3. into the vnison.   The passages not allowed.

Secondly, the lesser third passeth into a fift, first in degrees
when they are seperated by contrary motions, then by leaps when
the lower part riseth by degrees, and the vpper part descends by
degrees, and thus the lesser tenth may passe into a fift.   Lastly
both parts leaping, the lesser third may passe into a fift, so that
the vpper part doth descend by leap the distance of a lesser third. 30
Any other way the passage of a lesser third into a fift, is disallowed.

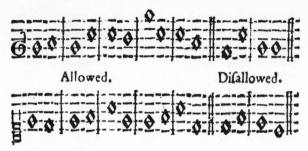

Allowed.   Diſallowed.

In the last disallowance, which is when the vpper part stands, and the lower part falls from a lesser third to a fift, many haue been deceiued, their eares not finding the absurdity of it: but as this way is immusicall, so is the fall of the greater third in the former manner, into a fift, passing harmonious; in so much that it is elegantly and with much grace taken in one part of a short aire foure times, whereas had the fift beene halfe so often taken with the lesser third falling, it would haue yeelded a most vnpleasing harmony.

He that will be diligent to know, and carefull to obserue the
true allowances, may be bolde in his composition, and shall proue
quickly ready in his sight, doing that safely and resolutely which
others attempt tymerously and vncertainely. But now let vs
proceede in the passages of the lesser third.

Thirdly, the lesser third passeth into an eight, the lower part
descending by degrees, and the vpper part by leaps; but very
seldome when the vpper part riseth by degrees, and the lower part
falls by a leap.

Fourthly, the lesser third passeth into other Concords, as when 10
it is continued as in degrees it may be, but not in leaps. Also it
may passe into the greater third, both by degrees and leaps, as also
into the lesser sixt if one of the parts stand still. Into the great
sixt it sometime passeth, but very rarely.

Lastly, adde vnto the rest this passage of the lesser third into
the lesser sixt, as when the lower part riseth by degrees, and the
vpper part by leaps.

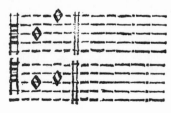

Of the greater or perfect Third.

The greater or perfect third being to passe into perfect Concords, first takes the vnison, when the parts ascend together, the higher by degree, the lower by leap; or when they meete together in a contrary motion, or when one of the parts stand still. Secondly it passeth into a fift when one of the parts rests, as hath beene declared before: or else when the parts ascend or descend together one by degrees, the other by leaps; and so the greater tenth may passe into a fift; seldome when both parts leape
10 together, or when they seperate themselues by degrees; and this is in regard of the relation not harmonicall which falls in betweene the parts. Thirdly, the greater third passeth into the eight by contrary motions, the vpper part ascending by degree.

The vnison.　　　　The fift.　　　　The 8.

The greater third may also passe into other Concords; and first into a lesser third, when the parts ascend or descend by degrees, or by the lesser leaps. Secondly it is continued, but rarely because it falls into Relation not harmonicall, thereby making the harmony lesse pleasing. Thirdly, into a lesser sixt, when the parts part asunder, the one by degree, the other by leap.
20 Fourthly, into a greater sixt one of the parts standing, or else the vpper part falling by degree, and the lower by leap.

Of the lesser Sixt.

The lesser sixt regularly goes into the fift, one of the parts holding his place: Rarely into an eight, and first when the parts ascend or descend together, and one of them proceeds by the halfe Note, the other by leap.

Howsoeuer the waies of rising and falling from the lesser sixt into the eight in the former example may passe, I am sure that if the Base be sharpe in *Ffavt*, it is not tollerable to rise from a sixt to an eight.

Lastly, the lesser sixt may passe into an eight in Crotchets, for they are easily tollerated. 10

It passeth likewise into other Concords, as into a greater sixt the parts rising or falling by degrees, as also into a greater or lesser third, the one part proceeding by degree, the other by leap; or when one of the parts stands. It selfe it cannot follow, by reason of the falling in of the Relation not harmonicall.

Of the greater Sixt.

The greater sixt in proceeding affects the eight; but it will hardly passe into the fift, vnlesse it be in binding wise, or when way is prepared for a close.

Finally, the greater sixt may in degrees be continued, or passe into a lesser sixt, as also into a greater third, or a lesser third.

These are the principall obseruations belonging to the passages of Concords, perfect and imperfect, in few parts; and yet in those few for fuge and formality sake, some dispensation may be graunted. But in many parts, necessity enforcing, if any thing be committed contrary to rule, it may the more easily be excused, because the multitude of parts will drowne any small inconvenience.

F I N I S.

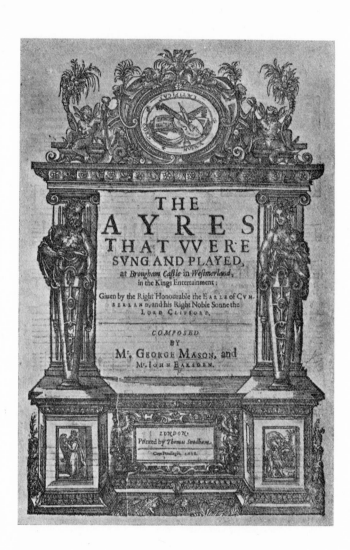

To face p. 226

I.

A Dialogue sung the first night, the King being at supper.

Tune thy chearefull voyce to mine;
  Musicke helpes digesting,
Musicke is as good as wine,
  And as fit for feasting.
Melodie now is needfull here;
It will helpe to mend our cheare
  Ioyne then, one ioy expressing.
Here is a guest for whose content
  All excesse were sparing
All to him present   10
  Hourely new delights preparing.

Ioy at thy board, health in thy dish,
  Mirth in thy cup, and in thy bed
Soft sleepe and pleasing rest wee wish.

Earth and ayre and Sea consent
  In thy entertaining.
All is old which they present
  Yet all choice contayning.
Musick alone the soule can feast
It being new and well exprest;   20
  Ioyne then sweet cords enchaining.
Could we our wisht ends aspire
  Ioy should crowne thy dishes
Proud is our desire
  If thou dost accept our wishes.

Ioy at thy board, health in thy dish,
  Mirth in thy cup, and in thy bed
Soft sleepe and pleasing rest wee wish.

II.

Another Dialogue, to be sung at the same time.

Now is the time, now is the hower
When ioy first blest this happy Bower:
Here is a sight that sweetens euery sower.
  So shines the Moon by night
    So looks the Sun by day
  Heauenly is his light
    And neuer shal decay.

There is no voice enough can sing
The praise of our great King:
  Fal showers of sweet delight,   10
    Spring flowers of plesant mirth;
What heauen hath beams that shine more bright?
  Here heuen is now; stars shine on earth.
    In one all honor groweth
    From one all comfort floweth
    Dutie saith that to this one
    All it hath it oweth.
Let then that one of all be praised
  That hath our fortunes raised.

III.

The Kings Good-night.

Welcome, welcome, King of guests
  With thy Princely traine,
With ioyful Triumphs and with Feasts
  Be welcom'd home againe.
    Frolicke mirth,
    The soule of earth,
  Shall watch for thy delight:
    Knees shall bend
    From friend to friend
  While full cups doe thee right: 10
  And so, great King, good-night.

Welcome, welcome as the Sunne
  When the night is past:
With vs the day is now begunne
  May it for euer last.

Such a morne
Did nere adorne
The Roses of the East,
As the North
Hath now brought forth: 20
The Northerne morne is best.
And so, best King, good rest.

IIII.

Come follow me, my wandring mates,
Sonnes and daughters of the Fates:
Friends of night, that oft haue done
Homage to the horned Moone,
Fairely march, and shun not light,
With such stars as these made bright;
Yet bend you low your curled tops,
Touch the hallowed earth, and then
Rise agen with anticke hops
Vnus'd of men.   10
Here no danger is, nor feare,
For true Honour harbours here,
Whom Grace attends.
Grace can make our foes our friends.

V.

A Ballad.

Dido was the *Carthage* Queene
And lou'd the *Troian* Knight
That wandring many coasts had seene
And many a dreadfull fight:
As they on hunting road, a shower
Drave them in a louing hower
Downe to a darksome caue
Where *Æneas* with his charmes
Lockt Queene *Dido* in his armes
And had what he could haue.   10

Dido Hymens Rites forgot,
Her loue was wing'd with haste,
Her honour shee considered not
But in her breast him plac't.

And when her loue was new begunne
Ioue sent downe his winged Sonne
  To fright *Æneas* sleepe;
Bad him by the breake of day
From Queene *Dido* steale away:
  Which made her waile and weepe.   20

Dido wept, but what of this?
  The Gods would haue it so:
Æneas nothing did amisse,
  For hee was forc't to goe.
Learne, Lordings, then, no faith to keepe
With your Loues, but let them weepe:
  'Tis folly to be true:
Let this Story serue your turne,
And let twenty *Didoes* burne
  So you get daily new.   30

VI.

The Dance.

Robin is a louely Lad,
No Lasse a smother euer had.
Tommy hath a looke as bright
As is the rosie morning light.
Tib is darke and browne of hue,
But like her colour, firme and true.
Ginny hath a lip to kisse
Wherein a spring of Nectar is.
Simkin well his mirth can place,
And words to win a womans grace.   10
Sib is all in all to me,
There is no Queene of Loue but she.

Let vs in a louers round
Circle all this hallowed ground
Softly, softly trip and goe,
The lightfoot Fairies iet it so.
Forward then and backe againe,
  Here and there and euerywhere,
Winding to and winding fro,
Skipping hye and lowting low;   20
And like louers hand in hand
March around and make a stand.

VII.

A Song.

The shadowes darkning our intents
  Must fade, and Truth now take her place:
  Who in our right *Ægyptian* race
A chaine of prophecies presents
With which the starry Skye consents,
And all the vnder-Elements.

Thou that art all diuine, giue eare,
  And grace our humble Songs
  That speak what to thy state belongs
Vnmasked now and cleare,   10
Which wee in seuerall straines diuide,
And Heauenborne Truth our Notes shall guide,
One by one while wee relate
That which shall tye both Time and Fate.

VIII.

  Truth, sprung from heauen, shall shine
      With her beames diuine
      On all thy Land,
  And there for euer stedfast stand
      Louely peace,
      Spring of increase
Shall like a precious gemme
Adorne thy Royall Diademe,
      Loue that bindes
      Loyall mindes   10
Shall make all hearts agree
To magnifie thy state and thee.
      Honour that proceeds
      Out of noble deeds
      Shall waite on thee alone,
And cast a sacred light about thy Throne.
Long shall thy three Crownes remaine
Blessed in thy long-liu'd raigne.
Thy age shall like fresh youth appeare,
And perpetuall Roses beare: 20
Many on earth thy dayes shall be,
But endlesse thy posteritie.
And matchlesse thy posteritie.

Truth, Peace, Loue, Honour and Long-life attend
Thee, and all those that from thy loynes descend:
With vs the angels in this *Chorus* meet;
So humbly prostrate at thy sacred feet,
Our nightly sports and prophesies wee end.

IX.
The Farewell Song.

O stay! sweet is the least delay
  When parting forceth mourning;
O Ioy! too soone thy flowers decay:
  From Rose to Bryer returning.
Bright beames that now shine here, when you are parted,
All will be dimme, all will be dumbe, and euery breast sad-hearted.
  Yet more, for true loue may presume
    If it exceede not measure.
  O Griefe! that blest houres soone consume,
    But ioylesse pass at leasure.   10
Since wee this light must loose, our loue expressing:
Farre may it shine, long may it liue, to all a publique blessing.

X.
The Lords Welcome, sung before the Kings Goodnight.

Welcome is the word
The best loue can afford;
  For what can better be?
Welcome, Lords, the time drawes neare
When each one shall embrace his deare
  And view the face hee longs to see.
Absence makes the houre more sweet
When diuided louers meet.

Welcome once againe,
Though too much were in vaine: 10
  Yet how can loue exceed?
Princely Guests, wee wish there were
Ioues Nectar and Ambrosia here
  That you might like immortals feed,
Changing shapes like full-fed *Ioue*
In the sweet pursuit of loue.

FINIS.

THO: CAMPIANI

EPIGRAMMATVM
libri II.

Vmbra.
Elegiarum liber vnus.

LONDINI
Excudebat *E. Griffin,*
Anno Domini. 1619.

THO: CAMPIANI
Epigrammatvm
Liber primus.

1   *Ad Excelsissimum Florentissimumque*
    CAROLVM, Magnæ BRITANNIÆ
        Principem.

LVDICRA qui tibi nunc dicat, olim (amplissime Princeps),
  Grandior vt fueris, grandia forte canet,
Quæque genus celebrare tuum et tua lucida possunt
  Facta, domi crescunt, siue patrata foris.
At tenues ne tu nimis (optime) despice musas;
  Pondere magna valent, parua lepore iuuant.
Regibus athletæ spatijs grati esse solebant
  Apricis; nani ridiculique domi.
Magnus Alexander magno plaudebat Homero,
  Suspiciens inter prælia ficta deos: 10
Cæsar, maior eo, Romana epigrammata legit;
  Sceptrigera quædam fecit et ipse manu.
Talia sed recitent alij tibi (maxime Princeps);
  Tu facias semper maxima, parua lege.
Enecat actiuam quia contemplatio vitam
  Longa, breuis, necnon ingeniosa, fouet.

2   *De libris suis.*
Nuper cur natum libro præpono priori?
  Principis est æquum Principe stare loco.

3   *Ad Lectorem.*
Nec sua barbaricis Galeno scribere visum est,
  In mensa nullum qui didicere modum;
Nec mea commendo nimium Lectoribus illis
  Qui sine delectu vilia quæque legunt.

4   *In Neruam.*
Ad cœnam immunis propter ioca salsa vocatur
  Nerua; suum fas est lingere quemque salem.

5   *In Tabaccam.*

Aurum nauta suis Hispanus vectat ab Indis,
    Et longas queritur se subijsse vias.
Maius iter portus ad eosdem suscipit Anglus,
    Vt referat fumos, nuda Tabacca, tuos:
Copia detonsis quos vendit Ibera Britannis,
    Per fumos ad se vellera cal'da trahens.
Nec mirum est stupidos vitiatis naribus Anglos
    Olfacere Hesperios non potuisse dolos.

6   *De auro potabili.*

Pomponi, tantum vendis medicabilis auri,
    Quantum dat fidei credula turba tibi:
Euadunt aliqui, sed non vi futilis auri;
    Seruantur sola certius ergo fide.

7   *Ad Berinum.*

Nomen traxit Amor suum, Berine,
A feruente mari, vnde diua mater
Est e fluctibus orta sals-amaris,
(Verum viuida si refert vetustas),
Credo non sine maxima procella.
Nec dici temere hoc putes, Berine;
Quippe instar maris æstuant amantes,
Sæpe et naufragium rei queruntur,
Plusque illa fidei; vorax Charybdis
Mœcha est, et furia acrior marina.   10

8   *In Villum.*

Discursus cur te bibulum iam musaque fallit?
    Humectas mentis lampada, Ville, nimis.

9   *In Neruam.*

Fratres, cognatos, natos, et vtrunque parentem
    Composuit constans Neruaque rectus adhuc;
Solus stirpe manens e tanta, sanguinis omne
    Iam decus in venis comprimit ille suis.
Ergo beatorum mensas vir prouidus ambit,
    Inde sibi sanguis crescat vt vsque nouus.
Iamque pater, mater, iam fratres, atque nepotes,
    Spreto est externo sanguine, Nerua, tibi.

10   *In Mathonem.*

Ebrius vxorem duxit Matho, sobrius horret,
    Cui nunc in sola est ebrietate salus.

11   *De bona Fama.*

Qui sapit in multis, vix desipuisse videri
    Vlla in re poterit; tam bona Fama bona est.

12 *Ad Caluum.*

Cantor saltatorque priori de ordine certant,
  Calue; sed ante choros musica nata fuit:
Dignior et motus animi quae temperat ars quam
  Corporis est, quanto corpore mens melior.

13 *Ad Cosmum.*

Plena boni est mulier bona res pretiosaque, Cosme:
  Rara sed esse nimis res pretiosa solet.

14 *In Lycum.*

Non ex officijs quæ mutua gratia debet
  Ferre per alternas atque referre vices,
Sed Lycus ex vsu priuato pendit amicos;
  Nec tacet; et solus quod sapit, inde putat.
Pectore vir bonus et sapiens cernetur aperto;
  Non itidem malus; is, quod sapit, omne tegit:
Sis licet ex fructu nummorum iam, Lyce, diues,
  Fictæ ne speres fænus amicitiæ.

15 *Ad Eurum.*

Multum qui loquitur, si non sapit, idque vetustum est;
  Caccula causidicus si sapit, Eure, nouum est.

16 *Ad Hædum.*

In multis bene cum feci tibi, non bene nosti;
  Si malefecissem, notior (Hæde) forem.

17 *In Barnum.*

In vinum solui cupis Aufilena quod haurit,
  Basia sic fælix, dum bibit illa, dabis;
Forsitan attinges quoque cor; sed (Barne) matella
  Exceptus tandem, qualis amator eris!

18 *In Cacculam.*

Caccula causidicus quid ni ditissimus esset?
  Et loquitur nemo magis, et verba omnia vendit.

19 *In Sabellum.*

Nummos si repeto (Sabelle) rides;
Cœnam si nego perfuris (Sabelle).
Vtrumuis pariter mihi molestum est:
In re non fero seria iocosum;
In re non fero serium iocosa.

20 *In Sectorem zonarium.*

Artifices inter Sector Zonarius omnes
  Lucrum non fallax solus vbique facit;
Namque opera expleta, cuncta sine lite moraue,
  Mercedem propria continet ille manu.

21 *In Neruam.*

Temperiem laudare tuam vis Neruaque tangi;
  Ex tactu tepidus, Nerua, fatebor, eras.
Sed quid homo tepidus sonat Anglis ipse docebo;
  Scilicet haud multum qui bonus aut malus est.

22 *In Tuccam.*

Non salue, sed solue tibi Lycus obuius infit;
  Vrbanus sed tu nil nisi, Tucca, vale.

23 *In Calum.*

Colligit, et scriptos Calus in se ridet iambos:
  Vix credas homini quam male dicta placent.
Inuidiamque viro ceu quid probat vtile magno;
  Quem metui potius quam placuisse iuuat;
Hæc Calus: at Genius quandoque susurrat in aurem,
  Est grauis Inuidiæ sæpe ruina comes.

24 *In Marinam.*

Docta minus, mœchis vt erat contenta duobus,
  Sic etiam bigis vecta Marina fuit:
Nunc eadem solis agitur fastosa quadrigis,
  Nunc igitur mœchos bis capit illa duos.

25 *In Tatium.*

Haud melior Tatio vir erat, nec amicior alter;
  Hoc tolerabilior iam Calus; aula docet.
Nam faciles nondum gustata potentia reddit,
  Et prima prohibet plurima fronte pudor.
Simplicitate sua sic virgo educta pudice
  Lusus declinat, verbaque nuda nimis:
Aptior hæc tandem licet obtrectante labello
  Basiolum discit reddere, parque pari;
Inde manum tangi patitur, tectasque mamillas,
  Nec refugit quamuis arctior instat amans. 10
Ast Venerem simul illa sapit, tacitosque Hymenæos,
  Inpune et fieri perdita quæque videt;
Perfricta quid non audebit denique fronte,
  Aut quem nequitiæ ponet aperta modum?
Pessimus ex prauo sic nascitur aulicus vsu;
  Nec mirum, cui non imperat vna Venus.

26 *In Acerrum.*

Cautus homo est, et Acerrus habet quot lumina quondam
  Argus, at hæc dubie cuncta nihilue vident.

27 *In Calum.*

Ne quem nunc metuas in te atros scribere versus;
  Nigrorem Æthiopi qui paret, ecquis erit?
Perfosso quid opus noua figere spicula corde?
  Quis dabit in misera pocula dira phthisi?
Omnis cura tibi, Cale, sit de funere, tanquam
  Mortuus, et speres iam bona verba licet.

28 *Ad Licinium.*

Vir bonus esse potest, Licini, cui fœmina nulla
  Imperat; at contra vir malus esse potest.

29 *In Gaurum.*

Causidicos in lite paras tibi, Gaure, peritos,
  Quorum tu meritis munera nulla negas:
In morbo medicos contra conducis inertes,
  Quamque potes minimo; sic tibi, Gaure, sapis?
Hæredi siquidem rem, vitam nemo relinquet;
  Hæredi potius viuitur, anne tibi?

30 *In Pardalum.*

Ex quibus existunt animalia spagyrus ijsdem
  Dicit ali; verum est, id ratioque docet.
Ex sale, mercurioque, et sulphure corpora constant,
  Vt Paracelsiacæ perstrepit aura scholæ.
Pardalus idcirco Chymicus tumidusque professor,
  Pro modico modium iam solet esse salis;
Idque agit assidue, magis vt se nutriat, inquit:
  Sulphur sic vtinam mercuriumque voret.

31 *In Coruinum.*

Bassano multum debet Coruinus; honorem
  Iure suo, gratum munificoque animum:
Bassanus ne hilum Coruino; qui male gratus
  Cunctorum amisit mutua iura hominum.

32 *In Histricum.*

Tritas rogo cur habeat Histricus vestes;
An deficit res, aut fides? negat: quæro
Nouis quid obstet? vestiarium non fert,
Ait, qui adaptet sibi: timet titillari.

33 *In Albium.*

An te quod pueri in via salutent
Ignoti, grauis intumescis, Albi,
Incedens veluti nouus Senator,
Fixis vultibus, et gradu seuero?

Erras; non honor hic, metus profecto est;
Nam tristis ferulæ memor puellus
Quid nî cogitet ex ineptiente
Ista te grauitate pædagogum?

34 *De Epigrammate.*

Sicut et acre piper mordax epigramma palato
Non omni gratum est : vtile nemo negat.

35 *In Coruinum.*

Quis non te, Coruine, omni iam munere dignum
Et gratum exemplo te celebrante feret?
Nam Venerem tibi dat Galla, idque palam omnibus effers,
Tanti ne meriti non videare memor.

36 *De Vtilitate.*

Vtilis est nulli semet qui negligit; omni
Vix vsquam spreta est vtilitate bonus.

37 *In Neruam.*

Vinum amat, horret aquam; qua visa Nerua recurrit,
Vt solet a rabido morsus, Amate, cane.
Porrecto vini cyatho fugitat canis; illi
Ostendas lympham quando fugare velis.

38 *Ad Ponticum.*

Argus habet natos sex, nullam, Pontice, natam;
Vulgo si credis, sobrius Argus homo est.

39 *Ad Cosmum.*

Versum qui semel vt generat nullum necat, idem
Non numeris gaudet, Cosme, sed innumeris.

40 *De Henrico 4. Francorum Rege.*

Henricum gladio qui non occidere posset,
Cultello potuit : parua timere bonum est.

41 *Ad Sereniss. Annam Reginam.*

Anna, tuum nomen si deriuetur ab anno,
Nominibus quadrant annua quæque tuis :
Annua dona tibi debentur, et annua sacra;
Atque renascendi per noua secla vices.

42 *Ad eandem.*

Quatuor Anna elementa refert, venerabile nomen;
Diuisus partes, Anna, tot annus habet.
Anna retro est eadem, sed non reflectitur annus;
Hic in se moriens, salua sed illa redit.

43 *Ad Sereniss. Carolum Principem.*

Scotia te genuit, cepit mox Anglia paruum ;
  Sed tu, quod spero, Carole, neuter eris.
Vnica te faciet nam magna Britannia magnum ;
  Nomina conueniunt factaque magna tibi.

44 *Ad Augustiss. Iacobum Regem.*

Curta tuum cur hæc metuunt epigrammata nomen ?
  Debetur famæ maxima musa tuæ.

45 *Ad Castricum.*

Acceptum pro me perhibes te, Castrice, ludis
  Admissum ; pro te captus at eijcior :
Esse mei similem non est tibi causa dolendi,
  Sed me tam similem pœnitet esse tui.

46 *Ad Rob. Caræum Equitem Auratum
nobilissimum.*

Olim te duro cernebam tempore Martis,
  In se cum fureret Gallia, qualis eras.
Teque, Caræe, diu florentem vidimus aula,
  Dux, idem et princeps, dum tua cura fuit.
Vnus erat vitæ tenor, et prudentia iuncta,
  Cum grauitate tibi sic quasi nata foret :
Nec mutauit honos, nec te variabilis ætas ;
  Qui nouit iuuenem, noscet itemque senem.

47 *In Tuccam.*

Consuluit medicum de cordis Tucca tremore ;
  Morbum (proh) talem miles habere potest !

48 *In Cacculam.*

Vulgares medici tussi febrique medentur,
  Et vitijs quorum causa cuique patet.
Morbi sed cerebri conuulso corpore, vel cum
  Non mouet, exposcunt haud leuis artis opem.
Æmulus hinc causam defendit Caccula nullam
  Quæ iusta, aut bona sit ; pessima sola placet.
Hanc agit intrepide semper, victorque triumphat,
  Tanquam is cuius ope est Attica pulsa lues.

49 *De Terminis forensibus.*

Anglorum Iurisconsulti quatuor vno
  Exposcunt anno, termini at ijs duo sunt :
Terminus a quo res trudunt, et terminus ad quem ;
  Mutua qui sumunt nomina sæpe sua.

50 *Ad Ponticum.*

Conuiuas alios quæras tibi, Pontice; cœno
    Lautius atque hodie tutius ipse domi:
Nam me qui monuit vester modo rufus olebat
    Ac si esset totus caseus, isque vetus,
Et tostus decies; atqui hunc meus horret vteruis
    Suffitum genius; Pontice, cœno domi.

51 *In Tabaccam.*

Cum cerebro inducat fumo hausta Tabacca stuporem,
    Nonne putem stupidos quos vapor iste capit?

52 *Ad Sabellum.*

Filia, siue uxor peccat, tua culpa, Sabelle, est;
    Per se nulla bona est; nulla puella mala;
Soli debetur custodi fœmina quicquid
    In vita spurce, siue decenter agit.

53 *De Gauro.*

Nil dum facit temere, nihil facit Gaurus.

54 *In Acmen.*

Est diues Titus, id fateris, Acme;
Et te coniugio expetit misellam;
Illum tu fugis, attamen beatum:
Quare? non sapit, inquis; et quid inde?
An si quis prior est Vlysse cœlebs,
Non reddes, simul hunc sinu maritum
Complexa es, stolidum magis Batillo?

55 *In Glaucum.*

Debilis eunuchus sit, sit castratus oportet;
    Tam Glauco inuisum est omne virile genus.

56 *In Laurentiam.*

Imberbi, si cui, Laurentia nubere vouit,
    Inuenit multos hæc sibi fama procos;
Impubes omnes, mora quos in amore pilosos
    Reddidit; ignoto sic perit illa viro.

57 *In Lalum.*

Ædes Lalo amplæ sat sunt, sed aranea telis
    Immunis totas inficit, ille sinit.
Quoque magis numero crescunt, gaudet magis, vnus
    Tetras bestiolas has amat atque fouet;
Non tamen vt bellas; nec quod medicina pusillis
    Vulneribus tela est; toxica nulla facit.

Verum est cum muscis lis non medicabilis; illas
   Insequitur demens, omnimodeque necat;
Idque opus imposuit misero festiua puella,
   Ala cui muscæ læsus ocellus erat.   10

58   *In Neruam.*

Dissecto Neruæ capite, haud (chirurge) cerebrum
   Conspicis; eia, alibi quære; vbi? ventriculo.

59   *Ad Aprum.*

Causidicus qui rure habitat, vicina per arua
   Si cui non nocuit, iam benefecit, Aper.

60   *Ad Pontilianum.*

Qua celebrata Lyco fuerant sponsalia luce,
   Captus homo tota mente repente fuit:
Idque velut monstri quid demiraris? at illo
   Quis non insanit (Pontiliane) die?

61   *Ad Berinum.*

Vidisti cacodæmonem, Berine;
   Qua tandem specie? canis nigri, inquis.
Vah; dicam melius, canem figura
   Vidisti cacodæmonis, Berine.

62   *Ad Aulum.*

Cum scribat nunquam Coruinus non satur, Aule,
   Tantum ieiuni carminis vnde facit?

63   *Ad Lauram.*

Egregie canis, in solis sed, Laura, tenebris;
   Nil bene fortassis non facis in tenebris.

64   *Ad Ponticum.*

Re nulla genio cum pigro (Pontice) noster
   Consentit genius; sed velut ignis aquæ
Miscetur, pariter suscepta negotia reptant
   Inuite, pariter somnus vtrumque premit.
Mens hebet, herba velut, vicino infecta veneno,
   Tota mihi; vel ceu flamma repressa furit.
Tale mihi tuus est solanum, Pontice, summus
   Patronus Decius, nescio quale tibi.

65   *De honore.*

Qui plus quam vires tolerant subit amplior æquo,
   Is merito dici possit honoris ὄνος.

66 *Ad Salustium.*

Hesterna tibi gratulor, Salusti,
De cœna magis ob iocos inermes,
Et suaues animo calente risus,
Hausto non timide nouo rubello;
Quam de istis auibus quater sepultis,
Selectis dapibus tuo palato;
Quæ mensa positæ, sed expianda,
Efflauere stygem, suoque nostrum
Tetro nunc feriunt odore nasum.
Sed me reprimo quamlibet grauatum,   10
Nam res candida fama mortuorum est.

67 *In Cossum.*

Condidit immenso puerilia membra sepulchro
   Filioli, multo marmore claustra tegens,
Cossus, quanta duos caperent satis ampla Typhæos,
   Solus consilij conscius ipse sui.
Ergo impar spectator opus miratur; at illud
   Ingenium authoris ceu leuis vmbra refert:
Ædes qui tantas habitat miser, vt bene possent
   Cum turba proceres sustinuisse duos.

68 *De Nuptijs.*

Rite vt celebres nuptias,
   Dupla tibi face est opus;
Prætendat vnam Hymen necesse,
   At alteram par est amor.

69 *Ad Guil. Camdenum.*

Legi operosum iamdudum, Camdene, volumen,
   Quo gens descripta et terra Britanna tibi est,
Ingenij fœlicis opus solidique laboris:
   Verborum et rerum splendor vtrinque nitet.
Lectorem vtque pium decet, hoc tibi reddo merenti,
   Per te quod patriam tam bene nosco meam.

70 *De suis.*

Rerum quæ noua nunc Britannicarum
Exorta est facies? Vetus recessit
Prorsus sobrietas; gula, insolensque
Cultu insania, futilisque pompa
Pessundant populum manu potentem;
Sic pauci vt bene de suoque viuant;
Vixque ex omnibus inuenire quenquam est
Qui non accipit ipse fœnus aut dat.

71 *Ad Glaucum.*

Exemplo quicquid fit, iustum creditur esse ;
Exemplis fiunt sed mala, Glauce, malis.

72 *De Medicis.*

Gnarus iudicat aurifex metalla,
Dat gemmis pretium et suum valorem :
Doctos sed medicos, bene et merentes,
Tantum ponderat imperita turba.

73 *In Ligonem.*

Inuideat quamuis sua verba Latina Britannis
Causidicis, docto nunc Ligo fertur equo.
Et medici partes agit vndique notus ; Alenum
Scenarum melius vix puto posse decus.

74 *De Senectute.*

Est instar vini generosi docta senectus ;
Quo magis annosa est, acrior esse solet.

75 *Ad Caluum.*

Insanos olim prior ætas dixit amantes ;
Non sanos hodie dicere, Calue, licet.

76 *Ad Maurum.*

Perpulchre calamo tua, Maure, epigrammata pingis ;
Apparet chartis nulla litura tuis.
Pes seu claudus erit, seu vox incongrua, nunquam
Expungis quidquam ; tam tibi pulchra placent.
Pulchra sed hæc oculis vt sint, tamen auribus horrent ;
Horrida vox omnis, lusce, litura fuit.

77 *In Cinnam.*

Notos, ignotos, celsos, humilesque salutat
Cinna ; ioco populi dicitur ergo salus.

78 *In Tuccam.*

Sit licet oppressus, licet obrutus ære alieno
Tucca, nihil sentit : quam sapit iste stupor !

79 *In Neruam.*

Coctos Nerua cibos crate aut sartagine torret
Vsque in carbonem ; deliciasque vocat.
Quid potius cuperet quam carbonarius esse
Helluo inops, cui plus quam caro carbo placet ?

80 *Ad Eurum.*

Solus pauper amat Macer beatas,
Lautas sed nimis atque fastuosas ;
Laudari cupit, Eure, non amari.

81 *Ad Ponticum.*

Propria si sedes iecur est et fomes amoris,
  Haud tuus esse potest, Pontice, sanus amor.

82 *In Ligonem.*

Ligo Latine vulnerarium potum
Dicere volebat; vuluerarium dixit.

83 *In Dædalum.*

Parua te mare nauigasse cymba
Magnum, Dædale, prædicas; quid ad me
Cymba si styga transmees eadem?

84 *Ad Iustinianum.*

Vir bonus et minime vis litigiosus haberi,
  Et lites coram iudice mitis ais,
Non amo, nec temere cuiquam struo; gratia causæ
  Maior vt accedat (Iustiniane) tuæ.
Inuidiam, ah, nescis quantam tua candida verba,
  Quas inimicitias, quæ tibi bella parant,
Quosue illic risus astantibus ipse moueres,
  Damnans iuridicis vtile litis onus,
Quamque patet turbis bonitas tua: tres tibi scribent
  Mane dicas aliqui; mox alij atque alij;   10
Nec succrescenti posthac a lite quiesces,
  Idque alieno etiam iudice: iamne tremis?

85 *In Cacculam.*

Legis cum sensum peruertis; forsitan illud
Iure facis, sed non, Caccula, iure bono.

86 *Ad Papilum.*

Papile, non amo te, nec tecum cœno libenter,
  Nec tamen hoc merito fit, fateorque, tuo:
Sed nimis ore refers miscentem tristia Picum
  Toxica, suspectum te tua forma facit:
Anguillam quisquis timet, esse hanc autumat anguem
  Et non esse sciat, cogitat esse tamen.

87 *In Lycum.*

Coniugio est iunctos qui separat execrandus;
Pugnantes dirimi non sinit ergo Lycus.

88 *In Bostillum.*

Magna Bostillus magnum se venditat aula;
Aulæ magna tamen plus bouis olla capit.

89 *Ad Eurum.*

Non laute viuis, sed læte; negligis vrbem;
    Attamen vrbani plenus es, Eure, ioci;
Tam lepido tibi fit rus ipsa vrbanius vrbe,
    Rusque tuum in se nil rusticitatis habet.

90 *In Mathonem.*

Martis vt affirmat, Veneris sed vulnere claudus
    It Matho, scit morbum dissimulare suum;
Et fictum narrat, medico indulgente, duellum;
    Prostrato inflictum sed sibi vulnus, ait.

91 *In Myrtillam.*

O dira pestis vtriusque Myrtilla
Sexus, liquescens dulcium ore Sirenum:
Parumne ducis credulos amatores
Si perdis omnes, artibus animos ijsdem
Quin optumarum polluas puellarum,
Vt nulla propter te indole ex sua viuat
Simul aure putrida hauserit tuos cantus?
O pestis omni pestilentior peste!
Haud sæuijt adeo Atticis senex Cous
A mœnibus quam depulit sacram tabem: 10
Madore nec quæ languido Britannorum
Terrebat animos omnium noua strage;
Crebraue sternutatione quæ lues longe
Grassata miseram solitudinem vidit;
Nec enim parem poeticis inaudire est
Scriptis, sed omnes vna pestis hæc pestes
Superat, sit illa vera, sit licet ficta.

92 *In Pseudomedicum.*

Inuento ex libro Medicus qui creditur esse;
    Fortunæ, non is filius artis erat.

93 *Ad Mantalum.*

Non satis est supra vulgus quod, Mantale, sentis,
    Consilium si non exprimis ore graui.
Distinguit ratio a brutis, oratio sed nos
    Inter nos, animæ lux et imago loquens.

94 *De Francisci Draci naue.*

En Draci sicco tabescit littore nauis,
    Æmula sed sphæræ, pulcher Apollo, tuæ.
Illa nam vectus vir clarus circuit orbem,
    Thymbræo et vidit vix loca nota deo.
Cuius fama recens tantum te præterit, Argo,
    Quantum mortalem Delia sphæra ratem.

95 *In Morachum.*

Mors nox perpetua est; mori proinde
Non suadet sibi nyctalops Morachus,
In solis titubans ne eat tenebris.

96 *In obitum Hen: Mag: Brit: Principis.*

Grandior et primis fatis post terga relictis,
  Concipiens animo iam noua regna suo,
Princeps corripitur vulgari febre Britannus;
  Hinc lapso vt cœpit viuere flore perit.
Sic moriemur? ad hæc ludibria nascimur? et spes
  Fortunæque hominum tam cito corruerint?

97 *De Fran: Draco.*

Nomine Dracus erat signatus vt incolat vndas;
  Dracum namque anatem lingua Britanna vocat.

98 *In obitum Iacobi Huissij.*

Heu non maturo mihi fato, dulcis Huissi,
  Occidis, heu, annis digne Mathusalijs;
Occidis ex morbo quem fraus et auara Synerti
  Sæuitia ingenuit; cui mala multa viro
Det Deus; et, lachrymis quotquot tua funera flerunt
  In diras versis, ira odioque necent.

99 *In Bostillum.*

Audijt vt cuculos comedi Bostillus in aula
  Mœchus, abit metuens prospiciensque sibi.

100 *In Fannium.*

Hispani bibit indies lagenam
Vini Fannius; vsque cruditatem
Causatur stomachi; nouem decemue
Ante annis cucumem vnicum quod edit
Maturum minus; isthic, isthic vsque
Hærens ventriculum grauat, nec esse
Hispani immemorem sinit Lyæi.

101 *In Aprum.*

Impurus, sexu nec Aper scortator in vno,
  Cum lotij clausus forte meatus erat,
Sic perijt; misero sua facta vrina ruina est,
  Et pœnæ causa in pene nocente fuit.

102 *Ad Caluum.*

Non Anglos carnis defectu, Calue, bouinæ
  Caletum Galli deseruisse ferunt,
Sed condimenti quod profert acre Sinapi;
  Hoc ioculoque sibi Gallia tota placet.
Coccineo hanc hosti nuper cum dederet vrbem,
  Neutrius Gallo copia, crede, fuit.

103 *In Coruinum.*

Effodiat sibi, Calue, oculos Coruinus, Homero,
Vt sperat, similis non tamen esse potest.

104 *In Cinnam.*

Dæmonis effigie compressit Cinna puellam;
Deinde sacerdotem se facit; atque fugat
Dæmonium vt voluit; grauida sed virgine, nescit
Anne pater Dæmon; vel sacer hospes erat.

105 *Ad Næuolam.*

Ebrius occurrit quoties tibi Næuola, vinum
Non nimium, dicis, sed bibit ille malum.

106 *In Caluum.*

Diuinas bona, Calue, tibi, sed sola futura
Semper; et hæc semper sola futura puto.

107 *Ad Eurum.*

Vocem Lyctus habet parem cicadis;
Aut qualem tenues feruntur vmbræ
Ad ripas stygis edere eiulantes.
Hunc si quis nouus audiat loquentem,
Exhaustum poterit phthisi putare;
Ipsum sin oculis metit, Cyclopum
Ceu spectans aliquem timebit auctis
Membris horribilem, atque ventricosum.
Vox tam disparilis fit vnde, dicam?
Sic, Eure, expediam: creasse mutum   10
Naturam voluisse credo Lyctum;
Errantemque dedisse semimutum.

108 *Ad eundem.*

Mentem peruertit grauis vt iactura Metello,
Sic inopinatum Lysitelique lucrum.
Harum quæ maior fuerit dementia quæris?
Damna ferens; curas nam petit, Eure, duas.

109 *Ad Ponticum.*

Qualiscunque suam contemnit fœmina famam,
Nullum, etsi decies, Pontice, iurat, amat.

110 *In Lychen.*

Græcia præclare pulchras vocat ἀλφεσιβοίας,
Quippe proci prestant munera, forma procos;
Sed formosa Lyche viuit neglecta; quot alma
Nam Cytherea trahit, fusca Minerua fugat.

111 *In Floram.*

Omnia consciolis, bona tantum narrat amanti
  Flora; ita flaccescit fama, virescit amor.

112 *Ad Areanam.*

Quod sis casta (Areana) nego, deciesque negabo,
  Credaris tota talis in vrbe licet.
Nam tuus insequitur dum putida scorta maritus,
  Dum turpi, et vario ruptus amore perit:
Crede mihi quotquot noti meretricibus illis
  Sunt homines, noti sunt, Areana, tibi:
Siue equites, seu magnatum de stemmate creti;
  Ruris an vrbis erit; pomifer, anne cocus;
Omnes, mille licet, te sunt, ô casta, potiti;
  Omnium et in morbos sic vitiata ruis.   10

113 *Ad Ponticum.*

Suspecto quid fure canes cum, Pontice, latrent
  Dixissent melius, si potuere loqui?

114 *Ad Labienum.*

Nonnullis medicina placet noua, notaque sordet;
  Sed tutas præfer tu, Labiene, nouis.

115 *In Album.*

Quem vitæ cursum, quam spem, sortemue sequaris,
  Quærendo tremulus factus es, Albe, senex,
Sic tumulo mox vt nequeas inscribere Vixi;
  Embrioque, aut minus hoc, cum morieris, eris.

116 *De Lycori et Berino.*

Gratis non amat, et sapit Lycoris:
Mœchæ dat nihil, et sapit Berinus.

117 *Ad Gallam.*

Cum loqueris resoni prodit se putrida nasi
  Pernicies: si vis, Galla, placere, tace.

118 *In Neruam.*

Et miser atque vorax optat sibi Nerua podagram,
  Solis diuitibus qualis adesse solet.
Errat si putat id voti prodesse gulosis;
  Nam quid lauta iuuat mensa, iacente fame?

119 *Ad Ponticum.*

Femina vindicta citiusne ardescit amore?
  Phœbo, si dicis, Pontice, maior eris.

120 *Ad Labienum.*

Vinum Theriacam magnam dixere vetusti
 Authores; gratum est hoc, Labiene, tibi.
Hinc te secure Baccho sine fine modoque
 Imples; visceribus sanus an æger idem est.
Sed ne delires; dirum namque ipsa venenum
 Theriaca est, sumas si, Labiene, nimis.

121 *In Lausum.*

Lausus vt æterna degit sub nube tabaccæ,
 Coniux ardenti sic sua gaudet aqua:
Vir fumum, hæc flammam bibit; infumata maritus
 Tanquam perna olim, frixa sed vxor erit.

122 *Ad Ponticum.*

Pœnituisse Mydam voti sat constat auari,
 Cumque cibus potusque aureus omnis erat.
Nunc aurum sed eum potare Chymista doceret,
 Iratosque sibi ludere posse deos.
Quid mirum tales auri si nectare lactet
 Immunes morbis, dijs similesque facit?
Sed non dijs similes sunt quos spes aurea fallit;
 Quales sint igitur (Pontice) dissimiles.

123 *In Aulum.*

Ex speculo pictor se pinxit vt Aulus, amicæ
 Dat tabulam; speculo mallet amica frui.

124 *De Henrico Principe.*

Occubuit primis Henricus clarus in annis;
 Nec spolium mortis, sed pudor ille fuit.

125 *Ad Paridem.*

Vt vetus adsciuit sibi magna Britannia nomen,
 Pingere se sexus cæpit vterque, Pari;
Haud sine vulneribus veteres tinxere Britanni
 Corpora, diuelli nec timuere cutem:
Parcere sed Pictos sibi præcipit aula nouellos,
 Et tenera leues arte polire genas.
Barbariem antiqui mores sapuere; recentes
 Mollitiem; neutrum mî placet ergo, Pari.

126 *In Vacerram.*

Damnatis quoties Vacerra turpe
Immiscet ioculis, id esse dictum
Non (vt velle videtur ore blaeso)
Imprudenter ait, sed impudenter.

127 *Ad Furium.*

Sub medium culpæ, Furi, cum coniuge mœchum
  Prendit Aper; taurum iam vitulumne vocas?

128 *Ad Berinum.*

Vxor quod nimium tua sit fœcunda, Berine,
  Conquereris; castæ sic tamen esse solent:
Addis vt implacido sit et ore, et more molesta,
  Et pugnax; castæ sic tamen esse solent:
Quin alijs lepidam dicis magis atque benignam
  Quam tibi: sic castæ non tamen esse solent.

129 *Ad Eurum.*

Mortuus Hermus abhinc tribus est aut quatuor annis;
  Immo viuit, ais; mortuus, Eure, mihi est.

130 *Ad Crispum.*

Mutua multa licet sestertia poscat amicus,
  Maxima relligio est, Crispe, negare tibi.
Sic numeras tamen vt lachrimis credaris obortis
  Quod facis officij pœnituisse tui.
Nil tibi, Crispe, deest nisi digni vultus amici;
  Nam, non vt decet, at quod decet vsque facis.

131 *Ad Chloen.*

Mortales tua forma quod misellos
Multos illaqueet, Chloe, superbis:
Hoc sed nomine carnifex triumphet.

132 *In Labienum.*

Pedere cum voluit potuit Labienus; Hybernum
  Virtute hac potuit perdere cum voluit.

133 *In Brussilium.*

Ardet Brussilij uxor histrionem;
Is funambulam; vtrinque flamma sæuit,
Nullo extinguibilis liquore, nullo.
Primum grande nemus vorauit, inde
Villas tres, ouium greges, boumque
Circum pascua tosta mugientum,
Vix aula furor abstinet paterna;
Et si fas miseris malum ominari,
Tandem cum domino domum cremabit.

134 *In Cacculam.*

Caccula cum tu sis vetus accusator, adaugens
  Crimina, quam causas dæmonis instar agis!

135 *In Cinnam.*

Dic sapere, et sapiet; stupidum dic, Cinna stupescet;
  Si furere, insanus; si premis, æger erit;
Dic modo, fiet idem quod dicis; nec simulare
  Nouit, habent vires verba veneficij.

136 *Ad Caluum.*

Ne tibi, Calue, petas socios in amore fideles,
  Si quod amas metuis perdere, solus ama.
Nocte suo fidum domino domuique molossum
  Vna salax cogit prodere cuncta canis:
Nocturni id fures norunt, quantumque libido
  Tentabit firmam deijcietque fidem.

137 *Ad Harpalum.*

Nec bene, nec belle, semper tamen, Harpale, cantas;
  Artem disce, canes sic minus, at melius.

138 *In Porcum et Neruam.*

Desinit auditis campanis meiere Porcus,
  Sit vesica licet mole molesta graui.
Haud lotium contra, sonuit si fistula, frænat
  Nerua; sed inuito sic ruit omne, miser
Vt penitus madeat; nec ei prodesse matella
  Possit, ita audaces euocat imber aquas.
Motus tam discors illis qua vi fit, Aquinus
  Quærat; nos risu res satis ipsa iuuat.

139 *In Poetastros.*

Sulphure vincenda est prurigo poetica nullo;
  Sed neque Mercurio, quem fugat illa deum.

140 *De Germanis.*

Germanus minime quod sit malus, efficit æquum
  Tota quod explosis gens amat effugijs.
Nam diuerticulis cum lex lætabitur, ansam
  Dat fraudi, multos nec sinit esse bonos.

141 *In Glaucum.*

Alas amisit Glaucus, draco nam fuit olim;
  Nunc serpens factus nec leue virus habet.

142 *In Aprum.*

Septem ciuis Aper degit, tot et aulicus, annos;
  Viuere scit melius quam, Labiene, mori.

143 *In Crispinum.*

Vxorem Crispinus habet, tamen indigus vnam
  Vix alit, extremam sensit vterque famem.
Ipsam diues amat Florus, fremit ergo maritus,
  Quanquam riuali nunc opus esse videt.

Mœchum sæpe vocat, sed cum, qui sustinet, ipse
    Qua fruitur, victu, vestibus, ære domum,
Dispeream nisi sit vere Crispinus adulter;
    Sponsus, qui sponsi munia Florus obit.

144   *De sudore Britannico.*

Quid nî pestis sit sudor malus Anglica? ciues
    Hybernis gaudent sole vigente togis.

145   *Ad Thespilem.*

Inferius labrum cur mordes, Thespilis? illi
    Ne noceas, si vis basia læta tibi.
Alterum iners cupido quamuis famuletur amanti,
    At magis hoc docta mobilitate placet.

146   *Ad Ponticum.*

Quanto causidicum magis arguo, si malus idem est,
    Tanto plus laudo, Pontice, si bonus est.

147   *Ad Gallam.*

An tua plus sitiat lingua, an plus, Galla, loquatur,
    Ardua res dictu plenaque litis erit.
Nam quoties sitit illa bibis; bene potaque garris;
    Procreat vnde nouam multa loquela sitim.
Dum bibis ergo inuita taces, mora nec datur illi
    Indefessa anima sed bibis, aut loqueris.

148   *De Londinensibus.*

Sunt Londinenses Coritani, siue Brigantes,
    Seu Cambri; raros vrbs alit ampla suos,
Sic Londinates producit mixta propago,
    Plurimus inter quos semicolonus erit,
Ægre mutandus; partis nam fœnore nummis
    Quantum quisque potest prædia ciuis emit,
In rus festinans, ætas ni præpedit, ipse;
    Hæredi saltem dant noua rura locum,
Qui, semiurbanus, velut hermaphroditus habetur
    Indigenis, nam nil rus nisi rure placet.   10
Quippe canes, vel equos semper, vel aratra loquuntur;
    Illis cætera sunt maxima barbaries.
O vtinam ciuis tantum ciuilia tractet;
    Rustica qui ruri non alienus erit.

149   *Ad Arethusam.*

Cernitur in niuea cito, si fit, sindone labes:
    Formosis eadem lex, Arethusa, datur.

150   *Ad Iustiniarum.*

Causidicos ditat, res perdit et vna clientes,
    Vno quæ verbo est, Iustiniane, mora.

151 *De horologio portabili.*

Temporis interpres, paruum congestus in orbem,
  Qui memores repetis nocte dieque sonos:
Vt semel instructus iucunde sex quater horas
  Mobilibus rotulis irrequietus agis:
Nec mecum quocunque feror comes ire grauaris,
  Annumerans vitæ damna, leuansque meæ.

152 *Ad Eurum.*

Nec turpe lucrum, nec decus, nec in plebem
Inuida potestas, pulchra sed poetarum
Votum pudicum est fama; nam bonis meta
Omnibus, at illis vnica, et mera, et sola;
Auferre quam merentibus furens nescit
Vis vulnerata diuitum: Aulus hinc viuit;
Liberque Iunius; et amabilis Flaccus;
Et vile quisquis vulgus, Eure, fastidit.

153 *Ad Labienum.*

Mentiri pro te seruo si sis bonus author;
  Pro se mentiri, cur, Labiene, vetas?

154 *Ad Haemum.*

Difficile est reperire fidem, si quæris in aula,
  Pene vbi delator tertius, Hæme, vir est.
Talem pone nouis nimium qui partibus hæret;
  Officiosus homo est? insidiosus erit.

155 *Ad Iustinianum.*

Quatuor et viginti Arthuri regia mensa
  Conuiuas aluit; quæque rotunda fuit.
Mensis iam reges longis vtuntur, at vni
  Vix est conuiuæ, Iustiniane, locus;
Augustus toto cum maximus esset in orbe,
  Illi conuictor sat Maro gratus erat.
Sed sine compare sit Maro, sic sine compare rex est
  Delicias populus quem vocat ipse suas.

156 *Ad Faustinum.*

Curuam habeat tua ceruicem, Faustine, puella:
  Sic, tanquam cupiat basia, semper erit.

157 *Ad Iustinianum.*

Si quæruntur opes, vel honores, siue voluptas,
  Vix est qui fruitur, Iustiniane, satis.
Nam satis est quicquid naturæ sufficit; vltra
  Quod poscit mens, est, Iustiniane, nimis.

158 *In Haedum.*

Causidicus bene dotatam cum duxerat Hædus,
    Nulla viro vigilis cura clientis erat.
Vere sed expleto, cum dote extinguitur vxor,
    Desertoque animi detumuere noui.
Hinc parat omnimodis pulsos reuocare clientes;
    Nam nunc si causas non agit Hædus, eget.

159 *Ad Eurum.*

Qui compotorem sibimet proponit amicum,
    Compos propositi non erit, Eure, sui.

160 *Ad Glubum.*

Hæres auari, Glube, fœneratoris
Viperea qui nunc flagra flet tua causa;
Prædia, age, vende, pasce scorta, scurrasque;
Disperde maleparta alea, gula, luxu,
Egensque quæras fœnore at triplo nummos;
Instesque, licet irrideant trapezitæ;
Nec desine vsque dum infimus rogatorum
Te filium fateare fœneratoris.

161 *Ad Amatum.*

Multas cum visit regiones Pætus et vrbes,
    In patriam læte deinde receptus erat.
Vt mos est, rogat hunc ciuis de mercibus, armis
    Miles; de ruris rustica cura bonis;
Aulicus ad vestes quod pertinet; aulica fucos,
    Atque oleum talci; singula quisque sua:
Solus qui solo nutritur iure Britanno,
    Externa de re quærit, Amate, nihil.

162 *In Tuccam.*

Plus æquo gladio pacis qui tempore credit,
    Tucca, suo, gladio sed sine, sæpe perit.

163 *Ad Luciam.*

Lucia, vir nihili est qui quanti virgo sit æris
    Curat: venalem sic sibi quærat equum.
Nequicquam magna certant de dote puellæ,
    Plus auro innuptas vita pudica beat.

164 *In Cacculam.*

Acturus causas amisit Caccula vocem,
    Inter præcones illico quærit eam,
Causidicosque illos qui vociferare solebant
    Ingenti strepitu; deserit inde forum,

Fœmellasque rogat sua quæ venalia clamant,
    Vrbanis seruis deinde molestus erat;
Turrim mox adijt, cunctos rogitansque, locosque
    Omnes vestigans : vox tamen vsque latet.
Bombarda tandem, quæ turrim euertere posset,
    Explosa, inuenta Caccula voce redit.   10

165   *De seruo suo.*

Seruo iter ingressus gladium committo ferendum;
    Mox soli atque omni cum sine teste sumus,
Aurum, noster ait, gestas, here; nec latet, id iam
    Auferre armati vis ab inerme potest;
Factum quis prodet? dominum spoliare sed absit;
    Sed facilis res est, si volo; nolo tamen.
Credo, aio, et laudo pro tempore; pergit ineptus
    Dicere qualis hero quamque fidelis erit.
Inde domum lætus redeo, gladioque recepto
    Eijcio vacuum, despicioque fidem;   10
Parque pari referens, fidum te sensimus, inquam,
    Et retinere licet, si volo; nolo tamen.
Nam neque credendus, nec habendus, talia seruus
    Aut qui concipere, aut non reticere, potest.

166   *Ad Hædum.*

Ignarum iuuenem nudum cur trudis in vrbem?
    Neglecto cæcum quis duce tentat iter?
Gnossia non totidem domus est erroribus, Hæme,
    Fallax, his filo quamlibet esset opus,
Ætati crudæ quot vita vrbana tenebras
    Obijcit, impuras et sine luce vias.
Ne duce destituas titubantem nocte dieque
    Filiolum, saluum si cupis, Hæme, tibi.

167   *Ad Labienum.*

    Tres nouit, Labiene, Phœbus artes;
    Vt narrant veteres sophi; peræque
    Quas omnes colui, colamque semper:
    Nunc omnes quoque musicum, et poetam
    Agnoscunt, medicumque Campianum.

168   *Ad Calathen.*

    Græcas, Latinas, litterasque Gallicas
    Laudo: puellæ lingua sed si sit bona,
    Cur vteretur, Calathe, alia quam sua?

169   *In Næuolam.*

Tres est pollicitus rationes Næuola Cinnæ,
    Nummos quî nollet reddere: reddit eas:
Nil quod debetur prima; altera nil quod haberet;
    Tertia non presto est: Næuola debet eam.

170   *Ad Eurum.*

Pro patria si quis dulci se dixerit, Eure,
　Velle mori, ridens vt sibi viuat, ais,
Ciuis auarus; et vt seruetur Caccula rostris;
　Splendeat ut picta veste rotaque Calus.
Sic tu; pro patria fortis cadet attamen omnis;
　Si bona sit, merita est; sin mala, dulce mori.

171   *In Crassum.*

Crassus ab vrbe profecturus, quam firmiter hærens,
　Ludorum causa, desidiosus amat:
Tres licet haud vltra noctes sit rure futurus,
　Idque absoluat iter dimidiata dies:
Solennem ad cænam primos inuitat amicos,
　Ceu natalitiam quam celebrare parat;
Magna cum pompa, curua resonante sedetur
　Buccina, et in vitrum plena refusa salus,
Conuiuas æquo quæ iure perambulat omnes;
　Auspicium fœlix hinc sibi sumit iter.   10
Crassus at extremis tanquam rediturus ab Indis,
　Mox testamentum perficit; inde noua
Nata salus, reditum faustum quæ spondet amico;
　Postremo edictum tempus euntis erat;
Maiæ nimirum (cœlo suadente) calendis
　Exibit; nonæ iamque Decembris erant.

172   *Ad Lollium.*

Vt locupleti addat pauper, præpostera res est:
　Diuitis est, Lolli, gloria sola, dare.

173   *Ad Lauram.*

Singula dum miror tua labra, oculosque, genasque;
　Quicquid id est verbis, Laura, modesta premis.
Crines sin laudo, perfusa rubore silescis;
　Quam misere non hos esse fatere tuos.

174   *Ad Ponticum.*

Hic, illic, et vbique, et nullibi, Pontice, lex est;
　Cumque tenes vinctam, te latebrosa fugit.
Pauciloqua antiquis constabat certa Britannis;
　At nunc ambigua est lex sine lege loquens.

175   *Ad Afram.*

Calcat sublimis vulgaria verba poesis,
　Nec narrat, sed res ambitiosa creat.
Ludere si libet, ætatis tibi reddere florem,
　Par Hecubæ quanquam sis, prius, Afra, valet,

Quadrupedis pigræ quam ros, cerussaue inuncta,
  Vel minium Venetum, fulua vel empta coma ;
Dentes seu vere quos inserit Argus eburnos,
  Totaque mangonis pharmacopœa Lami.
Suauiter illa tibi canet optatos Hymenæos,
  Et gratis faciet ; quod tamen, Afra, veta :   10
Oscula det iuuenis, sed anus ferat aurea dona,
  Carminibus celebris quæ cupit esse bonis.

176   *Ad Albericum.*

  Res est quemlibet vna quæ benignum
  Et gratis facere (Alberice) possit ;
  Nullum lædere, quamlibet merentem.

177   *In Largum.*

Vendit Largus oues, laudatque emptoribus illas
  Vt teneras ; teneras sed sibi laudat aues.

178   *Ad Carolum Fitzgeofridum.*

Iamdudum celebris scriptorum fama tuorum,
  In me autem ingenue non reticendus amor.
Frustra obnitentem si non fortuna vetasset,
  In veteres dederat, Carole, delicias :
Hæc tibi qualiacunque tamen noua lusimus, ut nos
  Vsque amplecteris non alieno animo.

179   *Ad Stellam.*

  Vis, Stella, nomen inseri nostris tuum
    Compendiosis versibus ?
  An sat tibi est, ô delicata, sidera
    Inter minora si mices ?

180   *Ad Ed. Mychelburnum.*

Immemor ô nostri quid agis ? nec enim tibi magnus
Natalis frustra redijt, monitorque vetustæ
Semper amicitiæ nouus, et iam debitor annus ;
Accipe nostra prior, tenui sed carmina cultu,
Qualia sunt domini longo de funere rapta ;
Posterior tua si compti quid musa resoluet,
Festinans lepido quod portet epistola versu,
Vnicus antidotos facile exuperaueris omnes.
Hæc pauca interea, leue tanquam munus, habeto,
Quæ nouus ex vsu merito tibi destinat annus,   10
Iusque sodalitij officio quocunque tuetur.
Quanta sit horrifici Iouis inclementia cernis ;
Vt valeas lignis opus est ; et si sapis, ipsi
Cum falce, et tento nolles parsisse Priapo.

181 *In Glaucum.*

Tempore mitescit quantumvis fructus acerbus;
  Fitque sapor gratus, qui modo crudus erat.
At Glaucus quanto euadit maturior annis,
  Austerus tanto fit magis atque magis.
Coniugis exemplo iam desinat esse malignus;
  Nam suauis, lepida est, nec grauis illa viris.

182 *Ad Rutham.*

Non satis hoc caute dixti modo, Rutha, sorori,
  Te tam formosam non pudet esse leuem?
Illud nam dictum subito sic læsa retorsit,
  Te non formosam non iuuat esse leuem.

183 *In Gaurum.*

Perpetuo loqueris, nec desinis; idque molestum
  Omnibus est; et scis; sed tibi, Gaure, places.

184 *In Auricium.*

Haud quenquam sinis, Aurici, te adire,
Quantumuis humili adlocutione;
At nos alloquimur poli vtriusque
Rectorem, et rutila manu tonantem:
An non tu nimium tumes, sacerdos?

185 *Ad Herennium.*

Alcinoo mortem toties minitatus (Herenni),
  Cur occurrenti postea mitis eras?
Effrænem quamuis nequeas compescere linguam,
  At te iam video posse tenere manum.

186 *Ad Augustiss: Carolum magnæ Britanniæ
  Principem, Walliæ Principatum pro veteri
  ritu auspicaturum, die 4. No:*

Lœtus Britannis, ecce, festinat dies,
  Quintumque nunc præoccupat
Sacrum Nouembris; perge, ter beata lux,
  Quam festa signabit nota.
Maturus annis, mente nec princeps minor
  Britanniarum Carolus,
Ornandus hodie regijs insignijs,
  Exibit vt sponsus nouus,
Puris ephæbis cinctus, et procerum choro,
  Ceu gemma pompa in aurea;   10
Exceptus hilari confluentum murmure,
  Clarisque vulgi plausibus.
Prodi, ô beate, rem capesse publicam,
  Vmbra nimis torpes diu:

Vestigijs iam assuesce maiorum inclytis
  Præstantioris æmulus.
Pulchram tibi hic sit primus ad famam dies;
  At nemo norit vltimum.

187   *Ad Magnam Britanniam.*

Reddidit antiquum tibi, magna Britannia, nomen
  Rex magnus, magnos dum facit ille suos.

188   *De Regis reditu e Scotia.*

Nil Ptolomæus agit, cælique volumina nescit,
  Nam nunc a gelido cardine (Phœbe) redis,
Et veris formosa rosis Aurora refulget:
  Hunc, precor, æternum reddat Apollo diem.

189 *Ad ampliss. totius Angliæ Cancellarium,*
Fr. Ba.

Debet multa tibi veneranda (Bacone) poesis
  Illo de docto perlepidoque libro,
Qui manet inscriptus Veterum Sapientia; famæ
  Et per cuncta tuæ secla manebit opus;
Multaque te celebrent quanquam tua scripta, fatebor
  Ingenue, hoc laute tu mihi, docte, sapis.

190   *Ad eundem.*

Patre, nec immerito, quamuis amplissimus esset,
  Amplior, vt virtus, sic tibi crescit honor.
Quantus ades, seu te spinosa volumina iuris,
  Seu schola, seu dulcis Musa (Bacone) vocat!
Quam super ingenti tua re Prudentia regnat,
  Et tota æthereo nectare lingua madens!
Quam bene cum tacita nectis grauitate lepores!
  Quam semel admissis stat tuus almus amor!
Haud stupet aggesti mens in fulgore metalli;
  Nunquam visa tibi est res peregrina, dare.   10
O factum egregie, tua (Rex clarissime) tali
  Gratia cum splendet suspicienda viro!

191   *Ad Hymettum.*

Sis probus vsque licet, timidus tamen ipse teipsum
  Deseris, obsequio debet inesse modus,
Vilis erit cunctis sibi qui vilescit, Hymette:
  Non omnis pudor aut vtilis aut bonus est.

192   *Ad Ed: Mychelburnum.*

Nostrarum quoties prendit me nausea rerum,
  Accipio librum mox, Edoarde, tuum,
Suauem qui spirat plenus velut hortus odorem,
  Et verni radios ætheris intus habet.

Illo defessam recreo mentemque animumque,
  Ad ioca corridens deliciasque tuas ;
Haud contemnendo vel seria tecta lepore,
  Cuncta argumentis splendidiora suis.
Hæc quorsum premis ? vt pereant quis talia condit ?
  Edere si non vis omnibus, ede tibi.   10

193   *Ad Sitim.*

Sitis malorum pessimum,
Aegris molestum sobrijs,
Sanis inutile ebrijs,
Si sanus vllo sit modo
Qui non nisi vt bibat, bibit,
Semper palude plus madens,
Sitiens tamen tosta magis
Multis arena solibus.
Nunc est benigna vt sis, Sitis,
Bustis auari Castoris   10
Diesque noctesque asside,
Qui te volens viuens tulit ;
Consors amicum protege,
Picto sedens in marmore ;
Qui nubilo cælo caue
Ne sic madescat, Castoris
Vt ossa sicca perluat ;
Sed vnicum te sentiat
Qui te colebat vnicus,
Sorore cum tua Fame :   20
At non amantem me tui
Cum febre pariter desere,
Sitis, malorum pessimum.

194   *Ad Lupum.*

Nemo virtutem non laudat, sæuit et idem
  In vitium, hoc hominum sed, Lupe, more facit.
Nam quis ob hoc drachmam virtuti præbet egenti ?
  Aut in·se vitium non amat, atque fouet ?

195   *Ad Eurum.*

Insanum cupidis labris ne tange Lyæum ;
  Sic minus audentem te trahet, Eure, Venus.
Nec Veneri indulge, quamuis bona forma vocabit ;
  Nam minus in votis sic tibi Bacchus erit.

196   *Ad Gallum.*

Quod nemo fecit sanus, neque fecerit vnquam,
  Tu facis, inuideas cum mala, Galle, Fabro ;
Sollicitus domini quod nunc terit atria magni ;
  At nescis hac quam conditione perit ;

Qui soli parat vsque adeo seruire patrono,
  Vt non prospiciat libera tecta sibi.
Idque cauet dominus, modice dum plurima donat;
  Perpetuo, at parco fomite spemque leuat.
Vixque solubilibus vinctum tenet vsque catenis,
  Exercens varijs nocte dieque modis,   10
De libertatis nequando cogitet vsu.
  Iam vice vis fungi, liuide Galle, Fabri?

197   *Ad Lecesterlandium.*

Amplis grandisonisque, Lecesterlandie, verbis
  Implacabiliter vociferare soles,
Vxor dum queritur quod fit tibi curta supellex;
  Fibula sed verbis æquiparanda tuis.

198   *Ad Hippum.*

Quanquam non simplex votum, facis attamen vnum;
  Nam præter vinum nil petis, Hippe, bonum.

199   *Ad Faustinum.*

Da mihi, da semper, nam quod, Faustine, dedisti
  Esse datum nollem; res cito parua perit.
Sin tædet, dandoque velis imponere finem;
  Da semel, vt nunquam cogar egere datis.

200   *Ad Phloen.*

Quid custodita de virginitate superbis,
  Iam licet annumeres ter tria lustra, Phloe?
Intactam nam te cum vix tria lustra videbas,
  Haud potuit cassa vendere lena nuce.
Gloria virginitas formosis, dedecus æque
  Turpibus est, ætas si sit vtrique grauis.

201   *Ad Volumnium.*

Rident rusticulam, anseremque multi:
Ignauos asinos, oues, bouesque;
At non est homine imperitiore
Irridendum animal magis, Volumni;
Tanto ridiculus magis, Volumni, est,
Quanto plus sapere obtinet videri.
Nam quis non medicum excipit Ligonem,
Vectum quadrupede, intimis chachinnis,
Coum qui colit atque Pergamenum?
Multis sed sapit, imperatque multis   10
Vt vitæ dominus, tremorque mortis
Tanto ridiculus magis, Volumni, est.

202   *Ad Mycillum.*

Nullos non laudas, Suffenos, siue Cherillos,
  Seu quos in circo cruda iuuenta legit;
Candidus hinc censor dici contendis, at omnes
  Qui laudat, nullum laude, Mycille, beat.

203   *Ad Furium.*

Semper ad arma soles, Furi, clamare; cubili
  Siue lates, seu te compita plena vident.
Sed nunquam profers Veneris sint, Martis an arma;
  Vtcunque infœlix, te duce, miles erit.

204   *In Helyn.*

Captat amatores quoties se dicit amare;
  Fallax obsequium est; non amat, hamat Helys.

205   *Ad Vincentium.*

Dum placeo tibi, Vincenti, mea plurima poscis
  Mutua, te simul at ceperit ira leuis,
Mox eadem quamuis male custodita remittis;
  Lucrum est, Vincenti, displicuisse tibi.

206   *In Hebram.*

Difficilis non est, nec amantem respuit vnum;
  Vnum vero vnum vix amat Hebra diem.

207   *Ad Cacculam.*

Dicere te inuitum cuiquam male, Caccula, iuras;
  Inuitus tune es (Caccula) causidicus?

208   *Ad Caluum.*

Lingua proterua, rapax manus, et gula, Calue, profunda;
  Hæc tria sunt Daui commoda sola tui.
Illo prætereunte fremunt quacunque molossi;
  Sentit et in primo limine nostra canis.
Adueniente coci remouent patinasque cibosque,
  Arctius et retinet pallia quisque sua.
Audito fugitant fœmellæ; Caccula quamquam
  Natus litigijs, illius ora timet.
Sæpe domi ne te nunc visam terret imago
  Orci, nam seruat Cerberus ipse fores.   10
Dijs genitos quæras, hunc ni dimittis, amicos,
  Clauisque accinctos Amphitrioniades.

209   *Ad Philochermum.*

Quæris tu quare tibi musica nulla placeret;
  Quæro ego, cur nulli tu, Philocherme, places?

210   *Ad doctos Poetas.*

Nullus Mæcenas dabit hac ætate Poetis
   Vt viuant; melius sed bona fama dabit.

211   *Ad Rusticum.*

Rustice, sta, paucis dum te moror, auribus adsis;
   Dic age, cuias es? Salsburiensis, ais?
Pembrochi viduam num tu Sidneida nosti?
   Non: saltem natos? cum sit vterque potens;
A thalamis alter regis celeberrimus heros;
   Alter at in thalamis? proh tenebrose, negas?
Inclitus ergo Senex Hertfordius an tibi notus?
   Tantumdem: coniux quid speciosa senis?
Non: non? anne tuum scis nomen? si id quoque nescis,
   Cætera condono hac conditione tibi.   10

212   *Ad Cacculam.*

Causidicus tota cum sis notissimus vrbe,
   Atque alienas res irrequietus agas,
Ducere cur cessas vxorem, Caccula? lites
   Non est vt fugias, litigiosus homo es.

213   *Ad Caluum.*

Atroniam vt pulchram laudas, vt denique bellam,
   At minor hac Rhodius forte colossus erat.
Et capite, ac humeris superaret Amazonas omnes;
   Ad quam, si confers, Penthesilea foret
Qualis cum vetula pappat nutrice puella;
   Sola gigantei est germinis illa fides.
Cum video, spectrum videor mihi (Calue) videre,
   Et vix luminibus cernere vera meis.
Cuius ne temere attentes tu basia, totum
   Eius in os poterit nam caput ire tuum.   10

214   *De sacra dote.*

Verba sacerdotem duo constituunt, sacer, et dos;
   Sæpe sed occurrit vir sine dote sacer.

215   *Ad Rufum.*

Quos toties nummos oras, tibi, Rufe, negare
   Relligio est; grauius, sed dare, forsan erit.
Nam meus infaustus cunctis solet aureus esse,
   Et semper damni plus mea dona ferunt.
Conciet hinc Bacchus, vel fallax alea bellum;
   Labe vel asperget non bene parta Venus;
Omnia sponte sua mala quæ vitabit egestas:
   Nescis quas turbas plena crumena dabit.

Damnosos iuueni currus inuitus Apollo
  Concessit, nummos sic tibi, Rufe, nego.   10
Nec promissa Deus potuit reuocare nociua,
  Sed tibi promitto, sed tibi dono nihil.
Tu fortunatos qui prosint, quære patronos;
  Ast ego, ne noceant nostra, cauebo tibi.

216   *Ad Gallum.*

Perdidit ebrietas multos, tibi proficit vni,
  Galle, licet valide membra caputque grauet.
Hinc morbum simulas et acuta pericula lecto
  Postridie stratus vix animamque trahens;
Tunc inimicitias componis et eximis iris
  Expositum pectus sollicitumque metu:
Et pacem accitis euincis ab hostibus, omnes
  Expiraturis nam decet esse pios;
Deinde reuiuiscis cuncto securus ab hoste,
  Et Martem Bacchum fallere, Galle, doces.   10

217   *Ad Cacculam.*

Quæ speciem instaurant partes has, Caccula, verum est
  Ad speciem quod habes; nec tamen ad speciem.

218   *Ad Stellam.*

Pictor formosam quod finxit, Stella, Mineruam
  Carpis; at hoc similis fit magis illa tibi.

219   *Ad Ponticum.*

Vxorem nosti Camerini, (Pontice,) quam sit
  Toto deformis corpore et ore tetro:
Casta tibi visa, et merito; sed mœcha reperta est;
  Hanc vir in hesterno prendit adulterio.
Proh quantum sæuisse putas? Nil, Pontice, lætus
  Ipsam sed laudans cœpit amare magis;
Nam credebat, ait, turpem prius; atque adeo vt, se
  Præter, qui ferret tangere nemo foret.

220   *Ad Blandinum.*

Immemor esse tui dicor, Blandine, mearum
  Nulla tuum siquidem pagina nomen habet.
Sed Blandine, iterum atque iterum, Blandine legaris,
  Ne, Blandine, ferar non memor esse tui.

221   *Ad Marianum.*

Prudens pharmacopola sæpe vendit
  Quid pro quo, Mariane, quod reprendis,
Hoc tu sed facis, œnopola, semper.

222 *Ad Tho: Munsonium, equitem Auratum et Baronetum.*

Quicquid in aduersis potuit constantia rebus,
　Munsoni, meritis accumulare tuis
Addidit, et merito victrix Dea, iamque sat ipse
　Fama et fortunis integer amplus eris.

223 *Ad Eundem.*

Ne te spes reuocet nec splendor vitreus aulæ ;
　In te, Munsoni, spes tua maior erit.

224 *Ad Gulielmum Strachæum.*

Paucos iam veteri meo sodali
Versus ludere, musa, ne graueris,
Te nec tædeat his adesse nugis,
Semper nam mihi charus ille comptis
Gaudet versiculis facitque multos,
Summus Pieridum vnicusque cultor.
Hoc ergo breue, musa, solue carmen
Strachæo veteri meo sodali.

225 *Ad Lectorem.*

Fit sine lege liber, saluo cui demere toto
　Particulas licet, aut apposuisse nouas.
Sat, Lector, numeri ; numeris si sat tibi factum est ;
　Cui numeri potius, quam numerosa placent.

THO: CAMPIANI

1   *Ad Sereniss.* CAROLVM *Principem.*

Non veterem tibi dono librum, clarissime Princeps,
    Tanquam donatum ; si tamen ire iubes,
Splendorem fortasse nouum trahet, et melior iam
    Prodibit cum se nouerit esse tuum.

2   *Ad Lectorem.*

Lusus si mollis, iocus aut leuis, hic tibi, Lector,
    Occurrit, vitæ prodita vere scias,
Dum regnat Cytheræa : ex illo musa quieuit
    Nostra diu, Cereris curaque maior erat :
In medicos vbi me campos deduxit Apollo,
    Aptare et docuit verba Britanna sonis :
Namque in honore mihi semper fuit vnicus ille,
    Cuius ego monitis obsequor vsque lubens.
Quid facerem ? quamuis alieno tempore, Phœbus,
    En, vocat, et recitat pulueris ore scelus.   10
Respondente cheli, metuendaque dulce sonanti,
    Quo sic perfudit mentem animumque meum,
Cogerer vt chartis, male sed memor, illa referre
    Quæ cecinit mira dexteritate deus.
Hinc redijt mihi musa vetus, sed grandior, et quæ
    Nunc aliqua didicit cum grauitate loqui ;
Et noua non inuita mihi, diuersaque dictat,
    Omnia quæ, Lector candide, reddo tibi.

3   *Ad Librum.*

I nunc, quicquid habes ineptiarum
Damnatum tenebris diu, libelle,
In lucem sine candidam venire
Excusoris ope eruditioris :
Exinde vt fueris satis polite
Impressus, nec egens noui nitoris,
Mychelburnum adeas vtrumque nostrum,
Quos ætas, studiumque par, amorque,
Mi connexuit optume merentes :

Illis vindicibus nihil timebis   10
Celsas per maris æstuantis vndas
Rhenum visere, Sequanam, vel altum
Tibrim, siue Tagi aureum fluentum.

4   *Ad Pacem de augustiss: Reg. Elizabetha.*

O pax beatis, vnicum decus terris,
Quam te lubens osculor, amabilis mater,
Rerumque custos, et benigna seruatrix!
Quæ sola te tuetur integram nobis,
Non illam amem, illam venerer omnibus dictis,
Factisque? pro illa vnquam mori reformidem?
Illam quis amens proditam exteris optet,
Domi suis quæ pacem et exteris donat?

5   *In Caluum.*

Risi, Calue, hodie satis superque,
Notorum quia quemque vt attigisti,
Currentem licet et negotiosum,
Sistebas, retinens, toga prehendens;
Tum demum rogitas equumne grandem
Empturus sit, et optimum, et valentem;
Nec cessas odiosus abnuentem
Vnumquemque trecenties rogare.
Quin me iam decies eras de eodem
Aggressus; memini, fuit molestum.   10
Si quisquam interea tuum caballum
Posset ridicule satis tabella
Pro re pingere, squallidum, vietum,
Morbosos timide pedes leuantem,
Pictor vendiderit prius tabellam
Quam tu vendideris tuum caballum.

6   *Ad Clonium.*

Fitne id quod petimus? mihi si persuaseris, inquis:
Siccine nos semper ludis, inepte Cloni?
Vnum nunc vtinam tibi persuadere liceret:
Vt cito suspendas te, miser, illud erit.

7   *In Crispum.*

Crispus amat socios, vt auara Lycoris amantes;
Vt libros Casinus bibliopola suos;
Ciuis vt emptores Vincentius; vtque clientes
Caccula causidicus; sacra sacrator Helix;
Non laudem, non quod verum mereantur amorem,
Sed prodesse magis quod sua cuique solent.

8 *In Caluum.*

In circo modo Calue te prementem
Vt vidi nitidæ latus puellæ,
Sermonique auide viam astruentem;
Mox diuam Venerem, Leporem, Amoremque
Orabam tibi, ne inficetus illam
De grandi quid equo tuo rogares.

9 *In obitum Gual. Deuoreux fratris clariss. Comitis Essexiæ.*

Pilas volare qui iubebat impius
Forata primus igne ferra suscitans,
Ei manus cruenta, cor ferum fuit.
Fenestra quanta mobili hinc deæ patet
Ferire possit vt malos, bonos simul.
Quid alta fortitudo mentis efferæ,
Toriue corporis valent? ruunt globi,
Præitque cæcitas, et atra nubila,
Sonique terror æthera, et solum quatit
Maligna fata, Deuoreux, et vnice,   10
Et alme frater incliti ducis, sacro
Tibi igne perdidere saucium caput,
Equo labansque funebri, heu, acerbum onus
Tuis, reuectus arduum ad iugum redis;
Rotaque subgemente curribus iaces
Molesta pompa fratri, et omnibus bonis.
Peribit ergo Rhona, pulsa corruet
Fero canente classicum tuba sono,
Et vlta stabis inter vmbra cælites.

10 *Ad Melleam.*

O nimis semper mea vere amata
Mellea, o nostri pia cura cordis,
Quanta de te perpetuo subit mi
    Causa timoris!

Eminus quanquam iaculetur altus
Aureos in te radios Apollo,
Torqueor ne fictus amans in illis
    Forte lateret.

Et procul cælo pluuias cadentes
In sinus pulchros agitante vento,
Horreo, insanum placidus tonantem   10
    Ne vehat imber.

Somnians, et res vigilans ad omnes,
Excitor; noctuque pauens dieque;
Sæpe si vestra potuit quis esse
    Quæro sub vmbra.

11 *De obitu Phil: Sydnæi equitis
aurati generosissimi.*

Matris pennigerum alites Amorum,
Quid suaues violas per et venustas
Nequicquam petitis rosas Philippum,
Dumis vsque Philip, Philip, sonantes?
Confossum modo nam recepit Orcus,
Omnes dum superare bellicosa
Fama audet iuuenis; renunciate
Funestum Veneri exitum Philippi,
Vatem defleat vt suorum Amorum.

12 *In Melleam.*

Mellea mi si abeam promittit basia septem;
 Basia dat septem, nec minus inde moror:
Euge, licet vafras fugit hæc fraus vna puellas,
 Basia maiores ingerere vsque moras.

13 *In Cultellum.*

Cultelle, Veneri te quis iratus faber
Tam triste dira contudit ferrum manu?
Labella bellæ cæsa funesto scatent
Per te cruore: ah nectaris quantum perit!
Heu, heu, puellæ personat planctu domus;
Furit, dolori tantus accessit timor;
Nec acquiescit vspiam; impotens loqui,
Et basiare iam, quod est miserrimum:
At tu sceleste frustulatim diffluens
Pœnas Amori, sed nimis seras, dabis. 10

14 *Ad Caspiam.*

Virgo compressa est, inuitaque, Mellea iurat;
 Furem cur nollet prodere voce, rogo.
Se mala respondit clamare cupisse, prehendi
 Solam cum solo sed metuisse viro.
O pudor insignis, facilisque modestia, qualem
 Optarem soli, Caspia dura, tibi!

15 *Ad eandem.*

Phœnicem simulas, Caspia, Persicam,
Quæ nunquam socijs ardet amoribus,
Flamma sed moriens nascitur e sua.
Exors tu pariter, solaque amantium
Congressus fugis, et contiguas faces;
Verum insana diem ne reparabilis
Expectes volucris, fataque viuida;
Formæ flamma etenim nulla tuæ parem
Quibit reddere, non si Venus aurea
Aut pulchrum in cinerem se Charites dabunt. 10

16   *Ad Labienum.*

Quæ celare cupit non peccat fœmina, dicis,
    Quæ celat, peccat; sed, Labiene, minus.

17   *In Carinum.*

Cogito sæpe, Carine, sed infœliciter, vnde
    Signarit vultus tanta rubedo tuos:
Nam sumptus ne sis vinosus terret, auaro
    Conditur gelida nec nisi cœna fame.
Porrho incœnatus nonnumquam, sordide, dormis,
    Aridulusque siti somnia vana vides.
Esurientis at ora magis pallore notantur,
    Et macilenta creat liuida signa fames.
Quæro igitur tanti quæ sit tibi causa ruboris;
    Forsitan hanc speciem pictus ab arte petis: 10
Sed reliqua vt pingas quare vis pingere nasum
    Non video; totusque hæreo et excrucior.

18   *In Melleam.*

Anxia dum natura nimis tibi, Mellea, formam
    Finxit, fidem oblita est dare.

19   *Ad Caluum.*

Italico vultu donas mihi, Calue, machæram;
    More Britannorum protinus accipio.
Id mi succenses; nunc ergo remittere conor;
    Quo more id faciam non tamen inuenio.

20   *Ad Næuolam.*

Desine, nam scelus est, neu perdere, Næuola, tentes
    Quod mihi suspirat Mellea basiolum.
Qui ferro necat, aut rigido cor transigit ense,
    Terrenam molem diuidit ille animæ.
Dulcia sed temere qui basia soluit amantum,
    Cælitus vnitas diuidit ille animas.

21   *Ad Caluum.*

Fœmina cum pallet ne dicas pallida quod sit,
    Si, Calue, ingenui munus obire velis:
Languentem reficit mulier laudata colorem,
    Totum quem formæ credita culpa premit.

22   *In Lycum.*

Cum, Lyce, vouisti serum tibi funus, opinor
    Te latuit lapidem rene latere tuo.

23   *Ad Lucium.*

Crassis inuideo tenuis nimis ipse, videtur
   Satque mihi fœlix qui sat obesus erit.
Nam vacat assidue mens illi, corpore gaudet,
   Et risu curas tristitiamque fugat.
Præcipuum venit hæc etiam inter commoda, Luci,
   Quod moriens minimo sæpe labore perit.

24   *Ad Marinum.*

   Parui tu facis optumos poetas ;
   Laudas historicos, amasque laxum
   Sermonem, pedibus grauis Marine ;
   Sparsas nec sale fabulas moraris.
   Cur mirabilis omnibus, Marine,
   Scriptor fit Plato ? quippe fabulosus.

25   *In Maurum.*

Tres elegos Maurus totidemque epigrammata scripsit,
   Supplicat et musis esse poeta nouem.

26   *In Cottam.*

Cotta per æstates vt in hortis dormiat vrgent
   Vxor obesa, Canis, torrida Zona, torus.

27   *De Catullo et Martiale.*

   Cantabat Veneres meras Catullus ;
   Quasuis sed quasi silua Martialis
   Miscet materias suis libellis,
   Laudes, stigmata, gratulationes,
   Contemptus, ioca, seria, ima, summa ;
   Multis magnus hic est, bene ille cultis.

28   *Ad Meroen.*

Scortatorem optes, Meroe nasuta, maritum ;
   Diminui nasum sic puto posse tuum.

29   *Ad Lupum.*

Aduersus fortem poterit vis nulla valere,
   Et fateor ; sed quis tum, Lupe, fortis erit ?

30   *Ad Hæmum.*

Notorum mandas morientum nomina libro,
   Atrum quem merito funereumque vocas :
Sin cupis, Hæme, pius lætusque notarius esse,
   Inscribas viuos ; sic liber albus erit.

31   *In Ottuellum.*

Promissis quoties videt capillis
Blanditur mihi tonsor Ottuellus,
Cum vix curticomo feret salutem.
An tonsoribus, vt suis puellis,
Chari sunt et amabiles comati,
His formæ studio, lucelli vtrisque?

32   *Ad Philochermum.*

Quæ potuit riuos retinere et saxa mouere
    Musica, te nulla parte, vel arte, mouet;
Quod facit ergo caue, Philocherme, tarantula vulnus,
    Ictus enim, ni fit musica grata, peris.

33   *Ad Ianum.*

Cur tibi displiceat tua, Iane, quod vxor ametur?
    An tibi quam nemo possit amare placet?

34   *Ad Laur: Mychelburnum.*

Quis votis tibi, somne, supplicabit
Tam surdo atque hebeti deo, clientem
Qui sex continuas iacere noctes
Molli me vigilem toro sinebas,
Disperdique vaga cor inquietum
Fessa et lumina cogitatione?
Sed postquam salibus cubilibusque,
Laurenti, excipior tuis, solutos
Cepit grata simul quies ocellos.
Quod sane ob meritum puella si quæ,   10
Laurenti, vigiles queretur horas
Dum pulchra speculo intuetur ora,
Mittam ad te, lepidum deum soporis.

35   *Ad Iustinianum.*

Tu tanquam violas, laurum, et thyma dicis olere
    Os consobrinæ, Iustiniane, tuæ;
Ac veluti minio buccas, et labra notari:
    Ipso quin minio picta labella rubent,
Atque genæ; floresque remansos spiritus halat;
    Ex vero omnia habet; sed nihil ex proprio.

36   *In Cottam.*

Non ego ne dicas vereor si quid tibi dico;
    Sed ne non dicas, Cotta, sed adijcias.

37   *Ad Caspiam.*

Asperas tristis minitetur iras,
Spemue promittat facies serenam,
Semper horresco, quoniam satis te,
    Caspia, noui:

Cum furis pulso retrahis capillos,
Euocas morsu rigido cruorem,
Quicquid occurrit, nimis ah perite
    Dextera torquet:
Fulmen hoc te terribilem, cruentam
Sed manus reddit furibunda, et hinc te   10
Siue ridentem metuo, benigne
   . Siue loquentem.

Forte sopitum haud aliter leonem
Conspicit siluis tremulus viator,
Et pedem flectens, cauet excitari
    Ne fera possit.

38   *In Galbam.*

Natum Galba suum, domesticumque,
Extremus quasi Persa sit, vel Indus
Tractat, quod nothus est; nec alloquendum
Censet, more nisi et stilo insolenti,
Et nudo capite, hospes vt videri
Omnino -nouus exterusque possit;
Annon Galba satis superque ineptit?

39   *In Neruam.*

Abstrahis a domini cœna te, Nerua, sacrati,
   Nec tamen vt cæcus numinis hostis abes;
Nec tibi quod panis vel vinum displicet: immo
   Inuitamenti vim leuioris habent.
Causa duplex prohibet; quia ventri nil emis vna;
   Altera quod nimis hæc sit sibi cœna breuis.

40   *Ad nobiliss: virum Gul: Percium.*

Gulelme gente Perciorum ab inclita,
Senilis ecce proijcit niues hiems,
Tegitque summa montium cacumina:
Et æstuosus vrget hinc Notus, gelu
Coactus inde Thracius, rapit diem
Palustris vmbra, noxque nubibus madet.
Tibi perennis ergo splendeat focus,
Trucemque plectra pulsa mulceant Iouem:
Refusus intumescat Euhius sciphis,
Nouumque ver amœnus inferat iocus;   10
Nouas minister ingerat faces, ruit
Glocestriensium in te amica vis, simul
Furorem vt hauriant leuem, facetijs
Simulque molle lusitent per otium.

41   *Ad Bassum.*

Indiget innumeris vir magnus; maior at illo est
   Omnibus his quisquis, Basse, carere potest.

42   *In Hyrcamum et Sabinum.*

Hyrcamum grauiter Sabinus odit,
Hyrcamusque male inuicem Sabinum;
Hyrcami cilia atque cæcitatem
Rides, ille tuam, Sabine, barbam
Hirsutam, indomitam, et quasi cacatam.
Alternis odijs peritis ambo,
Incondite itidem superbientes
Ambo, tum tetrici, atque curiosi,
Exortes comitum, tenebrici ambo;
Vos sic vnanimes, fere ijdem et ambo,   10
Quare tam male conuenitis ambo?

43   *In Rufum.*

Nupsit anus, sed amans dentes non Isba malignos
     Sustinet vt possit, Rufe, nocere tibi.
Nam quem tritum habuit fœlix modo despuit vnum,
     Iamque suus passer, iamque columba tua est.
Et tenero faciet lepidissima murmura rostro,
     Basia per morsus nec metuenda dabit.
Fœmineo placeant mala immatura palato,
     Sed rugosa viros canaque poma iuuent,
Rufe, nouo fas sit tantum vouisse marito,
     Ne reparet dentes viuida nupta suos.   10

44   *Ad Accam.*

Partem das animæ, sed quæ tibi tota fruenda est;
     Tu, mihi da partem qua licet, Acca, frui.

45   *In Carinum.*

Puluilli totidem colore, vultu,
Textura, imparilique sectione
Distincti, in tenebras tuas, Carine,
Mirabar quibus artibus venirent.
Perspexi modo; scilicet tabernas
Omnes despolias, trahens ab illis
Ornamenta tuum in cubilulillum:
Quæ postquam subigis tuis rapinis
Ignotos penitus lares subire,
More istic faciunt, nec est stupendum,   10
Puluilli siquidem tui, Carine,
Iam spectent varie se, et insolenter.

46   *De morte canis.*

Desinite, o pueri, ientacula vestra timere,
     Non eritis nostræ postea præda cani:
Quod lacera scit plebs errans per compita veste,
     Cur manet ex huius parta quiete quies.

47 *In credulos ciues.*

Bis sex Londinum vita concedit in vna,
  Bis sex iuratos urbs speciosa vocat.
Dispeream præter speciem vocemque virorum
  Bis sex istorum millia si quid habent.
Nam sensus, animosque suos in iudice ponunt;
  Ex se non norunt ore fauere reis:
Seruatum quis enim, cui iudex defuit, vnum
  Secula per bis sex vidit in vrbe reum?

48 *Ad Melleam.*

Scelesta, quid me? mitte, iam certum est, vale:
Longe repostas persequar terræ plagas,
Tuis vel vmbras Tartari fucis procul.
Nec me retentare oris albicans rubor,
Nec exeuntem lucidum hinc et hinc iubar
Lenire speret: Circe, in æternum vale.
Rides inepta? siccine irati stupes
Minas amantis? sic genas guttis lauas?
Magisne rides? tam meus suauis tibi est
Discessus? at nunc non eo, vt fleas magis.   10

49 *In Turbonem.*

Turbo, deos manes celsi tu pondere gressus
  Tota in se terres ne sua tecta ruant.

50 *Ad Caspiam.*

Si quid amas, inquis, mea Caspia, desine amare;
  Flammas ne caleant sic prohibere potes.
Ecquando cœlum frondescit? terra mouebit
  Astra? vel auditis non tremet agna lupis?
Omnia naturæ iam se contraria vertant;
  Aspera sic tandem Caspia mitis erit.

51 *In Lycum.*

Quod pulcher puer est, potes videre;
Quod te blandus amat, potes videre;
Quod tecum bibit, et potes videre;
Sed quæ Lesbius impudenter audet
A tergo, Lyce, non potes videre.

52 *Ad Afram.*

Purgandæ præfectum vrbis notat, Afra, lutosa
  Frons tua neglecti muneris esse reum.

53 *Ad Caspiam.*

Ne tu me crudelis ames, nec basia labris
  Imprime, nec collo brachia necte meo.

Supplex orabam satis hæc, satis ipsa negabas,
  Quæ nunc te patiar vix cupiente dari.
Eia age iam vici, nam tu si fœmina vere es,
  Hæc dabis inuito terque quaterque mihi.

54 *Ad Amorem.*

Cogis vt insipidus sapiat, damnose Cupido,
  Mollis at insipidos qui sapuere facis.
Qui sapit ex damno misere sapit; o ego semper
  Desipuisse velim, sis modo mollis, Amor.

55 *Ad Paulam.*

Grates, Paula, tuis ago libenter
Magnis pro meritis, anus iocosa;
Languenti mihi quæ diem diemque
Assidens, strepitu et leui cachinno
Sustentare animum obrutum solebas.
Nec certe ingenium moror retusum,
Absurdumque satis; valere apud me
Debet plus animi tui voluntas;
Hausta non pharetra facetiarum,
Ridendam quoque te dabas amico.   10

56 *Ad Caspiam.*

Cur istoc duro lachrimæ de marmore manent
  Quæris, naturæ, Caspia, sacra docens.
Docta sed in causas nimium descendis inanes,
  Nam lacrimas hæc flent saxa miserta meas.

57 *In Berinum.*

Demonstres rogo mi tuos amores,
Non vt surripiam tibi, Berine,
Sed tanta vt scabie abstinere possim.

58 *In Erricum.*

Tene Lycus fæcem dicit? tene, Errice, fæcem?
  Ah nimis indigne dicit, et improprie,
Fæx a materia siquidem meliore creatur,
  At tua stirps tecum sordida tota fuit.

59 *In Æmiliam.*

Cum sibi multa dari cupiat, multisque placere,
  Quo probior tanto est nequior Æmilia.
Namque operam accepto Thais pro munere reddit;
  Illa nihil, sed lucrum ex probitate facit.
Ora, manus, oculosque gerat matrona pudicos;
  Vnius haud partis sola pudicitia est.
Omnibus arridere, omnesque inducere amantes,
  Quanquam intacta potest, nulla pudica potest.

60   *In Lycium et Clytham.*

Somno compositam iacere Clytham
Aduertens Lycius puer puellam,
Hanc furtim petit, et genas prehendens
Molli basiolum dedit labello.
Immotam vt videt, altera imprimebat
Sensim suauia, moxque duriora;
Istæc conticuit velut sepulta.
Subrisit puer, ultimumque tentat
Solamen, nec adhuc mouetur illa
Sed cunctos patitur dolos dolosa.   10
Quis tandem stupor hic? cui nec anser
Olim, par nec erat vigil Sibilla;
Nunc correpta eadem nouo veterno,
Ad notos redit indies sopores.

61   *In eosdem.*

Assidue ridet Lycius Clytha vt sua dormit;
Ridet et in somnis sed sua Clytha magis.

62   *In Ouellum.*

Dedecori cur sit multum quod debet Ouellus?
Nam fidei quis non esse fatetur opus?

63   *Ad Melleam.*

Insidias metuo quoties me, Mellea, pulchrum
Dicis, sic capitur non bene cautus amans;
Formosusque sibi visus se credit amari,
Nequicquam; specie luditur ipse sua.

64   *In gloriosum.*

In caput, Herme, tuum suggrundia nocte ruebant,
Haud istoc essent scilicet ausa die.

65   *In Pharnacem.*

Pharnax haud alij vt solent nouellum
Si quando famulum sibi recepit
In tectum, faciem viri, torosque
Inspectat; studia ingeniue dotes;
Sed quantum esuriens edat bibatque.

66   *Ad Caspiam.*

Per nemus Elisium Dido comitata Sichæum
Pallida perpetuis fletibus ora rigat;
Et memor antiqui semper, Narcisse, furoris
Vmbram sollicitas per vada nigra tuam.
Debet ab aduerso quisquis tabescit amore
Supplicium stygia ferre receptus aqua.
Caspia, si pro te morientem pœna moratur,
Esto tuis semper iungere labra labris.

67   *In Coruinum.*

Coruinus toties suis iocatur,
Nullum reddere suauiora posse,
Seu nymphas cecinit, trucesue pugnas,
Seu quicquid cecinit bonum, malumue :
Hoc de se toties refert facetus,
Vt tandem fatuus sibi ipse credat.

68   *Ad Melburniam.*

Olim inter siluas, et per loca sola, Dianam
   Cum nymphis perhibent abstinuisse viris ;
Votiuasque sacris seclusas ædibus, atram
   Fama quibus pepulit relligiosa notam.
Tu sed pulchra, diserta, frequens, Melburnia, viuis ;
   Virgo et anus nullis nota cupidinibus.

69   *Ad Tho: Mychelburnum.*

Tu quod politis ludere versibus
Fratrum elegantum tertius incipis,
Thoma, nec omnes occiduas sinis
Horas relabi prorsus invtiles ;
Dijs sic beatis me similem facis,
Vt læter vna iam numero impari.
Ergo peræque diuiduum tribus
Me dono vobis, quilibet integrum
Vt Campianum possideat sibi,
Primus, secundus, tertius inuicem :   10
De parte ne sis sollicitus tua.

70   *Ad Carolum Fitz Geofridum.*

Carole, si quid habes longo quod tempore coctum
   Dulce fit, vt radijs fructus Apollineis,
Ede, nec egregios conatus desere, quales
   Nescibit vulgus, scit bona fama tamen.
Ecce virescentes tibi ramos porrigit vltro
   Laurus ; et in Lauro est viuere suaue decus.

71   *Ad Menum.*

Te quod amet, quantumque, palam solet omnibus Hermus
   Dicere, sic fratres, sic quoque, Mene, patrem,
Et quoscunque tuos ; tacet is de coniuge tantum,
   Horum quam vestrum plus tamen extat amor.
Exemplo quis enim chari liuescit amici ?
   Multorum inuidiam sed trahit omnis amans.
Ergo leues populi contemnas, Mene, susurros :
   Vero vis testi credere ? crede tibi.
Liuida vix vnquam proprijs innititur alis
   Fama, sed Icarijs ; dum volat illa, perit.   10

72   *Ad Papilum.*

Cum tibi barba foret quam Zeno, quamque Cleanthes
    Optaret, totam deputat Hanno tibi,
Ingentem in te vindictam meditatus vt hostis;
    Quod damnum vt repares, Papile, iure paras:
Causidicosque graui turgescens consulis ira,
    Quam spe lucrifici lætitiaque fouent:
Ex notis fore iuratos, quod perditur oris
    Qui decus agnoscent, rem grauiterque ferent;
Et mulctam statuent inimici nomine grandem:
    Hoc suadent illi, Papile, tuque voras.   10
Sed mihi, quantumuis in neutro iure perito,
    Auscultato parum: sint, age, dicta prius
Omnia vera, tamen, citius quam causa adolescet,
    Tota renascetur, Papile, barba tibi.

73   *Ad Philomusum.*

Ridiculum plane quiddam facis atque iocosum,
    Et surdo et stupido dum, Philomuse, canis.
Omnia nam surdus miratur, sed nihil audit;
    Contra audit stupidus cuncta, probatque nihil.

74   *In Miluium.*

Quam multa veluti somnia accidunt viuis,
    Quæ cum palam vident libenter haud credunt!
Quis sat stupescit? toruus et senex ille,
    Profectus ima ex sorde, Miluius terram
Vt nauseet, equesque vrbe nobilis tota,
    Matronam et hanc, et illam, et alteram stupret?
Est nostra tanquam turpe somnium vita;
    Id comprobat mors ipsa, cuius aduentu
Expergefacta mens suum petit cœlum,
    Terrestriumque infra superbias ridet.   10

75   *Ad Crispum.*

Crispe mones vt amem, sed caute, ne mihi probro
    Sit quod amem; caute nunquis amare potest?
Est velut ignis amor, nihil est detectius illo,
    Protinus indicio proditur ipse suo.

76   *Ad Caluum.*

Nunquam perficies, testeris vt omnia, Calue,
    Numina, quin minus assentiar atque minus.
Credita quæ primo res est, repetita rubescit,
    Labitur et nimium sollicitata fides.
Tam multis homini nemo se purgat amico:
    Inuidiam toties deposuisse parit.

z

77 *Ad Ed: Mychelburnum.*

Ibit fraternis elegis ornata sub vmbras,
 Munia si ad manes perueniunt superum ;
Et multum veneranda leues, Edoarde, tenebit
 Aspectuque animas exequijsque soror.
O fœlix si non fata importuna fuissent,
 Si non immature optima deficerent !
Quid nunc perpetuum fas est sperare beatis ?
 Quid connubia ? quid floridæ amicitiæ ?
Ætas quid ? nondum sex luna impleuerat orbes
 Deseruit iuuenem cum malefidus Hymen :   10
Cum desiderio sed enim decedere vita,
 Non mors, longa mora est ; non obit æger, abit.

78 *In obitum Fran: Manbæi.*

Quid tu ? quid ultra, Phœbe, languenti diem
 Aperis ? beatos ista lux magis decet ;
Sordes et vmbras semper infœlix amat
 Ærumna, misero nulla nox atra est satis.
Heu, heu, sequar quocunque me rapiet dolor,
 Et te per atra Ditis inferni loca,
Manbæe, lachrimis ora perfusus, petam ;
 Flectamque manes planctu et infimos deos,
Liminaque dira molliam, ac vsque horridas
 Acherontis vndas ; cuncta nam pietas potest :   10
Quaqua redibis mœror inueniet viam.
 Tum rursus alma luce candebit polus,
Vltroque flores terra purpureos dabit ;
 Omnia virebunt ; sentiet mundus suum
Decus renasci, sentiet tremulum mare,
 Suumque flebit ipse Neptunus nephas.
Ah, siste vanos impetus, demens furor,
 Ostiaque mente ficta Ditis excute,
Occlusa viuis, nec reclusa mortuis :
 Fac iure tu quod quilibet miser potest,   20
Luge ; supersit hic tibi semper labor.

79 *De homine.*

Est homo tanquam flos, subito succrescit et aret ;
 Vis hominem floremque vna eademque rapit.
Ceu flos est ? minus est : nam mors vt vtrumque coæquat,
 Quam bene flos, hominis tam male funus olet.

80 *In Barnum.*

Mortales decem tela inter Gallica cæsos,
 Marte tuo perhibes, in numero vitium est :
Mortales nullos si dicere, Barne, volebas,
 Seruasset numerum versus, itemque fidem.

81 *In Lupum.*

Cum tacite numeras annos patris improbus hæres,
  Sic, Lupe, succlamas, omnia tempus habent;
Sumptus siue grauet, seu te mulctauerit vxor,
  Concludis vehemens, omnia tempus habent.
Sic semper; chymico nunc te committis Orello,
  Mox vere vt dicas, omnia tempus habent.

82 *Ad Caspiam.*

  Nescio quid aure dum susurras, Caspia,
  Latus sinistrum intabuit totum mihi.

83 *Ad Turanium et Nepheium.*

  Mî Turanule, tuque, mi Nephêi,
  Quin effunditis intimos chachinnos.
  Hem, murum prope dirutum videte
  Coram qui peragit domi latenter
  Quod debent saturi; ecce seruus autem
  Caute præmonitus, caputque nudus
  Stat præfixus hero, ne obambulantes
  Spectent luminibus parum benignis;
  Dextra composite tenet galerum
  A tergo dominum lubens adorans;   10
  Nasum sed grauiter premit sinistra
  A tergo dominum haud lubens adorans.
  O seruum lepidum, probum, pudicum,
  Vultu qui superat tacente mimos,
  Tarltonum et streperi decus theatri!

84 *In Ianum.*

Sabbato opus nullum nisi per scelus igne piandum
  Posse exerceri, feruide Iane, putas:
Iane, voras medice pilulas, at non operantur,
  Has puto te sacro sumere posse die.

85 *In Sannium.*

Quæ ratio, aut quis te furor impulit, improbe Sanni,
  Fœmineum vt sexum mente carere putes:
Cum mea diffusas fœlix per pectus amantum
  Vnica possideat Caspia centum animas?

86 *Ad Arnoldum.*

Non si displiceat tibi vita, Arnolde, graueris;
  Hac vt displiceat conditione data est.

87 *Ad Genium suum.*

Quid retines? quo suadet Amor, Iocus atque Lyæus,
  Ibo; sed sapiam; iam sine, chare Geni.

88 *Ad Nassum.*

Commendo tibi, Nasse, pædagogum
Sextillum et Taciti canem Potitum,
Teque oro tua per cruenta verba,
Et per vulnificos sales, tuosque
Natos non sine dentibus lepores
Istudque ingenij tui per acre
Fulmen, ridiculis et inficetis,
Irati vt tonitru Iouis, timendum ;
Per te denique Pierum serenum,
Parnassumque, Heliconaque, Hippocrinenque,   10
Et quicunque vacat locus camænis,
Nunc oro, rogoque, improbos vt istos
Mactes continuis decem libellis ;
Nam sunt putiduli atque inelegantes,
Mireque exagitant sacros poetas,
Nasonemque tuum et tuum Maronem,
Quos vt te decet æstimas, tegisque
Ne possint per ineptias perire.
Quare si sapis, vndique hos latrones
Incursabis et erues latentes ;   20
Conceptoque semel furore nunquam
Desistes ; at eos palam notatos
Saxis contuderit prophana turba.

89 *Ad Caspiam.*

En miser exclusus iaceo, ceu montibus altis,
    Caspia, nix nullo respiciente cadit :
Meque tuus liquefecit amor violentius absens,
    Sol teneram iniecto quam solet igne niuem.

90 *Ad Caluum.*

Est quasi ieiunum viscus tua, Calue, crumena ;
    Id bile, hanc vacuam seruat amore iecur.

91 *In Byrseum.*

Multis ad socerum queritur de coniuge Byrseus,
    Nupta quod externos suescit amare viros :
At breuiter socer, Et talis mi, ait, illius olim
    Mater erat ; credo, fœmina et omnis erit.
Commune et iuuenile malum est, quod serior ætas
    Sanabit, spero, sanctaque canities.
De me nec socero verum est hoc, Byrsee, clamas :
    Sed potuit, sed habet fabula ficta salem.

92 *Ad Caspiam.*

Ecquando vere promissam, Caspia, noctem,
    Præstabis, cupido facta benigna mihi ?
Nox ea, si moriar, sat erit mihi sola beato ;
    Si viuo, non sunt millia mille satis.

93 *In Bretonem.*

Carmine defunctum, Breto, caute inducis Amorem;
Nam numeris nunquam viueret ille tuis.

94 *Ad Coruinum.*

Sextum perfidiæ haud satis pudenter,
Coruine, insimulas, redarguisque
Nequaquam meminisse quod spopondit
Æquali, vel enim potentiori;
Quin eludere, si sit vsus, ipsum
Audere intrepide suos parentes.
Læsam dic age vi'n fidem experiri?
Hunc ad cœnam hodie vocato, vel cras,
Vel tu postridie, perendieue,
Sin mauis vel ad vltimas calendas;   10
Ni præsto fuerit, per et tabernas
Omnes vndique quæritans volarit,
Quas te nec meminisse iam nec vnquam
Vsurpasse oculis in hunc diem vsque
Audacter mihi deierare fas sit:
Postremo nisi præbeat vocanti
Conuiuam memorem se, et impigellum,
Cœnam coxeris hanc meo periclo.
Nullumne hoc specimen fidelitatis?

95 *Ad Hyspalum.*

Sanum lena tibi promittat vt, Hyspale, scortum,
Puram sentina quis sibi quæret aquam?

96 *Ad Licinium.*

Non quod legitimum id bonum necesse
Censetur, Licini; bonum sed ipsum
Semper legitimum putare par est:
Fœnus nam licitum fatemur omnes,
Nemo non malus at bonum vocabit.

97 *In auarum.*

Omnia dum nimium seruas, miser, omnia perdis,
Nec tua sunt toties quæ tua, Paule, vocas.

98 *In Lupercum.*

Vxorem Lycij senex Lupercus
Strato admouerat, imminens puellæ;
Absentis domini exilit molossus
Subuenturus heræ, vagasque morsu
Partes mollis adulteri reuulsit.
Stat mœchus lachrimans sine eiulatu,

Testes nequitiæ suæ recusans,
Testes nequitiæ suæ requirens.
O rem ridiculam! magisne dicam
Hanc plane miseram? canem viro esse   10
Plus quam femina, quam vxor est, fidelem.

99   *In Erricum.*

Cum stygio terrere vmbras vultu, Errice, possis,
Dic per Plutonem quid tibi cum speculo?

100   *Ad Tuccam.*

Nil æris, magnam sed habes tu, Tucca, crumenam;
Atque animum, quantum nulla crumena capit.

101   *Ad Pontilianum.*

Quod iuuenis, locuplesque sibi consciscere ipse
Eutrapilus mortem, Pontiliane, stupes;
Nam neque spretus amor, nec dedecus impulit atrum,
Non iactura grauis, nec sine mente furor;
Haud dolor excrucians, tetri aut fastidia morbi;
Cunctos causa fugit, sed mihi vera patet;
Hanc voco desidiam, quam res accendere nulla
Cum potuit, vitæ nausea summa fuit.

102   *De Puella ignota.*

Regalem si quis cathedram prope percutit hostem,
Exigitur sonti vindice lege manus.
Impune ergo feret quæ cor mihi figit amicum,
Virgo, oculis feriens quo stetit illa loco?
Parce tamen rigidumque nimis summitte vigorem,
Sacrosanctum ius: arbiter assit Amor,
Ille Amor æthereos qui non violarit ocellos;
Non ego, non tanti funera mille forent.

103   *Ad Chloen.*

Mittebas vetulam, Chloe, ministram,
Lippam, tardipedem, et febriculosam
Ad me luce noua aureos rogatum;
Si tu cur redijt rogas inanis,
Mane istuc mihi non placebat omen.

104   *In Philonem.*

Dulcis cum tibi Bassiana nupsit,
Nemo non male clamitans ferebat
Tam pulchram illepido dari puellam,
Toruus quique adeo et nigellus esses.
Cædis te, Philo, post reum malignæ
Suspensum populus frequens Tyburni

Spectans, et querulam expiationem,
Occasumque tuum pie gemiscens,
Turmatim redit; obuijsque narrat
Exemplum iuuenis viri, et torosi,   10
Perdigna facie artubusque pulchris:
Sic præbet miseris nimis popellus,
Detrectatque male imprecans beatis.
At vobiscum agitur satis benigne
Os durum quibus, horridique vultus,
Aut distorti oculi, patensue nasus,
Pulchri nam fieri, vt lubet, potestis;
Si de quercu aliqua, per aut fenestram,
Vultis prætereuntibus parumper
Pendere horribili modo intuendi.   20
De vobis bona multa prædicabunt
Omnes, quique etiam solent in omnes
Quæuis dicere turpiora veris,
Vitæ qui leuibus bonis fruuntur.

105   *Ad Paulinum.*

Non agros, Pauline, tibi, non splendida tecta,
   Non aurum inuideo, ferripedes nec equos;
Sed tam casta thoro, tam pulchra quod obtigit vxor,
   Tam lepida, alternoque obuia melle tibi;
Moribus apta tuis et ficta per omnia votis:
   Inuidiam faceret nî prohiberet amor.

106   *De se.*

Nos quibus vnanimi cura est placuisse puellæ,
   Quam multa insipide dicimus et facimus?
Quæ simul ad sese redijt mens, omnia ridet,
   Afficiturque videns ipsa pudore sui:
Sicut ego hesterna; sed quid mea crimina stultus
   Profero? non faciam, tuta silentia sunt.

107   *In matronam.*

Abscidit os Veneris famulæ matrona, marito
   Ne mutuum rursus daret:
Quid fecit? culpæ cupiens occludere portam,
   Insulsa patefecit magis.

108   *Ad Cosmum.*

Cernit Aper vigilans annos post mille sepultos;
   Talia sed cæcus cernere, Cosme, potest.

109   *De Mellea et Caspia.*

Vror amat plures quod Mellea, Caspia nullos;
   Non sine riuali est aut amor, aut odium.

110 *Ad Sabellum.*

Tuus, Sabelle, lippus iste cum furit
Cunctis minatur clam venena Colchica,
Et atra quicquid ora Cerberi vomunt.
Ab India vsque virus omne colligit,
Per vda stagna, perque murcidos lacus,
Emitque pluris aspidem, quam tu bouem :
Hyberniam odit, namque ibi nusquam nocens
Bestia timetur, pabulum quæ toxicis
Præbere dirum possit, id Pico graue est.
Quin imprecari Tartarum deo solet   10
Lernæ quod olim tabidam extinxit feram.
Hunc ego, Sabelle, rideo veneficum,
Tu vero ab istoc perdito retrahe pedem ;
Vlcisci amicum tutius, quam hostem potest.

111 *In Miluum.*

In putrem vt sensit se Miluus abire saliuam
    Seruatam testa condidit aureola ;
Et super inscripsit, Milui non ossa, cinisue,
    Sed Miluus, Milui hîc siue saliua sita est.

112 *In Calpham.*

Ridicule semper quantum mihi, Calpha, videtur,
    A multis iactas te sine dote peti ?
Nam quis quod nusquam est petat ? aut captabit inani
    Siccum spe patrem, pumiceum vel auum ?

113 *Ad Caspiam.*

Caspia, laudatur feritas in te, tua quicquid
    Atrum in candorem vertere forma potest.

114 *In amicum molestum.*

Non placet hostilem nimium propensus ad iram,
    Quiue leues grauiter fert inimicitias ;
Nec placet eructans odiose plurima quisquam,
    Fretus iam veteris nomine amicitiæ.

115 *In Hannonem.*

Diuitias vocat Hanno suas sua carmina, tales
    Morsus diuitias Irus habere potest.

116 *Ad Cambricum.*

E multis aliquos si non despexit amantes,
    Si tua non fuerit rustica nata fremis ?
Aut tam formosam tibi, Cambrice, non genuisses,
    Aut sineres nato munere posse frui.
Castæ sint facies sua quas sinit esse pudicas,
    Pulchrior huic forma est quam decet esse probis.

117 *Ad Leam.*

Priuato commune bonum, Lea, cum melius fit,
 Obscurum plane est fœmina casta bonum.
Nam nulli nota, aut ad summum permanet vni,
 Omnibus atque alijs est quasi nulla foret;
Sin se diuulget, mala fit; quare illa bonarum
 Aut rerum minima est, aut, Lea, tota mala.

118 *De Amantibus.*

Olim si qua fidem violasset fœmina, quanquam
 Tunc extra legem viueret, inque nota;
Vna nocte nouo si forte vacaret amanti,
 Materies elegis plena furoris erat.
Questus causa fides taceat iam lubrica, nostris
 Sat firma est, si sit sana puella satis.

119 *De Venerea Lue.*

Ægram producit Venerem mundana Senectus,
 Contractamque noua perditione Luem;
Suspectam quæ nunc Helenam fecisset, et omnes
 Laidis arceret iure metuta procos.

120 *In Crassum.*

De socijs loquitur præclare Crassus, et illis
 Quæ non sunt tribuit prædia, rus, et agros;
Ingenium, formam, genus, artes, omnia donat;
 Tale sodalitium Tucca libenter amat.

121 *Ad Ed: Mychelburnum.*

Prudenter facis, vt mihi videtur,
Et sentis, Edoarde, qui optumum te
Longe pessima ab vrbe seuocasti,
Vix anno ter eam aut quater reuisens;
Tum Pauli simul ac vides cacumen,
Ad notos refugis cate recessus,
Vrbis pestifera otia, et tenaces
Vitans illecebras, lubidinesque,
At nos interea hinc ineptiarum
Portenta vndique mille defatigant;
Conuentus, ioca, vina, bella, paces,
Ludi, damna, theatra, amica, sumptus;
Inclusos itidem domi fabrorum
Aurigumque tonitrua, eiulatus,
Vagitusque graues agunt Auerni
Vsque in tædia; rursus ambulantᵉ
Occursu vario in via molestant
Curti causidici, resarcinatis
Qui gestant manibus sacros libellos;

10

Horum te nihil impedit diserto   20
Quo minus celebres lepore musas
Sub iucunda silentia: o meorum
Cunctorum nimis, o nimis beate!

122   *In Gallam.*

Ilia cur tenue vsque sonent tua nescio, Galla,
    Te nisi quod cantor Tressilianus amet.

123   *In Fuscinum.*

Contrectare tuos nequeam, Fuscine, puellos
    Non myrrham, non si thura, rosasque cacent.
Pro turpi est quicquid facilis natura negauit;
    Si faciem demas, nec placet ipsa Venus.

124   *Ad Caspiam.*

Admissum tarde, cito, Caspia, læsa repellis:
    Constans ira, leuis sed muliebris amor.

125   *Ad Candidum.*

Sis licet ingenuis nunc moribus, æquior ipso
    Socrate, vel minima, Candide, labe carens,
Nescis qualis eris cum tu nouus aleo fias,
    Teque auctum lucrum qualibet arte trahat.
Victor vt euadas, nullum vt ferat alea damnum,
    Attamen ingenium polluet illa tuum.

126   *In Gallam.*

Poscit amatorem feruens sibi Galla Priapum,
    Frigida sed castum Thespilis Hippolitum:
Hinc ego Lampsacides fieri tibi, Thespilis, opto,
    Gallæ sed gelido purior Hippolito.

127   *In Berinum.*

Credita quæ tibi sunt mutato nomine prodis,
    Nomine mutato cuncta licere putas;
Cur tibi nil credam iam si vis, quære, Berine;
    Mutari nomen nolo, Berine, meum.

128   *Ad Sybillam.*

Nil non a domino bonum creatum,
Audacter satis hoc, Sybilla, dicis;
Nec non ergo bonam creauit Euam;
Illam sed tamen oscitante Adamo,
Nequa perciperet bonam creari.

129   *In Gallam.*

Tactam te, ad viuum sed nunquam, Galla, fateris;
    Vah, quota pars carnis mortua, Galla, tuæ est!

130 *Ad Eurum.*

Rerum nomina, resque mutat ipsas
Vsus multimoda vicissitate;
Id si vis lepide æstimare dictum,
Inspectes capita, Eure, fœminarum;
Nam pars illa noui satis dat vna,
Ne quid de medijs loquar, vel imis.

131 *Ad Paulinum.*

Quid, Pauline, meas amationes
Inclamas? Quasi sit parum perire,
Ni tu hanc insuper ægritudinem addas.
At si quid ratio ista promoueret,
Declamare aliquot dies polite,
Pulchre, et sobrius ipsemet potessim,
Depingens graphice proterui amoris
Mille incommoda, vel deinde mille,
Quæ nusquam tibi dicta, scripta, picta
Occurrunt, neque visa somnianti   10
Vnquam; sed tamen vsque me moleste
Castigas miserum, diu perorans;
Obtundis, scio, perditum sinam me
Consulto fieri, lubet perire,
Suaues dum peream per ipse amores.

132 *In Cornutos.*

Vxoris culpa immeriti cur fronte mariti
   Cornua gestari ludicra fama refert?
An quia terribilem furor irritus, atque malignum
   Efficit, armatis assimilemque feris?
An quod ad hanc faciem satyros, vmbrasque nocentes
   Fingimus, atque ipsum Dæmona cornigerum?
An quod apud populum tantum fortuna nocentes
   Reddit, nec verum crimina nomen habent?

133 *Ad Hermum.*

In re si quacunque satisfacis omnibus, Herme,
   Cur hoc vxori non facis, Herme, tuæ?

134 *Ad Aufilenam.*

En dat se locus arbitris remotis,
Aufilena, meo tuoque amori:
Quam nunc suaue rubent repente malæ,
Inuitoque etiam rubore candent!
Quam mollis manus, et benigna colla!
Tam belli poterunt pedes latere?
Vicina et genua, inuidente palla?
Quid me tam male pertinax repellis?

Nempe est fœmineum parum efferari,
Sed tandem furor hic recedet vltro.　　10
Aufugisti etiam? vale, proterua,
Deformis, pede sordido et fugaci:
Vultus ergone tam feros probaui?
Ceruices rigidas? manus rapaces?
Non mi esset melius carere ocellis,
Quam sic omnia perperam videre?

135　　*Ad Battum.*

Qui tibi solus erat modo formidatus adulter,
　Iam, Batte, excruciat prodigiosa Venus.
Quæuis Pasiphae est cogente libidine; tu si
　Riualem admittas denuo tutus eris.

136　　*Ad Melleam.*

Quid mæres, mea vita, quidue ploras?
Nec fraudem paro, quod solent prophani
Caros qui male deserunt amantes;
Nec, prædator vti, arduum per æquor
Hispanas reueham Indicasque nugas:
Expers sed Veneris, Cupidinisque,
Siluæ iam repeto virentis vmbras,
Et dulcem placidamque ruris auram,
Vt memet reparem tibi, et reportem
Lucro millia mille basiorum.　　10

137　　*Ad Thelesinam.*

Expressos Helenæ vultus Paridisque tabella
　Fœdarunt quædam sicut ab vngue notæ;
Hoc, Thelesina, doles, sed et hoc bene conuenit illis,
　Iurgia nam quouis esse in amore solent:
Quid cum te vrgerem solam, quod amantis in ore
　Sæua impinxisti vulnera facta manu?

138　　*In Fabrum.*

Heus, puer, hæc centum defer sestertia Fabro;
　Quid stas, quid palles? quid lachrimas, asine?
Curre, inquam: pueros quamuis præcidat inanes,
　De nummo poterit lenior esse tibi.

139　　*In Afram.*

Cum tibi tot rugis veterascat nasus, vt illi
　Surgere Spartanus debeat, Afra, senex:
Cumque tuos dentes emat antiquarius Hammon,
　Prosint et tussi pharmaca nulla tuæ;
Nubere vis puero, primo moritura Decembri:
　Sic facere hæredem non potes, Afra, virum.

140   *Ad Cosmum.*

Ad vitam quid, Cosme, facit tua mortis imago?
  Esse vt te miserum, puluereumque scias?
Cum sit certa tibi satis, obliuiscere mortis;
  Res vitæ incertas has age; viue, vale.

141   *Ad Aten.*

Reginæ cum tres pomi de iure coirent,
  Te salebris, Ate, delituisse ferunt,
Et miseras risisse: quid hic, dea, si licuisset
  Pro pomo rigidam supposuisse tibi?

142   *In Aprum.*

  Crispo suasit Aper febricitanti
  Pestem protinus hanc inebriatis
  Tolli, sed penitus furente Baccho.
  Assensum est; bibitur simul; valere
  Crispus cœpit, Aper febricitauit.

143   *In Fuscum.*

Quasuis te petere et sectari, Fusce, puellas
  Credis, ridiculus nec reticere potes.
Haud aliter cymba vectus puer ire carinas
  Ad se omnes dicit garrulus, atque putat.

144   *Ad Lucillum et Manbæum.*

Charior, Lucille, anima vel illa
Esse si quidquam pote charius mi;
Tuque, Manbæe, vnanimi sodalis
  Delicium et mens.
Ecquid accepistis, eratne lætum,
Otia exegisse, Cupidinemque,
Et suos iam denique Campianum e
  Pectore amores?
Nam sat illuxisse dies videtur
Illa mi festiuiter, et beate,   10
Quæ breui tantas penitus fugauit
  Luce tenebras?
I fuge hinc, abiecte Amor, exulatum!
Tam ferum haud par est hominum imperare
Mollibus curis, ad eas redi vnde es
  Rupibus ortus.

145   *In Mamurram.*

Pediculosos esse quis sanus negat
Versus Mamurræ Satyricos, si quis legit?
Mordent, timent vngues, pedes et sex habent

146   *In Vincentium.*

Astrictus nunc est Vincentius ære alieno;
   In proprio nimium hic ante solutus erat.

147   *Ad Æmylium.*

Ægris imperat vsque possitallam
Impostor Litus, Æmyli : quousque?
Nummos ridicule vsque dum dat æger.

148   *In Parcos.*

Parcos ingenui non est laudare poetæ,
   Cui vetus horrendos antipathia facit.

149   *Ad Marcellum.*

Scilla verecunda est ; Scilla est, Marcelle, venusta
   Si verum vtrumque est, vix habet illa parem.

150   *Ad Mathonem.*

Arguo cur veram ficto sub nomine culpam
   Quæris, nec titulis te quoque signo tuis.
Nunquam si fingit non est epigramma poema ;
   Vix est simpliciter cui, Matho, vera placent.

151   *Ad Cosmum.*

Laudatus melior fiet bonus, et bona laus est ;
   Solis at quæ sit debita, Cosme, bonis :
Re turgente mali quamuis, et honore fruantur,
   Laudem ne sperent, non vacat illa malis.

152   *In Olum.*

Sat linguæ dedit, Ole, sator tibi ; parte sed vlla
   Hanc potuit melius figere quam capite :
Nam sentit tanquam lapis hoc ; tua voxque palati est,
   Faucis, pulmonis, denique mentis egens :
Si foret, Ole, tuam mihi fas disponere linguam,
   Hæreret qua tu pedere parte soles.

153   *In eundem.*

Summo vt significet patrem sedisse Senatu,
   Hoc aliquando quod is pederat, Olus ait.

154   *In Hipponem.*

Lites dum premit Hippo fœnerator,
Imam ad pauperiem redit, nec vllus
Ex omni magis est ei molestus
Sumptus, quam misero diu roganti
Assem quod dederat semel minutum,
Solum quem sibi nunc egenus optat ;

Lætus causidicis volensque cuncta
Præbebat siquidem, daturus et iam
Esset copia si secunda votis :
Inuitus, genioque retrahente,
Solum sed tribuit grauatus assem.

10

155 *Ad Eurum.*

Eure, bonum, non ordo facit, non res, locus, ætas :
    Fit licet his melior, nascitur ipse bonus.

156 *In Mycillum.*

Flagris morio cæditur, Mycillum
Pullum consiliarij Mycilli
Quod stultum vocitauit, at merentem ;
Dicat de patre iam, nihil pericli est.

157 *Ad Lalagen.*

Corpora mille vtinam, Lalage, mea forma subiret ;
    Vnum spes esset cedere posse mihi.

158 *Ad Hæmum.*

Quasdam ædes narras vbi certis, Hæme, diebus
    Vilia de summo culmine saxa cadunt.
Dæmonij hoc opera fieri contendis, at illud
    Vix credo ; credam si pretiosa cadent.

159 *Ad Argentinum.*

De gallinarum genere est tua fertilis vxor,
    Argentine, viro nam sine sæpe parit.

160 *Ad Telesphorum.*

Nec tibi parca placet, nec plena, Telesphore, mensa ;
    Amplior hæc auida est, ut minor illa, gula :
Quantus enim cibus est aliena in lance relictus
    Expleto quereris tu perijsse tibi.

161 *Ad Cassilianam.*

Cur proba, cur cunctis perhibetur casta Nerine ?
    Assueuit nondum, Cassiliana, tibi.

162 *Ad Hermum.*

Ad latus, Herme, tuum spectans, siquando machæram
    Laudo, tumes, dicens illa paterna fuit.
Si vel equum celerem pede, siue armenta, vel ædes
    Miror, et hæc fuerant omnia patris, ais.
Si vultum commendo tuum, fuit ille paternus ;
    Seruumque et scortum, et singula patris habes.
Sed cum nulla sit, Herme, tuæ constantia linguæ,
    Hanc bene maternam, si fateare, licet.

163   *In Marcellinam.*

Virgo olim cinerem et lutum solebat
Marcellina auido ore deuorare ;
Nunc mœchos amat, at lutosiores
Ipso, Calue, luto ; quid esse credam?
Annon pica animi quoque hæc laborat?

164   *Ad Eurum.*

Sacras somniat, Eure, conciones,
Et pronunciat ore sem' aperto
Pyrrhus ; dissimulat, nec est sacerdos.

165   *Ad Pontilianum.*

Nascitur in lucem primo caput, vnde gubernat
Pars senior, cœlo proxima, sphæra animæ :
Huic decor oris inest, huic sermoque, mentis imago,
Et prope totus homo est, Pontiliane, caput.

166   *Ad Cosmum.*

Sub specie mala, Cosme, boni dominantur : honesti
Vsus ut exoluit, sic decus omne perit.

167   *Ad Papilum.*

Non sapit in tenui qui re ius, Papile, sperat ;
Solis id magnis diuitibusque datur.

168   *Ad Eurum.*

Dilutum iudex vinum bibat, vt sonet ore
Ius quoque dilutum ; displicet, Eure, merum :
At nunc iuridicus ius dicit, negligit æquum ;
Ius ita qui iudex dicet iniquus erit.

169   *Ad Caluum.*

Et lare ridiculum est, aliena et quærere terra
Pacem animi ; nusquam est, sit nisi, Calue, domi.

170   *In Melissam.*

Sex nupta et triginta annis, sterilisque, Melissa
Nata ex se tandem prole triumphat anus :
Cura dei reges vobis proceresque cauete,
Portentum statua parturiente fuit.

171   *Ad Daunum.*

Carmen, equestris homo, cur fingis, Daune ? poeta
Si vis esse nimis forte pedester eris.

172   *Ad Cosmum.*

Cosme, licet media tua pangas carmina nocte,
Affulget schedæ dexter Apollo tuæ.
Metrica scripturo sal vel sol adsit oportet
· Perpetuo ; insulsa et frigida nemo sapit.

173 *Ad Eurum.*

Qui se, nec multis præter se gaudet amicis,
  Si nihil, Eure, vetat noster amicus erit.

174 *Ad Labienum.*

Dum nimium multis ostendere quæris amorem
  In mensa, et positas extenuare dapes,
Obtundis; nec cœna gulæ bene competit, in qua
  Plus condimenti est quam, Labiene, cibi.

175 *In Pollionem.*

Magnificos laudat, misere sed Pollio viuit;
  Laudem fortassis rem putat esse malam.

176 *Ad Sybillam.*

Omnes se cupiunt omni ratione valere;
  Attamen est verbum triste, Sybilla, vale.

177 *Ad Papilum.*

Bellam dicebas Bellonam, Papile, sensi,
  Suauius hospitium castra inimica darent:
Inveniat quicum pugnet, mihi præfero pacem;
  Vt tua sit soli Penthesilea tibi.

178 *Ad Gallam.*

Assurgunt quoties lachrimæ tibi, si placet humor
  Vt diuertatur, mingere, Galla, potes.

179 *Ad Labienum.*

Quæris completo quot sint epigrammata libro;
  Sit licet incertum, sic numerare potes:
Plus minus, hebdomada quotquot nascuntur in vna
  Londini, faciunt tot, Labiene, librum.
Nobiliumque minor numerus censetur vtrinque,
  Turba sed obscuræ plurima plebis erit.

180 *In Marcellinam.*

Laruas Marcellina horret, Lemuresque, sed illa
  Nil timet in tenebris si comitata viro est.

181 *Ad Linum.*

Henrico, Line, septimo imperante,
Nondum pharmacopola quintus vrbem
Infarsit numero, nec œnopola;
Ingens nunc tribus vtriusque creuit:
Primo sed præit ordine œnopola,
Ac tanquam alterius parens videtur,
Morbos dum creat, inficitque nostra
Sensim corpora dulcibus venenis.

A a

Quo tandem ruet hæc vicissitudo?
Quid dicam? nisi Dæmonas trecentos   10
Sementem facere his superfluorum,
Omnes quos patimur licentiatos?

182   *In Gallam.*

Galla melancholicam simulans, hilarare Lyæo
  Se solet, et fit non ficta melancholica.

183   *In Tabaccam.*

Haud vocat illepide meretricem Nerua Tabaccam,
  Nam vendunt illam, prostituuntque lupæ.

184   *Ad Mauriscum.*

Nullam Brunus habet manum sinistram,
  Nec mancus tamen est; sed est quod aiunt,
Maurisce, vt caueas tibi, ambidexter.

185   *Ad Phillitim.*

Phillitis, tua cur discit saltare priusquam
  Firmiter in terra stare puella potest?
Non metuis mox ne cadat immatura? caducas
  Næ sua sic pupas membra rotare facit.

186   *Ad Lalagen.*

Lingua est Gallica lingua fœminarum;
Mollis, lubrica, blandiens labellis,
Affundens, Lalage, decus loquenti:
Terra est Anglica terra fœminarum;
Simplex, suauis, amans, locis honestans
Semper præcipuis genus tenellum.

187   *Ad Cyparissum.*

Ne nimis assuescas carni, Cyparisse, bouinæ,
  Cornua nam quis scit num generare potest?

188   *Ad Hermum.*

Castæ qui seruit si sit miser, Herme, quid ille
  Scortum qui metuit? perditus, et nihili est.

189   *Ad Chloen.*

Pulchras Lausus amat; Chloe, quid ad te?
Pulchras non amat ergo Lausus omnes.

190   *Ad Pasiphylen.*

Qui te formosam negat haud oculos habet; at te
  Nauci qui pendit, Pasiphyle, cor habet.

191   *In Hermiam.*

Hermia cum ridet tetros hahahalat odores ;
  Herme, ferenda magis si pepepedat erit.

192   *In Mycillum.*

  Cantat nocte Mycillus ad fenestras
  Formosæ dominæ, vigil, frequensque ;
  Et cantat lepide, et patent fenestræ
  Voci, at ianua clausa sola surda est.

193   *Ad Caluum.*

Ex reditu lucrum facturus Næuola, præsens
  Quod sperat recipit ; quam cito, Calue, redit ?

194   *Ad Hæmum.*

  Augeæ stabulum, Hæme, non inique
  Londinum vocitas ; scatet profecto
  Multa impuritie ; hæc vt eluatur
  Iam plane Herculeo est opus labore ;
  Nam nunc vndique fœtidum est, at illic
  Non fœnum male olet, sed, Hæme, fenus.

195   *In Tuccam.*

Nil refert si nulla legas epigrammata, Tucca ;
  De te scribuntur, non tibi ; Tucca, tace.

196   *Ad Nisam.*

Quod melius saltas insultas, Nisa, sorori,
  Vtraque at melior quæ neque saltat erit.

197   *Ad Publium.*

  Publi, sola mihi tacenda narras,
  Sed quæ si taceam, loquuntur omnes :
  Dic tu tandem aliquid meri nouelli,
  Plane quod liceat loqui, aut tacere.

198   *Ad Cosmum.*

Qualis, Cosme, tuæ est hæc excusatio culpæ ?
  Suasit Amor ! quasi non pessima dictet Amor !
Ille deus natos ferro violare parentes
  Fecit, patronum quem tibi, inepte, paras.
Dic odio potius factum, dum mittis Amorem ;
  Dic aliud, dic tu quicquid, amice, lubet.

199   *In Harpacem.*

Fœnore ditatus ciuis, nunc rusticus Harpax
  Fœno ditescit ; re minor, at melior.

200 *Ad Olum.*

Nupsisse filiam, Ole, fœneratori
Gestis; quid ita? corrupta num datur? prorsus
Vt dicis, ais, et grauida; te, Ole, iam laudo
Qui fenus addis tale feneratori.

201 *Ad Daunum.*

Sponsam, ne metuas, castam tibi, Daune, remisi
 Ipsam, ni credis tu mihi, Daune, roga.

202 *In Lagum.*

Cum vix grammatice sapiat tria verba ligare,
 Dijs Lagus inuitis versificator erit:
Euenit ebriolis vitium par, protinus omnes
 Saltare incipiunt cum titubare timent.

203 *In Vergusium.*

Nil amat inuectum Vergusius, extera damnat;
 Nec, vicina licet, Gallica vina placent:
Haud piper attinget crudus, procul aurea poma
 Hesperidum calcat, nec pia thura probat.
Bombycis deridet opes, et patria laudat
 Lanea, re vera non aliena sapit.
Sed tamen vxorem Rufini, iamque maritus,
 Ardet: at hæc trita et non peregrina putat.

204 *In Hipponacem.*

Terget linteolis genas manusque,
Vix toto lauat Hipponax in anno,
Rugas dum metuens cutem puellis
Seruat, sed bona perdidit paterna.
Non est lautus homo: quid ergo? tersus.

205 *Ad Calliodorum.*

Sollicitus ne sis signum fatale cometa
 Vt quid portendat, Calliodore, scias;
Expectes cladem (domini natale propinquat)
 Non hominum, sed tu, Calliodore, boum.

206 *Ad Glaucum.*

Ius qui bonum vendit cocus
Melior eo est qui polluit
Ius omne fucis non bonis;
Sit, Glauce, turgidus licet,
Raucisque sæuior Notis.

207 *In Hannonem.*

Carmina multa satis pellucida, leuia, tersa;
 Naturæ vitreæ sed nimis Hanno, creat.

208 *In Librarios.*

Impressionum plurium librum laudat
Librarius; scortum nec hoc minus leno.

209 *Ad Gaurum.*

Pollio tam breuis est, tam crassus, vt esse Gigantis
Secti dimidium credere, Gaure, velis.

210 *Ad Ligonem.*

Cur non salutem te rogas equo vectum?
Ne equum tuum videar, Ligo, salutasse.

211 *Ad Albium.*

Dextre rem peragens, vel imperite;
Vera an ficta, loquens, iocosa vel tu,
Albi, seria, semper erubescis:
Hinc te ridiculum, leuemque reddis.
At tandem vitium pudoris omne
Vis deponere? vis? adi lupanar.

212 *In Olynthum.*

Dum sedet in lasano dormescit prætor Olynthus,
Et facit in lecto quod facit in lasano.

213 *In Pandarum.*

Scrotum tumescit Pandaro; tremat scortum.

214 *In Hannonem.*

Scorti trita sui vocat labella
Non mellita, sed Hanno saccaranta;
At nescit miser extrahi solere
Ex dulci quoque saccaro venenum.

215 *Ad Ligonem.*

Purgandus medici non est ope Cæcilianus,
Purgandus tamen est; num, Ligo, mira loquor?
Purgandus grauidæ de suspitione puellæ,
Ne te detineam, Cæcilianus adest.

216 *In Mundum.*

Mundo libellos nemo vendidit plures,
Nouos, stiloque a plebe non abhorrenti;
Quos nunc licet lectoribus minus gratos
Librarij emptitant, ea tamen lege
Ne Mundus affigat suis suum nomen.

217 *Ad Lausum.*

Non si quid iuuenile habeant mea carmina, Lause
Sed vulgare nimis, sed puerile veto.

218 *Ad Bassum.*

Seruum quando sequi cernit te, Basse, cinædum
Vxori te vult Cinna preire tuæ.

219 *Ad Lamianam.*

Nequidquam Lamiana cutem medicaris, et omni
Detersam tentas attenuare modo:
Innocua illa satis per se manet; eripe luxum,
Eripe nocturnæ furta nociua gulæ.
Pulcher vt in venis sanguis fluat atque benignus,
Cures; curabis sic, Lamiana, cutem.

220 *In Ligonem.*

Funerea vix conspicimus sine veste Ligonem:
An quia tam crebri funeris author erat?

221 *In Marsum et Martham.*

Marsus vt vxorem, sic optat Martha maritum:
Ambos quid prohibet quod voluere frui?

222 *Ad Pontiliānum.*

Iste Bromus quis sit qui se cupit esse facetum,
Plane vis dicam, Pontiliane? planus.

223 *Ad Syram.*

Vna re sapere omne fœminarum
Se credit genus: illa res negare est.
Vna re sapere ut magis studeret
Optandum foret: illa res tacere est.

224 *In Hermum.*

Omnibus officij ritu se consecrat Hermus,
Talia sed nunquam sacra litare solent.

225 *In Cambrum.*

Cum tibi vilescat doctus lepidusque Catullus;
Non est vt sperem, Cambre, placere tibi.
Tu quoque cum Suffenorum suffragia quæras;
Non est vt speres, Cambre, placere mihi.

226 *In Eundem.*

Disticha cum vendas numerasti, Cambre, bis vnum;
Pastor oues cuperet sic numerare suas.

227 *Ad Graios.*

Graij, siue magis iuuat vetustum
Nomen, Purpulij, decus Britannum,
Sic Astræa gregem beare vestrum,

Sic Pallas velit ; vt fauere nugis
Disiuncti socij velitis ipsi,
Tetræ si neque sint, nec infacetæ,
Sed quales merito exhibere plausu
Vosmet, ludere cum lubet, soletis.

228   *Ad Librum.*

Verborum satis est, oneri sunt plura libello;
  Sermo vel vrbanis multus obesse potest.
Partibus ex breuibus quæ constat inepta figura est
  Si sit longa nimis ; par modus esto pari.

THOMÆ

CAMPIANI

Vmbra.

Fœmineos dea quæ nigro sub Limine manes
Occludis, cœlo ostentans, iterumque reducens
Vmbriferum per iter; quanquam crudelis amanti,
Sis mihi tu facilis; quanquam non æqua resumis
Formosarum animas, festina morte peremptas.
Abreptas solus resonante reducere plectro
Threicius potuit, lucique ostendere amores;
Non potuit tamen; ad tristes deuoluitur vmbras
Quicquid formosum est, et non inamabile natum.
O Sacra Persephone, liceat tua regna canenti,   10
Lucifugasque vmbras, aperire abscondita terris
Iura, tenebrarumque arcana adoperta silentum.
Respice qui viridi radiancia tempora lauro
Comprimis; insidias, et furtiuos Hymenæos,
Et Nympham canimus, sed quæ tibi prodita somno
Nupsit; facta parens, etiam sibi credita virgo.
    Est in visceribus terræ nulli obuia vallis,
Concaua, picta rosis, variaque ab imagine florum;
Fontibus irrorata, et fluminibus lapidosis:
Mille specus subter latitant, totidemque virenti   20
Stant textæ myrto casulæ, quibus anxia turba
Nympharum flores pingunt, mireque colorant.
Nec minus intenta est operi Berecynthia mater,
Instituens natos frutices quo syderis ortu
Aerio credant capita inconstantia cœlo.
Admonet immaturæ hyemis, gelidæque pruinæ,
Imbriferumque Austrorum, horrendisonumque Aquilonum;
Grandine concussam Rhodopen, Taurumque niualem,
Concretosque gelu prohibet transcendere montes;
Tantum qui placido suspiras ore, Fauoni,   30
Arboreos tibi commendat dea sedula fœtus.
Fraga, rosas, violasque iubet latitare sub vmbris;
Forma rosis animos maiores indidit, ausis
Tollere purpureos vultus, et despicere infra
Pallentes odio violas, tectasque pudore.
Diua rosas leuiter castigat, et admonet æui
Labilis; aspiceres folijs prodire ruborem,
Et suspendentes ora annutantia flores.

Accelerant Nymphæ properata ex ordine matri
Pensa ostentantes, quarum pulcherrima Iole   40
Asportat gremio texturas millecolores.
Hanc olim ambierat furtim speciosus Apollo ;
Muneribus tentans, et qua suasisse loquela
Posset ; sæpe adhibet placidam vim, sæpe et amantum
Blanditias cupidus, sed non cupiente puella.
Brachia circumdat collo, simul illa repellit ;
Instat hic, illa fugit ; duplicant fastidia flammas ;
Ardet non minus ac rutilo Semeleia proles
Cum curru exciderat, totumque incenderat orbem.
Spes sed vt illusas vidit deus, et nihil horum   50
Virginis auersam potuisse inflectere mentem,
Dira subinde vouet peruertens fasque nefasque ;
Illicitumque parat spreto medicamen amori,
Lactucas humectantes gelidumque papauer,
Cyrceiæque simul stringit terrestria mala
Mandragoræ, condens sudatos pixide rores.
   Nox erat, incedit nullo cum murmure Phœbus,
Nulli conspiciendus adit spelæa puellæ ;
Illa toro leuiter roseo suffulta iacebat,
Sola struens flores varia quos finxerat arte.   60
Candida lucebat fax, hanc primum inficit atra
Nube, deinde linit medicati aspergine succi
Puluillosque leues et picti strata cubilis ;
Terque soporiferas demulcet pollice cordas
Plectripotens, nectitque Hecateio carmine somnos.
Virgineos oculos vapor implicat, excipit artus
Alta quies, et membra toro collapsa recumbunt.
Vidit et obstupuit deus ; inter spemque metumque
Accedit, refugitque iterum ; suspirat ab imo
Pectore ; nec pietas, nec siderea ora puellæ   70
Plura sinunt ; sed amor, sed ineffrænata libido
Quid castum in terris intentatumue relinquit?
Oscula non referenda serit, tangitque, premitque ;
Illa (quod in somnis solet) ambigua edidit ore
Murmura, ploranti similis nec digna ferenti ;
Sæpe manu vrgentem quamuis sopita repellit,
Nequidquam, raptor crebris amplexibus hæret,
Vimque per insidias fert, indulgetque furori.
Nec satis est spectare oculis, tetigisse, fruique,
Ingratum est quicquid sceleris latet ; illaque turpe   80
Quod patitur vitium quia non sensisse videtur,
Mæstus abit (reuocante die) spoliumque pudoris
Tanquam inuitus habet ; semper sibi quod petat vltra
Inuenit ingeniosus amor, crescitque fauendo.
   Tandem discusso noua nupta sopore resurgit,
Illam sed neque turba vocat, neque clari Hymenæi

Illius ante fores iuuenum non inclita pompa
Conspicitur, placide charis commista puellis.
Omnia muta tacent, pariter tacuisset Iole,
Verum nescio quæ morborum insignia terrent;   90
Nec valet a stomacho, nec non tremulum omnia frigus
Membra quatit: cubito incumbens sic anxia secum:
Numquid et hoc morbi est? nam quæ mutatio sanas
Attentat vires? nec enim satis illa placebant,
Postrema quæ nocte timens insomnia vidi.
Quos ego præterij fluctus! quæ prælia sensi
In somnis! quantis, o dij, transfixa sub hastis
Occubui! vereor diros ne iratus Apollo
In me condiderit parientia spicula morbos.
Sed nec Apollineas pestes, nec respicit iras   100
Hic in corde pudor meus; hoc solamen, Iole,
Semper habes, moriare licet, moriere pudica.
Assurgit, cingitque operi se, candida fecit
Lilia, quæ gustare cupit, quia candida fecit:
Quidque oculi cernunt animus desiderat; ægrum
Pectus ferre moras nescit, votisue carere.
Singula quæ grauidæ possunt ignara ferebat;
Torpores lassata graues, fastidia, bilem;
Luminaque in morbum veniunt, putat illa fuisse
Obtutu nimio; causas ita nectit inanes.   110
Sed simul atque impleri vterum, sensitque moueri
Viuum aliquid, potuitque manu deprendere motus;
Exanimata metu nemorum petit auia tecta
Tristis, vt expleret miserando pectora planctu.
    Crudeles, ait, et genus implacabile, Diui,
Quas tandem ærumnas animique et corporis hausi
Immerita? assurgunt etiam noua monstra; tumere
Cœpit vter nobis; iam virgo puerpera fiam;
Nec dubitat natura suas peruertere leges
Quo magis excrucier possimque horrenda videri,   120
Demque pudicitiæ, sceleris sed nomine, pœnas.
Quo fugiam? quæ nunc vmbræ? quæ nubila frontem,
Vel tumulum hunc defuncti animi tectura cupressus?
Quam bene cum tenebris mihi conuenit! horreo Solem;
Iam culpa possum, sed non caruisse timore;
Frangitur ingenuus pudor, et succumbit in ipsa
Suspicione mali, scelerisque ab imagine currit,
Ceu visis fugiunt procul a pallentibus vmbris.
Infœlix partus, nisi quid monstrosius illo est,
Absque tuo genitore venis, nomenque paternum   130
Si quis quærat habes nullum; patrem assere primum,
Post tibi succedam grauis atque miserrima mater.
    Talia iactantem venti læua arbitra risit
Inuida populea latitans sub cortice Nais;

Lætaque per sentes repit, tenuesque myricas ;
Sed simul explicuit se, proditione superba,
Præcipitique gradu loca nota perambulat, omnes
Suscipiens nymphas, referensque audita, nec illa
Per se magna satis, reddit maiora loquendo ;
Et partes miserantis agit, vultusque stupentes   140
Effingit, monstrumque horret, crimenque veretur.
Inde per alternos rumores fama vagatur,
Flebiliorque·deæ tandem florentia tecta
Peruenit, illa nouo temere conterrita monstro
Exilijt, natamque animo indignata requirit.
Sed procul vt matrem approperantem vidit Iole
Concidit exanimis, gemitus timor exprimit altos,
Exortosque vtero creat ingeminatque dolores.
Continuo silua effulsit velut aurea, et omne
Per nemus auditur suaue et mirabile murmur.   150
Diua pedem, perculsa soni nouitate, repressit,
Interea sine ploratu parit, ipsaque tellus
Effudit molles puero incunabula flores.
Occurrit natæ Berecynthia, prima nepotem
Suscipit, ille niger totus, ni candida solis
Hæserat effigies sub pectore, patris imago.
    Sed non ambiguo iam personat omnia cantu
Phœbus, et ardentes incendit lumine siluas,
Dum sua furta canens miseram solatur Iolen ;
Obstupuit dea, nunc lucos, nunc humida natæ   160
Lumina suspiciens, vultusque pudore solutos.
Proditor, exclamat, non hæc, si Iupiter æquus,
Probra mihi vel tecta diu, vel inulta relinquam.
Quo fugis ? infestum caput inter nubila, Phœbe,
Nequicquam involuis ; scelus et tua facta patebunt,
Nec mihi surripiet fuga te, sequar ocior Euris,
Maternusque dolor vires dabit, iraque iusta.
Nec mora, per nubes summi ad fastigia cœli
Contendit ; nymphæ tristi exanimæque sorori
Circumfusæ acres tentant lenire dolores,   170
Et placidis dictis tristes subducere curas.
Illa immota sedet, tacitoque incensa furore
Ardet, et ingenti curarum fluctuat æstu.
    Fœlices quibus est concessum, ait, intemerata
Virginitate frui ! mea iam defloruit ætas
Immature ; heu maternos sensisse dolores,
Gaudia non potui ; sed me nec gaudia tangunt ;
Nec duri, si non infamia iuncta, dolores.
Nox et somne, meo pars insidiata pudori,
Hos mihi pro meritis partus, hæc pulchra dedistis   180
Pignora, formosique patris referentia vultus ?
Nempe ego, Phœbe, tuos amplexus dura refugi,

Et simplex, tali quam posses prole beare.
Atque vtinam caruisse tuo, speciose, liceret
Munere! quantumuis indocta et stulta putarer,
Non tamen infamis, turpique cupidine læsa,
Cogerer ad nigros animam demittere manes.
Sic effata, aliquid vultu letale minanti,
Deficit, excipiunt Nymphæ, manibusque leuatam
Celsa ferunt intecta deæ stratisque reponunt.   190

    Cuncta Ioui interea narrauerat ordine Phœbus,
Factaque lasciuis prætexuit impia verbis;
Addiderat Cycnumque, et terga natantia tauri,
Furtiuumque aurum, et duplicatæ præmia noctis.
Iupiter officij tanti memor irrita risit.
Vota deæ, iustumque odium in ludibria vertit.
Illa sed ingenti luctu confusa recedit,
Conqueriturque fidem diuum, sæuoque vlulatu
Indefessa diu languentes suscitat iras;
At nulla in terris tanti vis nata doloris   200
Quam non longa dies per amica obliuia soluat.

    Iamque puer, tacite præter labentibus annis,
Paulatim induerat iuueniles corpore vultus;
Cui quamuis nullo variantur membra colore,
Multus inest tamen ore lepos, tinctosque per artus
Splendescit mira nouitate illecta venustas.
Si niger esset Amor, vel si modo candidus ille,
Iurares in vtroque deum; non dulcior illo
Ipsa Venus, Charitesque, et florida turba sororum.
Huic olim nymphæ nomen fecere Melampo,   210
Lucentesque comis gemmas, laterique pharetram
Aptarunt, qualem cuperet gestare Cupido.
Ille leuem tenera sectatur arundine prædam
Auroræ vt primo rarescit lumine cœlum;
Mox feruente æstu viridantes occupat vmbras,
Aut ab euntis aquæ traducit murmure somnum.

    Tempus erat placidis quo cuncta animalia terris
Soluerat alta quies, solita cum Morpheus arte
(Somnia vera illi nullo mandante deorum)
Florigeram penetrat vallem, sopitaque ludit   220
Pectora nympharum, portentaque inania fingit,
Horribilesque metus; mox lætis tristia mutat,
Inducitque leues choreas, conuiuia, lusus,
Secretosque toros, simulataque gaudia amoris;
Sæpe alias Satyro informi per deuia turpes
Tradit in amplexus, alias tibi, pulcher Adoni,
Aut, Hyacynthe, tibi per dulcia vincula nectit.
Sic deus effigies varias imitatus, opaca
Dum loca percurrit, sopitum forte Melampum
Cernit odorato densoque in flore iacentem: 230

Accedit prope, spectanti dat Cynthia lumen.
Et quid, ait, mira nostram dulcedine mentem
Percellit? meue illudis, formose Cupido?
Sideream nigra frontem cur inficis vmbra?
Iam placet iste color? vilescunt lilia? sordent
Materni flores? sed vbi nunc arcus et auro
Picta pharetra tibi? cui tu, lasciue, sororum
Hac struis arte malum? tua quem noua captat imago?
At si non amor es, quis es? an furtiua propago
Atrigenæ noctis? num crescit gratia tanta   240
E tenebris, iucunde, tibi? tam viuidus vnde
Ridet in ore lepos? tale et sine lumine lumen?
Vt decet atra manus, somno quoque mollior ipso,
Qui te sed leuiter tangi sinit, aptus amori!
O vtinam quæ forma tuos succenderet ignes
Cognorim! puer illa foret, seu fœmina, seu vir;
Quam cupide species pro te mutarer in omnes!
Vtcunque experiar, spes nulla sequetur inertes.
Induit ex illo facies sibi mille decoras,
Versat et ætates sexumque, cuilibet aptans   250
Ornatus varios; nequicquam, immobilis hæret
Spiritus, et placido pueri mens dedita somno est.
Iamque fatigatus frustratum deflet amorem
Morpheus, indulgens animo pronoque furori.
    Luce sub obscura procul hinc telluris in imo
Persephones patet atra domus, sed peruia nulli;
Quam prope secretus, muro circundatus æreo,
Est hortus, cuius summum prouecta cacumen
Haud superare die potuit Iouis ales in vno.
Immensis intus spacijs se extendit ab omni   260
Parte, nec Elisijs dignatur cedere campis,
Finibus haud minor, at lætarum errore viarum
Delicijsque loco longe iucundior omni.
Et merito, his vmbræ nam diuersantur in hortis
Quot nunc pulchrarum sunt, sæclo quotue fuere
Primo, quotue alijs posthac visentur in annis.
Vallem vulgus amat, quarum peragendaque syluis
Fabula sit, liquidis spectant in fontibus ora,
Aut varias nectunt viuo de flore corollas;
At quibus vrbanæ debetur turgida vitæ   270
Mollities, studijs alijs, alioque nitori
Assuescunt animos, nil simplicitatis habentes.
Altior, et longe secretior heroinis
Contingit sedes, Parnasso suauior ipso;
Gemmarum locus, atque oculorum lumine lucet.
Non huc fas cuiquam magnum penetrare deorum;
Soli sed Morpheo, cui nil sua fata negarunt,
Concessum est, pedibus quamuis incedere lotis:

Illum durus amor, sibi nil spondente salutis
Arte sua, tandem his languentem compulit hortis,   280
Tot puero ex formis vt fingat amabile spectrum.
  Primo fons aditu stat molli fultus arena,
Intranti, gradibus varijsque sedilibus aptus.
Hic se cum redeunt, labem si traxerat vllam
Vita, lauant, puræ remeantque penatibus vmbræ.
Morpheus hac vtrumque pedem ter mersit in vnda,
Et toties mistis siccat cum floribus herbis ;
Inde vias licitas terit, et velatus opaca
Nube, lubens saturat iucundis lumina formis.
Aspicit has tacita sua mutua fata sub vmbra   290
Narrantes, choreis certantes mollibus illas
Quas olim didicere, vel ignes voce canentes
Quales senserunt dum lubrica vita manebat.
Sed deus obliquo species sibi lumine notas
Præterit, Antiopam Nycteida, Deiphilemque,
Tyndaridemque Helenam, desponsatamque priori
Hermionem, calido dotatam sanguine nuptam ;
Argiam, et Rhodopen, victoris et Hippodamiam
Expositam thalamis, pomis captasque puellas,
Roxanamque, Hieramque, ut cognita sydera spectans   300
Negligit, innumerasque pari candore micantes.
Hinc dorsum sublime petit per amœna roseta
Euectus, picta et multo viridaria flore.
Vndanti circum locus est velut insula valle
Inclusus, formis aptus priuusque Britannis,
Densis effulgens tanquam via lactea stellis.
Prima suo celerem tenuit Rosamunda decore
Ingenti, cui Shora comes rutilantibus ibat
Admiranda oculis, grauis vtraque conscia sortis.
Inde Geraldinam cœlesti suspicit ore   310
Fulgentem, Aliciamque caput diademate cinctam,
Casti constantisque animi lucente trophæo.
Nec tamen his contentus abit deus, altius ardet
Accelerare pedem, fulgor procul aduocat ingens
Apparens oculis, maioraque sidera spondet.
Emicat e viridi myrteto stella Britanna,
Penelope, Astrophili quæ vultu incendet amores
Olim, et voce ducem dulci incantabit Hybernum.
Constitit eximiæ captus dulcedine formæ
Morpheus, atque vno miratur corpore nasci   320
Tot veneres, memori quas omnes mente recondit.
Proxima Franciscæ diuina occurrit imago,
Eiaculans oculis radios, roseisque labellis
Suaue rubens, magni senis excipienda cubili
Mollis odoriferis prope Catherina sedebat
Fulta rosis, tacitam minitantur lumina fraudem,

Chara futura viro, toto spectabilis orbe.
Coniugibus lætæ minus huic speciosa Brigetta
Succedit, radijs et pulchris Lucia feruens.
Formam forma parit, noua spectantemque voluptas   330
Decipit oblitum veteris, placidæque figuræ.
Vtque satur conuiua deus rediturus, apricam
Planitiem duo forte inter nemora aurea septam
Cernit, et in medio spaciantem, corpore celso,
Egregiam speciem, magnæ similemque Dianæ.
Nube sed admota propius dum singula spectat ;
Digna sorore Iouis visa est, aut coniuge ; sola
Maiestate leuis superans decora omnia formæ,
Hæc comitata suis loca iam secreta pererrat,
Conscia fatorum, dicetur et Anna Britanna   340
Olim, fortunæ summa ad fastigia surgens.
Altera subsequitur fœlix, et amabilis vmbra,
Cui Rheni imperium, et nomen debetur Elizæ.
Morpheus hic hæret, capiunt hæ denique formæ
Formarum artificem, nec se iam proripit vltra.
Gratia, nec venus vlla fugit, congesta sed vnam
Aptat in effigiem, Policleto doctior ipso.
Sic redit ornatus, tenero metuendus amico,
Cuius in amplexus ruit, haud renuente puello.
Quo non insignis trahis exuperantia formæ   350
Humanum genus ? hac fruitur, Iunonis vt vmbra
Ixion, falso delusus amore Melampus.
Sed patris aduentu, somno iam luce fugato,
Gaudia vanescunt, atque experrectus amata
Spectra puer quærit nequicquam, brachia nudum
Aera circundant, nil præter lumina cernunt.
Sæpe repercussis cœlo conniuet ocellis,
Amissi cupidus visi, dulcisque soporis ;
Et caput inclinat, sed acutas vndique spinas
Curæ supponunt tristes, arcentque quietem.   360
Nusquam quod petit apparet, nec præmia noctis
Permittit constare dies, vt inania tollit.
Sæuit at introrsum furor, et sub pectore flammas
Exacuit, subditque nouas ; inimica dolori
Lux est, oblectat nox, et loca lumine cassa.
Siluarum deserta subit, clausosque recessus
Insanus puer, et dubio marcescit amore ;
Sperat et in tenebris aliquid, terraque soporem
Porrectus varie captat ; tum murmure leni
Somne, veni, spirat ; prodi, o lepidissime diuum ;   370
Et mihi redde meam, prope sponsam dixerat amens ;
Redde mihi quæcunque fuit, vel virgo, vel vmbra,
Qualiscunque meo placuit, semperque placebit
Infœlici animo ; veri, vel ficti Hymenæi

Quid refert? vitæ domina est mens vnica nostræ,
Sed non talis erat quem vidi vultus inanis,
Quod sensi corpus certe fuit, oscula labris
Fixa meis hærent; si quid discriminis hoc est,
Nunc frigent, eadem cum præbuit illa calebant.
Illa, quid illa? miser quod amo iam nescio quid sit: 380
Hoc tantum scio, conceptu formosius omni est.
Terra siue lates, suspensa vel aëre pendes,
Vel cœlum, quod credo magis, speciosa petisti;
Pulchra redi, et rursus te amplexibus insere nostris.
Pollicita es longum, nec me mens fallit, amorem.
Dic vbi pacta fides nunc? nondum oblita recentis
Esse potes voti cum me fugis, et reuocari
A charo non lætaris, quem spernis, amante.
Sic varias longo perdit sermone querelas,
Atque eadem repetit, nec desinit; igne liquescit   390
Totus, et ardenti cedit vis victa dolori.
Mente sed ereptam vigili dum quæritat vmbram,
Vmbræ fit similis; tenui de corpore sanguis
Effluit, et paulatim excussus spiritus omnis
Deserit exanimum pectus, motusque recedit;
Optatumque diu fert mors, sed sera, soporem.
Corpus at inuentum terræ mandare parabant
Lugentes nymphæ, flores, herbasque ferentes
Funereas plenis calathis; quæ vidit Apollo
Omnia, et iratus puero hunc inuidit honorem: 400
Vtque erat in manibus nympharum non graue pondus,
Labitur, obscuram sensim resolutus in vmbram;
Et fugit aspectum solis, fugietque per omne
Tempus perpetuo damnatus luminis exul.

THOMÆ

CAMPIANI

ELEGIARVM LIBER

Elegia 1.

Ver anni Lunæque fuit; pars verna diei;
  Verque erat ætatis dulce, Sybilla, tuæ.
Carpentem vernos niueo te pollice flores
  Vt vidi, dixi, tu dea Veris eris.
Et vocalis, eris, blanditaque reddidit Eccho;
  Allusit votis mimica nympha meis.
Vixdum nata mihi simulat suspiria, formam
  Quæ dum specto tuam plurima cudit Amor.
Si taceo, tacet illa; tacentem spiritus vrit:
  Si loquor, offendor garrulitate deæ.   10
Veris amica Venus fetas quoque sanguine venas
  Incendit flammis insidiosa suis.
Nec minus hac immitis Amor sua spicula nostro
  Pectore crudeli fixit acuta manu.
Heu miser, exclamo, causa non lædor ab vna;
  Vna, Eccho resonat; Quam, rogo, diua, refers?
Anne Sybillam? illam, respondit: sentio vatem
  Mox ego veridicam, fatidicamque nimis:
Nam perij, et verno quæ cœpit tempore flamma,
  Iam mihi non vllo frigore ponet hyems.   20

2

Cum speciosa mihi mellitaque verba dedisti,
  Despectisque alijs primus et vnus eram:
Mene tuos posuisse sinu refouente calores
  Vana putas? an sic fœmina nota mihi?
Errabas, fateor, veros non sensimus ignes,
  Nec mihi mutandus tam cito crescit amor.
Nos elephantinos nutrimus pectore fœtus,
  Qui bene robusti secula multa vident;
Dum tua diuersis varie mens rapta procellis
  Nescit in assueto littore stare diu;   10
Qui mihi te pactam vidit per fœdera sacra,
  Cum redijt, vidit fœdera nulla dies.

Ottale, successor meus, haud inuisa tenere
  Per me regna potes, non diuturna tamen.
Si promissa semel constaret semper amanti,
  Non cuperet tua nunc esse, sed esse mea :
Pacta prius nostris penitus complexibus hæsit,
  Illius illecebrans gratia nota mihi est ;
Nota sed ante alijs, mecum quos expulit omnes ;
  Teque eadem quæ nos, Ottale, damna manent.   20
Nec tibi proficiet quod sis formosus, habendi
  Fœmina non semper pendet ab ore viri.
Carbones aliquæ, vel si quid tetrius illis,
  Delicijs spretis, sæpe vorare solent.
Vidi ego quæ cinerem lingua glutiret avara,
  Iamque in amaritie quam mihi suauis ! ait.
Multa suis mulier sentit contraria votis,
  Prendere quæ nemo præ leuitate potest.
Ottale, nullus eris si tu sincerus amator.
  Ni malus et fallax, Ottale, nullus eris.   30
Nam quis eam teneat, cuius leuis ante recurrit
  Sidere quam firmo pectore possit amor ?

3

Ni bene cognosses, melius me nemo meorum,
  Hoc condonassem nunc ego, Calue, tibi.
Nec mihi dum constat satis hoc quo nomine signem ;
  Erroremne tuum, stultitiamne vocem.
Irascor veteri, quod me magis vrit, amico ;
  Nec nos vulgari fœdere iunxit amor.
Ira loqui cogit quam vellem durius in te ;
  Es nimis incautus ; nec tibi, Calue, sapis ;
Formosam qui cum dominam sine teste teneres,
  Raro qua, fateor, pulcrior esse solet ;   10
Quæque tuis multo tibi charior esset ocellis,
  Pro qua vouisses forsan, amice, mori :
Hanc mihi, quemque adeo nosti, tu credere bardus
  Vt velles ? talem siccine, crude, mihi ?
Quid facerem ? quis vel potuit minus ? illico captus
  Ostendo ingenium, nec bene sanus amo.
Muneribus tento, cunctaque Cupidinis arte,
  Qua non est, et scis, notior vlla mihi.
Vici, et iam (testis mihi sit chorus omnis Amorum)
  Osculor inuitus, quod tua sola foret.   20
Iste voluptatem mihi scrupulus abstulit omnem,
  Et summe iratus tunc tibi, Calue, fui,
Quod tua culpa minus fidum te fecit amico ;
  Qua nisi te purges, non cadet ira mihi.

4

Ille miser faciles cui nemo inuidit amores,
  Felle metuque nimis qui sine tutus amat;
Noctes atque dies cui prona inseruit amica,
  Officijs, regno, et nomine pulsa suis.
Nam quis te dominam post tot seruilia dicet?
  Ora quis ignauæ victa stupebit iners?
Imperet, et iubeat quæ se constanter amari
  Expetit; vtcunque est, obsequium omne nocet.
Qua (bene quod sperabat) amantes reppulit arte
  Penelope, docta scilicet vsa mora,   10
Hac magis incendit, cupidosque potentius vssit;
  Deceptamque sua risit ab arte Deus.
Nec minus ipsa dolos persensit callida, vinci
  Fraude sua voluit, dissimulare tamen:
Discite, formosæ, non indulgere beatis,
  Fletibus assuescat siquis amare velit.
Nec tristes lachrimæ, cita nec suspiria desint,
  Audiat et dominæ dicta superba tremens:
Sit tamen irarum modus, haud illæta labori
  Nox fessum reparet, pacificusque torus;   20
Quæque minas misero iactarunt pulchra labella
  Mordeat, et victor pectora dura premat;
Tum leuiter. niueis incumbens ore mamillis
  Sanguineam exugat dente labroque notam:
Sic velut acer eques per pascua læta triumphet,
  Femina iam partes sola ferentis agat.
Sed simul orta dies peruerterit otia noctis,
  Cum veste antiquos induat illa animos:
Iamque assurgenti speculumque togamque ministret,
  Præstet aquam manibus, calceolumque pedi.   30
Postilla assideat, fessus si forte videtur;
  Sin minus, actutum proijciendus erit.
Custos regni amor est; dominantes seruat amores
  Sæuitia, et nullo iure inhibente metus.
Odi quod nimium possim, truculenta sit opto,
  Dum mea formosa est, dummodo grata mihi.
Turbato quot apes furem sectantur ab alueo,
  Tot mihi riuales displicuisse velim.
Dulce nec inuitam foret eripuisse puellam
  E medio iuuenum triste minante choro,   40
Multorumque oculis pariter votisque placentem
  Posse per amplexus applicuisse mihi.
Spartanæ nomen tantum famamque secutus
  Primus apud Graios ausus amare Paris;
Quodque vir ille palam, timide petiere Pelasgi,
  Crimine vtrique pares, vnus adulter erat.
Quoue animo Troiæ portas subijsse putatis

Cum rapta insignem coniuge Priamidem?
Aurato curru rex, et regina volentes
    Accurrunt; fratres, ecce, vehuntur equis;   50
Et populus circum, iuuenesque patresque, globantur,
    Æmula spectatum multa puella venit.
Vnam omnes Helenam spectant, gratantur ouantes
    Omnes vni Helenæ; sed Paris ipse sibi.
Illi vel fratres talem inuidere, sed illi
    Suaue fuit, quod res inuidiosa fuit.
O fœlix cui per tantos nupsisse tumultus
    Contigit, et dignum bello habuisse torum.
Vt tam pulchra meis cedant quoque præmia cœptis,
    Optarem pugnas et tua fata, Pari.   60

5

Prima suis, Fanni, formosis profuit ætas,
    Solaque de facie rustica pugna fuit;
Donec vis formæ succreuit, viribus aurum,
    Quo sine nunc vires, et bona forma iacet.
Ergo sapis triplici nummos qui congeris arca:
    Semper quod dones, quodque supersit habes.
Vltro te iuuenes, vltro petiere puellæ,
    Riuales de te diraque bella mouent.
At non arenti color est tibi lætior aruo,
    Labra sed incultis asperiora rubis.   10
Vel nulli, vel sunt atri rubigine dentes,
    Iamque anima ipsa Stygem et busta senilis olet.
Forsitan ingenium quod amabile ducis amantes;
    Hei mihi, quod nimium est hæc quoque causa leuis!
Sit tamen ampla satis per se; tibi nulla fuisset,
    Qui nihilo plus quam magna crumena sapis.
Ceu lepidus coleris tamen et formosus, Adoni,
    Nec fugit amplexus lauta puella tuos.
Nonnullæ accedunt quas tu, furiose, repellis;
    Pulsisque, vt par est, lachrima crebra cadit.   20
O fœlix, si non odiosa podagra grauaret!
    Neruus et effetus, membraque inepta senis.
Si non ingratæ Veneris funesta puellæ
    Supplicia afflictus pesque manusque daret.
Te tamen haud vlli possunt arcere dolores
    Cum petit amplexus fœmina cara tuos.
Plurima possit amor; verum si olfecerit aurum
    Mulcebit barbam Mellia nostra tuam.

6

Caspia, tot pœnas meruit patientia nostra?
    Culpa erat insistens primo in amore fides?

Mene fugis quod iussa feram? quod fortis amator
 Non succumbo malis quæ dare multa potes?
Troile, non illud nocuit tibi, Cressis acerbas
 Eripuit tandem commiserata moras,
Non illud solis in terris questa puella est
 Dum rapit infidum mobilis aura virum,
Sæpe 'alios leuitas, sed nos constantia lædit;
 Supplicium pietas et benefacta timent.   10
Forsan erit miserorum aliquis grauis vltor amantum,
 Cui longa pœnas pro feritate dabis,
Ah memini ignoto languentia membra dolore,
 Et speciem ereptam pene fuisse tibi;
More meo lachrimans aderam, fidusque minister,
 Tum mihi facta malis lenior ipsa tuis;
Protinus insensum tibi supplex inuoco numen,
 Et subita ex votis est reuocata salus.
Tanti erit in nostro semel ingemuisse furore,
 Tanta erat in proprijs pax aliena malis.   20
Quid precibus valeam tua pectora ferrea norunt,
 Et nossent melius, sed mea fata vetant.
Multa tamen cupiam pro te discrimina inire,
 Multa iube, dulcis nam labor omnis erit.
Dulcis erit, sed erit labor; heu miserere laboris;
 Noster ab hac nimium parte laborat amor.
Sæuitiam natura feris, sed moribus apta
 Corpora, et arma manu, fronte, vel ore dedit;
Humana includi formoso pectore corda
 Iussit, in hac specie quæritur vnus amor.   30
Quo speciosa magis tanto tu mitior esses:
 Me miserum! tanto sæuior ira tua est.
Ingentesque animos assumis conscia formæ,
 Virtutes nouit fœmina quæque suas.
Si lubet accedat reliquis clementia, palmam
 Vt sine riuali me tribuente feras.
Dotibus ingenij superas et corporis omnes,
 Hoc vno vinci nomine turpe puta.

7

Tene ego desererem? mater velit anxia natum,
 Vnanimem aut fratrem prodere chara soror?
Delerem ex animo tam suaues immemor horas?
 Delicias, lusus, basia docta, iocos?
Desine iam teneros fletu corrumpere ocellos;
 Ante calor flammis excidet, vnda mari,
Et prius a domina discedent sidera luna,
 Quam te destituat, me violante, fides.
Ista manus nobis æqualia fœdera sanxit,
 Quam tu nunc lachrimis suspiciosa lauas.   10

Semper habes aliquid querulo sub corde timoris,
  Fœmineo multi sunt in amore metus.
Sæpe mihi Thesei memoras fugientia vela,
  Vtque erat indigno Dido cremata rogo.
Neglectis quæcunque solent miserisque nocere,
  Hæc tua sed nondum pectora læsa dolent,
Quid feci? mea tu, cum non sint, crimina ploras;
  Hocne fides? mores hoc meruere mei?
Forte licet miseras fiducia fallat amantes,
  Plus illa insanus possit obesse metus.   20
Lugubri exemplo Cephali sat fabula nota est,
  Ne nimium ex Procri sit tibi, nostra, caue.

8

Parce, puer Veneris, parce, imperiose Cupido,
  Iam nimis intentas vertis in ora faces:
Ah pudet, abiectus cecidi, miserere iacentis;
  Quem modo læsisti, nunc tueare, timor.
Rusticus ille prior fuit, ingratusque puellæ,
  Hic tamen ingenue signa fatentis habet.
Vixdum prima diem reserarant lumina solis,
  Cum thalamum subij, pulchra Sybilla, tuum.
Horrida rura virum, sed non metuenda, tenebant;
  Tutum riuali fecit in vrbe locum.   10
Ipsa etiam speciosa toro sed sola recumbens
  Aduentum primo visa probare meum.
Dissimulans sic fata, Quid hoc? absente marito
  Ad nuptæ iuuenem stare cubile decet?
Ast ego, virgineum diffundens ore ruborem,
  Respondi blandus quæ mihi iussit Amor.
Longa dehinc varijs teritur sermonibus hora
  Dum votis obstat sola ministra meis:
Optabam tacitus, licet haud inamabilis esset,
  Membra feris miseræ diripienda dari.   20
Discedant famulæ, quoties locus aptus amori,
  Nec domina sistant vel reuocante gradus;
Aduersatur heræ si quæ crudelis amanti est,
  Inuidiamque sibi diraque bella parit.
Iamne vacat monstrare alijs præcepta pudoris
  Cum reus indoctæ rusticitatis agar?
Forte ministra moras, sed quas abitura, trahebat,
  Mansit et illa diu vt posset abesse diu.
Sed nec eat prorsus, iusta illam causa morata est,
  Quæ discedenti tum mihi nulla foret.   30
Verbis affari, nudos spectare lacertos;
  Cætera ne liceant, hæc quoque pondus habent.
Dum velut iratæ cupio non esse molestus,
  In me odia incendi credulitate mea.

Tu tamen hanc veniam vati concede, Cupido,
  Perque tuas iuro, flammea tela, faces
Nulla leues posthac conatus verba repellent;
  Cassibus exibit fœmina nulla meis.
Candida seu nigra est, mollis seu dura, pudica
  Siue leuis, iuuenis siue adeo illa senex;   40
Qualiscunque datur, modo sit formosa, rogare
  Non metuam, et longa sollicitare prece.
Quæ nolit, poterit satis illa negare petenti;
  Quæ velit, illa tamen sæpe petita, velit.
Nolit, siue velit, semper repetenda puella est;
  Hoc ferri grate munus vtrique solet.
Si peruersa, tamen formam placuisse iuuabit;
  Si cupida, optato conuenit apta viro.
Annuit, et vultu probat hæc ridente Cupido,
  Iamque noua incedo mactus amator ope;   50
Indico tamen hoc vobis, mala turba, puellæ,
  Cum peto vos, culpam ne memorate meam.

9

Ergo meam ducet? deducet ab vrbe puellam
  Cui rutilo sordent ora peruʃta cane?
Mellea iamne meo valedicere possit amori,
  Vrbeque posthabita vilia rura colet?
Anne fides, sensusque simul periere? sequetur
  Post tot formosos illa senile iugum?
Pauperis vxor sim potius quam regis amica,
  Sic ais; ah stulte relligiosa sapis!
Verum habeas; quid enim tibi, perfida, tristius optem
  Quam tali dignam concubuisse viro?   10
Vtrique et similes parias; patris exprimat ora
  Progenies; mores ingeniumque tuum.
Vitam igitur nobis pingui de rure maritus
  Eripiet, miseræ, perfugiumque animæ?
Tam tristes tædas poterit nox vlla videre?
  Endimeoneis raptaue Luna genis?
Igneus horrentes inducat turbo procellas,
  Et rapiat flores aura prophana sacros;
Tartareique canes diros vlulent Hymenæos,
  Prædicat lites scissaque flamma facum.   20
Strataque cum lecti genialis sponsa recludit
  Per totum videat serpere monstra torum.
Vos paruique Lares, nocturni et ridiculi dij,
  Terrea Pigmæo gens oriunda Obera;
Raso qui capitis, cilij, mentique capillo
  Luditis indignos, turba iocosa, viros:
Raptaque per somnum vehitis qui corpora, et altis
  Fossis aut vdo ponitis illa lacu:

Confluite huc, vestro nimium res digna cachinno est,
    Eia agite, o lepidi, protinus ite, Lares,   30
Pulchramque informi positam cum coniuge sponsam
    Eripite, haud vllo conspiciente dolos ;
Amplexumque meos cum se sperabit amores,
    Stramineam pupam brachia dura ferant ;
Aut tritum teneat carioso pene Priapum,
    Præclare vt miserum rideat omnis ager ;
Fabula nec toto crebrescat notior orbe,
    Huic cedant claudi probra venusta dei ;
Ipseque nescierim, quamuis dolor intus et ira
    Æstuet, in risus soluar an in lachrimas.   40

10

Illa mihi merito nox est infausta notanda,
    Qua votum veneri spreuit amica torum.
Sic promissa fides ? reditum sic ausa pacisci
    Improba deque meo vix reuocanda sinu ?
Credideram, persuasit Amor, suasere tenenti
    Quæ mihi discedens oscula longa dedit.
Ergo vigil, tacitusque tori de parte cubaui ;
    Esset vt infidæ fœdifragæque locus.
Adieci porrho plumas et lintea struxi,
    Mollius vt tenerum poneret illa latus :   10
Nulla venit, quamuis visa est mihi sæpe venire ;
    Quæ cupidos oculos falleret vmbra fuit.
Audito quoties dicebam murmure lætus
    Iam venit ! extendo brachia, nulla venit.
Me strepitu latebrosa attentum bestia lusit,
    Spemque auido ventis mota fenestra dedit.
Sic desiderio tandem languere medulla
    Cœpit, inassuetis ignibus hausta fuit.
Iamque erat vt cuperem gelida de rupe, Prometheu,
    Expectare tuas, vulnere crudus, aues.   20
At quanto leuior iam tum mihi pœna fuisset
    Captasse impasti ludicra poma senis.
Ecquis erit miser ? inueniat quam possit amare,
    Quam cupide indicta nocte manere velit.
Me videat quisquis sponsæ periuria nescit ;
    En lachrimis oculi liuidaque ora tument,
Insomnique horrent artus, dum forsitan illa
    Immemor, et dulci victa sopore, iacet.
Nec metuit promissa ; fidem nam perdidit et me ;
    Nec timuit, quorum est numine abusa, deos.   30
Conuentum in siluis statuit Babilonia Thisbe
    Cum iuuene ardenti, sed prior ipsa venit :
Cumque viro perijt, qui si potuisset abesse,
    Haud scio nox miseræ tristior vtra foret.

Non iter in siluas, nec erat tibi cura cauendi
  Custodes, potuit tota patere domus;
Si velles saltem, si non periura fuisses,
  Basia si veri signa caloris erant.
Nam quid detinuit? famulis pax vna: quid ergo?
  Sex septemue gradus? ianua aperta? torus,   40
Et qui te misere remoratus quærat in illo?
  Hæccine tam fuerat triste subire tibi?
Quam vellem causam vel inanem fingere posses,
  Inuito vt faceres ista coacta metu:
Sed nihil occurrit, res est indigna, nefasque;
  Impia, fecisti dirum in amore scelus;
Quod nullis poterit precibus lachrimisue piari,
  Ni mihi sex noctes sacrificare velis.

11

Qui sapit ignotas timeat spectare puellas;
  Hinc iuuenum atque senum maxima turba petit.
Incautos nouitate rapit non optuma forma,
  Quemque semel prendit non cito soluit Amor.
Quod pulchrum varium est; species non vna probatur,
  Nec tabulis eadem conspicienda Venus.
Siue lepos oculis, in vultu seu rosa fulget,
  Compositis membris si decor aptus inest;
Gratia siue pedes, leuiter seu brachia motat;
  Vndique spectanti retia tendit Amor.   10
Distineat iuuenem neque pompa, nec aurea vestis,
  Nec picti currus, marmoreæue fores:
Raro vrbem solus prouecta nocte pererret,
  Nox tenebris fieri multa proterua sinit;
Siqua die placita est, noctu pulcherrima fiet:
  Adde merum, Phædram possit amare gener.
Hæc ego: cum contra est telis facibusque minatus,
  Ni sileam, triplex pectore vulnus Amor.

12

Qui gerit auspicijs res et, nisi consulat exta,
  Nil agit, hic subitos nescit abire dies.
Suspiciosa mora est, fortuna irridet inertes,
  Omnia præcipiti dans redimensque manu.
Dum Menelaus abest, Helenen Priameius vrget,
  Vrgentique aderant numina Fors et Amor.
Herus æque omnes voluere cubilia, solus
  Læander Cypria sed duce victor amat.
Solus congreditur dubia sub luce puellam
  Defessam sacris ante ministerijs.   10
Sæpe opportune cadit importuna voluntas,
  Insperataque sors ad cita vota venit.

Parua sed immemoris sponsi cunctatio Thisben
　　Seque per vmbrosum præcipitauit iter.
Vna dies aufert quod secula nulla resoluent,
　　Secula quod dederint nulla, dat vna dies.
Mane rosas si non decerpis, vespere lapsas
　　Aspicies spinis succubuisse suis.
Dum iuuat, et fas est, præsentibus vtere; totum
　　Incertum est quod erit; quod fuit, inualidum.　　20

13　*Ad Ed: Mychelburnum.*

Ergone perpetuos dabit vmbra sororia fletus?
　　Inque fugam molles ossea forma deas?
Sic, Edoarde, situ ferali horrenda Thalia
　　Antiquosque sales deliciasque abiget?
Carmina nequaquam tangunt funebria manes.
　　Impetrabilior saxa ad acuta canas.
Parce piam cruciare animam, si chara sorori
　　Extinctæ superest, ne sit iniqua tibi.
Aspice, distortis Elegeia lassa capillis
　　Procubuit, lachrimis arida facta suis;　　10
Ecce, premit, frustraque oculos exsoluit inanes:
　　Prodiga quod sparsim fudit, egena sitit.
Sic proiecta graues Istri glacialis ad vndas
　　Dicitur emeritum deposuisse caput.
Sic exhausta sacri vatis lugubre canendo
　　Exilium, et tardos ad meliora Deos.
Iam satis est, Edoarde, tui miserere, deæque;
　　Fessa dea est nimium sollicitata diu.
Assueti redeant animi, solatia, lusus;
　　Exuat atratam vestra Thalia togam.　　20
Nec te detineat formæ pereuntis imago;
　　Ad manes abijt non reditura soror.
Neue recorderis quæ verba nouissima dixit;
　　Præsidio illa minus proficiente iuuant.
Verba dolorem acuunt, soluunt obliuia curas;
　　Immemores animos cura dolorque fugit.
Sed tua si pietas monitis parere recusat,
　　Ægraque mens constans in feritate sua est,
Nulla sit in terris regio, non ora, nec ætas
　　Inscia ploratus, insatiate, tui.　　30
Non Hyades tantum celebrent fulgentia cœlo
　　Sidera, fraternus quas reparauit amor;
Quantum fama tuas lachrimas, obitusque sororis;
　　O bene defleto funere digna soror!
Et, tibi, si placet hoc, indulge, Edoarde, dolori;
　　Singultuque grauem pectore pasce animum.
Tristitiam leuat ipsa dies; gaudebit et vltro
　　Ascitis tandem mens vegetare iocis.

FINIS.

APPENDIX TO THE
LATIN POEMS.

Thomas Campion's 1595 edition of Latin verse to a very large extent consists of poems which appeared in his subsequent (1619) collection. For this reason it has not been thought necessary to reprint it in full; but as it contains many poems which were not subsequently reprinted, and in some cases the modifications which the poet made in reprinting are of interest, I have given in this Appendix all such poems as were not included in the subsequent edition together with notes of all readings in which the earlier text differed from the later, in the form of a running commentary. It will thus be found possible by incorporating the passages of the 1619 edition alluded to and making the changes specified to reconstruct the entire actual text of the 1595 *Poemata*.

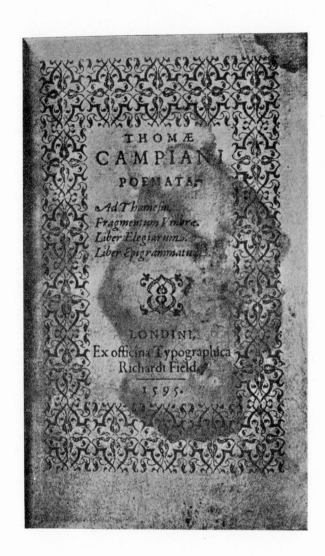

AD *DIANAM.

* Serenissi-
mæ reginæ
laudes sub
Dianæ
nomine
cele-
brantur.

Dij nemorum, et vati Thamesinæ adsistite nymphæ,
Dum struit herbosum vestras altare Dianæ
Propter aquas, iaculantis apros, vulpesque Dianæ.
Post hiemes aliquot solita inter sydera sydus
Natiuo candore deam splendescere læti
Suspicietis, iniqua arcentem frigora vultu,
Qua formosa poli glacialis parte relucens
Seruatos lustrarit agros, populumque suarum
Virtutum memorem, nec dedignabitur alte
Despectare suos proiecta cacumina colles.   10
Illa aquilam (cernetis enim) rigidumque leonem
Frustra obnitentes roseis trahet armamentis,
Atque leui filo spumantia colla refringet.
  Ocius ô nymphæ quin fertis ad illius aram
Gramineos flores, mentam, violasque latentes,
Et folijs quæ caltha suis se prodit agente
Sole diem, frustra nymphis se illisa requirens
Cum gelidam fugeret retrahens sibi brachia noctem?
Præcipue asportate rosas, prata ampla rosarum,
Diua suos flores agnoscet debita sacra.   20
Congerite has frondes, stipulaque arente fouete
Candentes prunas, animisque educite flammam;
Has olim ad Thamesin sparsas in littore voces
Certum est in cineres dare, quid conspergitis undas
O nymphæ? quid iniqua pios manus enecat ignes?
  Parce dea, extinctam superant mea sacra fauillam,
Quasque adolere fuit satius, *fecere sororum

* Ne qua
pars Eliza-
bethæ
laudis
interiret.

Agmina relliquias, et mi monumenta pudoris.
Sed tibi seu cœlum est animus, seu visere terras,
Ad Thamesin tua sceptra canam, tua sceptra canenti   30
Adcurrent nemora, et laurus simul omnia fient.

AD *DAPHNIN.

* Claris-
simus
Essexiae
comes sub
Daphnidis
persona
adum-
bratur.

Ecquis atat superum? nec enim terrestris in illo
Effulsit splendor, certe aut Latous Apollo
Per virides saltus teneros sectatur amores,
Aut Daphnis formosus adest, quem sordida terra,
Quem nemus abductum, quem si fas Cynthia fleuit.
Illi nequicquam Fauni, Charitesque quotannis
Ornarunt, festosque dies suauesque Hymenæos,
Montibus et siluis immania lustra ferarum
Eruit, innuptæ veneratus sacra Dianæ.
Ah nimium intrepidus toruo occursare leoni   10
Gestit, et ingentes ad pugnam incendere tauros.

Quam modo qua Tagus auriferis incumbit arenis,
Per vaga dorsa freti iuuenum longo agmine cinctus,
Vastatoris apri fugientia terga cecidit !
Non Atlante satæ (fœlicia sydera munus
Hoc pietatis habent) magis infœlicis Hyantis
Confusæ ex abitu steterant, trepidæque volarunt
Per siluas, resonantibus vndique Hyantida siluis ;
Quam te, Daphni, super duplicantes vota Britanni,
Quam te, Daphni, super pendentibus anxia fatis   20
Diua, notos metuens, longumque quod æstuat æquor.
Sed postquam sospes tandem patria arua reuisas,
Terra nemusque viret, veteresque ex ordine cultus
Solenni instituunt siluestria numina pompa,
Nec tibi tantum ausit decus inuidisse Menalcas.

AD THAMESIN.

ARGVMENTVM.

Totum hoc poema gratulationem in se habet ad Thamesin de Hyspanorum fuga, in qua adumbrantur causæ quibus adducti Hyspani expeditionem in Angliam fecerint. Eæ autem sunt, auaritia, crudelitas, superbia, atque inuidia. Deinde facta Apostrophe ad Reginam pastoraliter desinit.

** Elisa-
bethæ.*

Nympha potens Thamesis soli cessura * Dianæ,
Cæruleum caput effer aquis, charchesia late
Quæ modo constiterant signis horrenda cruentis,
Ecce tuos trepide liquere fugacia portus.
Non tulit Hispanos crudelia signa sequentes
Neptunus pater, et multum indignantia spumis
Æquora, non deus ætherea qui fulminat arce,
Nubila qui soluit, ventorumque assidet alis.
Ille suos cultus, sua templa, suosque Britannos
Proteget, vltricemque suam victricibus armis.   10
Nec Romana feret purgatis Orgia fanis
Reffluere, aut vetitas fieri libamen ad aras.
O pietas odiosa deo, scelerataque sacra,
Quæ magis inficiunt (damnosa piacula) sontes.

** Americæ
poetica
descriptio.*

Est * locus Hesperijs, Diti sacer, abditus vndis,
Quem pius occuluit Nereus, hominumque misertus
Oceanus, quemque ipse deis metuendus Apollo
Luminis inditio quod detegit omnia, sensit
Ignotis sub aquis melius potuisse latere.
At pater vmbrarum cui nox parit horrida natos   20
Terribiles, nigro vultus signante corymbo,
Ille per obscuras petit antra immania siluas
Aurea, siluarum Stygiæ sub tegmine nymphæ
Atra tenebrosis spectant in fontibus ora.
Eumenides regem comitantur, et ortus Echidna
Cerberus, et quæ monstra tulit furialis origo,
Quos caput horrendum quatiens sic alloquitur Dis :
  Paci inimica cohors, nunc iras sumite pleno
Pectore, nunc totas penitus diffundite vires,

Exululate sacros, et quos horrere susurros   30
Ipse velim, collecta simul conflate venena,
Tabe Promethea riguus quas Caucasus herbas,
Tantaleæue ferunt limphæ, Phlegetonue, Acheronue,
Lætificas armate manus, Anioque, Tyburque
Sentiat infusum virus, Duriusque, Tagusque,
Diraque Auernales exuscitet vnda furores,
Irarumque minas, auidique incendia belli.
  Dixit, et effugiunt quassantes ore colubros
Anguicomæ, Ditem dolor excitat, euolat antro,
Et vagus excurrit sinuosi margine ponti   40
Atra velut nubes ventis agitata, senemque
Oceanum vocat, et rauco clamore remugit.
Constiterant fluctus, egere silentia venti,
Cyaneis os tollit aquis venerabile numen
Æquoreum, madidasque comas a fronte remouit,
Ismarias superare niues albedine visas.
Quamuis nulla senis subijt reuerentia Ditem,
Sic tamen affatur, mollitque astutia vultum :
O qui luctantes ciuiliaque arma gerentes
Imperio fluctus componis, et æquora late   50
Fusa, et sidentes ruptis de montibus amnes,
Cur inuisa iacet? cur hæc vacat insula cultu?
Pondere terra gemit, fœto maturuit aluo
Resplendens aurum, ferit hoc mortalia sydus
Pectora, tu solus prohibes quod amabilis auri
Suadet amor facinus ; non has Romanus ad oras,
Non venit Hispanus castris assuetus et armis,
Nec quisquam Italiæ, tua monstra natantia terrent.
Esto precor facilis, quosque ingens gloria Martis
Extulit Hesperios, animis rebusque potentes   60
Excipe, conde sinu, nostroque in littore siste.
Quem contra Oceanus: Tibi, Dis, patet orcus, et omnis
Vis terrena, nocensque ægris mortalibus aurum,
Verum siquid habent, et habent tua munera pulchri,
Sunt Angli, sunt Troiana de gente Britanni,
Qui pacem, numenque colunt, et templa fatigant.
Sin longa spectes serie numerosa trophæa,
Has etiam spectes immensæ molis arenas.
Ingemuit, traxitque imo suspiria corde
Tartareus, spumaque oris barbam albicat atra.   70
Aggressumque tuas, decus ô regina Britannûm,
Virtutes narrare, fremens occœpit acutis
Obturbare senem stridoribus, et ferus ira
Concussit piceos scabra rubigine dentes.
Ardebant oculi, vultu pax exulat omnis,
Excidit obsequium et meditata precamina, diras
Euomit atque minas quales irata Medea ;
Et tibi, ait, quoniam leuis est mea visa potestas,
Rumpam fundamenta maris quæ tegmine nostras
Obfuscant ædes, post imas quære sub vmbras   80
In fluctus requiem, sedemque cadentibus vndis.
Horruit Oceanus (vitium formido senile est)
Sed quid non ausit demens furor, et mala præceps
In sua, vix motum longa mulcedine Ditem

Lenijt, et malus impetratis rebus abiuit.
Carbasa tenduntur subito venientibus Euris,
Et ruit æquoreos male gratum pondus in armos :
Cogitat Oceanus rapido nunc mergere ponto,
Nunc grauibus scopulis, in acutaque figere saxa.
Cauta iram cohibet mens, at vindicta dolentem   90
Oblectat, sensitque animo te, Drace, futurum
Exitio Hispanis, clarumque insignibus ausis
Frobucerum, pariterque nouis successibus oras
Ampla reportantem ad patrias spolia auripotentem
Candisium, audaces animos fortuna secundat.
   Excipit Hesperios Dis quem tegit aurea palla,
Corporis et tenebræ vestis fulgore coruscant,
Vix hunc credideris cæcas habitare cauernas,
Squallentemque situ Stygijs sordere sub vmbris.
O quam splendescit Venus aurea! suauis in auro est   100
Gratia, multus honos, absque auro gratia nulla est.
   Propter Auarities stat inhospita, lumine læta
Sollicito, mirum, hoc lætatur in hospite, nullum

* Auaritiæ
domus.

Quæ colit hospitium ; * Libica est procul inuia Syrtis
Per vada, stant tacitæ longa insuetudine siluæ,
Semper et obdormit tranquilla in montibus Eccho,
Dissimilisque sui, non est qui suscitet illam..
Mœnibus obsepta est sublimibus ærea turris,
Mulciber hanc vario torquens errore viarum
Æternum statuit non expugnabile tectum.   110
Hæc domus, hìc misera insomnis noctesque diesque
Thesaurum obseruat cæca tellure sepultum.
Et quia causa deest, fingit sibi monstra timenda,
Formidatque animo quas non præsenserat vmbras.
Turribus aërijs tuta est si credere posset,
Tuta loco, extructisque ingens super æquor arenis.
Alta per exiguam clauduntur mœnia portam,
Hanc sola ingreditur, nunquam egreditur nisi Plutus
Euocet, eximium hunc spretis habet omnibus vnum.
   Proxima purpurea succedit cuspide Cædes   120
Suspitiose oculos obliquans, atque cruentum
Vix animo halato cor in ilia gurgitat atra,
Atra æstu, rabieque insana fellis adusti.
   Vltima subsequitur manifesta Superbia curru,
Fastiditque solum, sellam haud dignatur eburnam
Qua vehitur, quam traxit auis Iunonia pompam
Pennarum expandens, gemmasque elata recludens.
Agmina conueniunt, dextras vtrinque dederunt,
Dis ait : Hesperij satis est dextræque moræque,
Mensa diesque vocant, perijt pars optima lucis: 130
Applaudunt regi vmbrarum portuque recedunt.
   Ecce fatigatos læuo curuamine cœli
Lentus agens Hyperion equos, curruque reclinans
Viderat Hesperios, et quis nouus incola terras
Venit in ignotas miratur, eoque morantes
Cursores animat, Tethidosque hortatur ad vndas.
Interea ingentem vino cratera propinant,
Indulgentque epulis Dis cum regaliter usis
Hospitibus, donec gelidis stipata tenebris

Induxit somnos nox, atque papauera sparsit.   140
  Postera deformes roseo velamine texit
Vmbras aurora, et simulatis fronte capillis.
Concurrunt stygiæ feriuntes tympana nymphæ,
Et recinunt miserum clamoso gutture carmen.
Ducentesque choros dominum, regemque requirunt.
Turba petit siluas somno experrecta madentes
Rore leui suauesque expirans gramen odores.
Valle sub obscura liquidis argenteus vndis
* Fons erat, Inuidiæ sacer, hunc, Narcisse, petisses   * Fons
Tutus, in aduersam quia nulla repercutitur lux   150   Inuidiae
Seu lucis radius speciem, sed quicquid in orbe   sacer.
Est vsquam limphis manifesto cernitur illis.
Fons mundi speculum est, sed qui speculatur in illo
Morbum oculis haurit macidum, et lethale venenum.
Huc diuertentes cum Dite Hyspana iuuentus
Immisere oculos auide putealibus vndis,
Et sub aqua mirantur aquas, vrbesque, domosque,
Agnouere suos portus, nemora, aruaque et aurei
Lucida signa Tagi: longe omnibus eminet vna
Cuncta mari tellus, celeberrima rupibus albis,   160
Hanc spectant, et agros, vrbes, vada, flumina, fontes
Laudant inuiti, hac vna regione morantur,
Quæque vident cupiunt, atque inuidere videndo.
Paulatim increuit pulmonibus ardor anhelis,
Liuidus ora color, macies cariosa medullas
Occupat, illi acres pugnant superare dolores,
Iamque odio locus est, nec iam discedere possunt.
Sic miseri cum flamma ædes circumflua vastat,
Excussi somnis media sub nocte pauentes
Corpora proriperent, obsistit at obuius ignis,   170
Cernentesque aduersa oculos, et cassa mouentes
Effugia exurit feralis tæda lacertos.
  Postquam irretitas acies, et vulneris æstu
Senserat arderi et frangi iuuenilia corda
Dis, arrisit aquis, lætusque silentia rupit,
Spectatæ satis, o iuuenes, nimiumque recedant
Cœlestes lymphæ, mens est et numen in illis.
Ecce ferunt violas, detexuale lilia nymphæ,
Ecce struunt in serta rosas fontemque coronant.
Nondum extrema grauis diuerberat ora loquentis   180
Imber, et obducto recidentia nubila cœlo.
Tristis hiems, et nox nullo suadente resurgit
Vespere, terrarumque orbem intempesta recondit.
Per iuga dissiliunt fluctus, voluuntur et imas
In valles, teretesque trahunt de montibus ornos.
Intremuere omnes, Dis autem interritus vmbras
Increpat, et facilem concussit arundine terram,
Terra tremit, nigrasque aditum patefecit ad arces.
  At dirupta iam ruituris subuolat Auster
Nube, pruinosisque cadentes sustinet alis.   190
Tænarium nemus vmbriferum, tacitæque cauernas
Noctis, et æternum quibus obdormire sepulchris
Adsueuit Morphei pater, hæc præteruolat æstu
Fulmineo, donec portas prope sensit opacas

Stantem Hecaten, medijs qua circumcingitur vmbris,
Desilit hic terramque vagis amplectitur vlnis.
Læta viro occurrit Plutonia, dumque stupescit
Haud expectatos comites, fugit imbrifer[1] Auster,
Et numerosa horret niueis concussa capillis
Styria, luctificique fluunt cum grandine nimbi.   200
 Delitias facit hospitibus, stygiosque lepores
Dis, et in obscuros Triuia comitante recessus
Monstrat iter, stant mensæ epulis vinoque repletæ,
Aureo et effulgent operosa cubilia tecto.
Accubuere, canente suam accumbentibus Orpheo
Euridicen, quæque olim inter Rhodopeia saxa
Fudit ad vmbrosas quercus, tenuesque miricas.
Quin etiam immites Thressas fleuisset, et Hebro
Dimersum caput et cytheram, si non dea mater,
Flens dea Calliope nati compresserat ora.   210
Conticuit, subitoque oritur miserabile murmur,
Quale sepulturis cum nænia flebilis inter
Affines canitur resono plangore gementes.
Lugentque Hesperij nequaquam in vatis honorem,
Pestiferi sed enim torquentur imagine fontis,
Visorumque memor furit ægris dira cupido
Pectoribus, totasque ædes singultibus implent :
Nec sua turpari mœsto conuiuia luctu
Sustinet vlterius Cereris gener, atque ita fatur :
 Ite leues vmbræ, celsas ad sydera pinus   220
Extruite, et fluidas lato super æquore turres.
Vosque nisi hospitij pigeat fortassis Iberi
Exhilerate animos, neu quem simulachra dolorem
Vana ferant, nam quæ niueis fonte insula saxis
Emicuit spectans Helecen gelidumque Booten
Insula, diues opum, sedes veneranda Britannis,
Ingentes diffisa suis horrere carinas
Discet, et Hispano tandem succumbere ferro.
 Cincta sub hæc aderat torto caput angue Megæra,
Horrida tela, ignes, et ahenea monstra ministrans.   230
Ergo incenduntur furijs, Stygiasque ad arenas
Armati incedunt, nigros vbi cernere manes
Littoribus tot erat, quot apes præsepia circum,
Aut æstate solent turmatim irrepere sulcis
Formicæ, cursansque ignito horrenda flagello
Vndique Tysiphone cessantes verberat vmbras.
Iam sed in immensum ceu turres seu iuga Pindi
Increuere rates, quas est mirata iuuentus
Hesperia, et Stygio faciunt vota impia regi.
 Incubuere omnes, et olenti littore classem   240
Diducunt mare per gelidum, Cynosuris euntes
Respicit, aspectu sed dedignante Calistho,
Iamque fremens, vt erat vultu illætabilis vrsa
Vnguibus immites nimbos concussit, et auras
Nubibus infestat, pugnamque Aquilonibus Austros
Aduersum instituit, veteresque resuscitat iras.
 At tu nympharum Thamesis pulcherrima limphis
Alta tuis, procul vt vidisti hostilia signa,

---
[1] Corrected in Bod. ed. to 'imbricus'.

Tu dea flumineam spaciosa gurgite frontem
Celata, æquoreas turbasti fluctibus vndas.   250
Donec Ibera cohors ventorum pulsa furore,
Et virtute virum, per Hybernica saxa refugit.
Illic dira fames Scythicas illapsa per auras,
Et Lybico vesana sitis de puluere nata,
Tum Phlegetonteæ pestes, rabidique furores,
Ingratusque sibi dolor, et sua funera Erinnis
Exornans, nigra Hyspanos sub tartara mittunt.
Sic ô sic pereant aduorsis vndique fatis,
Ira Calisthoniæ trepidisque impendeat vrsæ,
Siue bibant Tyberim, vel aquas torrentis Iberi,   260
Siue Aurora nouo, sero vel sole recedens
Hesperus illustret gentes, vmbrasque repellat.
Sic pereat, quicunque tuas fleturus in oras
Vela inimica dabit, Brutique nepotibus, et dijs
O vetus hospitium, sanctumque Britannia nomen.
   Tuque viresce diu dea ceu Daphneia laurus,
Tu dea, tu fœlix Anglorum numen Elisa.
Non aconitum in te virus, non ensis acumen,
Nec magicum vim carmen habet, nec flamma calorem.
Scilicet integrum diuina potentia pectus   270
Firmat et humano dedit inuiolabile ferro.
Ergo diu vigeas, procul hinc fuge, pigra senectus,
Ismarioque cuba glaciali frigida saxo,
Vel steriles inter quas alluit Ister arenas,
I fuge, cœlestes animas tentare nefandum est.
Fallor? an excessit tardo per inane volatu?
Ecce autem rigidam trahit inter nubila pallam,
Et tremit, et cani recidunt horrore capilli.
At te diua rosis ambit formosa iuuenta,
Atque Heliconiacas aspergit floribus vndas,   280
O diua, ô miseris spes Elisabetha Britannis
Vna, senectutem superes, pulsisque superstes
Hostibus, innumeros gemines virtutibus annos.

FRAGMENTVM VMBRÆ.

ARGVMENTVM.

  Iole Berecynthiæ filia magicis carminibus sopita ab Apolline vitiatur, et ex eo grauida fit, puerumque nigrum parit nomine Melampum. Hunc, postquam adoleuerat, Morpheus amare cœpit, dormientemque varijs imaginibus cum diu frustra tentasset, Proserpinam adit, cuius sub ditione formosarum omnium manes habentur. Ibi Troianas, Græcas, Romanas, aliarumque gentium formas cum satis spectasset, tandem ad Britannicarum exemplum figuram sibi longe pulcherrimam effingit eaque indutus Melampum denuo aggreditur, qui falsa pulchritudinis specie deceptus in miserrimum amorem dilabitur, siquidem patris interuentu mox expergefactus vmbræ ipsius quam per somnium viderat desiderio tabescit, et in vmbram mutatus est.

  1619 *text to* Et quid ait., *reading* l. 1 O dea fœmineos nigro quæ: l. 79 Nec saturat spectando sitim, tangendo, fruendo: l. 114 Tristis, vt expleret miseros plangendo dolores.

ELEGIARVM

LIBER.

ELEGEIA 1.

Ite procul tetrici, moneo, procul ite seueri,
    Ludit censuras pagina nostra graues.
Ite senes nisi forte aliquis torpente medulla
    Carminibus flammas credit inesse meis.
Aptior ad teneros lusus florentior ætas,
    Vel iuuenis, vel me docta puella legat.
Et vatem celebrent Bruti de nomine primum
    Qui molles elegos et sua furta canat.
* Probro nec semper fax sit tua, Phœbe, remota,
    Feruet ab innato flamma calore magis.   10
Nobis * egelidas Neptunus mollijt auras
    Qui fouet amplexu litora lata suo.
Et nos Phœbus amat, quantumque hieme abdicat, *ardens
    Tanto plus facili conspicit ore pater.
Quid sacras memorem nymphis habitantibus vndas,
    Siue tuas Thamesis, siue, Sabrina, tuas?
Mille etiam Charites siluis, totidemque Napææ,
    Tot Veneres, tot eunt Indigenæque deæ.
Vt taceam musas, toto quas orbe silentes
    Chaucerus mira fecerat arte loqui.   20
Ille Palæmonios varie depinxit amores,
    Infidamque viro Chressida Dardanio.
Prodigiosa illo dictante canebat arator
    Ludicra, decertans cum molitore faber.
Sic peregrinantum ritus perstringit aniles,
    Riualemque dei deuouet vsque papam.
Quis deus, ô vates magnis erepte tenebris,
    Admouit capiti lumina tanta tuo?
Fabula nec vulgi, nec te Romana fefellit
    Pompa, nec Ausonij picta theatra lupi.   30
Imperio titubante nouos sibi finxit honores
    Quæ mundi dominos callida Roma tenet.
Iuris sola sui gentes procul Anglia ridet
    Tendentes Latio libera colla iugo.
Sacra libertate dea regnante potimur,
    Quæ dare iam nobis otia sola potest.
Omnia nunc pacem, montesque vrbesque fatentur,
    Cum Venere et nudo qui pede saltat Amor.
Pacis amans deus est, quamuis fera bella Cupido
    Corde gerens nostro semper ad arma vocat.   40
Alme puer, teneris adsit tua gratia musis,
    Paces siue deæ, seu tua bella canunt.

Marginal notes:

* Arguuntur enim Septentrionales quantum a sole absunt tantum abesse ab humanitate & litteris.

* Aer insularum iuxta Philosophos perpetuo aestu maris calescit.

* Æstate.

ELEGEIA 2. *Ad amicam quæ promissum fefellerat.* El. 10 of 1619
ed. Var.: l. 1. Illa diei nox iam sit contermina nulli : l. 20 pectore
ruptus aues : l. 22 Captasse exanimi : l. 35 erant tibi decipiendi :

l. 38 Si tua non dederas basia signa necis. ELEGEIA 3. *Aditum ad amorem sibi difficilem optat.* El. 4 of 1619 ed. Var.: l. 3 Infœlix etiam cui stulta: l. 9 propulit arte: l. 10 Scilicet adducta Penelopea mora: l. 11 ardentius vssit: l. 16 Fletibus insuescat: l. 23 ore papillis: l. 31 Post læua dominam assidat: l. 35 possim, date dij truculentam: l. 36 Dummodo formosa est: l. 39 Mellifluam pulchrum est te diduxisse: l. 40 torua tuente choro: l. 42 appropriare tibi: l. 44 Primo inter Græcos cœpit amare: l. 47 intrasse putatis: l. 56 Dulce fuit.

ELEGEIA 4.

De Mellea lusus.

Pulchra roseta inter mea Mellea pulchrior illis
   Dum legit vmbroso mollia fraga solo:
Venit Amor, qui iam pharetra positisque sagittis
   Gestitat igniuomo ferra forata cauo.
Puluis agit sine voce pilas vbi concipit ignem,
   Et niuis in tacito puluere candor inest.
Audax ô nimium puer! ô versute Cupido!
   Tu ne ferebaris cæcus? at ipse vides,
Argutoque minax intendis acumine ferrum.
   Intueor, licet hac fronde latere velis.   10
Erubuit deprensus Amor, risuque fugauit
   Mollitiem, et dixit tu mihi miles eris.
Si confirmandus de more poposceris aurum,
   Aurea virgo tibi hæc oscula quinque dabit.
Post illa vt nostris possit succedere castris,
   Aurea iam de te basia quinque feret.
Immo etiam de me centum, vel millia centum,
   Et placeas mage si prodigus esse velis.
Dixi, aufugit Amor, pictasque reuerberat alas,
   Nos veriti numen mutua labra damus.   20
Gessimus acre dehinc ductore Cupidine bellum,
   Et reparat noua nos in noua bella dies.

ELEGEIA 5. *Ad Cambricum.* El. 5 in 1619 ed. Var.: l. 1 Cambrice, prima fuit formosis aptior: l. 9 Nec tamen arenti: l. 15 Sed sit magna satis: l. 16 Qui pariter trito cum pugione sapis: l. 18 Fletque superciliis læsa puella tuis: inserts after l. 20 Non solum ingenium tibi formamque indidit aurum, Verum in formosas regna beata dedit: l. 22 Penis et effœtus. ELEGEIA 6. *Non differendum tempus.* El. 12 in 1619 ed. Var.: l. 12. vota ad inempta venit. ELEGEIA 7. *Ad Caspiam.* El. 6 in 1619 ed. Var.: l. 10 virtus et: l. 11 Est aliquis cœlo facilis spectator amantum: l. 17 Sedulus orabam (præsentia numina) diuos: l. 20 Tanti erat: ll. 35 and 36 reliquis virtutibus vna, Et facilis palmam: ELEGEIA 8. *Ad infidam.* El. 2 in 1619 ed. Var.: l. 1 Cum mihi blanditias et credula: l. 3. Mene statim sub corde tuos posuisse calores: l. 7 Nos elephæ longos: l. 18 Illius interior nota medulla mihi est: l. 22 spectat in ora viri: l. 25 digitis immitteret ori: l. 31 Sed quid eam metuo, cuius. ELEGEIA 9. *Ad Edouardum Mychelbornum de obitu sororis.* El. 13 in 1619 ed. Var.: l. 7 piam temerare: l. 30 Inscia mœroris, mœstitiæque tuæ. ELEGEIA 10. *Ad amicam de sua fide sollicitam.* El. 7 in 1619 ed. Var.: l. 4 Tot noctesque tuo munere, totque dies? l. 8 Quam manus

ista tuo possit abire sinu : l. 9 Illa manus : l. 13 Iamque mihi : l. 14
Conclusam rapidis sæpe Ariadnen aquis : l. 15 Et quæcunque solent
miseris in amore : l. 19-21 Quod superest has trado manus, innecte
catenas, Implexosque meis artubus adde tuos. Sic ego nec faciam,
nec tu patiere, sed vna Tecum et res fuerit, si nequit esse fides.
ELEGEIA 11. *Ad Cupidinem.* El. 8 in 1619 ed. Var.: l. 8 Intraui
thalamum : l. 15 ego purpureum : l. 19 quamuis formosa fuisset.
ELEGEIA 12. *Melleæ nuptias execratur.* El. 9 in 1619 ed. Var.:
l. 3 iamne potest nostro valedicere : l. 4 Cum furcis procul vt degat et
arboribus ? l. 6 montibus Æthiopem : ll. 11, 12 Moxque tui similes
parias, vultusque paternos, Maternamque fidem progenies referat :
l. 24 gens Obera geniti : l. 33 se sperarit : l. 34 Inuoluant pupam
brachia stramineam : l. 40 Æstuat.

ELEGEIA 13.

Caspia potitus lætatur.

Quos cupiam lætus ? quos alloquar ? anne deorum
    Formosorum aliquem noster adibit amor ?
Tutius an manes tacitasque exuscitet vmbras ?
    Sors erit inuidiæ facta beata nimis.
Tum neque Shora suos audebit prodere lusus,
    Errore implexos nec Rosimunda Lares.
Nocte immortalem me Caspia reddidit vna,
    Tanta extirpabit gaudia nulla dies.
Quas ego, quam cupide vidi tetigique papillas !
    Quam formosa inter brachia molle latus !   10
Qualia inhærenti spirauit basia labro !
    Qualia, sed castis non referenda viris !
Delitias tantas miratus et ipse Cupido est,
    Quasque dedit nobis optat habere vices.
Iniectis igitur miser asseruare lacertis
    Cogor, pectoribusque insinuare meis.
Sed miserum iuuat esse diu, sed sæpius illo
    Riualem cupiam posse timere loco.
Quæ mihi per longos venit exorata labores,
    Non nisi per magnos est retinenda metus.   20
Nox est, si moriar, satis hæc mihi sola beato ;
    Si viuo, non sunt millia mille satis.

ELEGEIA 14.

Ad amicos cum ægrotaret.

Æger eram, non vua[1] meos lenire dolores,
    Nec condita modis mille operosa Ceres,
Non dulces potuere ioci, comitumue lepores,
    Ex angore animi mens hebetata fuit.
Deciderat manibus lyra, nec suspiria crebris
    Exitibus numeros sustinuere suos.
Horrebam procul obscuræ confinia noctis,
    Nec lassos artus mollia fulcra iuuant.
Illætos querimur tarde proserpere soles,
    Noxque die grauior fit mihi, nocte dies.   10
Excutiunt placidos insomnia dira sopores,
    Somnia non vllam post habitura fidem.

[1] This is the MS. corr. in the Bodl. ed. for the original reading 'vna'.

In me sæpe ruunt armatis agmina turmis,
Sulphureisque boant ænea monstra cauis.
Hispidus hinc serpens inter deserta relicto
Fit mihi, vel frendens obuius ore leo.
Et quæ nulla ætas tulerit portenta videmus,
Excurrit vario flexilis orbe timor.
Iam iam lapsuras capiti impendere ruinas
Suspicor, aut tremulo sub pede sidit humus.   20
Iam mare, iam ventos metuo, saxa aspera terrent,
Antennas video fractaque transtra ratis.
Amisos etiam comites in littore flemus,
Et cadit ex oculis lachrima vera meis.
Te modo spectabam tumidas, Hatecliffe, per vndas
Ægre versantem brachia fessa salo.
Iamque tuos, Stanforde, tuos, Thurbarne, volutos
Exanimes artus per vada summa lego.
Collectos manibus mœrens amplector, et omnis
Flebilibus resonat quæstibus ora meis.   30
Si mihi displiceant somni mirabile non est,
Quos misere afflictos tam ferus horror habet.
Nec minus illepide nocturnis territa visis
Mens vigilans toto somniat illa die.
Sed vos ô chari multum valeatis amici,
Differor externis dum miser ipse locis.
Inuidiosa via est quæ nos disiungit amantes,
Nec socijs socio iam licet esse mihi.
Verum vos video absentes et somnio, somnis
Anxia turba meis non onerosa tamen.   40
Vestra vel in somnis lachrimaui funera, flentes
Vos quoque si moriar tymbon adite meum.

ELEGEIA 15. *A puellarum aspectu penitus abstinendum.* El. 11 in
1619 ed. Var.: l. 6 Nec templis : l. 11 non pompa.

ELEGEIA 16.

Postquam Vulcanus Veneris nudarat amores
Fertur frons teneræ diriguisse deæ;
Fracto dedidicit stupra occultare pudore,
Iamque odit fabricas conditor ipse suas.
Ah Venus exclamat, spumosa fusior vnda
Quæ non nuptibiles vndique miscet aquas:
Nos coniunxit Hymen, nos festa corona deorum,
Nos Charites, tua nos non violanda fides.
Cur non alternos simul exercemus amores?
Hostibus externis cur mea regna patent?   10
Sanguineam ex acie referens Mars horridus hastam
Ibit in amplexus, ô Cytherea, tuos?
Proditione illam victor possederit arcem
Quam mihi connubij iure remisit Hymen?
Dispeream si non pereat male perditus ille
Qui iacit in nostras nubila nigra faces.
Protinus induitur monichorum more cucullum,
Et cadit a fusco vertice rasa coma.
Candorem vultu simulat, Germanaque claustra
Ingreditur simplex, quam minimeque malus.   20

Insidias intus struit, inconcessa recludens
  Arcana, Ætnæo sacraque operta cauo.
Fulmina syderei Iouis arma micantia, et altos
  Quod superos tonitru tartaraque ima quatit,
Amens committit miseris mortalibus, amens
  Sulphureoque ardens igne odioque deus.
Et quid Thracis, ait, clipeusue vel hasta iuuabit
  Inter fulminei concita tela Iouis.
Ecce Neapolitas Galli obsidione recingunt
  Arces, hæc Marti suaserat arma Venus,   30
Quos mollis comitatur Amor ; sed vt inclita cernunt
  Fulmina, et æratos igne volare globos,
Stragibus hinc atque hinc diris, fœdoque cruore
  Intrepidus totos sparsit adulter agros.
Insidias risit dea coniugis, atque superbum
  Candido amatorem suscipit apta sinu.
Infremuit Lemni pater, eque voragine fumos
  Colligit Ætnæa tartareaque Styge.
Hos consopitis aspergat, fata vetabant
  Tangere fœlices spurca venena deos.   40
Aere sed læso feriunt contagia Gallos,
  Atque Neapolita cœpit in vrbe lues,
Quam vitare satis poterat nec fœmina, nec vir,
  Dum redit in seriem transitione malum.
Debuerat saltem formosis parcere, at illis
  Et color et vires interiere simul.
Respexit tandem Venus, et miserata puellas
  Corticibus sacris nigra venena fugat.
Restauratque toris vires, membrisque colorem,
  Lacteolumque genis purpureumque decus.   50
Ergo vbi nec cessisse dolos, nec viribus æquum
  Vidit se Marti qui paret arma faber
Obticet, indulgens Veneri et riualis amori,
  Si decuma obtingat nox sibi, lætus habet.

EPIGRAMMATVM LIBER.

The references are to the numbered Epigrams in Book II of the
1619 ed.
Ad Librum, Ep. 3. Var.: l. 2 Damnate in tenebras: ll. 3 and 4
Dedas Feldisio[1] male apprehensum Prælo ne quis ineptior prophanet :
l. 5 Deinde vt: l. 12 visere, lubricumue Tybrim: l. 13 Aut
hostile Tagi. *Ad pacem de serenissima Regina Elisabetha*, Ep. 4.
Var.: l. 1 O pax potentis maximum dei munus : l. 4 Quæ te tuetur sola
perstitem nobis. *In obitum fratris clariss. comitis Essexij*, Ep. 9.
Var.: l. 1 quisque iussit impius : l. 18 Canentque Nemesin fero tubæ
sono. *In Hornsium*, Ep. 5. Var.: l. 1 Hornsi risi hodie: l. 11
Siquis interea : l. 14 Morbosos male humi pedes : followed by a
variation of Ep. 8 as follows :

> Verum sollicitabat vna me res
> Plurimum, modo videram assidentem

---

[1] Feldisio is the correction in the errata for the text's Felsidio.

Te iuxta nitidissimam puellam,
Sermonique auide locum aucupantem;
Hei mihi vt metui ne identidem illam
Grandem equum si emeret tuum rogares?

Ad Melleam, Ep. 10. Var.: l. 7 ne doctus. *De interitu Philippi Sydnei,* Ep. 11. Var.: l. 1 Passeres Cypriæ alites petulci: l. 2 per et niuentes: l. 3 Et rubras petitis: l. 4 Usquequaque Philip: l. 5 to end:

Mars illum insidijs modo interemit
Riualem metuens, renunciate
Flebiles Veneri exitus Philippi,
Victus inuoluit caput tenebris.

In Melleam, Ep. 12. *In Cultellum,* Ep. 13. Var.: l. 3 Discissa dominæ labra funesto madent: l. 4 cruore, sanguine exundant Lares: l. 5 puella personat totam domum: l. 6 Amens, dolori: l. 7 Nec vspiam potest quiescere, nec loqui: l. 8 Nec basiare: l. 9 sceleste fractus, vt decuit prius: l. 10 Supplicia Veneri, sera sed nimium dabis. *Ad Melleam* resembles Ep. 14:

Mellea, te inuitam virgo cum vera fuisses
Raptam ais, et cur vox non fuit inditio?
Respondit lepide mala se clamare cupisse,
Sed miseram audiri se vt nimium metuit.

Ad Caspiam, Ep. 15. *In Robertum Th.,* Ep. 17. Var.: l. 1 Cogito saepe Roberte. *Ad Melleam* Ep. 18. *Ad Caluum* Ep. 19 shoulder-note on left margin—Italorum comitas est laudanti quiduis amico obtrudere, si autem acceperit tanquam sordidissimum respuere. *Ad Bibricum* Ep. 20. Var.: l. 1 Bibrice tentes. *In tonsorem* Ep. 31. Var.: l. 1 Promissis sicubi: l. 3 dabit salutem: l. 4 instar et puellis: l. 6 His propter speciem, ibus ob lucri spem? *In Largum:*

Scripserit historiam bene Largus, nam scit apud se
Quis per sex annos ederit aut biberit.

Ad Laurentium Mychelbornum, Ep. 34. Var.: l. 5 Conficique: l. 9 grata statim: l. 10 Quod quidem: l. 12 Pulchra dum. *Ad Iustinianum,* Ep. 35. Var.: l. 2 Consobrinæ animam: l. 3 Et veluti. *In Cottum,* Ep. 36. Var.: l. 2 dicas, Cotte.
Ad Caspiam, Ep. 37. Var.: l. 7 nimis heu perite. *Ad Franciscum Manbæum:*

Dum vagus ignotas veheris, Manbæe, per oras
Noctes atque dies vela notosque queror.
Quam vellem misero qui te mihi surpuit illi,
Si liceat, vento diripuisse caput.
Effossisque oculis iugulum incidisse prophano,
Ne cui tale dehinc spiret ab ore malum.

Ad Gu. Percium, Ep. 40. *De Th. Grimstono & Io. Goringo:*

Miror apud Gallos quid fortis pectore et armis
Noster Grimstonus quidue Goringus agat.
Nulli vnquam bello melius potuere mereri,
Nusquam virtuti terra maligna magis.

Ad Ed. Spencerum:

Siue canis siluas, Spencere, vel horrida belli
Fulmina, dispeream ni te amem, et intime amem.

In Hyrcamum et Sabinum, Ep. 42. Var.: l. 7 Inficete itidem.
In Prettum, Ep. 43. Var.: l. 2 possit Prette: l. 9 Pretté nouo.
In Caspiam.

> Si vnquam quæ me odit semper male Caspia amaret,
> O quam firma ipso contra in amore foret!

Ad Iacobum Thu: Ep. 45. Var.: l. 2 imparabilique: l. 3 tuas
Iacobe: l. 11 tui, Iacobe. *In Rusticum:*

> Glandem in fatidicam mutatum stultus amator
> Riuali insultans a Ioue finxit auum;
> At riualis ait, nequid mirere puella,
> De quercu ob facinus nempe pependit auus.

In Berinum:

> Tres baccas ederæ vorat Berinus,
> De repente fit inclitus poeta.

Iræ resembles Ep. 48 in its opening lines:

> Scelesta quid me? mitte, iam certum est, vale,
> Longe remotas persequar terræ plagas,
> Tuis, vel vmbras tartari, insidijs procul.
> Nec me retentare oris albicans rubor;
> Nec exeuntem lucidum hinc et hinc iubar
> Reuocare poterit, improba æternum vale.
> Vt dubia certas sensit irarum minas,
> Perculsa tremulo cecidit ad pedes metu;
> Quid misera dixit sum merita dignum nece?
> Amans quod in te tam tetrum admisi nephas,   10
> Vt me relinquas perditam, vt pro me tuos?
> Ah siste, sæuis imperes iris modum,
> Nec te immerentem perde, quid paras vide
> A me iam vt abeas poscis exilium tibi.
> Mane per has lachrymas, ocelle mi, precor,
> Resipisce tandem, amans ne amantem deseras.
> Sub hæc furenti mi redardescit dolor,
> Pluraque parantem dicere his resequor prius:
> Periura nullos æthere horrescis deos,
> Nec vindicantis scelera Adrasteæ faces?   20
> Impura non tu maria, terras, sydera
> Adhibita falso polluis, spreta fide?
> Ah dulce nostros fœdus ignes alligans
> Per te caducum cecidit, et tamen rogas
> Cur triste pectus opprimat silentium?
> Deuota labra, mique sacratum femur
> Eiectus æquore naufragus miles premit,
> Disrumpor, eheu primulo vidi die
> His exeuntem foribus ipsum militem,
> His ipse ocellis militem, et tamen rogas   30
> Cur triste pectus opprimat silentium?
> Vale scelesta, vafra, fœdifraga vale,
> Nec me retentes, nec per hanc guttam obsecres
> Summis natantem palpebris, corde inscio.
> Obfirmor, intuere, postremum vides,
> Nunc abeo, iam nunc vltimum dico vale,
> Iam taceo, pectus opprimit silentium.
> Continuo volucres excipit pedes furor,

Effugio solus deuijs errans locis
Illam perosus, me, meos, diris agent ;   40
Quicquid moræ spem dederat in fugam date.
Iras inanes risit æthereus puer,
Frustraque pectus æstuans emollijt :
Respicio, lenis imber irrorat genas,
Quid hoc? amores dissidens odium parit,
Sedantque nimbi porro fluctiuomum mare.
Amo, peruror, redeo, miseram sordibus
Et lachrymis oppletam et vmbris conspicor,
Supremus animum vix retardauit pudor
Quin impotentiæ suæ inditium daret.   50
Tandem facetam texui somnis moram,
Horrenda referens visa, cædes, vulnera,
Vultus relictæ luridos, tabo illitos,
Aut insequentem summa per iuga montium.
Hæc comminisci verus edocuit amor,
Assensit illa, et sensit artem subdola,
Sed tacita simulat vda nectens oscula ;
O suaue amoris dissidium ! ita turtures
Pugnando iungunt rostra dulci murmure.

In gloriosum [Ep. 49] :

Shæcherlæe, deos tua celsa gradatio manes
Terret ne *tectum corruat in capita.

Ad Caspiam, Ep. 50. Var. : l. 4 Sydera? vel sæuos. *In Lytum*,
Ep. 51. Var. : l. 5 tergo, Lyte. *In Merinum* [Ep. 52] :

Ista * Scauingerulum tua frons lutulenta Merine
Desidiæ semper vendicat egregiæ.

* Terra
enim inferis
pro tecto
est.

* Magi-
stratuum
genus apud
Londinen-
ses qui
defæcandæ
vrbis curam
habent.

Ad Caspiam, Ep. 53. *Ad Amorem*, Ep. 54. *Ad anum*, Ep. 55.
Var. : l. 1 Gratias refero tuis libenter : l. 3 Ægroto mihi : l. 5 Subleuare
animum : l. 7 valebit vsque : l. 8 Grata apud me animi. *Ad Caspiam*,
Ep. 56. Var. : l. 1 Quæris cur durum hoc marmor lachrimare videtur :
l. 2 Caspia naturæ viribus attribuens : l. 4 Nam lachrimat tu me quod
miserum excrucias. *In Berinum*, Ep. 57. *In Erricum*, Ep. 58.
Var. : l. 2 Indigne dicit, dij boni, et improprie : l. 4 At te sordidior
gens tua tota fuit. *In Æmiliam*, Ep. 59. *De Thermanio & Glaia*
[Ep. 60] :

Somno compositam iacere vidit
Glaiam Thermanius puer puellam,
Diducit tacita manu solutas
Vestes, illa silet, femur prehendit,
Suauiumque leui dedit labello,
Illa conticuit velut sepulta :
Subrisit puer, vltimumque tentat
Gaudium nec adhuc mouetur illa,
Sed lubens patitur dolos dolosa.
Quis nouus stupor? ante Glaya molli   10
Ansere, aut vigilans magis Sybilla,
Lethargo quasi iam graui laborans
Noctes atque dies trahis sopores.

Ad Melleam, Ep. 63. Var. : l. 2 Dicis, sic facile stultus amans capitur.
In Onellum, Ep. 62. Var. : l. 1 sit quod multum : l. 2 Nam quantum
debet tantum habuit fidei. *Ad Edo. Mychelbornum :*

Cum tibi tam cordi est, age, perdito arundine pisces,
  Fleuerit hoc quamuis Pythagorea anima.
Fleueris ipse licet cum febricitaueris alga,
  Aut penitus lapso cum pede tundis aquas.
Vis vera? hoc studio, ne sit iucundius, at te
  Tempora in hoc nolim tam bona conterere.
Quanto elegis melius teneros captabis amores,
  Vel tua siluestrem ludet arundo deam.

In gloriosum, Ep. 64. *In Largum*, Ep. 85. Var.: l. 1 Largus haud
alij vt solent nouellum : l. 3 In domum, faciem statim, torosque :
l. 4 Inspicit, studia. *In Cottum :*

> Ille miser Cottus quid agit nisi cassa canendo
>   Vt placeat nulli dum placet ipse sibi?

Ad Caspiam, Ep. 66. Var.: l. 1 complexa Sichæum : l. 2 Flebilis
æternas soluitur in lachrymas : l. 3 Attonitusque nouæ Narcissus
imagine formæ : l. 4 Vmbram sollicitat. *Ad Hymettum :*

> Vnde tibi ingratæ subeunt fastidia vitæ,
>   Dulcis Hymette, tua non nisi sponte miser?
> Nec pede transuerso incedis nec poplite torto,
>   Non oculo lippis, non tibi naris hiat :
> Nullus ab iniusto crescit tibi fœnore census,
>   Non tua mens fraudis conscia nec sceleris :
> Funera non fratris, non sunt tibi flenda sororis,
>   Nec catulum audiui condoluisse tuum.
> Per te igitur nostros referas obtestor amores
>   Quo demum inuisa est nomine vita tibi?   10
> Iam scio, tu taceas, causæ nimium esse recordor,
>   Vxorem duxti, iam morere, haud veto te.

In Berinum, Ep. 67. Var.: l. 1 Berinus toties: l. 2 Nullos reddere.
Ad Melborniam, Ep. 68. *In Thermannum &* *Prucium*, Ep. 73.
Var.: l. 2 dum canis, Hermopile. *Ad Tho. Smithum*, Ep. 75.
Var.: l. 1 Smithe mones: *In Caluum*, Ep. 76. l. 5 Neu te tam
multis homini purgabis amico : l. 6 Inuidiam toties discutiendo paris.
In Miluium, Ep. 74. Var.: l. 6 Puellam & hanc. *Ad Edo. Mychel-*
bornum, Ep. 77. Var.: l. 9 Quidue ætas ? l. 10 Deseruit miseram
cum iuuenilis Hymen : l. 12 non obitus, abitus. *De rerum humanarum*
inconstantia :

> Constat nulla dies, anno superimminet annus,
>   Quicquid mortale est hora propinqua rapit.
> Sic moriemur ? ad hæc ludibria nascimur ? et spes
>   Fortunæque hominum tam cito corruerint ?

Francisci Manbæi epicedium, Ep. 78. Var.: l. 7 ora suffusus : l. 8
planctu et immites deas : l. 15 Decus reuerti, sentiet tremulum mare :
l. 18 Sperare nostrum nemini tantum licet : [line 19 of 1619 ed.
omitted :) l. 19 Fac ergo quiuis iure quod miser potest : l. 20 as l. 21 in
1619 edition. *De homine*, Ep. 79. Var.: ll. 3, 4 Quid dixi vt flos est?
minus est, siquidem examinatis, Dulcis odor flori, pædor inest homini.
In Barnum, Ep. 80. Var.: l. 4 Seruassent versus et numerum atque
fidem. *In Petrum Ha.*, Ep. 81. Var.: l. 2 Sic, Petre : l. 3 Nummus
siue deest : l. 5 iam carnifici mox culpa futurus : l. 6 Vere illud dices.
Ad Caspiam, Ep. 89. *Ad Castellum & Braceium*, Ep. 83. Var.: l. 1 Mi
Castellule, tuque mi Braceie : l. 3 Murum non prope dirutum videtis : l. 4
Qui palam peragit : l. 5 Quod solent saturi : l. 6 Doctus haud dubie :
l. 7 Occultauit herum. *In Bæcum*, Ep. 84. Var.: l. 1 nullum certe sine

pernicioso : l. 2 Bæce, exerceri posse putas scelere : l. 3 Bæce voras. *In Caluum*, Ep. 85. Var. : l. 1 improbe Calue : l. 2 Vt dubites animam fœmina an vllam habeat ? l. 3 Cum mea conclusas fœlici pectore amantum. *Ad Erricum*, Ep. 86. Var. : l. 1 displiceat vita, Errice, discrucieris. *De se :*

> Vsus et hoc natura mihi concessit vtrinque
> Vt sim pacis amans, militiæ patiens.

Ad Nashum, Ep. 88. Var. : ll. 1 & 2 tibi, Nashe, Puritanum Fordusum, & Taciti canem Vitellum : l. 4 Perque vulnificos : l. 7 insipidis et : l. 8 Perinde ac tonitru : l. 9 denique candidam Pyrenen : l. 16 Publiumque tuum : l. 17 Quos amas vti te decet, fouesque : l. 18 Nec sines per : l. 19 Ergo si sapis. *Ad Caspiam*, Ep. 89. *Ad Melleam :*

> Dente vel vngue petat me Mellea perfero : credas
> Qui impatienter amat, tam patienter amet?

Ad Dolorem :

> Si deus est aliquis dolor, aut in vallibus atris
> Cum dijs infernis vt perhibent habitat.
> Illi ter centum cæpes mox sacrificarim,
> Desinat vt nobis cor miserum exedere.

In Byrseum, Ep. 91. *In Bretonem*, Ep. 93. Var. : l. 2 Nempe tuis nunquam viueret in numeris. *Ad Ge. Chapmannum*, Ep. 94. Var. : l. 1 Cottum perfidiæ : l. 2 Chapmanne, insimulas : l. 3 Neutiquam meminisse : l. 7 Responde mihi, vin' ? : l. 8 I iam, ad cœnam : l. 10 Si lubet, vel : l. 16 nisi præberit.

In socerum fraudulentum :

> Qui iacet ad pontem nudus, Thurbarne, rogator
> Filius Hepsis erat, sed gener Eudiuali.

In Tricium :

> Tres habuit, quartamque potest sperare nouercam,
> Et Tricius miserum se tamen esse negat.

In Gellam :

> Pura basia fert refertque Gella,
> Et puram venerem, salesque puros,
> Verum est, non nego, Gella Puritana est.

Ad Io. Dauisium :

> Quod nostros, Dauisi, laudas recitasque libellos
> Vultu quo nemo candidiore solet :
> Ad me mitte tuos, iam pridem postulo, res est
> In qua persolui gratia vera potest.

In auarum, Ep. 97. Var. : l. 1 seruas stulte. *Ad Ed. Braceium* [Ep. 98] :

> O nimis lepidam, Braceie, sortem
> In re ludere cum solet iocosa !
> Vxorem Bromij senex Morachus
> Strato impegerat insuper recumbens,
> Intonansque ferociter puellæ.
> Actutum Bromij exilit molossus
> Subuenturus heræ, vagasque testes
> Impotentis adulteri reuulsit.
> Mœchus illachrimat sine ululatu[1]
> Testes nequitiæ suæ recusans,
> Testes nequitiæ suæ requirens.

---

[1] The text reads ' æiu latu '.

Quas tandem vt resuat puella suadet,
Nec posse intimat imbecilliores
Sutura fieri, ac prius fuere.
In Erricum, Ep. 99. *In Hermum & Hermiam :*
Adria nec fluctus, Lybicum nec littus arenas,
Hermia nec mœchos, scorta nec Hermus habet.
Ad Thusimellam :
Si sapis increpitare meam, Thusimella, cauebis
Nequitiam, referet multa tacenda dolor.
Seque tuis thalamis reperisse fatebitur, olim
Quæ sibi famosus prætulit arma deus.
In puellam, Ep. 102. Var.: l. 1 Magnum intra delubra deum qui
perculit hostem : l. 2 Illi sons merito cæditur ense manus : l. 4 qua stetit
ara dei : l. 5 Parce tamen paulumque tuo de iure recedas. *In Prettum :*
Vna tibi manus est, vnus pes, Prette, sed vnus
Pes ad potandum sufficit, vna manus.
Quin lippis oculis quoque potio multa nocebit,
Tu quasi non posses absque oculis bibere ?
At clementer edunt qui potant, tu satur ipso
Nec quo nupsisti diceris esse die.
In Petrum Ha., Ep. 104. Var. : l. 1 Bella cum : l. 3 pulchram stupido :
l. 5 Paulo post Petre te malam ob rapinam : l. 7 et subitam calamita-
tem : l. 8 Fortunasque tuas pie : l. 9 Redit, flebile prædicatque amicis :
l. 11 Decora facie : l. 12 Sic fauet misero nimis : l. 13 Inuidetque male :
l. 15 Os quibus rigidum : l. 17 fieri statim : l. 23 Cuncta dicere. *Ad
Coruinum*, Ep. 105. Var. : l. 1 Coruine tibi : l. 3 Sed tibi tam tenera et
formosa quod obtigit uxor [ll. 4 and 5 of 1619 ed. omitted]. *De se*, Ep.
106. *In matronam*, Ep. 107. Var. : l. 1 Decidit famulæ cunnum
matrona : l. 3 sceleri cupiens. *In Marsium :*
Marsie, gente tua quam dudum indigna tulisti,
Quis vel tibicen tam misere vnquam habitus?
De Mellea & Caspia, Ep. 109. *Ad Sabellum*, Ep. 110. Var. : l. 9 id
Pretto graue est : l. 10 Quin Herculem subinde stomachari ferunt :
l. 12 temno veneficum nimis : l. 13 Tu vero ab homine perdito actutum
fuge. *In Miluum*, Ep. 111. *In Calpham*, Ep. 112. Var. : ll. 3 & 4
Nam quis quod nusquam est petat, aut dracmam exprimere vllam
Posse ex te speret, vel patre se, vel auo? *Ad Caspiam*, Ep. 113.
Ad Io. Dolandum :

O qui sonora cœlites altos cheli
Mulces et vmbras incolas atræ Stygis,
Quam suave murmur ! quale fluctu prominens
Lygia madentes rore dum siccat comas,
Quam suaue murmur flaccidas aures ferit
Dum lenis oculos leuiter inuadit sopor !
Vt falce rosa dissecta purpureum caput
Dimittit, vndique folijs spargens humum,
Labuntur, hei, sic debiles somno tori,
Terramque feriunt membra ponderibus suis.   10
Dolande, misero surripis mentem mihi,
Excorsque cordi pectus impulsæ premunt.
Quis tibi deorum tam potenti numine
Digitos trementes dirigit ? is inter deos
Magnos oportet principem obtineat locum.

Tu solus affers rebus antiquis fidem,
Nec miror Orpheus considens Rhodope super
Siquando rupes flexit et agrestes feras.
At, ô beate, siste diuinas manus,
Iam, iam, parumper siste diuinas manus!　　　20
Liquescit anima, quam caue exugas mihi.

In Amicum molestum, Ep. 114. *In Berinum :*

Pegaseo dum se miratur fonte Berinus,
Interijt misere captus amore sui.

Ad Cambricum, Ep. 116. *In Cottum :*

Scire cupis Cottus quid agat Lyte? cogitat Hermo
Curandam tradat mentulam, an Hersilio.

In Caluum, Ep. 120. Var.: l. 1 præclare Caluus : l. 4 Dispeream huic
ni mox Prettus amicus erit. *Ad Ed. Mychelbornum*, Ep. 121. Var. :
l. 2 Et sapis mi Edouarde qui procul te : l. 3 Optumum mala ab vrbe
seuocasti : l. 6 Ad tuos refugis : l. 7 Vrbis immodica : l. 13 Hæc foras;
itidem : l. 22 Sub æterna silentia : l. 23 Omnium nimis. *In Gellam*,
Ep. 122. Var.: l. 2 cantor Pyrrimanus futuit. *In Gulsonum*, Ep. 123.
Var.: l. 1 Exagitare tuos nequeam, Gulsone, puellos : l. 4 Nec fas
auersas nec iuuat ire vias. *Ad Caspiam*, Ep. 124. Var. : l. 1. Caspia
tam cito me eijciet culpa vna receptum. *In Prettum :*

Prette, non ita dico, te vt putarim
Seruitutis egere, siue reges,
Siue sceptrigeri ambiant monarchæ ;
Hoc tantum moneo, nec obsecrantem
Te seruire potesse apud sagacem
Vicinumque meum, tuumque Largum ;
Putrem nam ferat vt pedem manumque,
Ferre non poterit voracitatem.

De Gella et Thespili, Ep. 126. l. 4 Gellæ autem rigido purior :
In Berinum, Ep. 127. *Ad Sybillam*, Ep. 128. Var.: l. 1 Cuncta erant
bona quæ deus creauit : l. 3 Bonam ergo dominus creauit Euam.
Ad Hallum :

Sors hominum dubitas auium an præstantior, Halle?
Perspicuum est, me odit Caspia, psittacum amat.

Ad Robertum Wo :

Noui dedecoris pudore ruptus
Ille Marsius, vt putas, Roberte,
Armatos homines quot aggregauit?
Quot conductitios? quot et clientes?
Quot summo genere inclitos amicos?
Tantum conijcito, nihil nocebit
Tam magno in numero parum vagari.
Vt putas rogo te quot aggregauit?
Ipsus si tibi dixero, Roberte,
Vis mi credere iam, profecto nullos.　　　10

In Gellam :

Ad viuum nunquam dicis te, Gella, fututam,
Vah quota pars cunni mortua, Gella, tui est.

Ad Melleam :

Anglia quotquot habet iuras mea Mellea soli
Muneribus Veneris cedere posse mihi,

Anglia quotquot habet qui scis mea Mellea quanti
Muneribus valeant fortipremæ Veneris ?

De vxore fabri :
Lemnia tardipedem dea vix tolerauerit vnum,
Vulcanos Venus hic sustinet vna duos.
Leno vir et faber est, pariter fabricatur adulter,
Ligneus hic pupos, æneus ille globos.
Notus vterque, satis, satis ô nimiumque puellæ,
Cui magis vt placeam iam faber esse velim.

Ad Ia. Thurbarnum, Ep. 131. Var.: l. 1 Quid Thurbarne : l. 4 At
certe modo promoueret istuc : l. 6 Et laute, et sobrie : l. 7 nefandi
amoris : l. 9 Quæ tibi neque dicta, picta, scripta. *In Cornua*, Ep. 132.
Var. : l. 2 Cornua plantari : 1595 ed. inserts before last couplet—Stipitis
anne aliena quod insita virgula sulco Cornutam speciem sæpe referre
solet. *Ad Hallum*, Ep. 133. Var. : Halle for Herme in both lines. *Ad
Thusimellam*, Ep. 134. Var.: l. 1 En vacat locus : l. 2 Thusimella,
meo : l. 3 Quam suaue : l. 7 Formosa et genua : l. 9 Nempe
fœmineum est : l. 10 Sed statim : l. 14 Manus, et toties retorta colla.

Ad Annam :
Das mi animam et Leio, non te bene diuidis, Anna :
Tu mihi da tantum corpus, et illi animam.

In Zelotipum, Ep. 135. Var.: ll. 3 and 4 Eijcis innocuos thalamo
furiose bacillos, Redde fututorem denuo tutus eris. *Ad Melleam*, Ep.
136. Var.: l. 2 Nec fugam : l. 3 Charas qui : l. 6 Verum expers : l. 8
Et pinguem : l. 9 Me tibi vt reparem et simul reportem. l. 10 Ter
centum validas fututiones. *Ad Thusimellam*, Ep. 137. Var. : l. 3 Hoc
Thusimella : l. 4 Iurgia enim : l. 5 quot amantis. *In Fabrum*, Ep. 138.
In Afram, Ep. 139. Var. : l. 1 Tam vetus, et grandis cum sit tibi cunnus,
vt illi. *In se :*

> Olim fungus ego, silex verebar,
> Ne non vtibilis viro emineret
> Penis, qui puero excitatus altum
> Momentis caput extulit torosis.
> Tum nec apposita manu fouere,
> Nec sum tangere, nec repellere ausus,
> Nimirum metuens adulta stirps hæc
> Vt posset pathico orbe comprehendi.
> Vos iam intelligitis, viri et puellæ,
> Multo sed magis improbæ puellæ,   10
> Quam stulte, illepideque rusticeque
> Summæ lætitiæ meæ dolebam.
> Nec si grandior exijsset alnu
> Idcirca fore mi magis verendam,
> Aut plus peniuoræ arduam puellæ.

In Norbanum :
Se stupidum semper dicit Norbanus, et est : hoc
Cum vere dicit, quomodo dissimulat ?

Ad Aten de pomo aureo, Ep. 141. Var.: l. 1 de iure coibant. *In
Aprum*, Ep. 142. *In Sharpum*, Ep. 143. *Ad Iaruisium et Stanfordum*.
Ep. 144. Var. : l. 1 Charior Iaruisi : l. 3 Tuque Stanforde. *Ad Librum:*

Desine, iam satis est, nimium lasciue libelle,
Et vix Romano qui pede tutus eas.
At vos ô Latiæ peregrinæ parcite musæ,
Et fiat vestri pars leuis illa chori.

FINIS.

OCCASIONAL VERSES

The following set of five poems is given in the *Poems and Sonets of Sundry Other Noblemen and Gentlemen* appended to Newman's surreptitious edition of Sidney's *Astrophel and Stella* [1591]. *Canto Primo* is identical with xviiii of *A Booke of Ayres*, Part II, with the exception of a few differences alluded to in the notes on that song. The first stanza only is given of *Canto tertio*: the remaining are supplied from Robert Jones's *Second Booke of Songs and Ayres*. See Introd., p. li.

Canto Secundo.

What faire pompe haue I spide of glittering Ladies ;
With locks sparckled abroad, and rosie Coronet
On their yuorie browes, trackt to the daintie thies
With roabs like *Amazons*, blew as Violet,
With gold Aiglets adornd, some in a changeable
Pale; with spangs wauering taught to be moueable.

Then those Knights that a farre off with dolorous viewing
Cast their eyes hetherward ; loe, in an agonie,
All vnbrac'd, crie aloud, their heauie state ruing :
Moyst cheekes with blubbering, painted as *Ebonie*   10
Blacke ; their feltred haire torne with wrathful hand :
And whiles astonied, starke in a maze they stand.

But hearke ! what merry sound ! what sodaine harmonie !
Looke looke neere the groue where the Ladies doe tread
With their Knights the measures waide by the melodie.
Wantons ! whose trauesing make men enamoured ;
Now they faine an honor, now by the slender wast
He must lift hir aloft, and seale a kisse in hast.

Streight downe vnder a shadow for wearines they lie
With pleasant daliance, hand knit with arme in arme,   20
Now close, now set aloof, they gaze with an equall eie,
Changing kisses alike; streight with a false alarme,
Mocking kisses alike, powt with a louely lip.
Thus drownd with iollities, their merry daies doe slip.

But stay! now I discerne they goe on a Pilgrimage
Towards Loues holy land, faire *Paphos* or *Cyprus.*
Such deuotion is meete for a blithesome age;
With sweet youth, it agrees well to be amorous.
Let olde angrie fathers lurke in an Hermitage:
Come, weele associate this iolly Pilgrimage!   30

Canto tertio.

My Loue bound me with a kisse
    That I should no longer staie:
When I felt so sweete a blisse
    I had lesse power to passe away:
Alas! that women do not knowe
Kisses make men loath to goe.

Yes she knowes it but too well,
    For I heard when Venus' doue
In her eare did softlie tell
    That kisses were the seales of loue: 10
O muse not then though it be so,
Kisses make men loth to go.

Wherefore did she thus inflame
    My desires, heat my bloud,
Instantlie to quench the same
    And starue whom she had giuen food?
I the common sence can show.
Kisses make men loath to go.

Had she bid me go at first
It would nere have grieued my hart,   20
Hope delaide had beene the worst;
    But ah! to kiss and then to part!
How deep it strucke, speake, Gods, you know
Kisses make men loth to goe.

Canto quarto.

Loue whets the dullest wittes, his plagues be such :
But makes the wise by pleasing, doat as much.
So wit is purchast by this dire disease.
O let me doat! so Loue be bent to please.

Canto quinto.

A daie, a night, an houre of sweete content
Is worth a world consum'd in fretfull care.
Vnequall Gods! in your Arbitrement
To sort vs daies whose sorrowes endles are!
  And yet what were it? as a fading flower :
  To swim in blisse a daie, a night, an hower.

What plague is greater than the griefe of mind?
The griefe of minde that eates in euerie vaine,
In euerie vaine that leaues such clods behind,
Such clods behind as breed such bitter paine,   10
  So bitter paine that none shall euer finde,
  What plague is greater than the griefe of minde.

Doth sorrowe fret thy soule? ô direfull spirit!
Doth pleasure feede thy heart? ô blessed man!
Hast thou bin happie once? ô heauie plight!
Are thy mishaps forepast? ô happie than!
  Or hast thou blisse in eld? ô blisse too late!
  But hast thou blisse in youth? ô sweete estate!

Prefixed to John Dowland's *First Booke of Songs or Ayres*
[1597].
Thomæ Campiani Epigramma.

De instituto Authoris.

Famam, posteritas quam dedit Orpheo,
Dolandi, melius Musica dat tibi,
Fugaces reprimens Archetypis sonos ;
Quas et delicias præbuit auribus,
Ipsis conspicuas luminibus facit.

From Francis Davison's *Poetical Rapsody* [1602].

A Hymne in praise of Neptune.

Of Neptunes Empyre let vs sing,
At whose command the waues obay :
To whom the Riuers tribute pay,
Downe the high mountaines sliding.
To whom the skaly Nation yeelds
Homage for the Cristall fields
 Wherein they dwell ;
And euery Sea-god paies a Iem,
Yeerely out of his watry Cell,
To decke great *Neptunes* Diadem.   10
The *Trytons* dauncing in a ring,
Before his Pallace gates, doo make
The water with their Ecchoes quake,
Like the great Thunder sounding :
The Sea-Nymphes chaunt their Accents shrill,
And the *Syrens* taught to kill
 With their sweet voyce ;
Make eu'ry ecchoing Rocke reply,
Vnto their gentle murmuring noyse,   19
The prayse of *Neptunes* Empery.   H. CAMPION.

Prefixed to Barnabe Barnes's *Foure Bookes of Offices* [1606].

In honour of the Author by *Tho: Campion*
Doctor in *Physicke*. To the Reader.

Though neither thou doost keepe the Keyes of State,
Nor yet the counsels (Reader) what of that?
Though th'art no Law-pronouncer mark't by fate,
Nor field-commander (Reader) what of that?
Blanch not this Booke; for if thou mind'st to be
Vertuous, and honest, it belongs to thee.
 Here is the Schoole of *Temperance*, and *Wit*,
Of *Iustice*, and all formes that tend to it ;
Here *Fortitude* doth teach to liue and die,
Then, Reader, loue this Booke, or rather buy.   10

EIVSDEM AD AVTHOREM.

Personas proprijs recte virtutibus ornas,
 (Barnesi) liber hic viuet, habet Genium,
Personæ virtus vmbra est ; hanc illa refulcit,
 Nec scio splendescat corpus an vmbra magis.

From Richard Alison's *An Howres Recreation in Musicke* [1606].

What if a day, or a month, or a yeare
Crown thy delights with a thousand sweet contentings?
Cannot a chance of a night or an howre
Crosse thy desires with as many sad tormentings?
    Fortune, honor, beauty, youth
    Are but blossoms dying;
    Wanton pleasure, doating loue,
    Are but shadowes flying.
    All our ioys are but toyes,
    Idle thoughts deceiuing;   10
    None haue power of an howre
    In their liues' bereauing.

Earthes but a point to the world, and a man
Is but a point to the worlds compared centure:
Shall then the point of a point be so vaine
As to triumph in a seelly points aduenture?
    All is hassard that we haue,
    There is nothing biding;
    Dayes of pleasure are like streames
    Through faire medows gliding.   20
    Weale and woe, time doth goe,
    Time is neuer turning:
    Secret fates guide our states,
    Both in mirth and mourning.

Prefixed to Alphonso Ferrabosco's *Ayres* [1609].

TO THE WORTHY AVTHOR.

Musicks maister and the offspring
    Of rich Musicks Father,
Old *Alfonso's* Image liuing,
    These faire flowers you gather
Scatter through the *Brittish* soile;
    Giue thy fame free wing,
And gaine the merit of thy toyle:
    Wee whose loues affect to praise thee,
    Beyond thine owne deserts can neuer raise thee.
        By *T. Campion*, Doctor in Physicke.

Prefixed to Coryate's *Crudities* [1611].

INCIPIT THOMAS CAMPIANVS MEDICINÆ DOCTOR.

IN PERAGRANTISSIMI, ITINEROSISSIMI, *Montiscandentissimique Peditis Thomæ Coryati,* viginti hebdomadarium *Diarium, sex pedibus gradiens,* partim vero claudicans, Encomiasticon.

Ad Venetos venit corio Coryatus ab vno
Vectus, et, vt vectus, pene reuectus erat.
Naue vna Dracus sic totum circuit orbem,
At rediens retulit te, Coryate, minus.
Illius vndigenas tenet vnica charta labores,
Tota tuos sed vix bibliotheca capit.
Explicit Thomas Campianus.

Prefixed to Thomas Ravenscroft's *A Brief Discourse of the true (but neglected) use of Charact'ring the Degrees by their Perfection, Imperfection and Diminution in Measurable Music* [1614].

Markes that did limit Lands in former times
  None durst remoue; so much the common good
Preuailed with all men; 'twas the worst of crimes.
  The like in Musicke may be vnderstood,
For That the treasure of the Soule is, next
  To the rich Store-house of Diuinity:
Both comfort Soules that are with care perplext,
  And set the Spirit Both from passions free.
The Markes that limit Musicke heere are taught,
  So fixt of ould, which none by right can change,   10
Though Vse much alteration hath wrought,
  To Musickes Fathers that would now seeme strange.
The best embrace, which herein you may finde,
And th' Author praise for his good Work and Minde.
                 THO: CAMPION.

NOTES.

A BOOKE OF AYRES.

PART I.

On the back of the title-page, a facsimile of which will be found in its place in the text, is a representation of Monson's crest and coat-of-arms.

PAGE 6. I. Both this poem and Jonson's 'Come, my Celia, let us prove', from *Volpone*, Act I, Sc. vi (1605), are imitated and partly translated from Catullus, v, 'Vivamus, mea Lesbia, atque amemus.'

The following verses occur in Corkine's *Second Book of Ayres*. They are also based upon the same poem of Catullus, and resemble Campion's verses very closely in the first three lines. I believe them also to be Campion's.

> My deerest mistrisse, let vs liue and loue
> And care not what old doting fools reproue.
> Let vs not feare their censures, nor esteeme
> What they of vs and of our loues shall deeme.
> Old ages critticke and censorious brow
> Cannot of youthful dalliance alow,
> Nor euer could endure that we should tast
> Of those delights which they themselves are past.

II. The first stanza of this song is found in Add. MS. 24665 without variation.

PAGE 7. III. This song occurs in Add. MS. 24665 without variation.

PAGE 8. IIII. The air to which this song is set does duty also for 'Seeke the Lord and in his wayes perseuer' (*Diuine and Morall Songs*, xviii, p. 126).

V. This song occurs in Add. MS. 34608 without variation.

PAGE 9. VI. A fragment of this poem, entitled 'Of Coruina Her Lute', and consisting only of the first stanza, omitting the second couplet, occurs in Add. MS. 22603. The poem is given in Davison's *Poetical Rapsody* (1602).

VII. The old edition gives this poem without division into stanzas, while the last two lines run :

> Then what we sow with our lips,
> Let vs reape, loues gains deuiding.

The arrangement of the text, however, which I believe to be Mr. Quiller-Couch's, has the merit of giving better sense and two stanzas of uniform structure. 'Sweruing', in line 19, is Mr. Bullen's excellent emendation for the old edition's 'changing'. The six lines from 'What haruest halfe so sweete is' occur again in No. X of *Light Conceits*.

PAGE 10. VIII. Campion wrote a Latin version of this poem which appeared in the 1595 *Poemata* under the title 'De Thermanio et Glaia' (p. 343). In a revised form it appeared in the 1619 edition as 'In Lycium et Clytham' (Book II, Ep. 60).

The following song, closely resembling this poem in idea, occurs in Add. MS. 24665, which contains several of Campion's poems. It may possibly be Campion's.

> As on a day Sabina fell asleepe,
> Unto her bower by stealth then I did creepe,
> And first spake softe, then loude vnto my deare ;
> And still Sabina heard, but would not heare.

> Then to myself more courage did I take,
> When I perceiued shee did both winke and wake ;
> Then downe I lay'd mee by her on the ground
> And still awake a sleepe Sabina found.

> Then shewed her sightes more strange to her than mee,
> Yet still Sabina sawe but would not see :
> Now when as I had try'd all waies but one,
> I lookt about and found myself alone.

> Then thought it best the best way for to wooe,
> And still Sabina did but would not doe :
> Then did I touch each part from head to heele
> Yet still Sabina felt but would not feele.

> Now from the doer whie should shee have hid it,
> Yf it be true that 'twas Sabina did it,
> But she saies nay : I sweare and saie so too :
> Shee did both heare and see and feele and doe.

PAGE 11. X. The air to which this song is set does duty also for ' Loue me or not, loue her I must or dye' (Fourth Booke, x, p. 180). The metre and rhythm, which are somewhat peculiar, are identical in both.

PAGE 12. XII. There is a version of this song in MS. Harl. 3991 (fo. 34) with three slight variations ; reading 'fancy' in l. 5, 'assure' in l. 7, 'now divine' in l. 8.

There are also two versions in Harl. 6910 (fo. 150 seq.), which are more interesting as they appear to be variant drafts of the poet's own composition. They are as follows :—

> dolus

> Thou shalt not loue mee, neither shall these eyes
> Shine on my soule shrowded in deadly night.
> Thou shalt not breathe on me thy spiceryes
> Nor rocke me in thy quauers of delight.
> Hould off thy hands for I had rather dye
> Then haue my life by thy coye touch reprived.
> Smile not on me, but frowne thou bitterly ;
> Slaye me outright : no louers are long-liu'de.
> As for those lippes reseru'd so much in store
> Their rosy verdure shall not meete with myne.
> Withhold thy proude embracements euermore ;
> I'll not be swadled in those arms of thyne.
>   Now shew it if thou be a woman right ;
>   Embrace and kisse and loue me in despight.
>   FINIS THO. CAMP.

[Then follows a version in sonnet form of ' Thrice tosse these oaken a.hes in the ayre', Third Booke, xviii (v. p. 366), signed *finis idem* ; and followed by]

BEAVTIE WITHOVT LOVE DEFORMITIE

Thou art not fayer for all thy red and white,
For all those rosye temperatures in thee ;
Thou art not sweet, though made of meere delight,
Nor fayer nor sweet unlesse thou pittie mee.
Thyne eyes are blacke and yet their glittering brightnes
Can night enlumine in her darkest den ;
Thy hands are bloudy thoughts contriu'd of whitnes,
Both blacke and blooddy if they murder men.
Thy brows wheron my good happe doth depend
Fayrer then snow or lyllie in the springe :
Thy Tongue which saues at euery sweete words end,
That hard as Marble, this a mortall sting,
I will not soothe thy follyes ; thou shalt proue
That Beautie is no Beautie without Loue.

FINIS IDEM

It will be seen that each of these three versions is a sonnet, the only sonnets with one exception—the lines prefixed to Ravenscroft's *Brief Discourse*—among the whole body of works attributed to Campion. In view of his condemnation of 'Quatorzens' in the *Obseruations* (p. 37) it may be that he found the sonnet form intractable both in prosody and music, and that this is the reason for his desertion of such fixed forms in favour of his own free metres. 'Thoughts' in l. 7 of the latter of the above-quoted sonnets, is clearly a scribal error for 'though'.

In accordance with his frequent practice (see Introduction, p. l), Campion wrote a Latin version of this idea, entitled *Ad Caspiam*, 1619 ed., Bk. II, Ep. 53.

This poem has been attributed both to Donne and Sylvester.

PAGE **13**. XIIII. This song occurs both in Robert Jones's *Vltimum Vale* (1608) and Davison's *Poetical Rapsody* (1602).

PAGE **14**. XVI. This song reappears in a slightly different form as 'Beauty, since you so much desire', in the *Fcurth Booke*, xxii, p. 186.

PAGE **15**. XVII. Compare 'Your faire lookes vrge my desire' (Fourth Booke, xxiii, p. 186), which is an improved version of this song.

XVIII. This song occurs in *Two Bookes* (*Diuine and Morall Songs*); Alison's *An Houres Recreation in Music* [1606] ; Sloane MS. 4128 ; Harl. MS. 4064 ; MS. 17 B.L. ; Rawl. MS. Poet. 31 ; and Chetham MS. 8012 (p. 79).

Sloane MS. (fo. 14) contains the following variations from the text: l. 17, 'care' ; l. 22, 'His life.' Harl. MS. reads : l. 2, 'life is free' ; l. 6, 'Harmless joy'; l. 9, 'tower' ; it omits the fifth stanza ; l. 21, 'But scorning all the chaunce.' MS. B.L. (fo. 2) reads : l. 8, 'Nor fortune' ; l. 21, 'care' ; l. 22, 'His life.' Both in Sloane MS. and B.L. MS. the verses are headed 'Verses made by Mr. Fra. Bacon'. It is quite clear, however, that this attribution is incorrect.

PAGE **16**. XIX. This poem occurs among the *Poems and Sonets of Sundry other Noblemen and Gentlemen* appended to Newman's surreptitious edition of Sidney's *Astrophel and Stella* (1591), where it is headed *Canto Primo* in a series of five poems signed 'Content'. This copy contains two misreadings : 'Holds watch' in l. 18, and 'Diana's Dove' in l. 24 ; and one variation which is an improvement upon the text of *A Booke*, and which I have adopted in this edition : 'They that have not yet fed' in l. 32, in place of 'They that yet have not fed'. The same poem with the same variant readings, obviously derived from the 1591 *Astrophel and Stella*, occurs in Add. MS. 28253 (fo. 5) endorsed 'A fantasye of Sir Phillype Sydnys out of his Astrophel and Stella '.

The history of the word ' paramour' is interesting. It was originally an adverb, 'paramours' (par amours) signifying 'by way of sexual love', and as such is found in Malory, *Le Morte d'Arthur*, e.g. Bk. X, Ch. 53 : 'And as for to say that I love La Beale Isoud paramours, I dare make good that I do.' In Chaucer:

> I lovede never womman herebiforn
> As paramours, ne never shall no mo.

—the word has mainly a substantival meaning, though not without a trace of the original adverbial sense. The final s survives in some passages where it is clearly a noun : compare Drummond's *Madrigal*, ' I saw, but fainting saw, my paramours,' where the word is, of course, singular in number.

It occurs in many authors in the same sense that it bears here, viz. a lover, without its offensive modern connotation. But surely Mr. Bullen is wrong in saying in his note on this passage (1889 edition) that it acquired this connotation at a later date. It certainly has it in *A Midsummer Night's Dream*, IV. ii (first published in 1600).

> *Quince.* ' Yea, and the best person, too, and he is a very paramour for a sweet voice.'
> *Flu.* 'You must say 'paragon'; a paramour is, God bless us, a thing of naught.'

' Apes in Avernus.' The idea that old maids were condemned upon death to lead apes in hell is alluded to elsewhere. Mr. Bullen quotes some lines of a song found in William Corkine's *Second Book of Airs* (1612).

> O if you knew what chance to them befell
> That dance about with bob-tail apes in hell
> Yourself your virgin girdle would divide—
> . . . Rather than undergo such shame ; no tongue can tell
> What injury is done to maids in hell.

Compare also Shakespeare, *Much Ado*, II. i : 'I will even take sixpence in earnest of the bearward, and lead apes in hell '; or *Taming of the Shrew*, II. i : ' And for your love to her lead apes in hell.'

PAGE 17. XX. As Mr. Bullen points out, this poem is reminiscent of Propertius, ii. 28.

> Sunt apud infernos tot millia formosarum :
> Pulchra sit in superis, si licet, una locis.
> Vobiscum est Iope, vobiscum candida Tyro,
> Vobiscum Europe, nec proba Pasiphae.

XXI. One of Campion's attempts at classical metres. Possibly its non-success warned him against such close imitations, for he does not counsel their adoption in his *Obseruations*.

PART II.

PAGE 21. II. This song occurs in Davison's *Poetical Rhapsody*, Harl. MS. 4286 and Add. MS. 34608. Harl. MS. (fo. 56) reads : l. 22, ' It is fayned '; l. 23, ' A face which '; l. 24, ' And this is it.'

PAGE 22. V. The last line in this poem in the Brit. Mus. copy is illegible owing to a crease in the paper, which has in consequence missed the impression of the type. At the eleventh hour, after several years' searching, I have found, with the kind assistance of Dr. T. L. Southgate, another copy, in the possession of Charles Letts, Esq., from which I have been able to supply the missing line.

PAGE 26. XIII. I believe the reading given in the text, l. 4, 'her selfe-delight,' is preferable to the hitherto accepted 'herself, delight'. The first, meaning personal vanity, is required by the context and especially by the reference to mirrors of various kinds in the preceding line.

PAGE 28. XVII. There is a copy of this song in Add. MS. 24665, with unimportant variations in the last two lines.

PAGE 29. XX. There is a copy of this song in Add. MS. 24665, with trifling variations due to corruption or careless transcription. A *varia lectio* worthy of notice occurs, however, in l. 8, where the MS. reads 'Time hath a wheele'. This is plausible, but on the whole I prefer the version of the text.

Notice the internal rhyme in the fourth line of each stanza, rhyming with the end-rhyme of the previous line. Campion seems rather fond of this effect. See also *Ayres that were sung and played at Brougham Castle* (IIII. l. 9).

OBSERVATIONS IN THE ART OF ENGLISH POESIE.

PAGE 33. Thomas Sackville, first Baron Buckhurst, was created Earl of Dorset in 1603, and died in 1608. He was author of the Induction to the *Mirrour for Magistrates*, and part-author of *Gorboduc*, while from Jasper Heywood's preface to his translation of Seneca's *Thyestes*, we learn that he had written sonnets, which were probably the private poems here referred to.

l. 5. *In two things.* Campion is quoting here from his own song, 'Awake thou spring of speaking grace', No. XIII of the *Third Booke*, or vice versa; one can not say which.

l. 24. *take in worth*, i.e. accept kindly.

PAGE 34. l. 1. *Whether thus hasts.* This poem is reminiscent of the opening lines of the first satire of Persius.

PAGE 35, l. 10. *discreta quantitas.* See Scaliger, *Poetice*, IV. i, and 45.

l. 32. *Rewcline.* John Reuchlin, of Pforzheim, the German humanist, 1455-1522.

l. 35. *Epistolæ obscurorum virorum.* A series of broadly humorous compositions mainly by Ulrich von Hutten and his friend Crotus Rubianus, which appeared in 1515-16, in the dawn of Humanism. They purported to be written by members of the obscurantist party, of which they were the cause of much ridicule.

PAGE 36, l. 29. *as Tully and all other Rhetoritians.* See Cicero, *De Orat.* iii. 54: Quintilian, ix. 3.

l. 34. *prœlia porcorum.* The reference is to the *Pugna Porcorum per P. Porcium poetam*, written by Joannes Leo Placentius, and published at Cologne or Antwerp in 1530.

PAGE 37, l. 11. *Carmina prouerbialia.* 'A volume of riming Latin proverbs entitled *Carminum Proverbialium . . . Loci Communes in gratiam juventutis selecti*, 8vo, published at London in 1577, passed through many editions' (Bullen.)

l. 12. *bables*=baubles.

l. 21. *a singing-man at Westminster.* Mr. Bullen states that Campion was wrong, and that the epitaphs were made upon a singing-man at Abingdon. But Abyngdon was the man's name, and he was master of the Royal Chapel at Westminster in 1465. More's *Epigrammata* were published at Basle in 1520.

l. 28. *Procrustes the thiefe.* This passage was in Ben Jonson's mind when he uttered the dictum reported in Drummond's *Conversations*: 'He cursed Petrarch for redacting verses to Sonnets, which he said were like that Tirrant's bed, when some who were too short were racked, others too long cut short.'

PAGE 38, l. 15. *ămŏr.* The second syllable of *amor* is not, of course, long by nature ; but possibly Campion is thinking of the line in Vergil's *Eclogues*, ' Omnia vincit amōr, et nos,' etc., where the *or* is long in thesis.

PAGE 41. l. 5. *paisd*=weighed.

l. 32. *last foote of the fourth verse.* The old edition has *fift verse*, by dittography.

PAGE 42, l. 14. *ayreable*, suitable for setting to music.

PAGE 45, l. 20. *Kate can fancy.* Cf. the Latin epigram *In Laurentiam* (p. 244).

l. 27. *Beaten sattin.* This expression, which is frequently met with, seems to mean embroidered satin.

l. 31. *huffcap ale*=strong ale.

PAGE 46, l. 6. *Barnzy stiffly vows.* Cf. the Latin epigram *In Crispinum* (p. 255). In spite of Campion's disclaimer of any personal point in these lines, they certainly seem to refer to Barnabe Barnes and Gabriel Harvey.

PAGE 48, l. 7. *glossy Pirop.* Red or gold bronze. Cf. Ovid, *Met.* ii. 2, 'flammasque imitante pyropo.'

l. 34. *A wise man.* Cf. *The man of life upright* (pp. 15 and 117).

PAGE 49, l. 2. *Thou telst me, Barnzy.* This and the seventh epigram both appear to refer to Barnes.

PAGE 51, l. 26. iet=strut, walk proudly.

PAGE 53, l. 16. *Epigramme of Earinon.* Martial, ix. 11.

THE DISCRIPTION OF A MASKE ETC. IN HONOVR OF THE LORD HAYES.

PAGE 57. James Hayes or Hay, the son of Sir James Hay of Kingask, was a Scotch gentleman who came to court upon James's accession and was a great favourite with the King. He was knighted, created Lord Hay of the Scotch peerage in 1606, Baron Hay of Sawley in 1615, Viscount Doncaster in 1618, and Earl of Carlisle in 1622. The dedication by Donne of his *Divine Poems* to him as the E[arl] of D[oncaster] was therefore an error. He married, first, on the occasion of this masque, Honora, daughter of Lord Denny, and secondly, in 1617, Lucy Percy. Clarendon has a character of him, and he is eulogized in Lloyd's *State Worthies.* He was employed on several important missions, to France in 1616, and to Germany in 1619 to support the Elector Palatine.

PAGE 59, l. 4. *The disvnited Scythians.* Campion appears to be thinking of a passage in Herodotus, Δ. 70.

PAGE 62, l. 17. *Basse and Meane lutes.* The lute was a sort of guitar with a rounded back. The *Bandora* resembled both the lute and orpharion, but little is known of it. The *sackbut* was a bass trumpet or trombone. A *consort* was a band or orchestra of musicians.

l. 31. *The State*=the chair of state, earlier referred to (l. 14), reserved for the guest of the evening, on this occasion the King.

PAGE **63**, l. 37. *The chiefe habit.* This illustration, which forms a sort of frontispiece to the old edition, is reproduced in Mr. Bullen's 1903 edition, Nichols's *Progresses of King James*, and the present edition.
PAGE **69**, l. 18. *Can musicke then ioye?* This line seems to be corrupt, but I cannot see how to emend it.
PAGE **75**, l. 30. *By the great*, i.e. wholesale.
PAGE **76**, l. 30. *M. Lupo* : this composer cannot be identified, as there appear to have been numerous musicians of the name at this time. *M. Tho. Giles* was organist of St. Paul's, and father of the better known Nathaniel Giles, chorister at Magdalen College, Oxford, master of the choristers at St. George's, Windsor, and master of the children of the Chapel Royal.

A RELATION OF THE LATE ROYALL ENTERTAINMENT GIVEN BY THE RIGHT HONORABLE THE LORD KNOWLES, ETC.

PAGE **77**, Title-page (imprint). *Britaines Bursse.* The New Exchange opened on 11 April, 1609, in competition with the Royal Exchange (The Bourse).
PAGE **78**. ' Sir William Knollys, second son of Sir Francis Knollys, was created Baron Knollys of Greys in Oxfordshire, by King James in the first year of his reign, Viscount Wallingford in 1616, and Earl of Banbury in 1626. He died May 25, 1632, at the age of eighty-eight. It was his second wife, Elizabeth, daughter of the Earl of Suffolk, who received Queen Anne on her progress towards Bath ' (Bullen).
l. 7. *her Progresse toward the Bathe.* This progress began on Saturday the 24th April (Pearsall's *Sir Henry Wootton*, II, No. 213).
l. 15. *The house is fairely built of bricke.* 'This fair brick house was pulled down in the reign of George I by the then possessor, Earl Cadogan, who erected the present elegant structure somewhat further from the Thames, and built a cedar room for the reception of the monarch. Capability Brown was employed in laying out the beautiful grounds ' (Nichols).
l. 20. *two flight-shots.* A flight was a light kind of arrow. Compare Beaumont and Fletcher's *Bonduca*, I. i, ' Not a flight drawn home.' Mr. Bullen says a flight-shot was about a fifth of a mile.
l. 22. *Bases*, i.e. skirts.
PAGE **80**, l. 19 foll. *Perpetuana*, ' a glossy cloth of durable substance. *Mommoth-caps :* a Monmouth-cap was a kind of flat cap. *Wings :* appendages to the shoulders of a doublet ' (Bullen).
PAGE **82**, l. 6. *Caroch*, i.e. coach, the French *carrosse.*
l. 18. *Gamachios*, ' loose drawers or stockings worn outside the legs over the other clothing ' (Halliwell). ' A northern word for short spatterdashes worn by ploughmen ' (Grose).
l. 30. *Rosemary for remembrance.* This recalls Ophelia's speech, ' There 's rosemary, that 's for remembrance ' (*Hamlet*, IV. v). The expression was probably, however, not original in Shakespeare, but a current proverbial saying.
PAGE **84**, l. 9. *A hall*, i.e. room ! give way ! See Shakespeare's *Romeo and Juliet*, I. v.
PAGE **85**, l. 11. *A la mode de France.* Mr. Bullen's emendation for the old edition's *A la more.* Possibly there was some confusion with the word *moeur.*
PAGE **87**, l. 6. *the presents.* ' The presents are described in Mr.

Chamberlain's letter as " a dainty coverled or quilt, a rich carquenet, and a curious cabinet to the value in all of £1,500 "' (Nichols).

THE LORDS MASKE.

PAGE 90, l. 26. *Obey Ioues will.* Mr. Bullen's emendation for the old edition's *Ioues willing,* the last word having been duplicated from the next line.

PAGE 92, l. 7. *Come quickly, come.* See *Light Conceits of Louers,* XVII, and note thereon (p. 365).

PAGE 95, l. 16. *That all which see may say.* Mr. Bullen's emendation for the old edition's *stay.*

PAGE 96, l. 31. *numerous,* i.e. rhythmical, keeping time.

PAGE 100, l. 21. I retain the old edition's *preuent excuse,* which Mr. Bullen emends to *present.* But *preuent* in its primitive sense of ' anticipate ' is perfectly good here.

SONGS OF MOVRNING.

PAGE 101. *Title-page.* Coprario was an Englishman named John Cooper who studied music in Italy and italianized his surname. He was Court Composer to Charles I, and died in 1626.

PAGE 103, l. 13. *Cunctatosque olim.* As Mr. Bullen points out, this promise was redeemed by Campion with the *Lords Maske.*

PAGE 104, l. 15. *dare*: the word has the meaning of 'stupefy', ' amaze ', here. It has the related sense of ' terrify ' in Peele's *Sir Clyomon and Sir Clamydes*: 'Shall such defamed dastards dared by knights Thus bear their name.'

PAGE 105, l. 42. *the French Lyon*; Henri IV, assassinated by Ravaillac in 1610.

l. 51. *Suruaying India.* Prince Henry had interested himself in the East India Company.

l. 53. *his sayles.* An expedition was fitted out by the East India and Muscovy Companies, and on the 26th July, 1612, a grant was made by James I constituting 'a body Corporate and politic' by the name of ' Governor and Company of the merchants in London, discoverers of the North-West Passage,' ' with our dear son immediately under ourselves (whose protection is universal) supreme protector of the discovery and company.'

PAGE 106, l. 19. *Is rauisht now.* Mr. Bullen reads ' fled ' in this line. I have kept the reading of the old edition, as I am not sure that the emendation is necessary.

PAGE 108, l. 7. *O why should fate :* Fate is the marginal correction, written in a contemporary hand, in the Brit. Mus. copy, for the text's reading ' loue '.

To Fredericke V, l. 1. *How like a golden dreame.* The Count Palatine landed at Gravesend on the 16th Oct., 1612, and Prince Henry died on the 6th Nov. following. Their acquaintance, therefore, did not last a month.

PAGE 109, l. 8. *Then now for ones fate.* ' Then ' is the reading of the old text in the music. The separate text of the poetry alone has ' Thou now ', an obvious misprint.

To the World, l. 6. *With doubts late by a Kingly penne decided.* As Mr. Bullen surmises, this is probably a reference to King James's *Premonitions to all most mighty Monarchs, Kings, Free Princes and States of Christendom,* written against Bellarmine, and published in 1609.

Notes. 363

TWO BOOKES OF AYRES.

PAGE **115**, l. 1. *Paysed* means weighed. Compare Marlowe's *Hero and Leander*, Sestiad II : 'Where fancy is in equal balance paised.'

FIRST BOOK (DIVINE AND MORALL SONGS).

PAGE **117.** I. The meaning of 'a stray' in l. 4 is obvious. See Drayton, *The Crier* : —

> If you my heart do see
> Either impound it for a stray
> Or send it back to me.

Or Tottel's *Miscellany* : 'Nor gadding as a stray.'

II. See *A Booke of Ayres*, Part I, XVIII (p. 15) and notes thereon (p. 357).

PAGE **119.** V. The old edition reads 'all in darke' in l. 8, an obvious misprint.

VI. This song refers of course to the Gunpowder Plot of 1605. The allusion in the last stanza is to the death of Prince Henry in 1612 and his consequent succession by Prince Charles as heir to the throne.

PAGE **122.** XI. This song appears to have been living as a devotional hymn as late as 1707, for the first stanza appears in Add. MS. 30023 (fo. 50). 'James Moulton, his Boock. Amen. November 21 1707. 16 years.' It seems to have been written down from memory by the youthful pietist, possibly as a Sabbath exercise. It is clear, too, from the thrice repeated 'O come quickly', that it was remembered as a hymn, and not as a poem, for this repetition occurs in Campion's setting.

PAGE **124.** XIIII. The old edition reads 'And stone and by stone' in l. 20, an obvious misprint.

PAGE **126.** XVIII. See notes on *A Booke of Ayres*, Part I, IIII (p. 355).

PAGE **127.** XX. *Tuttyes* (l. 19) meant nosegays. The word seems to have survived until recently in the Dorset dialect. See Barnes's *Uncle an' Ant* (*Poems of Rural Life*).

PAGE **128.** XXI. This poem clearly refers to the death of Prince Henry in 1612.

SECOND BOOKE (LIGHT CONCEITS OF LOVERS).

PAGE **132.** I. The first line of this song occurs with the air in Add. MS. 33933.

PAGE **134.** V. Mr. Bullen, unnecessarily, in my opinion, reads in l. 10 'Her loue thought to obtaine'. The original text, however, gives far better sense. There is the usual antithesis between love, i.e. affection, and grace, i.e. material favours; and the lover complains that while he has the first, no entreaties can win the latter. Line 17 in the old edition contains a misprint, 'prayes' for 'prayers', possibly by anticipation of the next line.

In l. 24 Mr. Bullen reads 'My words of zeale'. I have retained the reading of the old edition, which in my opinion is equally good.

PAGE **135.** VI. The old edition has a misprint in l. 16 : 'most recure', presumably for 'past recure', Mr. Bullen's emendation.

PAGE **136**, VII. 'Swelling' in l. 8 is Mr. Bullen's emendation for the old edition's 'smelling'.

VIII. The first line of this song occurs together with the air in Add. MS. 33933.

PAGE **138.** X. The first six lines of stanza 1 have already appeared in No. VII of *A Booke of Ayres*.

E e

XI. Mr. Bullen quotes the following poem from a MS. Commonplace Book of the middle of the seventeenth century belonging to the Duke of Buccleugh, which appears to be a draft or version of this song.

> Hide not, sweetest Love, a sight so pleasing
> As those smalls so light composed,
> Those fair pillars your knees gently easing,
> That tell wonders, being disclosed.
> O show me yet a little more:
> Here's the way, bar not the door.
>
> How like sister's twines these knees are joined
> To resist my bold approaching!
> Why should beauty lurk like mines uncoined?
> Love is right and no encroaching.
> O show me yet a little more:
> Here's the way, bar not the door.

'Smalls' means the round parts of pillars. 'Sister's [or sewster's] twines' = sewing thread. 'Mines uncoined' is Mr. Bullen's emendation for the MS. 'mine eyes vncoyned'.

PAGE **139.** XII. There is a version of this song in Add. MS. 15117, which runs as follows :—

> The peacefull westerne winde
> The wintry stormes hath calmde,
> And nature hath in every kinde
> The vital heate inflam'de.
> The flowers so sweetly breathe
> Out of the earthlye bowers,
> That heaven which seethe their pompe benethe
> Would faine be decte with flowers ;
>   To grace the lyvely springe
>   Let all the shepheards singe
>   Fa la la.
>
> See how the morninge smyles
> Out of the easterne Cell ;
> And softly stealinge forthe beguiles
> Them that in sleepe do dwell.
> The frolicke birds do come
> From cliffs or rocks vnknowne,
> To see the treese and briers blow
> That late were overflowene.
>   All things do vs invite
>   To sing with sweet delite
>   Fa la la.
>
> What Nature did destroye
> Renewes, revives againe ;
> And now the wanton naked boye
> Doth in the woods remain :
> Where he such Change doth Vewe
> In everye livinge thinge
> As if the worlde were borne a newe
> To gratifie the springe.
>   To Cynthia then lett vs
>   Recorde our musick thus—
>   Fa la la.

This exceedingly charming version proves that the old edition's reading 'ouerflowne' is correct, and that there is no necessity to accept Mr. Bullen's emendation 'overthrown', which indeed seems inapplicable on grounds of sense. 'Ouerflowne' is quite good, and means 'flooded', 'drenched'. Compare Mortimer, *Husbandry* (1707–12): 'Foul food, as overflown Hay, Grass rotted by the long standing of water on it in wet summers.' Assuming, however (which is not the case), that the word is corrupt, the nearest conjecture, typographically, would be 'ouerblowne' in the sense of 'overblossomed'. But this is not necessary.

PAGE 141. XV. The old edition gives the same rhyme, 'mouing,' in both lines 6 and 8 of stanza 3. I have ventured to correct it in l. 8 to 'rouing', which I believe to be what was intended.

PAGE 142. XVI. This song occurs in Jones's *Musical Dream* (1609). The first line with air is found in Add. MS. 33933, and Eg. MS. 2230 contains a copy with trifling divergences due probably to transcription only. The old edition reads: 'Some else your secret friend' in l. 23, and as Eg. MS. above mentioned has 'Or else some your secret friend', I am inclined to think that the correct version is 'Or else some secret friend'.

XVII. Lines 5 and 6 (*Come quickly, come*, &c.) closely resemble a passage in *A Song, The Lords Maske* (p. 92). The meaning of lines 3 and 4 (which depends upon that of 'sticklers') is not clear, but I do not think it is improved by Mr. Bullen's reading, 'when love and longing fights,' which is ungrammatical. Line 6 in the old ed. reads 'pleasures', doubtless a misprint.

PAGE 143. XVIII. I have felt somewhat diffident as to whether the word 'trustlesse' in line 20 of this poem is not a corruption of 'thrift-lesse'. But as Professor Murray very kindly pointed out to me on my submitting the matter to him, there are numerous instances of the usage of the word in the sense of 'untrustworthy', and it may accordingly be construed here as 'fleeting'. What has added to my doubts is a copy in Add. MS. 24665, which, without variation in other respects, reads 'so fruitles', suggesting that 'trustlesse' was not a well-established reading. But according to my practice I have refrained from emending unless absolutely required.

THE DESCRIPTION OF A MASQUE ETC. AT THE MARIAGE OF THE EARLE OF SOMERSET.

PAGE 148, l. 2. *Tandem nubit amans.* For a narration of the long history of intrigue and sordid crime of which this bridal was the consummation, see Introduction (p. xlii).

l. 3. *Veræ vt supersint.* Cp. Ep. 68, Book I, 1619 collection (p. 246).

PAGE 149, l. 18. *Architect to our late Prince Henry.* To Constantine de Servi Prince Henry assigned a yearly pension of £200 in July, 1612.

PAGE 150, l. 23. *From euery quarter.* I see no reason for adopting Mr. Bullen's emendation 'twelve' for the old edition's 'three knights'. 'Quarter' is to be construed strictly, and three from every quarter of the globe would amount to twelve, the number required by the subsequent text. This interpretation is supported by the introduction later of the four winds, the four continents, etc.

PAGE 152, l. 42. *Bring away this Sacred Tree.* It is worthy of notice that according to J. Stafford Smith's *Musica Antiqua* this song occurred in Lanier's masque entitled *Luminalia,* or *The Festival of Light,* played by Queen Henrietta Maria and her ladies on Shrove Tuesday, 1637. From the *Ayres made by seuerall Authors* appended to the old edition we learn that this song was 'made and exprest by Mr. Nicholas Laneir', and indeed the music there given is that printed by Stafford Smith. As the latter states in connexion with the song in *Luminalia* that it was sung by *Eternity,* and that 'Towards the end of the song the Three Destinies set the Tree of Gold before the queen', and that 'The other songs set by Coprario were sung by Mr John Allen and Laneir', statements which are mere quotations from the stage directions in Campion's masque, the reference to *Luminalia* appears to be due to a confusion of the two. Beyond the reference in *Musica Antiqua* nothing seems to be known about *Luminalia,* and, as already shown, Stafford Smith's remarks thereon relate to Campion's masque.

THE THIRD AND FOVRTH BOOKE OF AYRES.

PAGE **160**, ll. 1–8. See Introduction, pp. xliii, xliv, and xlv. l. 28. See Introduction, p. xlv.

THE FIRST BOOKE.

PAGE **161**. II. This song occurs in Add. MS. 29291, headed 'Francis Pilkington, 1605', with that musician's setting.

PAGE **163**. VI. This song is given in Playford's *Introduction* with Campion's music. Line 3 therein reads 'nature or a curious eye can see', probably a mere error in transcription. Stanzas 3–4 were made the subject of a Latin epigram by the poet (*Ad Leam,* Book II, Ep. 117, 1619 ed., p. 291).

PAGE **165**. XI. This song occurs with Campion's music in Playford's *Introduction* and in his *Musical Companion* (1672). The first stanza is also found in Add. MS. 29386 (fo. 85), which is a collection of Henry Lawes's compositions, superscribed 'Dr Campion. 1652'.

PAGE **166**. XIII. Stanza 3. Compare the first paragraph of the Preface to the *Obseruations* (p. 33).

PAGE **168**. XVII. Versions of this song are found in both Add. MSS. 24665 and 29431. The copy in MS. 24665 contains 4 stanzas to the old edition's three, the penultimate line of each stanza being slightly lengthened. Line 5 reads 'for pity any more'. The additional stanza comes second:—

> When I first of loue did thinke
> As a toy I it esteemed ;
> Neuer from it did I shrinke,
> Cupids darts of lead I deem'd :
> Now I find dispaire pursues the game,
> Night and day it doth inflame.

Stanza 3 reads in ll. 4 and 5 : —

> Or betray me through dispight :
> Soe alas shall I die vnredrest.

Stanza 4 reads in l. 5 :—

> Only do not mocke me in thy bed.

PAGE **169**. XVIII. The following version of this poem in sonnet form occurs, together with several other versions of Campion's poems, in Harl. MS. 6910 (v. note on *A Booke,* &c., Part I, XII, p. 356):—

Thrice tosse those oaken ashes in the ayer
And thrice three tymes tye up this true lou's Knot ;
Thrice sitt you downe in this inchanted chaire
And murmure softe Shee will or shee will not.
Goe burne those poysoned weeds in that blew fyre,
This Cypres gathered out a dead mans graue,
These Scretchowles fethers and the prickling bryer
That all thy Thornye cares an end may haue.
Then come you fairyes, daunce with mee a round,
Dance in a circle, let my loue be center.
Melodiously breathe an inchanted sound,
Melt her hard hart that some remorse may enter.
In vain are all the Charmes I can deuise ;
She hath an arte to breake them with her eyes.

The poem is included among the *Remains never before imprinted* in the 1633 edition of Joshua Sylvester's *Works*, but the attribution is, of course, like that of other poems in the *Remains*, incorrect.

PAGE 170. XX. This song occurs in Morley's *First Book of Ballets* (1595), *Select Ayres and Dialogues* (1599), and Eg. MS. 2013, Harl. 6917, and Add. 10337.

The copy in Eg. MS. is set by Nicholas Lanier, and differs very slightly from the version of the text; it reads 'Fyer, fier' in l. 1 ; 'Loe, how I burne', l. 2 ; 'my empty loue-sicke Braine', l. 4 ; 'Humber, Trent and siluer Thames', l. 6 ; 'Fyer', l. 10 ; 'See how the Riuers', l. 12 ; 'his ayde denye', l. 13 ; 'like me fall', l. 18. Harl. MS. contains many similar divergences : 'Fire, Fire', in ll. 1 and 10 ; 'Oh, how I burne in hott desire', l. 2 ; 'For all the teares', l. 3 ; 'From an empty loue-sick brain', l. 4 ; 'Humber, Trent, and siluer Thames', l. 6 ; 'Great Ocean', l. 7 ; 'Then drown', l. 9. The variation in l. 11 is interesting and plausible, 'There is noe helpe for my desire' ; l. 13, 'The Oceans do their ayde denye' ; l. 14, 'Least my heat' ; l. 15, 'Come pouring down' ; l. 16, 'Yee that once' ; ll. 17 and 18 are repeated from ll. 8 and 9 of the previous stanza. Both these versions differ from the text in much the same ways and are probably drawn from another draft of the poem, or, at any rate, from the same original. The version in Add. MS. 10337 is substantially that of the text.

XXI. This song occurs in Eg. MS. 2013 (fo. 9), where the reading in l. 7 is 'Golden Age', and in l. 12, 'Which till eyes ache, let you fond men enuye.'

PAGE 171. XXIIII. There are two versions of this poem in Add. MS. 10309 (Brit. Mus.), one of which, that on fo. 85, does not differ materially from the version of the text ; reading, however, 'can' for 'could' in l. 4 ; 'men' for 'mindes' in l. 7 ; 'hope or joy' in l. 9 ; 'should demeane man soe' in l. 11 ; 'As she should all thinges foreknow' in l. 12 ; 'But no thought nor' in l. 13 ; 'Grow on affections easie' in l. 14 ; 'it' for 'he' in l. 16. In addition to these variations the first four lines of stanza 2 are given as the first four lines of stanza 3, and vice versa.

The other version, which occurs on fo. 94, is, however, quite different. It runs :—

Could my poore hart whole worlds of toungs employ,
The greifes it ownes that number would out goe ;
Its so enured to greife, s' estranged from ioy
That it knows not, how it releife should know.
Discurteous facts are cor'sives to true hearts,
And those are pronest to dispayring smarts

Noe caution, thought, nor alteration can
Assume affections place ; change harder is
Fancied to be ; use Lords it soe ore man
That it brooks worst what's strange, as being amisse.
  And soe much witt should men in this age have
  As they might chuse what's good and what's not leaue.

Those men are blest that can their freedom get
Whensoere they will, and free themselves from thrall ;
That hope disdaines, on ioy a rate dot(h) set
Inferiour far to th' blisse that ease men call :
  A blest estate had better nere been knowne
  Then from the height thereof, downe to be throwne.

The first version is unimportant, as the variations are probably due
to errors in transcription only ; the poem being one of those 'as
coine crackt in exchange, corrupted'. The second version is almost
certainly, however, an earlier draft from the poet's own pen. It is
markedly inferior, its involved language and awkward inversion con-
trasting unfavourably with the straightforward fluency of the final copy.

PAGE **172.** XXVI. This song occurs in Add. MS. 24665. The
version is that of the text.

PAGE **173.** XXVIII. I have retained the reading of the old edition in
l. 7, ' But roofes too hot would proue for men all fire,' not being convinced
that Mr. Bullen's emendation, 'for me all fire ', is an improvement. Both
are obscure, but the reading of the text maintains the parallel con-
struction between lines 7 and 8, in which ' too hot ' and ' too high ' are
both predicates. The lady is excusing herself from an assignation by
raising objections to every possible rendezvous : ' roofes ' (which
mean a dwelling-place or habitation as opposed to the al fresco
meeting-places objected to in the subsequent lines) are ruled out as too
hot for such fiery natures as that of the suitor. The excuses are
intended to be understood as mere excuses. This appears to make
tolerable sense. For ' roofs ' in this sense (not the metaphorical use
which demands the preposition ' under ', but the sheer metonymy) see
Chapman, *Rev. of Bussy d'Ambois*, I. 1, ' To move such bold feet into
others' roofs '.

FOVRTH BOOK OF AYRES.

PAGE **175.** *To the Reader.* l. 27, *Cloathed in Musicke by others,* e.g.
VII, IX, and XVII.—*Some three or four Songs that haue been published
before,* &c., e.g. XVII, XVIII, XXII, and XXIII. *All these Songs
are mine* : As Mr. Bullen points out, this is a reminiscence of Martial,
i. 38 :—

Quem recitas meus est, o Fidentine, libellus,
  Sed male cum recitas, incipit esse tuus.

PAGE **177.** V. Line 9 in the old edition contains the misprint ' serue'.
The Pawn was a corridor of shops in the Royal Exchange built by Sir
Thomas Gresham, and opened by Queen Elizabeth on Jan. 23,
1571. The Pawn met the special admiration of the Queen. Gresham's
Exchange, also called the Bourse, is not to be confused with the New
Exchange, or ' Britain's Bourse ' (see p. 361).

PAGE **178.** VII. This song occurs in Alison's *Houre's Recreation
in Musick,* Jones's *Vltimum Vale,* and Add. MS. 17786. It may possibly
have suggested Herrick's ' Cherry Ripe'.

PAGE **179.** IX. This song occurs in Ferrabosco's *Ayres,* Harl. MS.

6917, Add. MSS. 14934, and 24665, and Advocates' MS. 5, 2, 14.
The second couplet of stanza 2 in the old edition repeats the second
couplet of stanza 1, the correct reading being supplied in the text from
Ferrabosco's copy. Harl. 6917 gives the version of the text; Add.
14934 omits stanza 2 (fo. 192). This copy is preceded by a Welsh
translation, entitled ' A translation into Welsh of an English song
Composed by Mr. N. Lannear (taken out of Playford's Musical Com-
panion, p. 204) '. Advocates' MS. subjoins the following further stanza
(as given by Mr. Bullen) :—

> Married wives may take or leave,
> When they list, refuse, receive;
> We poor maids may not do so,
> We must answer Ay with No.
> We must seem strange, coy, and curst,
> Yet do we would fain if we durst.

PAGE **180.** X. See the note on *A Booke of Ayres*, Part I, X.

XI. ' Diseased ' in l. 8 means, of course, ' discomforted '. Line 11
repeats l. 7 by a printer's error. I regret that I have been unable to
trace another copy of this song so as to supply the correct version.

PAGE **181.** XII. ' Force ', in l. 4, has the meaning ' desire ', ' care
for '. Compare Surrey: ' The shipman forces not the gulph,' or
Tottel's *Miscellany* :—

> For Corin was her only joy,
> Who forced her not a pin.

The following poem occurs in William Corkine's *Ayres*. I take it
to be a version by Campion of the above on account of its general
tendency and l. 4 in particular, which is almost identical with l. 12
of the song in the text. ' Diuine concent ' has, besides, a distinctly
Campianian flavour. [See *Rose-cheekt Lawra*: p. 50.]

> Some can flatter, some can faine;
> Simple trueth shall pleade for mee.
> Let not beautie trueth disdaine;
> Trueth is euen as faire as shee.
>
> But since Paires must equall proue
> Let my strength her youth oppose :
> Loue her beautie, faith her loue;
> On eu'n terms so may we close.
>
> Corke or Leade in equall waight
> Both one iust proportion yeeld ;
> So may breadth be pays'd with height,
> Steepest mount with plainest field.
>
> Vertues haue not all one kind,
> Yet all vertues merits bee :
> Diuers vertues are combind
> Diff'ring so Deserts agree.
>
> Let then loue and beautie meete,
> Making one diuine concent,
> Constant as the sounds, and sweete,
> That enchant the firmament.

PAGE **183.** XVII. This song occurs in Dowland's *Third Booke*
and Add. MS. 15117. The version in the latter has some slight
differences in reading: ' Beauties parts,' l. 2 ; ' Hence,' l. 3 ; ' To

frame her,' l. 5; 'Should I have grieved and wished', l. 7; 'This kindles,' l. 10. But an additional stanza is given as follows:—

> Thus my complaints from her vntruths arise,
> Accusinge her and nature both in one.
> For Beautie stainde is but a false disguise,
> A Common wonder that is quickly gone.
> A false faire face cannot with all her feature
> With out a trew hart make a trew fair creature.

Further, Mr. Bullen quotes a version found in Christ Church MS. 1, 5, 49, which consists of the first stanza of the old edition, followed by that quoted above and a third not found in either the old edition or the MS. It runs as follows:—

> What need'st thou plain if thou be still rejected?
> The fairest creature sometime may prove strange:
> Continual plaints will make thee still rejected,
> If that her wanton mind be given to range:
>   And nothing better fits a man's true parts
>   Than to disdain t'encounter fair false hearts.

The two main points in the poem in the text, embodied in the concluding lines of each stanza, are neatly turned into Latin verse in Epigrams 18 and 116 respectively of Book II (1619 edition). See pp. 274 and 290.

XVIII. The following version of this song occurs in William Corkine's *Ayres*:—

Thinke you to seduce me so with words that haue no meaning?
Parets can learne so to speake, our voice by peeces gleaning:
Nurses teach their Children so about the time of weaning.

Learne to speake first, then to woe: to woeing much pertaineth:
He that hath not Art to hide soone falters when he faineth,
And as one that wants his wits he smiles when he complaineth.

If with wit we be deceiued, our fals may be excused:
Seeming good with flatterie grac't is but of few refused,
But of all accurst are they that are by fooles abused.

PAGE **186.** XXII and XXIII. See *A Booke*, Part I, XVI and XVII respectively, and notes thereon (p. 357). The refrain to XXII is quoted in Marston's *Eastward Ho* III. 2, from which it may be conjectured that the song was popular.

A NEW WAY OF MAKING FOWRE PARTS IN

COVNTER-POINT.

The main value of Campion's addition to the musical knowledge of his time is the rule of thumb which it affords for the harmonization of a continuous piece of music. The rule is embodied in the table given on p. 197, which is to be used as follows: Given the progression of the bass and the first chord, to find the second and succeeding chords. The first chord of the melody is, as usual, the tonic major or minor. The possible progressions of the bass are through intervals of a second, third, or fourth up or down, all larger progressions being resolved into these six: thus a fifth below is equivalent to a fourth above, a major third above to a minor sixth below, and so on. The rúle of the diagram is applied thus: If the bass go $_{down}^{up}$ the interval above for the *given* chord in each other part is to be looked for in the $_{upper}^{lower}$ line of the diagram, and the interval above the bass for the required chord will be found in the corresponding $_{lower}^{upper}$ line of the diagram, intervals for this purpose including compounds, the third including the tenth, and the fifth the twelfth.

PAGE **219**, l. 4. Sethus Calvisius, born at Groschleben, in Thuringia (1556–1615), was a German astronomer and chronologer. He conducted a school of music established at Pforte, and another at Leipsic later. He wrote five different works on the theory of music, including a *Melodiæ condendæ ratio*, which is very possibly the book to which Campion refers. He also published a number of compositions in various styles. A song of his was popular in Germany for many years.

AYRES SVNG AND PLAYED AT BROVGHAM CASTLE.

PAGE **230** III, l. 16. *Such a morne.* Compare Ep. 188, Book I, 1619 edition of Latin poems, which contains the central thought of this stanza, and convinces me that Campion wrote these *Ayres*. (See Introduction, p. li).

PAGE **231**. IIII, l. 9. *Rise agen.* The internal rhyme here resembles that in *A Booke of Ayres*, Part II, XX.

V. This 'Ballad' is found in Add. MS. 27879, fo. 220, Bishop Percy's famous 'folio MS.', which reads: l. 1, 'a Carthage queen'; l. 8, 'Whereas'; l. 10, 'would haue'; l. 15, 'their loues were'; l. 18, 'Who bade'; l. 28, 'And let'.

EPIGRAMMATVM LIBRI II.

LIBER PRIMVS.

PAGE **237**, 2. The first book was a new collection of epigrams previously unpublished; the second a *réchauffé* of the 1595 collection.

PAGE **239**, 15. It is tempting to conjecture that *Eurus* may be one of the Easts or Estes, either Thomas Este or his better known son Michael Este, the composer. There appears to be little individuality to be gleaned, however, from the epigrams addressed *Ad Eurum*, of which there are several.

17. This epigram ridicules Barnabe Barnes's Sonnet LXIII, which was pilloried by Nashe in *Haue with you to Saffron Walden* and Marston in the *Scourge of Villainy* also. [Sat. viii, ll. 126, 127.]

PAGE **242**. 40. Henri IV was assassinated by Ravaillac in 1610. I gather this to mean that whereas the assassination could not have been effected with a sword, it was successfully attempted with a knife, which was the case.

PAGE **243**. 45. The name *Castricus* suggests that there was some person with a name involving the syllable *Camp*, which was confused with that of the poet and led to the *contretemps* related.

46. See Introduction, p. xxxiii.

48. *Tanquam is*, &c., i. e. Hippocrates, who is said to have put an end to the plague at Athens by burning fires and other means. See also Ep. 91.

PAGE **244**. 56. Compare the epigram in the *Obseruations*, 'Kate can *fancy only berdles husbands*' (p. 45), and Introduction, p. l.

PAGE **246**. 68. See Note on *Veræ vt supersint nuptiæ, Maske at the Mariage of the Earle of Somerset* (p. 365).

PAGE **247**. 73. Edward Allen or Alleyn, the famous actor, is, of course, referred to.

PAGE **249**. 91. *senex Cous*, i.e. Hippocrates. *Madore.* In 1563 the Sweating Sickness raged violently; but the reference may be to a more recent visitation. *Crebraue sternutatione.* 'In 1580 an influenza of a virulent type passed over Europe' (Bullen).

94. The *Golden Hind*, Drake's famous vessel, was preserved at Deptford for some years.

PAGE **250**. 98. I regret that I cannot trace the circumstances to which this epigram relates. Who was 'Synertus' or 'Synertius' whose 'fraus et auara sæuitia' had such fatal consequences? James Huishe, 'son of James Huishe of London, citizen, deceased,' was admitted to Gray's Inn on February 4, 1594–5. His father was apparently very wealthy, and owned property in St. Pancras (London), South Brent, Sidbury (Devon), Shepperton (Middlesex), Surrey and Essex. In his will proved in the Prerogative Court of Canterbury in 1590 (69 Drury) he is described as a grocer, and directions are given *inter alia* for his sons James and Thomas to be brought up at school till the age of seventeen.

102. In view of the change of title of Ep. 94 of Bk. II, *Ad Coruinum* which in the 1595 edition is addressed *Ad Ge. Chapmannum*, I am inclined to think that this epigram also refers to Chapman in allusion to his translation of Homer.

PAGE **255**. 143. This epigram has a strong resemblance to an epigram in the *Obseruations*, Barnzy *stiffly vows* (p. 46), and embodies the same idea. I have emended *vnum* in l. 1 to *vnam*.

PAGE **257**. 151. This epigram must refer not to a striking clock, which was no novelty, but, as the word *portabili* implies, a form of repeating watch.

152, l. 3. This line will not scan in its original form. I have inserted *nam*, metri gratia.

PAGE **258**. 161, l. 6. *Oleum talci.* 'Oil of talc—an esteemed cosmetic when these epigrams were written' (Bullen).

PAGE **261**. 175, l. 5. *Quadrupedis pigræ quam ros.* As Mr. Bullen points out, this must mean asses' milk, used for the complexion. *Cerussa*, cp. Jonson, *Sejanus*: *His Fall*, II. i: ''Tis the sun Hath giv'n some little taint unto the *ceruse.'* Ceruse, originally white lead, was the term applied both to that substance used as a cosmetic and more generally to other whitening cosmetics.

PAGE **262**. 186. *die* 4 *No.*, i.e. Nov. 4, 1616.

PAGE **263**. 188. Compare with this epigram *Ayres sung at Brougham Castle*, No. III, stanza 2, and see Introduction, p. li.

192. Edward Mychelburne's resolution not to make his writings public was similarly deplored by Charles FitzGeoffrey in his *Affaniæ* (see Introduction, p. xlix). Mychelburne apparently kept his resolution, for nothing seems to be known of them.

PAGE **265**. 201, l. 8. *Quadrupede.* 'At this time doctors usually rode on mules when they went to visit their patients' (Bullen). *Coum*: Hippocrates. l. 9, *Pergamenum*: Galen.

PAGE **267**. 211, l. 3. *Pembrochi viduam.* Mary, daughter of Sir Henry Sidney; widow of Henry Herbert, second Earl of Pembroke; 'Sidney's sister, Pembroke's mother.' l. 4, *natos*, William Herbert, third Earl of Pembroke, and Philip Herbert, created in 1605 Earl of

Montgomery. l. 5, *A thalamis alter*, The Earl of Montgomery, who was Gentleman of the King's Bedchamber. l. 6, *Alter at in thalamis*, The Earl of Pembroke, who had married the daughter and heiress of the Earl of Shrewsbury. l. 7, *Hertfordius*, Edward Seymour, Lord Hertford, b. 1547, d. 1621, eldest son (by the second marriage) of the Protector Somerset. The 'coniux speciosa' was his third wife, Frances, daughter of Thomas, Viscount Howard of Bindon' (Bullen).

PAGE **269**, 222, 223. See Introduction, p. xlv.

224. There was a William Strachey known as a colonist and writer on Virginia who was shipwrecked in the *Sea Venture* on the Bermudas in the great storm of 1609, and who wrote an account of it to a lady of rank in London which was published in *Purchas his Pilgrimes*. There was a William Strachey who wrote commendatory verses prefixed to Ben Jonson's *Sejanus*, and from the epigram it would seem likely that this was Campion's friend. There was also a William Strachey of Saffron Walden, who was married in 1583 and alive in 1620.

LIBER SECVNDVS.

PAGE **270**. 1, l. 1, *Non veterem*. This book is an edition of the 1595 collection, revised and added to (see Appendix).

PAGE **272**. 9. See Introduction, p. xxxii.

PAGE **273**. 12. This epigram is a Latin version of the song ' My Loue bound me with a kisse.' See p. 350, and Introduction, p. li.

PAGE **274**. 18. Compare *Fourthe Booke*, XVII, ll. 3–6, and see note.

19. This Italian custom is alluded to in Jonson's *Cynthia's Revels*, I. i. *Aso*: ' By heaven, sir, I do not offer it you after the Italian manner ; I would you should conceive so of me.' The custom is fully explained in a shoulder-note to the corresponding epigram in the 1595 edition (see p. 341).

PAGE **275**. 23. This epigram contains the only hint we have of the poet's personal appearance.

PAGE **276**. 32. 'After being bitten by the Tarantula, there was, according to popular opinion, no way of saving life except by music. . . . It was customary, therefore, so early as the commencement of the seventeenth century, for whole bands of musicians to traverse Italy during the summer months, and, what is quite unexampled either in ancient or modern times, the cure of the *Tarantati* in the different towns and villages was undertaken on a grand scale' (Hecker's *Epidemics of the Middles Ages*: apud Bullen).

PAGE **277**. 39, l. 1. *Domini cœna*, i. e. the Lord's Supper.

40. See Introduction, p. xxvii. *Glocestriensium*. Percy was a member of Gloucester Hall, Oxford, now Worcester College.

PAGE **278**. 45, l. 7. I have kept *cubilulillum*, as Campion insists upon it in his Errata. *Cubiculillum* is a more likely form.

PAGE **279**. 53. This epigram is a Latin version of XII, *A Booke of Ayres*, Part I, q. v. (p. 12) and note thereon.

PAGE **280**. 54. This epigram is a Latin version of the epigram ' Loue whets the dullest wittes, his plagues be such ', on p. 351.

PAGE **281**. 60, 61. Compare *A Book of Ayres*, Part I, VIII, and see note thereon.

PAGE **282**. 69. See Introduction, p. xlviii.

70. See Introduction, p. xxxvii.

PAGE **284**. 78. Francis Manby was the son and heir of Francis Manby, of Elsham, co. Lincoln, gent. Francis Manby, senior, whose will was proved in the Consistory Court of Lincoln in 1587, was (per MS. Rawl. B. 77, fo. 138) eldest son of William Manby, who married, in 1563, the daughter and heiress of Thomas Gibthorpe and his wife, the widow of J. Dacomb of Elsham, Esq. Francis Manby, senior, married Anne, daughter of Sir Francis Chough, and had issue *Francis*, William, Robert, and Thomas. Francis Manby, junior, matriculated at Magdalen College, Oxford, in 1581, and was admitted to Gray's Inn on Jan. 31, 1583-4. From l. 16 of this epigram it would seem that he was drowned at sea, and on Nov. 10, 1596, letters of administration of his personal estate issued from the Prerogative Court of Canterbury to his next eldest brother, William.

In the epigram in the 1595 edition *Ad Franciscum Manbæum* (p. 341), Campion bewails the fate which had severed his friend from him, and execrates some person who had been the cause of the separation. The reference to *ignotas oras* looks as though Manby had been induced to join one of the numerous exploring or colonizing expeditions, and, as we have already seen, he seems to have perished at sea. As this epigram *In obitum Francisci Manbæi* occurs with a slightly varied title in the 1595 edition, his death must have occurred before that date, and no doubt it was necessary to defer the issue of the grant of letters of administration for some time, in order to support the presumption of his death.

80. See Introduction, p. xxxv.

PAGE **285**. 85. There seems to be considerable resemblance between this epigram and a short poem in A. Ferrabosco's *Ayres* :—

> Had those that dwell in error foule
> And hold that women haue no soule
> But seene those moue, they would haue then said
> Women were the soules of men :
> So they doe moue each heart and eye
> With the worlds soule, their harmonie.

This song is obviously corrupt, and I should begin by emending 'then said' in l. 3 to 'said then', and possibly 'those' to 'thee' in the same line. It looks as though it were another instance of Campion's habit of versifying the same idea in both English and Latin.

PAGE **286**. 88. This epigram figures in the 1595 edition with the title *Ad Nashum*. The alteration is possibly due to the death of Nashe in 1601. See p. xxvii.

PAGE **287**. 93. This epigram is, of course, levelled at Nicholas Breton. Breton is fond of introducing Cupid, but I cannot come across the particular instance where he is represented 'carmine defunctum'.

94. This epigram is addressed in the 1595 edition *Ad Ge. Chapmannum* (p. 345).

PAGE **290**. 116. *Pulchrior huic.* Compare the last line of XVII, *Fourthe Booke*, and see note thereon.

PAGE **291**. 117. With this epigram compare VI, *Third Booke*, q.v. (p. 163), and note thereon.

121. *seuocasti.* Edward Mychelburne, the poet, was a member of St. Mary Hall, Oxford, whence he migrated to Gloucester Hall. He continued to reside in Oxford, as it would appear, and died there in 1626. He was buried in the church of St. Thomas the Martyr.

PAGE 302. 205, l. 3. *domini natale.* Christmas Day, the connexion of which with feasting and good cheer was never closer than in the seventeenth century. *cometa.* There were three comets in 1618, but the great comet, to which reference is probably made, began to be observed on Nov. 27 (N. S.). It created much concern, as the epigram suggests ; some thinking it to be a presage of the death of the Queen, some a warning against the Spanish Match, while others thought it to be connected with the fall of Barneveldt.

PAGE 303. 216. The reference would seem to be to Anthony Munday, who wrote a little that was good among much that was very indifferent.

PAGE 304. 227. *Graij*, i. e. the members of Gray's Inn, also called *Purpulij*, or natives of the ' State of Purpoole ', as the Inn was jocularly intituled in the *Gesta Graiorum*, on account of a local place-name Portpool. Porte Pool was the old name for Gray's Inn Lane ; and the name still survives in Portpool Lane, running out of the east side of Gray's Inn Road. *Disiuncti socij* : see Introduction, p. xxxi.

VMBRA.

PAGE 312, l. 310. *Geraldinam* : Lady Elizabeth Fitzgerald, the 'Geraldine' of Surrey's sonnets. l. 311, *Aliciam* : Alice, daughter of Sir John Spencer, of Althorpe. She married (1) Ferdinando, fifth Earl of Derby, (2) Thomas Egerton, Baron Ellesmere, Lord Chancellor. l. 317, *Penelope* : Lady Penelope Rich, the ' Stella ' of Sidney's sonnets. The next line refers to her marriage (if marriage it was) with Charles Blount, eighth Lord Mountjoy, Lord-Lieutenant of Ireland. l. 322, *Franciscæ* : Frances, daughter of Thomas Viscount Howard of Bindon. ' Magni senis excipienda cubili ' refers to her marriage with the old Lord Hertford. l. 325, *Catherina* : Doubtless Catherine Parr, whose third husband was Henry VIII. She had four husbands ('coniugibus lætæ minus '). PAGE 313, l. 328 : *Brigetta* may be Bridget Fitzgerald, daughter of the twelfth Earl of Kildare ; she married (1) Earl of Tyrconnel, (2) Viscount Kingsland. l. 329, *Lucia* : ' The famous Lucy, Countess of Bedford ' (Bullen).

APPENDIX TO THE LATIN POEMS.

ELEGIARVM LIBER.

PAGE 329. *Ad Daphnin.* This poem appears to have been written at the time of the Queen's reconciliation with Essex in April, 1592, and his return home soon after from the French wars. PAGE 330, l. 12, *qua Tagus.* This appears to be a reference to the ' Journey of Portugal ' of 1589, undertaken against Spain and Portugal, chiefly the latter, by Sir John Norris and Sir Francis Drake almost entirely at their own expense. Essex's part in this expedition was likewise carried out at his own expense, and without the Queen's knowledge or consent. l. 25, *Menalcas* : Lord Burleigh is probably indicated.

PAGE 336. Elegeia 1, l. 7. *Et vatem celebrent.* Campion seems to take credit here for being the first English writer of Latin elegies. In FitzGeoffrey's verses (see p. xxxvii) he gets credit for being the *second* Latin epigrammatist in England.

PAGE 338, Elegeia 14. See Introduction, p. xlviii.

PAGE 340. *Ad Librum.* As will be seen on the title-page, the printer of this book was Richard Field of Stratford-on-Avon, the printer of Shakespeare's *Lucrece* and *Venus and Adonis*, and it is to him that allusion is made in *Feldisio*. The epigram had to be adapted in the 1619 edition, which was printed by Griffin.

In Hornsium. Nicholas Hornsey of Bonby, co. Lincs., was admitted to Gray's Inn on Nov. 7, 1586, the year of Campion's admission.

Page 341. *Ad Franciscum Manbœum.* See note on Ep. 78, Book II, 1619 ed. (p. 373).

Ad Gu. Percium. See note on Ep. 40, Book II, 1619 ed.

De Th. Grimstono &° Io. Goringo. See Introduction, p. xxxiii.

Page 342. *In Prettum.* Can this be William Pretiman who was admitted to Gray's Inn in 1583? See also two other epigrams with the same title, pp. 346, 347.

Ad Iacobum Thu. 'James Thurbarne, of New Romsey, Kent, gent., late of Barnard's Inn' was admitted to Gray's Inn on Feb. 10, 1584-5. See also, *Ad Ia. Thurbarnum* (p. 348).

Page 343. *In gloriosum.* There were several Shakerleys at Gray's Inn. Thomas Shakerley of Ditton, Surrey, gent., late of Staple Inn, was admitted in 1585. 'Syr Peter Shackerley,' who was admitted in 1576, took a part in the 'Comedy' performed at the Inn on Jan. 16, 1587-8. It is not clear which of these is to be identified as the 'gloriosus' of the epigram, but this latter is obviously the person referred to in the following passage in Nashe's *Epistle Dedicatorie* to *Strange Newes*: 'Nor do I meane to present him and Shakerley to the Queen's foole taker for coatch horses, for two that drew more equallie in one Oratoricall yoke of vaine glorie there is not under heaven.'

Page 344. *Ad Tho. Smithum.* Thomas Smith of London was admitted to Gray's Inn on May 13, 1586.

Francisci Manbœi epicedium. See note on Ep. 78, Book II, 1619 ed. (p. 373).

Ad Castellum et Braceium. Robert Castell, of East Hatley, co. Cambridge, was admitted to Gray's Inn on Nov. 8, 1588. Edmund Bressy or Bracy (to whom allusion is probably made), of Brainford, Middlesex, was admitted on May 17, 1588. See also, *Ad Ed. Braceium* (p. 345).

Page 345. *De Se.* See Introduction, p. xxxii.

Ad Nashum. I cannot identify the persons alluded to here. Mr. Bullen suggests that the epigram refers to the imitations of classical metres perpetrated by Gabriel Harvey and others.

In Bretonem. See note on Ep. 93, Book II, 1619 ed. (p. 374).

Ad Ge. Chapmannum. See note on Ep. 94, Book II, 1619 ed. (p. 374).

Ad Io. Dauisium. Sir John Davies, the author of *Orchestra.*

Ad Ed. Braceium. See *Ad Castellum et Braceium*, supra.

Page 346. *Ad Io. Dolandum.* The famous musician John Dowland, to whose *First Booke* Campion contributed an epigram (p. 351).

Page 348. *Ad Iaruisium et Stanfordum.* These intimate friends of the poet are alluded to in Elegeia 14, *Ad amicos cum ægrotaret.* George Gervis of Peatling, co. Leicester, gent., late of Barnard's Inn, was admitted to Gray's Inn on Nov. 24, 1585. John Stanford, of Leicester, gent., was admitted on Nov. 21, 1586, some months after Campion. Stanford took part in the 'Comedy' played at the Inn on Jan. 16, 1587-8.

OCCASIONAL VERSES.

Page 349. *What faire pompe*, &c. For this set of five poems see Introduction, p. li.

Page 350. *Canto tertio.* The three final stanzas are supplied from Robert Jones's *Second Booke of Songs and Ayres* (1601), the first only appearing in the set. The first stanza was probably the original extent of the poem, for it alone was turned by Campion into the Latin epigram *In Melleam* which appears in both collections (Ep. 12, Book II of the 1619 edition). *Seales of loue.* The same phrase occurs in the song 'Take, oh take those lips away' from Shakespeare's *Measure for Measure,* IV. i (acted in 1604). When Campion wrote the additional verses, and whether either he or Shakespeare originated the phrase, cannot be decided. Add. MS. 29409 (fo. 265) contains a version of this song in Scots dialect, with unimportant scribal differences.

    Canto quarto. Campion made a very close translation of these lines in his Latin epigram *Ad Amorem,* which appears in both collections (Ep. 54, Book II of the 1619 edition).

    Canto quinto. A copy of this poem occurs in Harl. MS. 6910, which contains copies or versions of several of Campion's pieces. This version (fo. 156), with the exception of the omission of ll. 3 and 4 owing presumably to a mere scribal error, is identical with that of the text. Stanza 2 is an example of the 'heel treading kind of verse', as Puttenham calls it, in which every line begins with the last words of the preceding.

    PAGE **351.** *Famam, posteritas.* Campion addressed another Latin epigram to Dowland in the 1595 *Poemata* (p. 346).

    PAGE **352.** *Of Neptunes Empyre.* This song was written for the masque *Gesta Graiorum,* performed by the members of Gray's Inn in 1594. Nichols (*Progresses of Queen Elizabeth*) gives a version which differs from Davison's in several details, reading : l. 3, 'To whom rivers '; l. 6, 'their crystal '; l. 8, 'sea-god praise again '; l. 13, 'The waiters with their trumpets '; l. 18, 'echoing voice '; l. 19, 'mourning noise '; l. 20, 'In praise'. Some of these variations are merely absurd corruptions, but 'trumpets' in l. 13 seems to me quite as plausible as Davison's text, the Triton's 'wreathèd horn' being his regular attribute.

    Though neither thou. These verses are not found in all copies of Barnes's book. Campion was presumably not on the best of terms with Barnes when his *Poemata* appeared in 1595 containing the epigram *In Barnum.* These prefatory lines may be regarded as evidence of a reconciliation, but if there was one it was not permanent, for Campion retained *In Barnum* in his 1619 collection of Latin poems and added another of the same title and equally derisive. Any reconciliation was presumably later than Campion's *Obseruations* (1602), which contains other scurrilous epigrams apparently directed at Barnes (pp. 46, 49).

    PAGE **353.** *What if a day.* This song seems to have had a most extraordinary vogue. It is quoted and referred to in the following MSS. and printed books of the sixteenth and seventeenth centuries.

    Add. MS. 33933, fo. 81 b (Brit. Mus.), *notes in flyleaves of a MS. Scottish Metrical Psalter* : date, early seventeenth century.

    Lans. MS. 241, fo. 49 (Brit. Mus.), *Diary of John Sanderson* : date of entry about 1592.

    Philotus, pub. Edinburgh, 1603.

    An Howres Recreation in Musick, Richard Alison, 1606.

    MS. K. K. 5. 30, fo. 82 b (Univ. Libr., Camb.), *a Scottish version copied by Sir James Murray of Tibbermuir* : date about 1612.

    Add. MS. 24665, fo. 25 b (Brit. Mus.), *Giles Earle his booke,* 1615. *Logonomia Anglica.* Alexander Gil, 1619.

    Golden Garland of Princely pleasures and delicate Delights. Richard Johnson, 1620.

Add. MS. 6704, fo. 163 (Brit. Mus.), *Richard Wigley's Commonplace Book* (1591–1643).
Cantus, Songs and Fancies. John Forbes, Aberdene, 1666.
Pepysian Library (Magdalene Coll., Camb.), vol. i, p. 52.
Psalmes or Songs of Sion (p. 36), by W. S. London, 1642.
Skene MS. (Advocates' Library), 1615–35.
Friesche Lust-hof, pp. 65, 77, and 141. J. Starter, 1634.
Stichtelyche Rymen. D. R. Camphuyzen, Rotterdam, 1639.
Lute MSS. Dd. iv, 23 (Camb. Univ. Libr.).
Citharen Lessons. Robinson, 1609.
Hudibras, I, 3, 9. S. Butler.
Nederlandtsche Gedenck-clanck. Valerius, 1626.
MS. Rawl. poet, 112, fo. 9 (Bodleian).

The version given in the text is that of Alison's *An Howres Recreation*, where the poem is signed 'Thomas Campion M.D.' This is the best, and in all probability the original, form, but the popularity of the song led to the composition of a vast number of additional stanzas in which Campion need not be supposed to have had a hand. Some of the versions referred to above contain three stanzas, some five, while some contain a second part with a further five stanzas. The abundance of the material makes it impossible to discuss the matter in detail in the limited space available, but those who are desirous of knowing more about the matter I would refer to Mr. A. E. H. Swaen's exhaustive monograph on the subject in *Modern Philology*, vol. iv, No. 3 (Jan., 1907), and vol. v, No. 3 (Jan., 1908). In his final conclusion, however, that this poem in its original form could not have been Campion's, Mr. Swaen is in error. He bases this conclusion upon the assumption that the date of Add. MS. 33933 cannot be later than 1578, but he is misinformed as to this. Whatever the date of the MS. Scottish Metrical Psalter, the jottings in the subsequent leaves (which are, by the way, in a different hand) contain, beside 'What if a day', other airs inscribed with the first lines of several poems which are undoubtedly Campion's, viz. 'Vain men, whose follies', 'Good men, shew', 'Though your strangeness', all three from *Two Bookes of Ayres*. This MS. cannot therefore be relied upon to contradict the attribution to Campion, which is directly supported by the subscription to the poem in Alison's song-book, and the categorical statement of Alexander Gil.

The allusion in Hudibras runs as follows :—

> For though dame Fortune seem to smile
> And leer upon him for a while,
> She'll after show him, in the nick
> Of all his glories, a dog-trick.
> This any man may sing or say
> I' th' ditty called, ' What if a day '.

The song, therefore, was still popular as late as 1663.

PAGE **353.** *Musicks maister.* 'Alfonso Ferrabosco, senior (1544 ?–1587 ?), was pensioned by Queen Elizabeth some time before 1567 : he appears to have lived at Greenwich. Peacham, in his "Compleat Gentleman" (1661), says of him, "Alphonso Ferrabosco, the father, while he lived, for judgment and depth of skill (as also his son yet living) was inferior to none ; what he did was most elaborate and profound and pleasing enough in Air, though Master Thomas Morley censureth him otherwise." ' He appears to have been a musician of the old school which by Campion's time had become obsolete. But

Peacham is wrong: his son was not living in 1661. The fact is that there were three Alfonso Ferraboscos, as Mr. Fuller Maitland points out in the Dictionary of National Biography. There was the one mentioned above ; his son, of the new school of monodists and composer of the *Airs* (1609), for which Campion wrote this poem, who succeeded Coprario as composer in ordinary, and died in 1628 ; and his grandson, son of the last named. This last was possibly the Master Alfonso Ferrabosco who sang in the ' Hymenæi ' on Twelfth Night, 1606: he ' was sworn as musician to his Majesty for the viols and wind instruments in the place of his father deceased' in March, 1627-8, and died in 1661 ' (Muses' Library Edition).

PAGE 354. *Markes that did limit.* One of the only four sonnets by Campion extant. ' Thos. Ravenscroft was born about 1592. He was a chorister of St. Paul's Cathedral, and obtained the degree of Mus. Bac. at Cambridge in 1607. He published *Pammelia* in 1609, in his infancy, as he tells us, the *Brief Discourse* in 1614, and his most famous work, the *Whole Book of Psalms*, &c., later. He is said to have died in 1635 ' (Muses' Library Edition).

BIBLIOGRAPHY.

Syr P. S. / His Astrophel and Stella. / wherein the excellence of sweete / Poesie is concluded / To the end of which are added, sundry / other rare Sonnets of diuers Noble / men and Gentlemen. / At London, / Printed for Thomas Newman. / Anno Domini 1591.

Thomæ Campiani / Poemata / Ad Thamesin / Fragmentum Vmbræ / Liber Elegiarum / Liber Epigrammatum / Londini / Ex officina Typographica / Richardi Field / 1595. [Text from Bodleian copy.]

The / First Booke / of Songes or Ayres / of foure partes with Ta / bleture for the Lute : / So made that all the partes / together, or either of them seue / rally may be sung to the Lute, / Orpherian or Viol de gambo / Composed by Iohn Dowland Lute / nist and Bacheler of musicke in both the Vniuersities / Also an inuention by the sayd / Author for two to play vp / on one Lute.

A / Booke of / Ayres, / Set forth to be song / to the Lute, Orpherian, and / Base Violl, by Philip Rosseter / Lutenist : And are to be solde at his house in Fleetstreete / neere to the Gray-/hound / At Lonond / Printed by Peter Short, by the assent / of Thomas Morley / 1601. [Text from Brit. Mus. copy: K 2 i 3.]

Obseruations / in the Art of English / Poesie. / By Thomas Campion./ Wherein it is demonstra / tiuely prooued, and by example / con-firmed, that the English toong is receiue eight seuerall kinds of num / bers, proper to it selfe, which are all / in this booke set forth, and were / neuer before this time by any / man attempted. / Printed at London by Richard Field / for Andrew Wise. 1602. [Text from Brit. Mus. copy: 1076 b. 18.]

A Defence of Ryme, Against a Pamphlet entituled Obseruations in the Art of English Poesie, wherein is demonstratiuely proued, that Ryme is the fittest harmonie of words that comportes with our Language. By Sa. D. At London : Printed by V. S. for Edward Blount.

A / Poetical Rapsody / Containing, / Diuerse Sonnets, Odes, Elegies,. Madrigalls, / and other Poesies, both in Rime, and / Measured Verse. / Neuer yet published. / The Bee and Spider by a diuerse power, / Sucke Hony & Poyson from the selfe same flower./ Printed at London by V. S. for Iohn Baily, and / are to be solde at his Shoppe in Chancerie lane, / neere to the Office of the six Clarkes./ 1602.

An Howres Recrea/tion in Musicke apt for Instru/mentes and Voyces. / Framed for the delight of Gentlemen / and others which are wel affected to that qualitie, / All for the most part with two trebles, necessarie for / such as teach in priuate families, with a pray/er for the long preseruation of the King / and his posteritie, and a thanks-giuing for / the deliuerance of the whole estate / from the late con-spiracie. / By Richard Alison / Gentleman and practitioner / in this Arte. / London / Printed by Iohn Windet the Assigne of William Barley, / and are to be sold at the Golden Anchor in / Pater Noster Row. 1606.

Foure Bookes / of Offices : Enabling Privat / persons for the speciall seruice of / all good Princes and Policies / Made and deuised by Barnabe Barnes / London / Printed at the charges of George Bishop, / T. Adams, and C. Burbie / 1606.

The / Discription of / a / Maske, Presented before the Kinges Maiestie / at White-Hall, on Twelfth Night / last, in honour of the Lord Hayes, and / his Bride, Daughter and Heire to the / Honourable the Lord Dennye, their / Marriage hauing been the same Day / at Court solemnized. To this by occasion other small Poemes / are adioyned. / Inuented and set forth by Thomas / Campion Doctor of Phisicke. / London / Imprinted by Iohn Windet for Iohn Brown / and are to be solde at his shop in S. Dunstones / Churchyeard in Fleetstreet. 1607. [Text from Brit. Mus. copy : C. 21, c. 43.]

Ayres / By / Alfonso Ferrabosco. / London: / Printed by T. Snodham, for Iohn Browne, / and are to be sould at his shoppe in S. / Dunstones Churchyard / in Fleetstreet / 1609.

Coryats / Crudities / Hastily gobled vp in five / Moneths trauells in France / Sauoy, Italy, Rhetia cõmonly / called the Grisons country, Heluetia alias Switzerland, some / parts of high Germany, and the / Netherlands ; / Newly digested in the hungry aire / of Odcombe in the County of Somerset, and now dispersed to the nourishment of the trauelling Mem/bers of this kingdome.

A / Relation / Of The Late Roy-/all Entertainment / given By The Right Hono/rable The Lord Knowles, At / Cawsome House neere Redding : to our most Gracious Queene, Queene Anne, in her / Progresse toward the Bathe, vpon / the seuen and eight and twentie / dayes of Aprill / 1613. / Whereunto is annexed the Description, Speeches and Songs of the Lords Maske, presented in the / Banquet-ing-house on the Mariage night of the High / and Mightie, Count Palatine, and the / Royally descended the Ladie / Elizabeth. / Written by Thomas Campion. / London / Printed for Iohn Bridge, and are to be sold at his Shop / at the South-dore of S. Pauls, and at Bri/taines Bursse. 1613. [Text from Brit. Mus. copy : C. 21, c. 48.]

Songs of Mourning : / Bewailing / the vntimely death of / Prince Henry. / Worded by Tho. Campion. / And set forth to bee sung with one voyce / to the Lute, or Violl : / by John Coprario. / London : / Printed for John Browne, and / are to be sould in S. dunstons / Churchyard. 1613. [Text from Brit. Mus. copy : K 2, g. 8.]

Two Bookes / Of / Ayres. / The First / Contayning Diuine and Morall Songs : / The Second, / Light Conceits of Louers. / To be sung to the Lute and Viols, in two, / three and foure Parts : or by one Voyce / to an instrument. / Composed / by / Thomas Campian / London : Printed by Tho. Snodham, for / Mathew Lownes, and I. Browne / Cum Priuilegio. [Text from Brit. Mus. copy : K. 2. i. 1.]

The / Description / of a Maske. / Presented in the / Banqueting roome at Whitehall, on / Saint Stephens night last, At the Mariage of / the Right Honourable the Earle of / Somerset : And the right noble / the lady Frances / Howard / written by Thomas Campion. / Whereunto are annexed diuers choyse Ayres composed / for this Maske that may be sung with a single voyce / to the Lute or Base-Viall / London. / Printed by E. A. for Laurence Li'sle, dwelling in Paules / Church-yard, at the signe of the Tygers head. / 1614. [Text from Brit. Mus. copy : C. 34, c. 7.]

A Briefe / Discourse / of the true (but neglected) vse of cha/ract'ring the Degrees by their Per / fection, Imperfection and Diminution / in Measurable Musicke, against the Common / Practice and Custome of these / Times. Examples whereof are exprest in the / Harmony of 4 Voyces Concerning the / Pleasure of 5 vsuall / Recreations. / 1. Hunting / 2. Hawking, / 3. Dauncing, / 4. Drinking, / 5. Enamouring. / By Thomas Rauenscroft, Bachelor / of Musicke. / London / Printed by Edw. Allde for Tho. Adams / 1614. / Cum priuilegio Regali.

The / Third / and / Fourth Booke / of / Ayres : / Composed / by / Thomas Campian / So as they may be expressed by one Voyce, / with a Violl, Lute, or Orpharion. / London : / Printed by Thomas Snodham. / Cum Priuilegio. [Text from Brit. Mus. copy: K. 2. i. 2.]

The / Ayres / That were / sung and played, / at Brougham Castle in Westmerland / in the Kings Entertainment : / Giuen by the Right Honourable the Earle of Cum/berland, and his Right Noble Sonne the / Lord Clifford / Composed / by / Mr George Mason, and / Mr. Iohn Earsden / London / Printed by Thomas Snodham / Cum Priuilegio 1618. [Text from Brit. Mus. copy: K. 8, h. 7.]

A New Way / of Making Fowre / parts in Counter-point, by a / most familiar, and infallible / Rule. / Secondly, a necessary discourse of Keyes, / and their proper Closes / Thirdly, the allowed passages. of all Concords / perfect, or imperfect, are declared / Also by way of Preface, the nature of the Scale is / expressed, with a briefe Method teaching to sing / By Tho: Campion / London / Printed by T. S. for Iohn Browne, and are to be / sold at his shop in Saint Dunstanes Church-yard, / in Fleetstreet. [Text from Brit. Mus. copy : 1042 d. 36.]

The Art of / Setting or Composing / of / Musick in Parts. / By a most familiar and easie Rule : / In Three several Treatises. / I. Of making four parts in Counterpoint. / II. A necessary Discourse of the several Keyes, / and their proper Closes. / III. The allowed passages of all Concords perfect / and Imperfect. / By Dr Tho. Campion. / The second Edition with Annotations thereon, by / Mr Christopher Simpson. / London, Printed for J. Playford and are sold at his / Shop in the Inner Temple. 1660.

A Brief / Introduction / To the Skill of / Musick. / In two Books. / The first contains the Grounds and Rules of Musick / The second, Instructions for the Viol, / and also for the Treble-Violin. / The Third Edition Enlarged. / To which is added a Third Book entituled, The Art of Descant, / or Composing Musick in Parts By Dr Tho. Campion. / With Annotations thereon by Mr Chr. Simpson / London, Printed by W. Godbid for John Playford, / at his Shop in the Inner Temple 1660.

A Brief / Introduction / To the Skill of / Musick. / In two Books. / The First contains the Grounds and / Rules of Musick / The Second, Instructions for the Viol / and also for the Treble-Violin / By John Playford, Philo-Musicæ / To which is added a Third Book, entituled, The Art of Setting, / or Composing Musick in Parts, By Dr Tho. Campion. / With Annotations thereon by Mr Chr. Simpson / London, Printed for J. Playford and are sold at his / Shop in the Temple in Fleetstreet. 1662.

A Brief / Introduction / To the Skill of / Musick. / In two Books / The First containes the General / Grounds and Rules of Musick. /

The Second, Instructions for the Viol / and also for the Treble-Violin. / To which is added The Art of Descant, or Composing / Musick in Parts, By Dr Thomas Campion. / With Annotations thereon by Mr Chr. Simpson. / The Fourth Edition much Enlarged. / London, Printed by William Godbid for John Playford, and are / to be sold by Zach. Watkins, at their Shop in the Temple / near the Church-Dore. 1664.

Tho. Campiani / Epigrammatum / Libri II / Vmbra / Elegiarum liber vnus / Londini / Excudebat E Griffin / Anno Domini 1619.

Excerpta Tudoriana, ed. Sir Egerton Brydges. 1814.

Ancient Critical Essays upon English Poets and Poesy, ed. J. Haslewood. 2 Vols. London; 1815.

The works of Dr Thomas Campion, ed. A. H. Bullen. Chiswick Press: privately printed ; 1889.

Fifty Songs By Thomas Campion. Chosen by John Gray. Ballantyne Press. 1896.

Lyric Poems of Thomas Campion, ed. Ernest Rhys: in Dent's Lyric Poets. 1896.

Thomas Campion, Songs and Masques with Observations in the Art of English Poesy, ed. and pub. A. H. Bullen. 1903.

Songs by Dr Thomas Campion. Astolat Press. 1904.

Elizabethan Critical Essays, ed. G. Gregory Smith. 2 Vols. Clarendon Press. 1904.

Poetical Works (in English) of Thomas Campion, ed. P. Vivian, in Routledges' Muses' Library. 1907.

LIST OF PRINCIPAL MSS. CONSULTED.

Add. MS. 6704. Richard Wigley's Commonplace Book (1591-1643).
,, 10309. Commonplace Book of Margrett Bellasys (Seventeenth Century).
,, 10337. Elizabeth Rogers's Virginal Book.
,, 14934. The miscellaneous collections or *Rhapsodia* of Lewis Morris.
,, 15117. A volume containing chiefly the treble-voice part of various English madrigals, psalms, &c., with Tablature for the Lute: date about 1630.
,, 15476. 'Nic. Oldisworth's book touching Sir Thomas Overbury.'
,, 17786. Vocal and instrumental music by English composers. Seventeenth Century.
,, 22603. Miscellaneous poems. Seventeenth Century.
,, 24665. 'Giles Earle his booke' (1615-1626).
,, 25707.
,, 27879. Bishop Percy's famous 'folio' MS.
,, 28253. Miscellaneous pieces of verse transcribed by members of the Caryll family and others: Sixteenth and Seventeenth Centuries.
,, 29291. Madrigals, catches, and canons by various composers. Seventeenth Century.
,, 29386. Glees, catches, and airs by various composers. Eighteenth Century.

Add. MS. 29409. A Collection of ancient Scottish and English ballads compiled by Peter Buchan (Nineteenth Century), fos. 256-277, copied from an unprinted MS. written by Lady Robertson of Lude in 1630.

„ 30023. 'James Moulton his Boock. Amen. November 21. 1707. 16 years.'

„ 33933. Scottish Metrical Psalter, with some additional (secular) words and airs.

„ 34608. Musical Commonplace Book of John Stafford Smith. (1785-9).

Harl. MS. 1072. Collections of coats of arms worn by persons of the same name.

„ 3991. A collection of songs and poems. Seventeenth Century.

„ 4064. A collection of poems and other miscellaneous matter.

„ 4286. Abbreviationes Placitorum in Banco Regis with various poems transcribed on the end leaves. Seventeenth Century.

„ 6910. A verse miscellany.

„ 6917. „ „ early Seventeenth Century.

Egerton MS. 2013. Miscellaneous words set by various composers, Lawes, Hilton, Laneir, &c., the greater part prior to 1644.

„ 2230. 'E libris Richardo Glouero, pharmacopol. Londinensi pertinensibus.' (1638.)

„ 2599. Book containing accounts and copies of the title-deeds of Augustine Steward.

Lansdowne MS. 55. 'The names of yᵉ Gentillmĕ of Grays In yᵗ playd ther a Cõmedy.'

„ 241. Diary of John Sanderson : entry on fo. 49, about 1592.

Stowe MS. 171. Miscellaneous collections, mainly eighteenth-century transcripts.

„ 795. Edmondes Papers, Vol VI. Miscellaneous letters.

Sloane MS. 1002. Account of the proceedings in the Countess of Essex's nullity suit, and the Overbury murder trials.

MS. Titus B. V.

MS. 17 B. L.

(All the foregoing MSS. are in the Brit. Mus.)

Rawlinson MS. Poet. 31. (Bodleian).

„ „ 112. „

Lute MSS. Dd. IV. (Cambridge Public Library.)

Skene MS. (Advocates' Library.)

Proceedings in Court of Requests. XXXVII. 71 ; LXIII. 67.

„ Chancery: Series II. Bundle XXXVI. 46; XLIV. 36.

„ Star Chamber. C. XXX. 35 ; C. XXXIX. 40.

State Papers : Dom. Eliz. CCXLI.

„ For. France. XXV, XXVI, and XXVII.

„ Dom. James I. LXXXII.

(These Proceedings and State Papers are in the Public Record Office.)

INDEX OF FIRST LINES.

This index comprises all the lyrics and epigrams, Latin as well as English. It has been found necessary, however, to draw a somewhat arbitrary line in the case of the masques against miscellaneous portions of verse, dialogue, or speeches, and to include only such pieces as are specifically songs.

CAMPION

G g

INDEX OF PERSONAL NAMES.

Ross, Thomas, xxx.
Rosseter, Philip, xxxviii, xlvii, xlix, lii,
3, 19,
Rowley, John, x.

Salisbury, Earl of, 156.
Sanderson, John, xxxvi, 377.
Sandfort (Sandforthe), Thomas, xxix.
Scroope, Lord, 156.
Searle, Alice, viii, xi; George, xxiii;
Henry, xi; Joan, xi; Laurence, viii,
xi, xii, xv; Leonard, viii, xi, xv;
Lucy, viii, xi, xii, xv; Mawde, viii,
x, xi; Nicholas, viii, xi, xv; Thomas,
viii, x, xi; Walter, viii, x, xi.
Shakerley (Shackerley), Sir Peter, xxix,
376; Thomas, 376; Shæcherlæus, 343.
Shakespeare, William, xxxviii, 358,
361, 377.
Sharpus, 348.
Shora (Jane Shore), 312, 338.
Shoyswell, Benjamin, xlix; Dorothy,
xlix.
Shrewsbury, Earl of, 373.
Sidney, Sir Henry, 372; his d. Mary,
372; Sir Philip, xxxvi, xxxviii, li,
lx, 273, 341, 349, 357, 358.
Sisley, Clement, viii, xxxv; Thomas,
xxv, xxvi, xxxi.
Smith, J. Stafford, 365, 366.
Smith, Thomas (Tho. Smithus), xl,
xlix, 344, 376.
Smyth, xxx.
Smythe, Sir Clement, xi.
Somerset, Robert Car, Viscount Ro-
chester, Earl of, xli, xlii, xliv, 149.
Sonning, Johan, viii, xi, xv; Robert,
viii, xi.
Southgate, Dr., 359.
Spencer of Althorpe, Sir John, 375;
his d. Alice (Alicia), 312, 375.
Spenser (Spencer, Spencerus), Edmund,
xxxviii, lx, 341.
Stanford, John (Stanfordus), xxviii,
xxx, xlix, 339, 348, 376.
Starkey, Peter, xxx.
Starter, J., 378.
Staverton (Stafferton), Francis, xxix;
Patrick, xxix.
Steward, Anne, viii, xix, xxv; Augus-
tine, viii, ix, xviii, xix, xx, xxi, xxii,
xxiv, xxv, xxviii, xxxi; Elizabeth,
xix; Luce, xxiv; John, xix; Mar-
garet, viii, ix, xix; Mary, viii, xix;
Nicholas, xviii, xix; Simeon, viii, ix,
xviii, xix; Thomas, viii, xix.
Stokys, xxxix.

Strachey, William (Gulielmus Stra-
chæus), xlix, 269, 373.
Sturton, John, Lord, xiv.
Suffolk, Earl of, 60, 361; Elizabeth,
his d., 361.
Surrey, lix.
Swaen, Mr. A. E. W., liii, 378.
Sylvester, Joshua, 357, 367.

Tabor, xl.
Tarlton (Tarltonus), xlvii, 285.
Tennyson, lxi.
Th., Robertus, 341.
Thurbarne, James (Thurbarnus, Iacobus
Thu.), xlix, 339, 342, 345, 348, 376.
Tolomei, Claudio, lix.
Toppham, xxix.
Tressilianus, 292.
Trigg, Lucy, x, xii; Mary, viii, xxi,
xxii, xxiv, xxv; Roger, viii, xii, xiii,
xiv, xv, xvi, xxiv; Thomas, xvi.
Turner, Ann, xliii, xliv; John, xvi, xix.
Tye, Dr. Christopher, xxi; Peter, xx.
Tyrconnel, Earl of, 375.

Villars, xxxii.
Vincentius, 296.

Wade, Sir William, xliii.
Wadylow, Hugh, xvii.
Wait, xxiii.
Walden, Theophilus Howard, Lord,
60, 63; Lord, 156.
Walgrave, Katherine, xii; William,
xii, xiv, xv.
Walker, John, xxii.
Walpole, Henry, xxvii.
Walsingham, Sir Francis, xxix.
Walterton, Nicholas, xix.
Warwick, Earl of, xxix.
Watson, Thomas, xxxvii, lx.
Webbe, lx.
Weme (Wembe), John, xvii.
Weston, xliii, xliv.
Wigley, Richard, 377.
Willey, xxxvii.
Williams, Elizabeth, xi; John, xi.
Williamson, Richard, xxx.
Whitgift, xxvii.
Wo., Robertus, 347.
Woofe, Nicholas, xxiii.
Wotton, John, xxxiii.
Wyat, lix.

Yelverton, Christopher, xxx; the Yel-
vertons, xxvii.

Zouch, E., xlv.

HARTFORDIÆ COMITATVS *noua, uera, ac particularis descriptio.*
Anno Dñi, 1577. *Christoferus Saxton descripsit et Nicholaus Londinensis*
sculpsit.

[In British Museum, pressmark, Maps 87 e 28: the right-hand half
only of the full opening is reproduced.]

To face p. 400